D1083867

WITHDRAWN

Indian Territory and the United States, 1866–1906

Legal History of North America

Indian Territory

Legal History of North America

General Editor
  Gordon Morris Bakken, *California State University, Fullerton*

Associate Editors
  David J. Langum, *Samford University*
  John P. S. McLaren, *University of Victoria*
  John Phillip Reid, *New York University*

and the United States, 1866–1906

Courts, Government, and
the Movement for Oklahoma Statehood

Jeffrey Burton

University of Oklahoma Press : Norman and London

Also by Jeffrey Burton
Dynamite and Six-Shooter (Santa Fe, 1970)
Portraits in Gunsmoke (with others) (London, 1971)
Bureaucracy, Blood Money, and Black Jack's Gang (London, 1984)

This book is published with the generous assistance of the
Wallace C. Thompson Endowment Fund, University of Oklahoma
Foundation.

Library of Congress Cataloging-in-Publication Data

Burton, Jeffrey, 1936–
    Indian territory and the United States, 1866–1906 : courts.
government, and the movement for Oklahoma statehood / Jeffrey
Burton.
        p.   cm. — (Legal history of North America ; 1)
    Includes bibliographical references and index.
    ISBN 0-8061-2754-6 (alk. paper)
    1. Indians of North America—Legal status, laws, etc.—Oklahoma—His-
ory—19th century.   2. Indians of North America—Indian Territory—History.   3. Oklahoma—Politics and government—To 1907. 4. Indians of North
America—Government relations—1869–1934. I. Title. II. Series.
    346.76601'3—dc20
    [347.660613]   94-41039
                                                                               CIP
Text design by Cathy Carney Imboden. Text typeface is Granjon. Display typeface is Snell Roundhand.

Indian Territory and the United States, 1866–1906 is Volume 1 in the series Legal
History of North America.

The paper in this book meets the guidelines for permanence and durability of the
Committee on Production Guidelines for Book Longevity of the Council on
Library Resources, Inc. ♾

2   3   4   5   6   7   8   9   10

FOR LINDSEY,
WHO FOUND THE STAR

[M]ankind being given to folly, it is clear that all its institutions must to a greater or a lesser degree be embodiments of that folly.—*Edward Crankshaw,* The Fall of the House of Habsburg *(1963), 56*

Contents

Maps

Explanatory Note

A serious difficulty was met in the answer to "Are you an Indian?"—Report on Indians Taxed and Indians Not Taxed in the United States (Except Alaska) at the Eleventh Census, 1890: *"The Five Civilized Tribes of Indian Territory."*

Some seventy years ago Joseph Thoburn allotted a single chapter of his two-volume *Standard History of Oklahoma* to "the Courts of Oklahoma and Indian Territory." Thoburn outlined the essential features of nearly all the congressional enactments which, after the Civil War, increased the authority and influence of federal courts in the Indian Territory; but he offered no assessment of the importance of this legislation in the political process that culminated in the creation of the State of Oklahoma.

Several historians since Thoburn's time have placed judicial reform among the factors which expedited the abolition of tribal government; none has submitted that general proposition to comparative analysis. The argument—or assumption—has always been that the foreclosure by the United States Government of the autonomy of the Five Civilized Tribes in Indian Territory was the political response to the demands of economic or demographic forces.

Some of this interpretative conformity, at least in the treatment of the Washington end of the transactions, may have originated in a predisposition to credit Roy Gittinger's pioneering text, *The Formation of the State of Oklahoma, 1803–1906,* with Domesday authority, where renewed recourse to the congressional and other official documents would not have been remiss. Good as Gittinger's book is, it is neither an exhaustive survey of the Government Printing Office sources nor an infallible review of the substantial range of material it does embrace.

The most persuasive assertion of the classic hypothesis, which Gittinger's book tends to suggest, that the impetus for the transition from Indian Territory to Oklahoma was provided by a coalition of interests between railroads, speculators, and homeseekers, was advanced by Carl Coke Rister in *Land Hunger: David L. Payne and the Oklahoma Boomers,* published in 1942. Rister's book is a vivid and highly able exposition of its own terms of reference; it has no reason to be more.

Standing apart from this tradition, in both a category and a class of its own, is *The Corporation and the Indian: Tribal Sovereignty and Industrial Civilization in Indian Territory, 1865–1907,* by H. Craig Miner. Innovative, perceptive, and brilliantly presented, it allows few grounds for serious dispute, outside its central thesis that the broad front of "industrial civilization," taken as a whole, was the wrecker of tribal sovereignty.

In our submission, neither interpretation reaches the core of the issue. This work will identify the federal Government, acting not for homestead or commercial interests but for itself as a political organism and engine of political change, as the prime instrument in the destruction of the institutional autonomy of the Five Tribes. It will show that the policy of the United States Congress and Executive toward Indian Territory was, predominantly, one of political expansionism for its own sake, and that it was accomplished through a series of reforms of the federal court structure.

Since the institutions of any free or even half-free society cannot be regulated into uniformity of outlook or object, the fruition of this policy was not, and could not be, the product of instantaneous unanimity within and between the various interested components of the federal Government. For some fifteen years after the imposition of the treaties of 1866 there was—beyond the Middle West and one or two Southern States— a general unconcern in government with the problems and prospects of Indian Territory. A campaign against the autonomy of the Five Tribes gathered strong support in the House of Representatives during the 1880s, but much less in the Senate. Until the turn of that decade most United States senators were either uncommitted on the issue or against any interference with the Five Nations. Success for the campaigners came only in the 1890s, when a majority in the Senate moved rapidly from acquiescence in judicial reform to exploitation of the breach it had thus opened in the already battered wall of tribal self-government. Before the old century had yielded to the new, the work of demolition was done, though as yet the old foundations were in no condition to support the architecture of a new State. Any question as to whether they may not have been ready even after 1906 is not a matter for this narrative, which ends with the passage of the Oklahoma Enabling Act in June of that year. There were, moreover, pressing reasons for bridging the political void opened up by the liquidation of the tribal governments.

As is well known, the compilation of authentic citizenship rolls in the

Five Nations, allotment of the tribal lands, and distribution of other tribal assets among tribal members, were the responsibility of the Commission to the Five Civilized Tribes, the so-called "Dawes Commission." Far less account has been taken of the fact that its decisions in citizenship cases could be appealed to the United States courts, making it an adjunct of the federal judicial system. It is not too much to say, therefore, as was often said at the time, that Indian Territory was under United States court government during those interim years. The Department of the Interior, through the Indian Office at Washington and the Union Agency at Muskogee, was not without influence; but, by the late 1890s, all the real authority in Indian Territory lay with the federal courts. This, to a swelling population, constituted a denial not only of good government but of the very justice that these courts had been established in Indian Territory to dispense.

The process that ended with the dissolution of tribal home rule had been helped along by diversities of attitude, ambition, and action in most of the five individual Nations and by the absence of any continuous common political front linking their governments. But even a concerted defense of tribal institutions could not have preserved them for more than a few further years. As well as the massive disparity in the strength of the two sides, there was the unassailable fact that the United States had, by treaty, reserved the right to install courts of law in the Five Nations country. A few Southern Democrats and Eastern Republicans stuck by the cause of tribal particularism until the fires were out; for America at large, suppression of the tribal governments and preparation of Oklahoma for statehood marked another step toward the fulfillment of a new Manifest Destiny—though few, probably, would have expressed it in those words.

Ancillary to the theme of political ends attained by judicial reform are questions relating to the nature and condition of the courts themselves. Here, again, little historical exploration has been essayed hitherto. Books of varying, but usually indifferent, quality have touched upon the work of the United States court at Fort Smith; but their emphasis has been biographical, the content devoted mostly to the career of the man who served for twenty-one years as district judge, and dwelling chiefly upon the more sensational of the cases that came before him. Those by Fred Harvey Harrington *(Hanging Judge)* and Glenn Shirley *(Law West of Fort Smith)* are good, up to a point. Samuel Harman's almost contemporaneous *Hell on the Border* is an American *Newgate Calendar*—a fascinating compilation in its way, and quite indispensable, but far from canonical (indeed, it has an amplitude of apocrypha). The best of the shorter pieces on Judge Parker and his court is an article by Harry Daily, published in *The Chroni-*

cles of Oklahoma more than sixty years ago. Wayne Gard's milestone volume *Frontier Justice* has room for fewer than a half-score pages on the subject; these, though not error free, are worth having to hand. Other writings about the Fort Smith court and its most famous judge are, for the most part, scrappy, folksy, or merely unhistorical. It would be venturing beyond our bounds of reference to consider the extensive literature on individual deputy marshals and criminals, except to remark that a little of it is excellent. Among the best of the genre is *Belle Starr and Her Times*, by Glenn Shirley (1982).

The other federal courts which, at sundry times, exercised jurisdiction in Indian Territory, have been overlooked almost entirely. Nor has there been any description or discussion of the admixture of common law and statute that formed the federal legal framework. Then, too, even the monographs on the Five Nations lack any adequate summary of the law code of the tribe concerned, while their appraisals of the tribal courts are too sketchy and superficial to be of much value. The subject is, indeed, a large and complex one; but in the following pages an effort will be made—though necessarily in a condensed form—to remedy this neglect.

Quite a lot will have to be said about court expenditures. These involved the allocation and outlay of amounts that mean nothing today. While changes in supply and demand—and in the composition of society—make it hard to match the economy of one era with that of another, we can at least bear in mind that one dollar then would do the essential work of fifty or sixty now.

Even in the nineteenth century, and among those in the United States who might have been expected to concern themselves with such matters, it was not recognized by all that the expression "Indian Territory" was doubly ambiguous. The second of its two terminological contradictions will be explained in the opening chapter; the first cannot be postponed until then.

"Indian" in this context was from the outset politically rather than racially descriptive, since most of the Eastern tribes that were resettled in the Western country between 1828 and 1842 had already experienced some infusion of European blood. After the tribes had arrived in the West, the European element became steadily larger in relation to the whole. In the interests of precision, and to obviate any possible confusion between ethnic and political denominators, the unqualified use of "Indian" and "white" will be avoided, as far as may be practical. Reference will generally be to "Indian citizen" and "United States citizen." When "Indian" or "white" do appear, the first will denote any citizen of one of the Five Tribes, irrespective of ancestry; the second, any individual of wholly European origin who was not a citizen of an Indian tribe.

Semantics are a curse on language; for as long as there are politics and polemics, words like "democracy" and "civilization" will mean everything, anything, or nothing. A further curse on the English language, in particular, has always been its shortage of personal pronouns. Now that social change has ushered the generic "he" towards retirement, writers have the opportunity to aim for greater clarity with fewer pronouns. We hope that, without making much use of the cumbersome "he or she" construction, we have succeeded in avoiding any ambiguity of expression. It should be recalled, all the same, that female suffrage had yet to arrive, and there were no women in either legislative chamber in Washington, none occupying elective posts in the tribal governments, none in any senior official administrative position. Of course many women appeared as plaintiffs or defendants in federal and tribal courts; but their numbers were proportionately small, and the cause at issue, as a rule, of comparatively little importance. Although several women were sentenced to hang for murder in Indian Territory, none was executed. There were a few female horse-thieves, but no female desperadoes: Belle Starr, the celebrated "bandit queen," was no more a bandit than she was a queen. Indian Territory had no female bank robber, unless we can count the Kansas woman who crossed and recrossed the northeast corner of the Territory between her home State and the bank she helped rob in Missouri.

But women were active in journalism, full time and part time. Some of the most percipient, searching, and perhaps even influential articles on Indian Territory and Oklahoma Territory were written by women. Quotations from two of these will be found in these pages; it is a matter for regret that room could not be found for a few lines from the writings of the ubiquitous Helen Churchill Candee (who later sailed in the *Titanic* and lived many years to tell the tale), or that irrepressible controversialist, Gail Hamilton. For almost every quotation or factual illustration chosen for this work, in whatever context, three or four—or a score or more—that might serve just as well have had to be set aside.

Slavery was an institution in the Five Nations before the Civil War, though there was always a minority of free blacks. Union Cherokees ordered the abolition of slavery in their nation while the war was still being fought; their Confederate opponents ignored the decree. After the war the process of formal liberation and emancipation was completed, at least on paper, by the federal Government; the intention was to secure full rights of tribal citizenship throughout the Five Nations for all persons of African descent who could qualify by birth or residence. In both official language and ordinary talk the term "freedman" was given not only to the ex-slaves and their descendants—irrespective of age and sex—but also to the minority of black citizens who, though not always accorded equality within their tribes, had never been slaves. To complicate matters a little further, ex-slaves from the United States, with no claim to citizenship and, in most instances, no right even of residence in the Five Nations, were sometimes called "freedmen" also. "Freedman," moreover, is a term musty with the antiquity of misleading historical antecedent: the "freedman" of Republican Rome never acquired all the rights of citizenship, and the "freedman" of Anglo-Saxon England needed a separate act of manumission before he was free enough to do more than enjoy the right, which was a duty, to pay certain taxes. None of this applied to the "freedmen" of the Five Nations; at least, it was not meant to.

Manifestly, then, there are multiple grounds for consigning the word "freedman" to desuetude. In this work "black" or "ex-slave" will be preferred to "freedman" in referring to Indian or United States citizens of African ancestry, except occasionally where adult males are plainly identifiable.

Objection may be made to references in the text to the United States Senate and House of Representatives as the "upper" and "lower" branches of Congress; certainly, the constitutional relationship between the two bodies gives no ground for such differentiation. Nevertheless, in the last third of the nineteenth century the Senate (still, be it remembered, an indirectly elected body) was commonly viewed as the senior of the two assemblies, not least by those who entered it after having served in the House. The point is well made in David Rothman's book, *Politics and Power.*

Acknowledgments

Almost all the printed publications needed for an undertaking such as this are available for study in the Bloomsbury district of London.

Thanks are due to several members or past members of the staff of the Official Publications library, at the British Library, for their help at various awkward junctures, particularly in locating one series of volumes whose whereabouts were concealed by the catalogue entry. Serial publications as voluminous as the *Congressional Globe* and *Congressional Record* cannot be consulted without great loss of time unless the shelves that accommodate them are within the direct reach of the researcher, as they are at the Institute of Historical Research. The Institute also holds, among much else, a good bibliographical collection and a useful selection of standard (and nonstandard) biographical works.

The manuscript records of the United States Department of Justice are on microfilm or may be microfilmed to order. For advice and assistance in this regard I am indebted to John W. Roberts of the Judicial, Fiscal, and Social Branch, Civil Archives Division, and Lula Lathan, Branch Chief, Publications Services Branch, National Archives, Washington, D.C.

The district and circuit court records of the United States Western Judicial District of Arkansas are not on microfilm. I am grateful to Kent Carter, Director of the Fort Worth, Texas, branch of the National Archives, who showed me everything I asked for and enabled me to leave Fort Worth with the right answers to nearly all the questions I had brought with me only a couple of days earlier.

Most important of all were the manuscript and newspaper collections of the Oklahoma Historical Society. I owe a great deal to the cordial cooperation and thoughtfulness of Mary Lee Boyle, then Senior Archivist, and William D. Welge, Archivist, Archives/Manuscripts Division (Indian Archives Division); and Mary Moran, Newspaper Librarian, at the Wiley Post Historical Building, Oklahoma City.

Professor Christine Bolt, of the University of Kent at Canterbury, offered several suggestions that were gladly taken. Our conversations made it easier for me to carry into practice my expressed intention of putting aside all preconceptions.

   I end, as I ought, perhaps, to have begun, by thanking my wife, not merely for ensuring that the jurisdiction of this project did not extend to the dinner table, but for her support throughout.

                                                                    J.B.

Synopsis

After the defeat of the Confederacy, the Five Tribes signed treaties which, in permitting the creation of a federal court within Indian Territory, could hasten the dissolution of tribal institutions and absorption of the Five Nations into the federal structure, with or without tribal consent. Some Indian citizens favored reform as strongly as others opposed it, but, until the 1880s, there was little support for it in Congress.

In 1889 congressional expansionists succeeded in installing the federal court. It became the axis of a political campaign to undermine the tribal governments by establishing a network of court towns.

Lands ceded by the Creeks and Seminoles in 1866 were, concurrently, opened to settlers, organized into Oklahoma Territory, and extended by the attachment of reservations occupied by Indian tribes that had not originated in the Southeast; but double statehood for the "twin Territories" was never feasible.

Before 1889 jurisdiction over crimes committed by or against United States citizens in Indian Territory rested with "outside courts" in Arkansas and elsewhere. These courts temporarily retained some of that jurisdiction even after 1889. Congress remedied defects in the criminal law, oversaw the eradication of flagrant malpractices, and introduced a civil code, but could not make a bad system good.

The Five Nations constructed legal codes that were adequate technically; but laxity, partiality, or corruption in office, amid political instability and social volatility, made a goodish system bad.

In 1896 the "outside courts" lost all jurisdiction in Indian Territory. Abolition of tribal courts and national autonomy soon followed, leaving the federal courts as the sole repositories of government.

Massive immigration, citizenship disputes, and liquidation of the Five Tribes' communal land titles generated so much judicial business that the new courts, overburdened, became worse than their predecessors. Statehood, the calculated outcome of judicial reform, came to Oklahoma as a judicial necessity.

*Indian Territory
and the United States,
1866–1906*

CHAPTER ONE

From Removal to Reconstruction

More difference of opinion seems to exist as to the matter of disposing of Louisiana than I had imagined possible—Thomas Jefferson to Dewitt [DeWitt] Clinton, December 2, 1803, with reference to the Louisiana Purchase.

The people are generally demoralized hence it will require years to bring us back to where we were at the commencement of the war.—Allen Wright, principal chief of the Choctaw Nation, inaugural speech, November 17, 1866 Records of the Choctaw Nation.

"Indian Territory" was a geographical expression which evolved from a policy. Its formal origins are found in an act of Congress of March 2, 1819,[1] which set the western boundary of the new United States Territory of Arkansas at the hundredth degree of longitude, and in the act of May 26, 1824,[2] defining the extent of the present State of Arkansas. All the land between the old and new western limits of Arkansas—bounded to the north by the thirty-seventh degree of latitude and to the south by the Red River—was reserved by the United States Government for the resettlement of the so-called Five Civilized Tribes.[3]

At first the sole legal identity of this area of more than 62,000 square miles was contained in the words "the Indian country," but it was commonly, and legitimately, written and spoken of as "the Indian territory." Thence it was but a short step to the general adoption of the style "the Indian Territory." This was the form that appeared in many congressional bills from the 1860s onward, though it was not until well into the 1890s that the term "the Indian country" was replaced by the newer phrase in prosecutions undertaken by the United States court. Even then it was no more than a regularized solecism: *the Indian Territory was United States territory, but it was never a Territory of the United States.* All the same, in everyday speech, residents of neighboring States habitually referred to the Indian country as "the Territory," without qualification or fear of being misunderstood. And, again in ordinary parlance, its eastern half was often styled "the Indian Nations"—or just "the Nations"—during the later decades of the nineteenth century, these terms being synonymous both with the Five Tribes and the area they inhabited.

West of the hundredth meridian is a neck of land containing 5,672 square miles now known as the Oklahoma Panhandle and formerly called the Public Land Strip, Neutral Land Strip, or No Man's Land. It was not part of the Indian Territory and was not attached to any State or Territory until it was included in Oklahoma Territory under the provisions of the Organic act of May 2, 1890.

A tract of 2,300 square miles enclosed by the Red River and its North Fork, nearly coextensive with the three southwesternmost counties of the present State of Oklahoma, was officially designated Greer County, Texas, until 1896 when after years of wrangling and litigation the Supreme Court of the United States awarded it to Oklahoma Territory. Greer County had never been in the Indian Territory. Otherwise, "the Indian Territory" (its definite article began to recede only during the closing ten or eleven years of the century and was not commonly omitted until the early 1900s) was identical with the area which, under the Enabling Act of June 16, 1906, was invested with the constitutional machinery to enter the Union with Oklahoma Territory as the forty-sixth State.

Benjamin Joseph Franklin, a Democratic Congressman from Missouri, in a speech delivered on March 1, 1879, traced the idea at the source of the Indian removal policy to Thomas Jefferson. Directly after the ratification of the Louisiana Purchase in 1803, Jefferson was supposed to have said, or written:

> The inhabited part of Louisiana from Pointe Coupée to the sea will of course be immediately a territorial government and soon a State, but above that the best use we can make of the country for some time to come will be to give establishments in it to the Indians of the east side of the Mississippi in exchange for their present country and open land offices in the last, and thus make this acquisition a means of filling up the eastern side instead of drawing off the population. When we shall be full on this side we may lay off a range of States on the western bank.[4]

This was an accurate vision of the political future, but it was not a germination of the Indian removal policy adopted by the United States Government shortly before and after Andrew Jackson became President in 1829. The travails of the Cherokee, Choctaw, Chickasaw, Muskogee (or

Creek), and Seminole tribes before and during their removal to the Indian country have been dwelt upon many times elsewhere; our concern is with the stresses in their domestic politics that were caused or aggravated by their removal. It is nonetheless germane that the Five Tribes were not offered a country that was to be their own merely "for some time to come."[5]

Political and social homogeneity had been lost to the Cherokees long before their emigration from Georgia, Alabama, and North Carolina to the Indian country. A section of the tribe had seceded in 1817 by entering into a treaty with the United States and moving to Arkansas Territory. In 1828, still in advance of the enunciation of a formal removal policy, these Western Cherokees, or "Old Settlers," continued westward to found the Cherokee Nation in the Indian country.

The Eastern Cherokees followed them west in accordance with the Treaty of New Echota concluded in Georgia on December 29, 1835, between representatives of the United States Government and leading members of the tribe. Those tribal leaders included several full-bloods who had aligned themselves with the "progressive" mixed-blood element; but they did not include the elected principal chief, John Ross, who was seven-eighths white but had identified himself with the interests of the "conservative" full-bloods. The "Treaty party" moved to the Indian Territory shortly after the ratification on May 29, 1836, of the New Echota agreement; the Ross party—the majority of the Eastern Cherokees—followed in 1838 and 1839 after the expiry of the period specified by the treaty, under duress and amid much hardship.

In June 1839 several leaders of the Treaty party were murdered by adherents of Ross, and others were driven into hiding. When, soon afterward, the Eastern and Western Cherokees amalgamated, Ross took control of the convention, which on September 6 drafted the new constitution of the Cherokee Nation.

Political unity made a poor screen for social fragility. In 1845–1846 the nation was rent apart by a vicious struggle between the Ross party and the combined interests of the Treaty party and the Old Settlers. The United States brought the contending factions to the table in 1846,[6] and the old divisions remained dormant until the Civil War.

Among the Creeks, a bloody contest between a treaty party and those who opposed removal had erupted in Alabama in 1825. Most of the McIntosh, or treaty, party belonged to the Lower Creeks; most of their adversaries to the Upper Creeks. The association between the two groupings ("towns") had never matured into unity; their differences over the removal issue may not have delayed the external political union of the

Upper and Lower Towns, but they robbed it of meaning until at least 1860, disrupted it until well into the 1880s, and afflicted it in some measure even in the 1890s.

Several hundred Lower Creeks reached the Indian Territory in 1828 and were joined by some thousand others over the next two years. In 1832 the Upper Creeks ceded their homelands to the United States and in the course of the next five years followed their kinsmen in the Indian country. Tentative steps toward political affiliation were taken in 1840, and in 1860 the Muskogee Nation adopted a new constitution which, dispensing with government by town, divided the nation into four judicial and administrative districts. With the coming of the Civil War, the frailty of the new constitutional framework was exposed: nearly all in the Lower Towns took sides with the Confederacy; nearly all the Upper Creeks, when they saw that neutrality was impossible, aligned themselves with the Union. The exceptions on either hand were quite numerous enough to render the difficulties more complicated.[7]

Removal of the Choctaws from Mississippi and western Alabama began in 1825 and was expedited in September 1830 by the Treaty of Dancing Rabbit Creek. A minority of the tribe exchanged Choctaw for United States citizenship to enable them to retain their homes in Mississippi, but these "Mississippi Choctaws" retained, and their descendants would inherit, the right to take land in the Indian Territory. A serious problem arose during the later 1880s, and worsened in the early 1890s, when several parties of Mississippi Choctaws, along with a number of false claimants, arrived in the Indian Territory to apply for admission to the tribal rolls.

The Choctaws who chose to emigrate in the 1830s were greatly in the majority. Several constitutions were successively adopted. The first, framed in 1834, gave the Choctaw Nation a general assembly; the last, promulgated at Doaksville on January 11, 1860, remained in force with little alteration until the extinction of tribal government.[8]

In 1832 the Chickasaws ceded their lands in Mississippi and rejoined their neighbors and kinsfolk, the Choctaws, in the Indian country. Under the Treaty of Doaksville, concluded in January, 1837, the Chickasaws purchased a tract on the western side of the Choctaw Nation, but their relegation to district status provoked dissension that led through several stages to the reemergence in 1855 of the Chickasaw Nation as a political entity.[9]

An important provision in the treaty of June 22, 1855, between the Choctaws, Chickasaws, and the United States conveyed the western portion of the tribal lands, lying between the ninety-eighth and hundredth degrees of longitude, conditionally to the United States for the consideration of $800,000, three-quarters of which was payable to the Choctaws, and the balance to the Chickasaws. The two nations retained a reversionary interest in this land, known thenceforth as the Leased District, which was to be used only for the settlement of Plains Indians. Nothing was done about introducing the Plains tribes into the district until after the Civil War.[10]

Although the Choctaw and Chickasaw nations were now separate, members of the two tribes enjoyed most of the rights of dual citizenship; and all the land in the two nations, taken together, was held for all the citizens of the two nations, again taken together.

Only after seven years of warfare in the Everglades was the relocation of the Five Tribes completed by the removal of the Seminoles during 1841–1842. When all but some two hundred of the tribe had been transported from Florida, fresh difficulties arose from the attempt to implement a clause of their treaty which assigned them a district within the Creek country. In August 1856 the Seminoles obtained their independence from the Creeks. Their new homeland was a tonguelike tract between the Canadian and North Canadian rivers as far as the intersection of the North Canadian and the southern boundary of the Cherokee Nation. The Seminoles were by far the least numerous of the Five Tribes and, having had little commercial, cultural, or sexual contact with white Americans, were reckoned the least "civilized." Until 1859 the Seminole Nation lacked a general council, and its constitution and laws were never published.[11]

The criteria for the adoption of white Americans or Europeans into the Five Tribes differed from tribe to tribe. A Choctaw law of October 1840 decreed that any white *man* (the language was specific) would become eligible for citizenship through marriage into the tribe after that marriage had subsisted for two years.[12] These regulations remained unaltered until 1875.[13] In the Chickasaw constitution of 1856 provision was made for the adoption of whites into the nation through intermarriage or by an act of the legislature.[14] Among the Creeks and Seminoles, a white person might be adopted into the tribe, whether he or she had married a "blood member" of the tribe; but intermarriage did not ensure admission. Even then, with certain exceptions adopted before the Civil war or by special act shortly after it, white adoptees in the Muskogee Nation were really only semi-Indians; they remained United States citizens.[15] The practice in the Seminole Nation was similar; but until the 1880s intermarriage between Seminoles and whites was rare, and adoption of white citizens much rarer still. In the other three tribes the white adoptees were full citizens, but the highest elective offices were not open to them, and they ceased to be citizens of the United States (although officials of the United States would sometimes contest this before and after the war, mainly in the Cherokee Nation). The Cherokees, among whom the quantum of white blood was always the highest, always permitted entry into the tribe through marriage upon fulfillment of certain conditions.

Slaves were held in all five nations. Marriage between Indians and persons of African descent was forbidden except, intermittently, in the Muskogee Nation. Even after the Civil War, marriage between Indians by blood and blacks was very uncommon except perhaps among the Creeks and Seminoles.

Comparatively few Indians owned slaves, but there was no political opposition to slavery as an institution except in the Cherokee Nation, where a quite small but determined and at times ruthless abolitionist and anti-Southern movement was built up by two white Baptist missionaries, Evan Jones and his son John. Overall, however, "slavery in the Cherokee Nation was little different from the surrounding slave holding areas with no increased freedoms under their Cherokee masters."[16]

When the Eastern Cherokees arrived in the Indian Territory in the late 1830s, they came with a judicial system which comprised district (lower) and circuit (higher) courts, whose judges were elected, and a supreme court of three appointed justices. Executive authority was in the hands of an appointed national marshal and a sheriff elected in each district.

Companies of tribal police, or "light-horse men," were formed by the Cherokees as early as 1797,[17] and in the first of its laws to be reduced to writing, dated September 11, 1808, the national council defined the composition of the tribal light-horse, their pay, and the punishment for theft ("one hundred stripes on the bare back" for stealing a horse, proportionately less for lesser thefts). The same law absolved the kin of any accused person who had been slain while resisting arrest from the traditional obligation to seek blood vengeance.[18]

In November 1825 the national council abolished the light-horse and provided a deputy sheriff and two constables for each of the eight districts, but the constitution of July 26, 1827, allowed only for the eight district sheriffs and the national marshal. After removal to the Indian country, the Cherokees divided their new homeland into nine districts, retaining in essence the judicial arrangements the council had drafted and approved in 1827.

During the renewed factional strife of 1845–1846 the rival leaders, John Ross and Stand Watie, recruited forces of so-called light-horse men that were really nothing better than gangs of "regulators," or vigilantes.

Because of the odium excited by the excesses of these organizations, the formation of light-horse companies was prohibited in the peace treaty the United States Government arranged in 1846.[19] Their revival was never permitted by any Cherokee government.

Until 1867 the Muskogee Nation had only a rudimentary constitution and a few crude laws, but there were light-horse men to enforce the fragmentary criminal code and to apply the judgments of the civil court. In 1860 the general council divided the nation into four districts, each with its own light-horse company.

It was the successful use of light-horse men by the Eastern Cherokees that led to their introduction into the Choctaw scheme of law enforcement. The thirteenth article of the Treaty of Doak's Stand committed the United States to include in the amount appropriated annually for its Indians the sum of $200 for each of the three Choctaw districts so that a corps of ten light-horse could be raised and supported for the district "to act as executive officers, in maintaining good order, and compelling bad men to remove from the nation, who are not authorized to live in it by a regular permit from the agent." Removal to the Indian Territory was followed by the formation of four districts (one of them for the Chickasaws); trial by jury was instituted and provision made for three judges to be elected for each district. The strength of the district light-horse was reduced from ten men to six in 1860.[20]

Upon resuming their separate national identity in 1856, the Chickasaws divided their country into four counties of very disparate size, each representing a judicial district. For execution of the laws, each county had a sheriff and as many constables as needed. The powers of the constable were concurrent with those of the sheriff. Light-horse were used before 1855 but had no place in the system of law enforcement that went into practice after the Chickasaw Nation had been reestablished.[21]

There was no agency for the pursuit and punishment of criminals in the Seminole Nation until after the Civil War.[22]

Neither before the Civil War nor later was it demanded of any tribal judge or lawyer that he should have had training in the law or even be able to read and write. It was expected that he should know and understand the tribal laws and be of good moral character; but sometimes even these qualifications were absent. The judges were paid, but not paid well; there were, from the time of the removals, lawyers with recognized professional credentials among the Cherokees and Choctaws, but the paltriness of the remuneration deterred them from seeking judicial appointments. In later years a number of tribal lawyers were licenced to practice in the federal courts.[23]

The need to regulate trading between Indian and white in the Indian country determined that the federal courthouse should become the legislative pressure point in the contest between tribal sovereignty and the centralizing inclinations of an expanding federal Government. That need was met by two acts of Congress approved on July 9, 1832, and June 30, 1834, and—derived from early postcolonial legislation—often called the Trade and Intercourse Acts.[24]

The earlier statute set out the conditions for the licensing of trade with the Indians, forbade the introduction of "ardent spirits . . . into the Indian country" and ordained that any person (white or Indian) "who sells, exchanges, gives, barters, or disposes of any spirituous liquors to any Indian under the charge of an Indian superintendent or agent," or who introduced, or tried to introduce, such liquors into the Indian country, should be punished upon conviction in the U.S. court by up to two years' imprisonment and a fine of not more than $300.

This law undermined the authority of the nascent tribal courts in Indian Territory by taking from them liquor-trafficking cases in which only Indians were concerned.

Among the provisions of the Act for the Government of the Indian Country of June 30, 1834, were three that further defined the role of the United States courts; Section 24 annexed the whole of the Indian country to the Territory of Arkansas for judicial purposes; Section 25 directed that "the punishment of crimes committed in any place within the sole and exclusive jurisdiction of the United States . . . shall extend to the Indian country"; and Section 26 excepted all cases within the sphere of the tribal courts. Together, these three provisions meant that the District Court for the District of Arkansas, with headquarters at Little Rock, would have full jurisdiction, and the tribal courts none, over crimes committed in the Indian country where at least one of the parties was a citizen.

Nothing was subtracted by the later act from the exclusive authority granted to the federal court by the earlier statute for the trial of all individuals charged with the introduction of liquor. Toward the end of the Civil War, Congress passed amendatory legislation to except "an Indian, in the Indian country," from the operation of the law of 1832; but this reversal of the general tendency for the federal courts to acquire jurisdiction would be canceled out by repeal a dozen years later.

By the 1840s, the federal court in Arkansas was ready to dispute the assumption that citizenship of the United States could be surrendered, or forfeited, by the acquisition of tribal citizenship. In 1846 the Supreme Court, considering a case where a white citizen of the United States who had married into the Cherokee Nation had been tried under federal law for the murder of another intermarried Cherokee, ruled that jurisdiction lay with the United States. In the opinion of Chief Justice Roger Taney:

> The country in which the crime is charged to have been committed is a part of the territory of the United States and not within the limits of any particular State. It is true that it is occupied by the tribe of Cherokee Indians. But it has been assigned to them by the United States, as a place of domicile for the tribe, and they hold and occupy it with the assent of the United States, and under their authority.[25]

This decision impinged upon the much greater issue of eminent domain—"the *dominium eminens,* or superior right, which of necessity resides in the sovereign power of all governments, to apply private property to public use in those great public emergencies which can reasonably be met in no other way."[26] Though the ruling, and its implications, stood unchallenged for some twenty years, both the general and the specific question were reopened after the Civil War.

Cases concerning members of different tribes were a matter for the nation in which the offense had occurred. It was long after the end of the Civil War when the difficulties that arose from the introduction of Plains Indians into the western areas of the Indian Territory impelled the United States to assume jurisdiction over all such cases.

When Arkansas became a State, in June 1836, the scope of the authority of the United States court in the Indian Territory was confirmed; but the remoteness of the Indian country from Little Rock, and the growth of the population of Arkansas itself, led Congress to enact a law, approved on March 3, 1851, which divided the State into an Eastern and a Western district.[27] The Western District, with Van Buren as its court town, comprised nine counties of Arkansas and "all that part of the Indian country lying within the present judicial district of Arkansas." Presently, by act of March 27, 1854, two more Arkansas counties were transferred from the Eastern to the Western District, and the singular status of the Van Buren court was emphasized by a provision that all prison sentences awarded there were to be served "with hard labor."[28]

The criminal laws of the United States were applicable "within any ford, arsenal, dock-yard, magazine, or in any other place or district of country within the exclusive jurisdiction of the United States" and "upon the high seas, or in any arm of the sea, or in any river, haven, creek, basin, or bay within the admiralty and maritime jurisdiction of any particular State."[29] It was a system derived from the common law of England, supplemented at intervals by items of statutory law, making a patchwork whose defects and limitations were exposed relentlessly as the rising numbers of white residents and transients were accompanied by an increase in the frequency of criminal acts committed by or against United States citizens in the Indian country.[30]

There was, besides, "the Arkansas side" of the jurisdiction encompassing offenses committed in the western counties of Arkansas against the statutes enacted for the operation of the United States Internal Revenue, Treasury Department, or Post Office Department; but there were never many of these, and the relative importance of this part of the court's work decreased with the growth of the white population of the Indian country.

Neither Congress nor the Executive had envisaged that the United States would exercise a mainly common-law jurisdiction for any length of time over an area of nearly 40 million acres which immigration from the United States would cause to become populous and industrially developed before the abatement of that jurisdiction. Once a manageable expanse of country had been pacified, had acquired the nucleus of a settled white population, and had developed at least the glimmerings of an economy, it could expect to be granted Territorial status, which earned the right to elect a legislature to formulate a code of criminal and civil law. This policy, and the assumptions which had shaped it—that the United States had acquired sovereignty by treaty, conquest, and settlement—could not easily be made to obtain in lands formally set aside for the Five Tribes and legally secured for them by patent in fee simple.

Conversely, the sovereignty of the Five Tribes was restricted by the constitutional limitations that prevented their courts from prosecuting, or protecting, United States citizens. As long as there were United States citizens in the Indian Territory, the Indian Territory would remain, for them, "within the exclusive jurisdiction of the United States." That, pre-eminently, is why, through the years, a long procession of jurists, lawyers, politicians, journalists, speculators, and entrepreneurs would assert with unwearying monotony that the Indian Territory was "an anomaly."

A second administrative link between Washington and the Indian Territory was provided by the local agencies of the Indian Office.

When the Department of the Interior was formed in 1849, it acquired from the War Department the responsibility for the management of Indian affairs. Further reorganization brought the Cherokee, Creek, and Seminole agencies within the Southern Superintendency, which was formed in 1851 and given headquarters in western Arkansas. At the same time the Choctaw Agency was subordinated to the Western Superintendency, near Skullyville. After their separation from the Choctaws, the Chickasaws were allotted their own agent, still within the Western Superintendency. The agent reported to the superintendent, the superintendent

to the Commissioner of Indian Affairs, the Commissioner to the Secretary of the Interior, and the Secretary to the President of the United
States. Later, on June 22, 1874, as part of the Indian Appropriation Act for
1874–1875, Congress combined the individual Five Tribes agencies into
the single Union Agency, with headquarters at the new railroad town of
Muskogee in the Creek Nation. The Southern Superintendency disappeared, placing the agent in direct contact with the Commissioner of
Indian Affairs.[31]

It was the agent's duty to ensure that the treaty stipulations between
the United States and the Indians under his charge were honored. Licenses to trade in the Indian country were issued to United States citizens
by the superintendent or the agent for not more than three years at a
time,[32] and it was the agent's right to withhold approval of permits to
reside in the Indian country granted to United States citizens by the tribal
governments.[33]

Where a United States citizen was living in one of the Five Nations
without license from either the tribal government or the federal Government, the tribal government could order him to leave, but it could not
legally enforce its own order.[34] After an act of Congress approved on
August 18, 1856, the task of enforcement belonged to the agent. He could
always call upon the United States Army for assistance, and, in the work
of excluding the liquor traffic from the reservation, his powers were
complementary to those of the United States marshal.[35]

Upon the agent, too, fell the informal but almost equally important
role of mediator in disputes over contracts, debts, and other matters where
at least one of the parties was a citizen and which would have been subject
to the processes of civil law had there been any. His success here would
depend wholly upon his powers of persuasion and the goodwill of the
disputants: a poor substitute, at best, for the machinery the federal law
system did not provide for settlement of civil controversies.[36]

More delicately, for semiofficial assistance and interference were separated by a very fine line, he could offer, or be invited, to serve as intermediary in disputes between one tribe and another where there was no
intertribal compact or where its terms had not been observed.[37] A letter of
1891, though written with a mind to the accrued complications of a half
century or more, includes a clear and concise statement on the ambiguities
that were inherent in the office of Indian agent among the Five Tribes.
Laws passed by Congress, said the writer,

> conferred upon the Indian agent powers judiciary and executive, author-
> ity to make and enforce such rules and regulations not inconsistent with
> law as, in his judgment, he deemed necessary for the interest or welfare of

the Indians under his charge, in arbitrary, monarchical power not now in keeping with the institutions of this free country, but which, on the other hand seemed necessary in the early period of Indian government when the Indians were far beyond the jurisdiction of the federal courts, and the conferment of intercourse laws was against the fugitive and outlaw only. The status of the Indian agent's authority is one that is undefined; that is to say, not so clearly defined as to relieve him from the embarrassments and entanglements which beset him in the discharge of his duty, from clashing with the federal courts claiming jurisdiction, which, if ever possessed by the agent, has never been taken away from him.[38]

Section 19 of the Intercourse Act of 1834 required of superintendents, agents, and subagents that they

endeavor to procure the arrest and trial of all Indians accused of committing any crime, offense, or misdemeanor, and of all other persons who may have committed crimes or offenses within any State or Territory, or have fled into the Indian country, either by demanding the same of the chiefs or of the proper tribes or by such other means as the President may authorize.[39]

This measure was as unsuccessful as the provisions for the expulsion of unauthorized residents, or "intruders." Its failure, or unenforceability, was the source of one of the most persistent arguments for the elimination of the five tribal governments, although most of the blame was not theirs.

Representatives of the Five Nations met in four Indian congresses between 1838 and 1845 to discuss matters of common concern and the possibilities of tribal confederation. In 1859, leading members of the Creek Nation organized an "international council" which, it was hoped, would clear the way for a consolidation of the Five Tribes before Congress could impose a Territorial government on them.[40]

It was not the onset of war but its outcome that wrecked the best chance the Five Tribes ever had of forming a loose federation where much of their autonomy, individual and collective, would be preserved. Under the treaties concluded in 1861 between the Confederate government and representatives of the Five Tribes, the Confederacy undertook to discharge all the obligations then owed by the United States (a promise it was never able to keep), and each of the nations assumed responsibilities and acquired rights which placed it in constitutional terms somewhere between the status of protectorate and that of Territory on the United States model. Each of the tribal governments was entitled to send a delegate to the Confederate Congress and did so.

Some of the provisions most favorable to the Indians were those concerned with the administration of justice. A narrow area of jurisdiction consisting of currency, postal, and liquor offenses was to be exercised by the Confederate government, leaving to the tribal authorities the pros-ecution of all other cases arising in the Indian Territory, including those where one or more of the parties involved was not an Indian citizen. For the first time (and the last), the tribes were empowered to enforce the orders of removal they had served upon intruders.[41]

While the Choctaw and Chickasaw nations were almost undivided in their support for the Confederacy, elsewhere the picture was rather differ-ent. The Creeks and Seminoles who joined the Confederate army were slightly outnumbered by their fellow tribesmen on the other side. Rather more than one-third of the Cherokee combatants, headed by Stand Watie and other members of the old Treaty party, lined up with the Secession movement, and a very much smaller number, mainly the "Pins"—the fol-lowers of the missionaries Evan and John Jones—were as committed to the Union. Between them, the majority, under John Ross, moved cau-tiously from neutrality to association with the Confederacy before finally attaching themselves to the Union, securing the abolition of slavery in the Cherokee Nation and instituting reprisals against the Confederate parti-sans who had evicted Ross from Tahlequah and from the post of principal chief.

A bill introduced in the Senate by James Harlan (R, Iowa) in Febru-ary 1865, although it was not proceeded with, marked the course that the United States might be expected to take with the Indian Territory after the collapse of the Confederacy.[42] Harlan himself, as Secretary of the In-terior between May 1865 and July 1866, became both the architect and instrument of that policy. Its aim was, in the word of the day, "territorial-ization": tribal unification under federal direction and with such a degree of subordination to Washington that white settlement of the Indian Terri-tory, reallocation of tribal lands, and Statehood must soon follow.

To a great extent, the wartime schisms in the Creek, Seminole, and Cherokee Nations were old feuds rekindled by new circumstances; still, whatever their motives, a good many citizens of those nations had re-mained loyal to the Union throughout the struggle. Some of them had endured great privation; some had perished.

These considerations carried little weight in the peace negotiations held at Fort Smith in September 1865, where the principal representative of the United States, Commissioner of Indian Affairs Dennis Cooley, was a placeman of Secretary Harlan. In its treatment of the nations en bloc as the ally of a defeated rebel regime, the Government showed it was much less interested in concluding a fair settlement than in exploiting the defeat of the Confederacy for the consummation of policy objectives that were being formulated before 1861.[43]

No settlement was reached at Fort Smith, but in the spring and summer of 1866 the Choctaws and Chickasaws jointly, and other tribes separately, signed Reconstruction treaties with the United States.[44] Our path will be eased at this point by a summary of the main treaty provisions and their outcome. The most conspicuous features of all four treaties were clauses relative to land cession, emancipation, progression to Territorial government, and the admission of railroads.

The Muskogee Nation ceded to the United States the western half of their country, an area containing some 3.4 million acres, in return for $975,000. Much of this sum, payable to the whole nation in consideration for the territory ceded, was to be allocated to the Loyal Creeks in consideration for the losses they had suffered during the War. This was the same as making the Loyal Creeks pay compensation to themselves.

The Seminoles ceded their entire reservation of about 2.17 million acres for a little over $325,000 and purchased from the United States 200,000 acres of the Creek cession for $100,000, a price per acre more than triple that which they had received from the United States for their former country; although the new land *was* better than the old.

The rest of the ceded lands were to be used by the United States for the resettlement of former slaves and western Indians. It was not absolute cession; by virtue of their patent in fee simple, the Creeks and Seminoles retained a reversionary interest which could operate if the United States failed to utilize the land as specified in the treaty or if for any reason the ex-slaves or Plains Indians in occupancy disposed of their holdings to the United States.

The ex-slaves were not interested in taking up allotments in the Creek and Seminole cession, but about 3.5 million of the available acreage of nearly 5.5 million was in the course of time converted into Government reservations for various Indian tribes. The Sac and Fox agreed to take up land in 1867; the Cheyenne and Arapaho in 1869; and the Iowa, Kickapoo, and Potawatomi in 1883. A small part of the Pawnee reservation, which was opened in 1876, also extended into the former Creek country. A block of territory in the center of the present State of Oklahoma, consisting of nearly 1.4 million acres from the Creek Nation and 0.5 million acres of former Seminole land, remained unassigned and became the nucleus of the State.

A lesser but still noteworthy consequence of the drastic redrawing of the boundaries of the Muskogee and Seminole nations was the resentment expressed by many Creeks at the transfer of a comparatively small slice of their domain to the Seminoles; it was commonly held, though without much apparent conviction on the part of those in charge of the Creek government, that the Seminoles did not own the tract, had only limited jurisdiction over it or none, and were there only on the sufferance of the Creeks.[45]

The United States offered to pay the Choctaws and Chickasaws $225,000 and $75,000, respectively, for the Leased District, provided that the tribes adopted their ex-slaves within two years of the date of the treaty. If the condition were not complied with, the money would be spent on the ex-slaves, who would, it was expected, be allotted land in the Leased District. If the tribes proceeded with the adoption, the Leased District would be applied to the purpose first intended for it, the settlement of "noncivilized" Indians.

Both the Choctaws and the Chickasaws declined to adopt the ex-slaves, but, owing mainly to the dilatoriness of the federal Government, there was no transplantation of the former slaves. Instead, more than 3.5 million acres went to the Cheyennes and Arapahos (forming six-sevenths of their reservation), almost 3 million acres to the Comanches and Kiowas (later joined by some Apaches), and nearly 0.75 million acres to the Wichita and Caddo tribes. Although the cession by the Choctaws and Chickasaws was absolute,[46] the United States paid them nearly $3 million in 1893 after the Cheyenne and Arapaho reservation had been allotted in severalty.[47]

The Cherokee Outlet, a sleevelike appendage of the Cherokee Nation extending from the ninety-sixth to the one-hundredth meridian and enclosing more than 8 million acres, was ceded conditionally by the Cherokees for the settlement of "friendly" Indians. In 1872 the United States allocated nearly 1.5 million acres directly west of the Cherokee Nation proper to the Osage Nation, and over the next few years smaller tribes were placed on correspondingly smaller reservations south and west of the Osage Nation. The Cherokees were "to retain the right of possession of and jurisdiction over" all portions of the Outlet not disposed of in this way. Constitutional and corporation lawyers would torture a variety of meanings from the plain and unambiguous language of this provision after the Cherokee government had decided to extract a return from land otherwise useless to them by leasing it to cattlemen.

Slavery was abolished. The Five Tribes had to adopt their former slaves into full citizenship or help with their removal to ceded or other specified areas. Compensation would be paid by the United States to the tribal government for the adoption of its resident ex-slaves and those who returned to their nation within six months of the date of the treaty; or, if the ex-slaves elected to take up allotments in the areas designated for them, the United States was supposed to bear all expense. In the event, very few ex-slaves ever moved; the Cherokees, Creeks, and Seminoles adopted their former slaves shortly after the treaties had been concluded; the Choctaws adopted theirs only in May 1883; and the Chickasaws (except for a period of less than four years from January 1873 when the ex-slaves were accorded partial citizenship) never adopted theirs.[48]

The sums payable by the United States for the land ceded by the nations remained in the United States Treasury, but the interest was credited to the tribal governments at the end of each fiscal year. The Seminoles alone drew a portion of their annual interest in cash for distribution among the tribe on a per capita basis; the other moneys due under this arrangement were reserved to meet the actual costs chargeable upon the tribal treasuries for the maintenance of government and were disbursed by Treasury bill. Citizens of the Five Tribes paid no taxes of any kind to the United States, and no direct taxes to their own governments. The Indian governments levied a few indirect taxes, but they affected only a small minority of citizens.

There was a set of provisions in the Cherokee treaty which, had they been acted upon, would have turned a section of the Cherokee Nation into a state within a state. Certain Cherokees (a clause in Article VIII confirms that Articles IV–VII were meant chiefly for former Confederate partisans), along with "freed persons who were formerly slaves to any Cherokee, and all free negroes not having been slaves, who resided in the Cherokee Nation prior to June 1st, 1861," could choose within two years to stay where they were, take up 160-acre allotments in Canadian district, or take up allotments in that part of the nation northeast of the Arkansas River and southeast of the Grand River.[49] (This last option would have placed the allottees in a slender strip of country in Illinois and Cooweescoowee districts, north of Canadian district, and adjacent to the northeast boundary line of the Muskogee Nation.) If the exercise of the removal options should exhaust all the land not occupied by those who were already living in these areas, room would be made elsewhere in Cooweescoowee district, touching the northern boundary of the Muskogee Nation.[50]

All who took up allotments in this fringe of the Cherokee Nation, together with the Cherokees already living there, would have the right "to elect all their local officers and judges . . . and to control all their local affairs, and to establish all necessary police regulations and rules for the administration of justice in said district, not inconsistent with the constitution of the Cherokee Nation and the laws of the United States." If any Cherokee law were to "operate unjustly or injuriously in said district", or any of the local "police regulations and rules" should "bear oppressively on any citizen of the nation," the President of the United States could "correct" it in the former instance or suspend it in the latter.

Further, the United States district court "the nearest to the Cherokee Nation" was to have "exclusive original jurisdiction of all causes, civil and criminal," in which residents of the special district were parties. Where one of the parties was resident elsewhere in the Cherokee Nation, the defending party could choose whether the case should be heard by the Cherokee court or the United States, the laws of the Cherokee Nation to apply. No court process from any other district of the Cherokee Nation could be served upon a resident of the special district unless it had been endorsed by the judge of the special district. Residents of the special district were to be represented in the Cherokee national council in the same ratio as their numbers bore to the population as a whole.

Owing to the disinclination of former Confederate families and ex-slaves to relocate themselves, and the preference of the standing populace for their existing status in the Cherokee Nation, an experiment that might have hampered government in the Cherokee Nation quite seriously never advanced beyond the statute book. Police regulations in Canadian district were unaltered, except that the district comprised a circuit of its own. The articles of the treaty of 1866 in regard to the special district were, however, construed to cover the conduct of civil and criminal cases occurring in Canadian district, which became, accordingly, an island of jurisdictional uncertainty.[51] In practice, however, most cases originating in Canadian district were dealt with by the Cherokee courts.

Rights-of-way were conceded by all but the Seminoles to allow for the construction of two railroads, one to run from north to south, the other from east to west. These railways would be granted land upon the extinguishment of the Indian title. This presupposed an expectation by the railway companies and the Interior Department of the early demise of tribal governments, and it was patently in the interests of the railways to expedite the journey of the tribal governments into oblivion; but the restrictive proviso was a vastly greater obstacle than was credited then, or a decade later, by either the railway companies or the cynics and pessimists among the Indians. The railroads received no grant of land, even after the tribal titles had been made defunct; the alarm that was excited in the nations on the question of railroad grants was a storm aroused by a specter. The Seminoles undertook to admit only one railway line, which they did not see until 1898.

All five tribes agreed to send delegates to a general council that was to meet annually to discuss matters of common cause. It was expected, but not stipulated, that the general council, to which all tribes in the Indian Territory were entitled to send delegates, would result in tribal consolidation and the formulation of a territorial constitution.

If the provisions that seemed to many to foreshadow the apportionment of large slices of the tribal domain to the railways and the Government posed a conspicuous but empty threat to tribal sovereignty, a subtler, but far deadlier and, indeed, fatal menace was coiled within certain other articles of the treaties. These articles, their implications, and their consequences are what has prompted the present inquiry.

Article VII of the Cherokee treaty, concluded on July 19, 1866, and proclaimed on August 11 that year, began: "The United States court to be created in the Indian Territory; and until such court is created there . . . " And, while the remainder of that article was devoted to the rights and responsibilities of inhabitants of the special district, the opening words embrace a specific intention.

Article XIII of the treaty was worded as follows:

> The Cherokees also agree that a court or courts may be established in the United States, in said Territory, with such jurisdiction and organized in such manner as may be prescribed by law: *Provided.* That the judicial tribunals of the nation shall be allowed to retain exclusive jurisdiction in all civil and criminal cases arising within their country in which members of the nation, by nativity or adoption, shall be the only parties, or where the cause of action shall arise in the Cherokee Nation, except as otherwise provided in this treaty.

Here the categorical purpose expressed in the Seventh Article is repeated and elaborated upon, with a restrictive proviso to exclude from United States jurisdiction all cases where all parties were Cherokee citizens. Nevertheless, the phrase excluding from the compass of the federal courts "members of the nation, by nativity or adoption," to every appearance unequivocal, did not put an end to attempts by the federal authorities to assume jurisdiction on cases involving white Cherokee adoptees. The exception in the proviso referred to the projected special district.

This single article in this one treaty would have sufficed for the installation of a United States court in the Indian Territory, but the other treaties yielded the same ground, or more. Article VII of the Seminole treaty, Article VII of the Choctaw and Chickasaw treaty, and Article X of the Creek treaty were framed in very similar language.

> The Seminole Nation agrees to such legislation as Congress and the President may deem necessary for the better administration of the rights of person and property within the Indian Territory: *Provided,* however, said legislation shall not in any manner interfere with or annul their present tribal organization, rights, laws, privileges, and customs.

> The Choctaws and Chickasaws agreed to such legislation as Congress and the President of the United States may deem necessary for the better

administration of justice and the protection of the rights of person and property within the Indian Territory: *Provided:* however, such legislation shall not in anywise interfere with or annul their present tribal organization, or their respective legislatures or judiciaries or the rights, laws, privileges, or customs of the Choctaw and Chickasaw Nations respectively.

The Creeks agree to such legislation as Congress and the President of the United States may deem necessary for the better administration of justice and the protection of the rights of person and property within the Indian territory; *Provided, however,* said legislation shall not in any manner interfere with or annul their present tribal organization, rights, laws, privileges, and customs.

Over and above all this, the article which set out the formula for the organization of a general council carried in every instance except that of the Cherokee treaty a section providing that "a court or courts may be established in said [Indian] Territory with such jurisdiction and organization as Congress may prescribe." This section was not dependent upon the operation of the other provisions of the article and left it open to Congress to prescribe that the court or courts should be administered by the United States.

These were the provisions through which the United States would dislocate and disarm the tribal governments before dispossessing them of all authority and, finally, dissolving them altogether.

The rationale was clear and simple. Its configuration was outlined before Congress again and again by advocates of court reform as a means of replacing tribal by Territorial or State government. Once a federal court had been established inside the region occupied by the Five Tribes, an argument could be put for the absorption of the duties and jurisdiction of the tribal courts; then the tribal courts would be subordinated, or abolished altogether; hence, without a judiciary or courts of law, the tripodal structure of government would collapse, and the nations would cease to command the respect or recognition of their citizens; so, though the outward forms of tribal government might linger for a while, it would have become a charade and a cipher.

The tribes whose allegiance to the Confederacy had been almost unqualified secured the best terms from the United States under the postwar treaties. Unity of purpose and ideal, even in a losing cause, may have won a trick or two for the Choctaws and Chickasaws at the negotiating table. In contrast, the personal rivalries and historic enmities which had split the Cherokees, Creeks, and Seminoles between Union and Confederacy ensured that each of these tribes would be represented by two opposing delegations with a single set of peace terms to treat for.

Illustrations of the easier usage accorded the Choctaw and Chickasaw delegation occur in the articles affecting the jurisdiction of the tribal courts. Article XXXVIII stated:

> Every white person who, having married a Choctaw or Chickasaw, resides in the said Choctaw or Chickasaw Nation, or who has been adopted by the legislative authorities, is to be deemed a member of said nation, and shall be subject to the laws of the Choctaw or Chickasaw Nations according to his domicile and to prosecution and trial before their tribunals, and to punishment according to their laws in all respects as though he was a native Choctaw or Chickasaw.

Nor (unlike what is to all appearances an equally plain proviso in the Cherokee treaty) was the Choctaw and Chickasaw jurisdiction much disturbed by the United States courts, although several instances of interference did occur during the 1870s and 1880s.[52] Traditionalists in the Choctaw and Chickasaw nations did not like the stipulation that a white person could be assured of admission into the tribe simply through intermarriage; in the 1870s a conservative government tried to mitigate the effects of this provision by placing a tax on all marriages between Choctaw women and white men.[53]

Under Article XLI, all Choctaws and Chickasaws "not otherwise disqualified or disabled" were to be "competent witnesses in all civil and criminal suits and proceedings in any courts of the United States, any law to the contrary notwithstanding." There was nothing to prevent members of the Cherokee, Muskogee, or Seminole nations from being called as a witness before a federal court, but their ability to give trustworthy testimony could more easily be challenged by opposing counsel.

Article XLVII, under which the Choctaws and Chickasaws would, upon requisition, deliver up any person "found within their respective limits" who was wanted in the United States for the commission of a criminal offense against federal or State laws, was so obviously an improvement upon the clumsy arrangement embodied in the Intercourse Act of 1834, involving the Indian agent, that it is hard to understand why similar provisions did not find their way into the other treaties. Yet there was no reciprocal clause even in the Choctaw-Chickasaw treaty.

Still, the success of the Choctaw and Chickasaw delegations in coming away from Washington with better terms than their counterparts from the other tribes meant only, in practice, that their two systems could function with a little more freedom from federal interference for as long as the United States Congress and Executive were controlled by men who were willing to allow the tribal governments to exist.

At this time, too, the progressive element was uppermost in the politics of the Choctaw and Chickasaw nations. Cyrus Harris, a mixed-blood, who was elected in 1866 to the first of three two-year terms as governor of the Chickasaw Nation,[54] believed that the best hope for maintaining tribal independence lay in allotment of the common lands by dividing them into homesteads, despite the risk of the unchecked "ingress of those who seek the downfall of our nationality."[55] Allen Wright, seven-eighths Choctaw, had been a member of the delegation to Washington that had negotiated the terms of the treaty of 1866 and had been elected principal chief later that year. He was less cautious than Harris in favoring a program of tribal modernization and consolidation.[56] It was he who first suggested that the Indian country should become the Territory of Oklahoma.[57]

Wright's attitudes were typified by an insistent belief in the supremacy of tribal law over the unwritten code of an earlier tradition which many Choctaws had not abandoned. Certain of his personal or political friends who were reported to be planning to avenge the death of an ally by killing the murderer, although he had been sentenced to hang,[58] received this warning, addressed to "Dear Friends":

> The information . . . comes in the form of a petition looking to a fair settlement according to due course of law, and early restoration of peace, order and harmony in the county [Jack's Fork]. And I deem it my duty to give you a word of caution. Therefore I would advise you to desist from doing anything in the way of seeking private revenge. So long as we exist as a Nation having Constitution, Laws, and officers to guide us, it is our imperative duty, as good and law-abiding citizens, to obey the laws of our Nation. Should you resort to retaliate upon the person of Stanford Ohohaya for killing Johnson Wash and kill him notwithstanding of the advice you have received from Friends—you and your confederates are liable to be prosecuted as murderers, and would in all probability be executed as such. . . . Hence to avoid bringing any trouble upon yourselves—the wisest course for you to pursue is, to rely upon the strong arm of the nation. It is her duty to investigate the extent of crime and guilt, and adjudicate it according to sense of justice.[59]

Outside the Choctaw and Chickasaw nations there was little overt support for progressive politics in the later 1860s, or, for that matter, until well into the 1870s. Cherokee affairs had been unsettled by the death of John Ross in August 1866, but the political regrouping that ensued did not alter the balance against any policy that might lead to allotment of the land and the establishment of a Territorial government, proposals congenial only to a minority of mixed-bloods. John Chupco, the Seminole principal chief, and John Jumper, the leader of the Confederate partisans, were both opposed to the encroachment of alien influences. Samuel Checote, a Confederate man who in the autumn of 1867 became the first elected principal chief of the Creeks, presided over a nation which, at that time seems to have been united in its antagonism to proposals for allotment and Territorialization, if it was united on nothing else.

All five governments, whatever their political complexion, had as their foremost concern the social and economic disruption that was the backwash of the Civil War.[60] A traveler who journeyed through the Indian Territory five years after the end of the war saw abundant evidence of the "waste and desolation": "The ruined plantations; the burned, charred remains of the farm-houses . . . the scanty and straggling herds of stock, now grown wild, in place of the great droves of cattle and horses.[61]

Three years later, however, a visitor observed that "the tribes have nearly as much [stock] as before the war."[62] By the early 1870s, then, the staple of the prewar economy had almost recovered its old position. Not much land had been under cultivation before the Civil War; its proportion to the whole was still insignificant, but was growing. Most of the Indians who had been dispersed by the war or the dangers of the war had returned to their old homes by March 1866, when the citizen population of the Five Tribes was estimated at 55,000, composed of 17,000 Cherokees, 22,000 Choctaws and Chickasaws, 14,000 Creeks, and 2,000 Seminoles.[63]

Servants of the Executive were not long in urging Congress to introduce legislation for the judicial reforms portended by the treaties. Newton Robinson, the Southern Superintendent of Indian Affairs, not only cited "the great inconvenience to persons in this Territory in attending the United States court now held in Van Buren" but expressed it as "the desire of these people" (the Indians) that a United States court should be set up in the Indian Territory; he suggested, most prematurely, that "the territorial seat of government" would provide the best site.[64]

A year later the Cherokee agent, Captain John Craig, reviewed the shortcomings of the existing arrangements and the stresses to which they were subjected. After condemning both the Van Buren court and the Cherokee courts for their partiality and inefficiency, Craig suggested reforms far more drastic than any that could have been introduced under the treaties. The cure, he thought, would be found in the establishment of military commissions in the Cherokee Nation with the power to try and, upon conviction, to "inflict a designated punishment on principals and accessories in cases of murder, robbery, assault and battery with intent to kill, and simple assault" in all instances, including those in which only Cherokees were involved.[65]

Measures as radical as those asked for by Craig had no chance of being considered in Washington, but it was because the treaty provisions for judicial reform did not reach nearly far enough to suit the most interested members of Congress that a generation was to pass before the federal court was installed among the Five Tribes.

These congressmen wanted nothing less than territorial government in the Indian Territory, and started to push hard for it when the tribal governments showed no disposition to draw up plans of their own for a closer association with the Union, as envisaged in the treaties. It was not until 1888 that the Territorializers were able to collect enough support in the House to pass an Oklahoma bill, and only after that had been stifled in the Senate did members of the two legislative branches enter into a coalition of objectives under which judicial would precede political reform in a gradated program that would inside a decade leave the edifice of tribal government in ruins.

CHAPTER TWO

An Imperium in Imperio?

Wondrous word; an anomaly!—George Colin McKee, Republican congressman, Mississippi, in House of Representatives, January 16, 1873, Congressional Globe, *42d Cong., 3d sess.*

What will be the next recourse, unless Oklahoma is established in the Indian Territory?—Theodora R. Jenness, "The Indian Territory," Atlantic Monthly, *April 1879*

It was not Congress, but an arm of the Executive branch of the United States Government, which struck the first blows at tribal pretensions to unfettered sovereignty within their national boundaries. These actions were, to begin with, lacking in legal and constitutional justification, and the Indians were able to gain the point. The Government's response was to frame a law which, for the next fifteen years, would be held as testimony to the hollowness of the Five Tribes' claims to local independence.

In the winter of 1866–1867 officials of the Internal Revenue Service of the Treasury Department assessed and collected taxes on certain Indians; one Choctaw citizen had to pay $16,000 out of the proceeds of his cotton crop. Chief Wright, in a memorial to Congress, protested, quite correctly, that Indians were exempt from federal taxation and requested the refund of the moneys exacted by the revenue men.[1]

That was the end of the Treasury's attempt to turn the Indian country into a general collection area. It decided instead to seek powers to levy taxation on certain specified products, and acquired that authority in July 1868 under Section 107 of "An act imposing taxes on distilled spirits and tobacco, and for other purposes."

[T]he internal revenue laws imposing taxes on distilled spirits, fermented liquors, tobacco, snuff, and cigars, shall be held and construed to extend to such articles produced anywhere within the exterior boundaries of the United States, whether the same shall be within a collection district or not.[2]

Almost directly after this, several tobacco factories were established in the Cherokee Nation, most notably one by Cornelius Boudinot, the lawyer-entrepreneur son of one of the leaders of the old "Treaty party." These manufacturers maintained that the provisions of the Cherokee Treaty of 1866 ensured that the Revenue Act could not be operative inside the nation. In 1871 the case went to the Supreme Court, which (with two justices dissenting) ruled that an act of Congress overrode a treaty.[3]

Although this ruling delivered a mortal thrust at the doctrine that the United States could reach into the Indian Territory only when the treaties so provided, it was instrumental in sealing the Territory against another threat, perhaps as great as the one it had presented. If the federal prosecution had failed, the Indian country would have furnished the site for a market-cornering scheme founded upon the bulk production of untaxed tobacco and financed from outside. Such heavy capital investment from the East or Middle West must have brought with it a wedge of political influence and promoted a need for associated industrial expansion—more railways, for instance, and in all probability more intensive farming methods—placing the tribal governments further in thrall. Government and society in the Indian country could not have withstood a rush of commercial and industrial expansion at this stage.

The tribal governments had made no move to take up the proposals for Territorialization embedded in the Reconstruction treaties when a bill similar to Harlan's Senate bill of 1865 was introduced in the House in March 1869 by Robert Van Horn (R, Missouri), a publisher and promoter from Kansas City.[4] No action on it was proposed by the Committee on Indian Affairs, but the fact that it had been introduced persuaded the leaders of the Five Tribes to accede to the first requisite of the consolidation proposals, which called for the drafting of a constitution. Similar bills were pending in Congress in the spring of 1870 when the principal chief of the Muskogee Nation, Samuel Checote, proposed an International Council "to take into consideration the present situation and adopt such a policy as will be beneficial to each Nation and citizen thereof":

> Deeply impressed with the great importance of our early action it behooves us to be alive to the progressive spirit of the age.
> The adventurous spirit of the white man warrants the assertion that unless we take measures to more fully secure the rich heritage so justly ours that ere long we will be surrounded by a flood tide of immigration we cannot resist and the settlement we cannot avoid.[5]

Later that year, delegations from the tribes met at Okmulgee, the Muskogee capital, and the text of a draft constitution was agreed upon and adopted in December.

A section of the Choctaw-Chickasaw treaty of 1866 had carried the proposal that the Indian country, when consolidated, should be given the name Oklahoma. Under the Okmulgee constitution, the tribal lands would be grouped together as "The Indian Territory," thereby conferring official recognition upon the name used informally by all.

Since the principal object of the delegates was avoidance of congressional plans to impose a constitution that would place the appointment of Territorial officials within the discretion of the United States Government, the Okmulgee proposals differed from those in the Harlan and Van Horn bills mainly by providing for the election of a governor by the qualified voters of each nation and for three district judges to be chosen by the governor.[6]

Van Horn responded by disinterring his bill from committee, where it had lain for almost two years. In reintroducing his bill, he referred to the recent completion of the transcontinental railway and set out the premise that would be reiterated by numerous expansionists and entrepreneurs in the course of the next twenty years:

> The Indian country, or the territory of the United States, owing to the construction of our Pacific railroads and the development of the material resources of the country, has become so circumscribed that we have now no country West to which these Indians can be removed. In the opinion of the committee the time has come for a new policy in regard to the Indians of this country.

Van Horn described the Okmulgee constitution as one for a State government (it was not far short of that) and observed that, in aiming for conformity with the main provisions of the peace treaties, the delegates had gone "further in some respects than the treaties themselves." In his opinion, the time had not yet come "for a movement to this extent." The Van Horn bill was designed as a vehicle for a continuing policy in Indian Territory. Its most important feature was a deliberate omission: "The land is yet owned in common, and the Committee on Indian Affairs have not thought it proper to disturb that state of affairs."[7]

Common ownership of land was the keystone of tribal society and of its agrarian economy. It allowed the individual citizen the *use* (not the ownership) of as much of the available land as he needed, provided that he kept his crops or stock at least a quarter mile (in the Chickasaw Nation, 444 yards) from his neighbor's fence or gate. Equality of opportunity would favor the more enterprising members of the tribe as long as there was enough good land to satisfy the requirements of all; but, as the land stock diminished, control of the land in use passed to a decreasing number of ranchers and farmers, leaving progressively less scope for the more energetic and intelligent of those outside the new cartelism.

In the 1870s, the agrarian structure of the Five Tribes had not run its full economic course from yeomanly communalism to syndicalism and monopoly; it was not until 1887 that Congress enacted legislation for the systematic allotment in severalty of the land, even of other Indian tribes. By then much of the common land of the Five Tribes belonged in effect to a comparatively few men, who, with their friends in Washington, were the stoutest upholders of the inviolability of tribal land title held in common.

Harlan, Van Horn, and their political associates were unconcerned with how the economic landscape of Indian Territory might be reshaped over the next fifteen or twenty years. They knew that the Five Nations could not be absorbed by the United States until the system of communal land tenure had been broken up and that, in their day, opposition in and out of Congress to the forcible dissolution of tribal titles could not be overcome. An early and direct assault upon the central rationale of the sovereignty of the Nations was therefore out of the question: the barrier would have to be planed away until conditions conducive to its total removal arose or could be created.

Extension of the federal Government through the application of the current treaty provisions would bring the Indians into closer contact with Washington. If the tribes would not accept a Territorial constitution in which the gubernatorial and judicial appointments were reserved for federal nominees, the United States would enter the nations through the legal tunnel afforded by the courts provisions of the Reconstruction treaties. During the debate on Van Horn's bill, Daniel Voorhees—an antiwar Union Democrat from Indiana, lawyer-orator, and subsequently, from the Senate, one of the foremost defenders of the sovereignty of the Five Nations—urged that the bill be enacted so that those provisions would be fulfilled:

> The bill . . . proposes certain legislation . . . if Congress shall deem such legislation "necessary for the better administration of justice, and the protection of the rights of persons and property within the Indian territory", [and] there can be no question of the power and duty of Congress to adopt such legislation, subject only to the stipulation of the provisos, that the tribal governments shall not be interfered with.[8]

Voorhees' remarks were accompanied by something that became one of the staples of debate on judicial questions affecting the Indian Territory: a reading of the seventh article of the Choctaw-Chickasaw treaty of

1866, thirteenth article of the Cherokee treaty, and tenth article of the Creek treaty. Only the seventh article of the Seminole treaty was, on this occasion, overlooked.

Voorhees pointed out that the administration of justice in the Indian Territory depended, for United States citizens, upon the Intercourse Act of 1834 and various pieces of emendatory legislation. All the officers and jurors of the United States court for the Western District of Arkansas were "selected from the citizens of Arkansas," making the Indians "the sport and prey of irresponsible United States officials."[9] As an example of this he cited the arrest of several prominent Cherokees, including two senators, on charges of which they were presently acquitted (although the verdict could as easily have been adduced as evidence of the impartiality of the Arkansas jury).

He went on to say that "at least one half of the arrests made in the Indian country by these deputy marshals are made without warrant or process of any kind whatever." The abolition of the Indian agencies in the Territory, as proposed by Van Horn, would save $20,000 per year and rid the country of "a useless corps of officers who, in nine cases out of ten, are inferior in point of education and ability to those whom they are supposed to have under their especial care and protection." The Okmulgee constitution, he finished, went too far in leaving the United States Government "no supervision whatever over the Indians or the Territory" and "no responsibility except to make the necessary appropriations." The Van Horn bill, however, would enable the Government to retain a certain control while giving the Indians "courts in their own country and juries of their own people."[10]

Neither the Van Horn bill nor the Okmulgee constitution became law. Efforts to keep the idea of voluntary consolidation a live issue with the tribal governments were made at five further annual meetings of the Indian general council, then abandoned. Even if the United States had agreed to give legal force to the Okmulgee constitution, the Cherokees and Chickasaws, for differing reasons, would have rejected it; and even if all the tribes had accepted it, the United States would not have allowed its adoption.

In February 1872, two unrelated requests for legislation to truncate the jurisdiction of the Western Arkansas court were received by Congress. Commissioner of Indian Affairs Francis Walker, asking for a term of the district court to be held annually at Okmulgee, stated erroneously that the court was "held by law only at Van Buren," but this scarcely damaged his argument because Fort Smith, which had been the court town for very nearly a year, was no more than a few miles west of Van Buren; hence the change had hardly mitigated the "inconvenience and expense attending the deportation of persons charged with crime, and the attendance of witnesses from so great a distance."[11]

The Kansas legislature saw another problem: criminal proceedings in which Cherokees and Kansans were the parties necessitated a troublesome journey to Fort Smith, and the State of Kansas was too big and was becoming too thickly settled to be served by the United States court at Topeka in federal cases arising domestically. These difficulties could be solved by dividing the State into two districts and attaching the Indian Territory to a new Southern District of Kansas, with the courthouse at Chetopa or Oswego.[12]

Both suggestions were pigeonholed by Congress. Even so, the Kansas resolution is of interest because beneath it were attitudes toward the Indian Territory and its inhabitants that persisted at least until 1889.

First, animosity for all Indians was commonly felt in Kansas, which was still a frontier State; the nearer the line marking the northerly limits of Indian Territory, the fiercer the enmity, so that it was intense in such ambitious little towns as Chetopa, Oswego, Sedan, Independence, Coffeyville, Parsons, Columbus, and Baxter Springs. It was an inimicality which, like the uninformed sentimentality that was its obverse, drew no distinction between the untutored nomad of the Plains and the transplanted Eastern agriculturalist, and it was aggravated by resentment of the Southern sympathies and associations of many Cherokees.[13]

A second factor was wholly commercial. As one observer explained,

> Let Congress pass an enabling act for that [Indian] Territory, and in three months these roads leading southward from Kansas City and Lawrence would double their business; in six months it would quadruple. Throw open the Territory next January [1874], and it would be ready for admission as a State by January 1875. . . . Settle it with white men, and the lands of Southern Kansas would nearly double in value. . . . I am led to think that the Kansians anticipate rightly, and that the Territory will be open to settlement before 1875.[14]

A third consideration grew out of the spoils system of political preferment. If Congress gave Kansas an additional federal district, it would have to appropriate funds for the payment of court officials. The district judge would almost certainly be a resident of the State and, almost certainly again, he would be politically influential in that State. The same was true on a diminishing scale of the United States marshal, district attorney, chief deputy marshal, clerk of the court, court commissioners, and so on down to the bailiff and stenographer. Such was the system that enabled a man to pay off old political debts and create new obligations.

Already, though, the proliferation of new judicial districts of the United States during President Grant's first term had provoked a storm of outrage from Congress, even though the creation of most of the new courts could be justified by circumstances.[15] Thus, while Congress could turn its back on the pleas of Commissioner Walker and the Kansas legislature, the pressures underlying them would build up until they could hardly be resisted.

During the immediate postwar years, the federal and tribal authorities were at odds because of the increased traffic in liquor. "Many complaints are made to me by Cherokees, regarding the proceedings of deputy marshals in making searches for spirituous liquors without warrant or writ," John Craig, agent for the Cherokees, noted in 1869.[16] But as he added in his report for the following year, "The quantity of whisky brought into the country is very large, and experience has clearly shown that it is beyond the power of the United States authorities to check its introduction."[17]

Many white men were profitably engaged in the whisky trade, and they were helped by Indians to elude detection. The Cherokee authorities, who could "repress its introduction" if they were so disposed, would "make no systematic efforts to that end."[18] Craig's successor, John B. Jones, the former missionary, reported, "frequent arrests have been made by United States marshals, where the parties were undoubtedly guilty, but they have escaped punishment by this process of intimidating witnesses."[19] Similar complaints were heard from the agent for the Choctaws and Chickasaws whose difficulties were aggravated by the influx of "a horde of roughs" who were following the line of the Missouri, Kansas and Texas Railway along its line of construction southward. The agent, with military aid, succeeded in removing these individuals, but it was not long before they were "getting up their heads again."[20]

The amendment in 1864 of Section 20 of the Intercourse Act so that an Indian who disposed of liquor to, or obtained it from, an Indian in the Indian country could not be reached by the federal courts,[21] had restored a portion of lost sovereignty to the Five Tribes, but the tribal authorities were not zealous in the exercise of the newly recovered right. In 1868, therefore, the United States prosecuted an Indian who had sold liquor to another Indian. The case failed, as it was bound to do, for want of jurisdiction; but attention had been called to a situation which, in the view of the Superintendent of Indian Affairs, was highly detrimental to the welfare of the tribes.[22] In spite of this, it was not until 1877 that Congress repealed the amendment of 1864.[23]

At the source of much of the jurisdictional dissension between the federal and tribal courts were their opposing interpretations of the citizenship clauses of the Reconstruction treaties. A prolonged tussle between the Van Buren court and the Chickasaw Nation ensued after Robert Love, a Chickasaw citizen serving as a deputy United States marshal, shot and killed a Chickasaw freedman whom he was attempting to arrest on a charge of murder. Love was charged and lodged in the United States jail. Cyrus Harris, the Chickasaw governor, tried to procure Love's release on a writ of requisition, but such a document served by an Indian government upon federal or State officials had no binding force, and the United States marshal disregarded it.

The case was reported to President Andrew Johnson and referred by him to Attorney General William Evarts, whose reply that the matter "must be left to judical control" suggests that he either did not know the law or did not care to lay it down.[24] In this instance, the federal court was in the right; although the Chickasaw Nation was obliged by the terms of the treaty of 1866 to extend citizenship to its ex-slaves, it had not done so. Hence the man killed by Love was not a Chickasaw citizen, and the Chickasaw courts could not take jurisdiction.

The Cherokee Nation was involved in far more of these disputes than any other. One such case was that mentioned by Daniel Voorhees in the debate on the Van Horn bill (although the Congressmen misunderstood or misrepresented some of the details). This controversy depended upon whether a man who had been killed by a Cherokee in the Cherokee Nation was a Cherokee or, as his mother maintained, a United States citizen. The Cherokee sheriff refused to surrender the defendant to a deputy United States marshal, and in due course the man was acquitted by a Cherokee jury. Some time later two Cherokee senators, who had been present when the sheriff had rejected the federal warrant, were arrested, charged with having resisted a United States officer, and taken to Van Buren. The charges were withdrawn; the mutual irritation ensured further friction. In the spring of 1872 the bitterness found an outlet in extreme violence.[25]

Ezekiel Proctor, a Cherokee mixed-blood, was said to have belonged to the Pin movement; but the Pins were mostly full-bloods, and one of the society's founders, John R. Jones, called Proctor "a most desperate character." Proctor's legal difficulties began when, trying to shoot an adopted white Cherokee named J. J. Kesterson, he missed his aim and killed the man's wife, a native Cherokee. Proctor surrendered to the sheriff of Going Snake district and was charged with murder; but the widower, perhaps abetted by his late wife's Cherokee relations, and believing that the jury had been packed with friends of the defendant, procured a warrant in Fort Smith for Proctor's arrest on a charge of attempting to murder Kesterson.

Word of this was relayed to Going Snake district. The district officers—and Proctor's friends—were forearmed as well as forewarned when a party led by two deputy marshals, but including relatives of the dead woman and other Cherokees hostile to Proctor, arrived while the trial was under way. Knowing that the federal officers were coming and who was with them, the Cherokee authorities held the trial in the schoolhouse, which was more suitable for defense than the courthouse. According to the more credible evidence, everyone in the temporary courthouse, including judge, jurors, and defendant, was armed or within easy reach of weapons. Armed men were also posted around the building by the sheriff.

As one of the marshal's party entered the courthouse, a gun was discharged from within, and general battle was joined. In the ensuing melee eleven men were killed, eight from the Fort Smith party. Proctor himself was among the many wounded.

If words have meaning, all jurisdiction in the Proctor-Kesterson case rested with the Cherokee Nation. Kesterson had acquired the right to live in the nation by marrying a native Cherokee and with it the responsibilities as well as the rights of Cherokee citizenship. A proviso in the thirteenth article of the Cherokee treaty of 1866 recognized Cherokee jurisdiction in "all civil and criminal cases arising within their country in which citizens of the nation, by nativity or adoption, shall be the only parties." Against this the federal authorities seem to have pitted the belief (for neither the first nor the last time) that a United States citizen did not lose United States citizenship by becoming a citizen of an Indian nation.

One set of principals was as much to blame for the carnage as the other. Evidence of precautionary measures, amounting perhaps to premeditation on the part of the Going Snake authorities, has been cited. It is apparent too that the Fort Smith party must have been caught between two fires. Their instructions were to make no move to arrest Proctor unless he was acquitted, and they said as much before the shooting started, although not everyone could have heard them. They may also have had grounds for thinking that the Going Snake officials were shielding the Cherokees who had murdered a deputy marshal nearby only a month earlier; but this makes it all the harder to excuse their clumsiness in putting on so conspicuous a show of force. Worse still was their recklessness, carelessness, or weakness in allowing Proctor's deadliest enemy to lead the way into the building heavily armed.

Proctor was acquitted of the murder of Polly Kesterson. Her relatives then charged that the jury had been selected from the defendant's friends, and they may have been right. Nonetheless, the question of justice malfunctioning was one for the Cherokees to resolve among themselves; and in 1877 their government, hoping to banish partiality from trials for serious offenses, made "all cases of manslaughter and all cases involving the punishment of death" the exclusive prerogative of the supreme court of the Cherokee Nation.[26]

The Cherokee side of the argument was concisely put by Principal Chief Lewis Downing in a letter to the tribal delegates dated April 17, 1872:

> [T]hough the course of the deputy marshals in this instance is indefensible in any light, even granting that they had a warrant for the prisoner, and might lawfully serve it at the time and place of the tragedy, the important fact remains that the right to do so is undetermined and disputed, as plainly conflicting with our treaty pledges, exclusive right to the unhindered administration of justice among ourselves as a nation. . . . I am assured that, though the conduct of the United States officers . . . was wholly unwarranted upon any ground, the calamity would not have occurred had they had a proper conception of their duty and authority in the premises.[27]

After the bloodletting there was a shower of indictments and warrants: the United States wanted to try, among others, nearly everyone who had been inside the improvised courthouse at the time of the fracas, and the Cherokee Nation was bent on bringing capital charges against its citizens who had joined or aided the deputy marshals en route from Fort Smith. The belated supervention of statesmanlike inertia prevented both the federal and tribal authorities from impaling themselves on the thorns of a luxuriantly tangled jurisdictional thicket.

President Ulysses Grant supported a request from the Department of the Interior for Congress to look favorably upon a pending bill for the creation of a judicial district in the Indian Territory, but Congress averted its eye.

Among the voices calling for the establishment of a federal court in the Indian country, none was louder than that of John Jones, the agent for the Cherokees and one of the most aggressive spokesmen for Cherokee sovereignty. Neither Jones, who in his reports to the Commissioner of Indian Affairs inveighed annually against the iniquities of the Arkansas court, nor the agent for the Creeks, who contented himself with the observation that it was "an imperative necessity" for United States courts to be brought into the Territory, indicated why they thought that the failings of the current system could be redressed simply by moving its base from Fort Smith to Tahlequah, Fort Gibson, or anywhere else in the Indian country. They may have assumed that courts in the Indian Territory, like courts anywhere else, would employ local men.[28]

Whatever the reasoning, there appears to have been unanimity among leading Cherokees that a federal court should be introduced into the Territory. The delegation that prepared a memorial urging the Senate to address itself to the creation of such a court, as "a matter of the gravest moment" in accordance with "the whole plan of our treaties of 1866," included two political opponents of Agent Jones.[29]

On May 1, 1872, barely a fortnight after the "Going Snake Massacre," Congressman Isaac Parker (R, Missouri) reported a bill "for better protection of the Indian tribes and their consolidation under a civil government, to be called the Territory of Oklahoma." Although Parker advocated the allotment of the tribal lands in severalty, he took care to emphasize that his bill made no provision for it. Like several other speakers, he cited the passage of the Revenue Act of 1868 and the judgment in the Tobacco case as fatal to any presumption that the terms of any treaty could place Congress under restraint. Even if the treaties had been graven in granite, Article VII of the Choctaw-Chickasaw treaty and its counterparts in the other peace treaties of 1866 were all wide enough to let in an act of Congress to turn the Indian country into a United States Territory.

Parker displayed supreme confidence in Congress as the fountain of governance whence all that was good must flow. Even if a treaty had been declared inviolable, Congress possessed the authority as "an inherent right of the Government" to "exercise this sovereign power whenever the Representatives of the people believe it ought to be exercised in the interests of humanity, in behalf of justice, and to give security to the property and lives of the people of this nation."

Turning, then, to the propaganda circulated by the delegations of the Five Tribes to connect this bill and its predecessors with the land-grabbing designs of the railroads, Parker reminded the House that the proffered grants were conditional upon the prior extinguishment of tribal title. Moreover, "[i]f it be true, as asserted by the Indians . . . , that their title is held in fee-simple, then I apprehend there need be no fear on their part about it."[30]

John Conner, a Union Democrat representing a Texas district and formerly a regular officer in the navy and the army, argued that the bill did not go nearly far enough. He wanted a bill that would abolish "these miserable Indian nationalities, for they are a burlesque on government"; for as long as the question remained unsettled, "a set of demagogues known as 'Indian delegates' will infest the Departments of this Government and squander the money belonging to their poor and deceived people." In four years the Cherokee delegation alone had run through more than $150,000 from the tribal coffers.

Conner had an answer to the allegation that the railroad corporations were the prime movers in a scheme for enforced territorialization: "[T]his territorial scheme originated ten years ago, long before the railroad companies so fiercely denounced had an existence." Just as noteworthy was his introduction, in a reading from the St. Louis *Missouri Republican,* of an argument that would be developed and refined by others. Here its force was more emotional than cerebral: writer and speaker apparently did not know that many Cherokees, Creeks, and Seminoles had fought on the Union side and that there had been no "act of war" since the treaties of 1866.

> Even if the treaties under which this territory was established were unalterable in character we believe their stipulations have been violated in various ways by the Indians themselves by internal crime and disorder, by acts of war against United States citizens on the frontier, and other matters unnecessary to enumerate.[31]

Michael Kerr, a Union Democrat from Indiana, but an opponent of the Reconstruction program, scornfully rejected the whole Indian policy of the last ten or twelve years as one "of weakness, of mere unmanly time serving, of maudlin sentimentality," a "kid-glove policy" foredoomed to failure while the Indian Territory stood "as an impassable barrier and obstacle in the way of needed American progress." "I say we have no right, unless we have made up our minds that we will be recreant to our duty, to maintain indefinitely a Chinese wall round about the very garden spot of this continent. We have no right to perpetuate over it a cloud of barbarism."[32]

From the Republican side of the House a member from Nebraska, John Taffe, succeeded in enunciating the creed of eminent domain without actually pronouncing those words:

> [N]othing like an actual sovereignty in Indian tribes was ever recognized in this country. As to land title, the ultimate fee or allodium has always been claimed and held by our Government, whether of the British Crown or of the United States. . . . Not the slightest pretension to the doctrine of *imperium in imperio* as ever been countenanced or tolerated."[33]

Only 138 members were in attendance when the motion was put to set the bill aside, and only 43 of these opposed the question, but the arguments heard then were among those that in later years would be bandied back and forth in debate after debate; some of the phrases minted in 1872 would be battered into clichés. The debate is also of interest as a record of the very decided views held by Isaac Parker a few years before a change of professional and personal circumstances would impel a change of attitudes.

Although the issues did not reach Congress again until almost the end of the decade, their topicality in the Indian Territory and in much of the country at large did not abate. Late in 1874, the Board of Indian Commissioners, a semigovernmental and semiphilanthropical organization formed in 1869 at the prompting of General Grant, returned from Muskogee with an endorsement of the view, firmly expressed by Secretary of the Interior Columbus Delano and his Commissioner of Indian Affairs, Edward Smith, that the lawlessness of the Indian country made the installation of Territorial government "an immediate necessity."[34] It was not so much this as the board's declaration that such action by Congress would elicit a hearty welcome from "a great majority of the inhabitants" which spurred the Cherokees, Chickasaws, Creeks, and Osages into coordinated and forceful protest.

"We respectfully deny," wrote Governor Frank Overton of the Chickasaw Nation, "that there is any considerable number of Indians in any tribe resident in the Territory, who desire the establishment of such a government by Congress." Overton commended to the attention of Congress the "protests and remonstrances emanating from time to time from the several national councils of the Territory, or from their respective, duly-authorized delegates," whom he advertised as "the true exponents of the sentiments of the people of this Territory."[35]

The tone of the memorial from the Osage Nation was bitingly acidic, its author scoffing at the arguments advanced for the extension of federal influence within Indian Territory and heaping ridicule upon the executive officers of the Fort Smith court:

> What! Can any person have the brass to look you in the face and say the Government of the United States cannot put down a few horse-thieves and murderers in the Indian country, when that Government has put down a rebellion of eight million people? . . . A great many of your deputy marshals, when they come into our country, look more after the quality of lands than they do after criminals, and they go smelling around hunting whisky, and, on finding the same, we are told that they spill it down their own throats.[36]

There was a further plea from the Kansas legislature for the creation of a federal court "at as early a day as possible . . . at as near a point as practicable to said [Indian] Territory,"[37] followed by a resolution submitted by Senator Powell Clayton (R, Arkansas) calling for an inquiry into the expediency of establishing one or more inferior courts in the

Indian Territory to relieve the Fort Smith court of the expense and trouble of trying petty larcenists and offenders against the liquor laws.[38] These proposals were, in part, a consequence of a recent scandal over the affairs of the Fort Smith court, and the one put forward by Clayton drew forth a furious response from some of the leading citizens of Arkansas.[39]

From the Indian Territory itself, suggestions were forthcoming for a quite different pattern of reform:

> Will the Committee on Indian Affairs and the Territorial Committee give us a little at a time. Homeopathic doses, as it were, of United States citizenship. We are not prepared to take it all at once, we know our people will object to so radical a change. . . .
>
> The five Nations . . . have a code of written laws. . . . We have District courts and Supreme courts already established for the trial of our own citizens—why not use them first? Enlarge their powers, give them full jurisdiction, civil and criminal over all persons who reside within the limits of either [*sic*] Nation with appellate powers to the United States courts. That would reach all cases. The White citizens of the United States now residing among us could not object, for they come here of their own free will. . . .
>
> Let them all be amenable to our laws, subject to arrest and trial the same as an Indian. If we have not laws enough to govern the country well, we will speedily follow your example, and erect more, as our Councils are capable. Make us first the peers of United States citizens, in the Territory, as a stepping stone to full equality hereafter. Then we should hear no more complaints of "want of law." . . . Try this method first, if you are afraid to trust us with this little stretch of power, can you blame us for refusing the "greater boon" you offer.[40]

And a few months later:

> The treaties of 1866 contemplated the establishment of a United States Court in the Territory, and why has it not been done? . . . Why not also extend the jurisdiction of the National Courts to all persons within their respective limits? A score of United States deputy marshals may stand by and witness a crime committed by one Indian upon another, or a Captain of the Light Horse and posse may see the law violated with impunity by white men, and both are powerless to interfere, for the question of jurisdiction stands in their way.[41]

Neither then nor later was there any support for this suggestion in either branch of Congress. Indeed, there was not a great deal of interest in the capital in any reforms for the Indian Territory, judicial or governmental, in 1877. All the same, those who were concerned with the issue were gaining in numbers and influence. Prominent among them in the late 1870s was John Patterson, Republican senator for South Carolina during the Reconstruction period and chairman of the Territories and Railroads committees. Others in the Senate were George Vest (D, Missouri) and Daniel Voorhees.

In November 1878, in accordance with a set of resolutions introduced by Voorhees, Patterson led a subcommittee of the Senate Committee on Territories into the Indian country. Their instructions were, first, to inquire into reports that the two railways which had laid track in the Indian Territory had issued bonds predicated upon their conditional land grants; secondly, to investigate allegations that moneys from the school funds of the Five Tribes had been diverted to finance delegations sent to Washington to work against attempts to organize a Territorial government, and lastly,

> to ascertain whether a civil form of government cannot be organized over the Indian Territory for the better protection of life and property; whether the lands now held in common by said Indian tribes cannot be divided in severalty among the Indians without confirming the conditional grants of land to certain railroad corporations.

Patterson and his colleagues confirmed the first proposition. They added that the title belonged to the Indians, anyway, until such time as they wished to surrender it, but that the "ill-advised" land grants should be repealed.

They rejected the second proposition, with the one qualification that they were not fully satisfied with the evidence relating to the Cherokee finances.

Most of the committee's time and interest was consumed by the third proposition. A good deal of testimony was taken about the tribal courts, much of it to their disfavor. There was adverse criticism of the Fort Smith court, too, but most of it followed a well-beaten path: the court was too far removed from the majority of the population of the Indian country to uphold the law effectively and for the attendance of witnesses. It was not, therefore, the collective testimony, but the preformulated views of the senators, which shaped their observations on the subject: "The chance of punishment by the courts of the United States is so remote and uncertain, and the negroes are so powerless and the whites so little disposed to hazard their lives in the effort to obtain justice, that there is an utter absence of that restraint which comes from a rigid enforcement of the laws."

Some of these criticisms can be answered, but the committee had reserved its chief concern for the lack of a court with jurisdiction over civil matters affecting United States citizens in the Territory, and here they left little room for argument:

[T]he property of whites and negroes, not Indians by adoption, is entirely without protection. The property of these persons and of the railroads which were constructed in the Territory by permission of the Indians amounts to many millions of dollars. To extend in some form a civil jurisdiction over the Territory by which the rights of property shall be adequately protected would seem the immediate duty of Congress.

They therefore recommended the establishment of a federal court in the Indian Territory with both civil and criminal jurisdiction over the United States citizens: "The authority for establishing these courts is not only found in the treaties, but in the general power given to Congress by the Constitution over all the domain and Territories of the United States."[42]

They could with equal clarity and far greater economy have asserted that the United States enjoyed the right of "eminent domain."

It has been maintained that "few Indians were interviewed" by the Patterson committee, that "the bulk of the testimony was taken outside the Territory proper," and that those full-bloods who did go before the committee merely "recited pro-territorial statements which the Union agent had written out for them."[43] None of these criticisms is well founded. Many Indians appeared before the committee when it reached the Indian country, and very few said anything in favor of Territorial government. Most, though by no means all, spoke out in support of the establishment of a United States court in the Territory, while several Creeks said merely that they could not oppose it because they were committed to its acceptance under the terms of the treaty of 1866.

Although slightly more than half the testimony had been taken in Washington in the spring of 1878 and a little of it in Kansas late in November—certainly not amounting to "the bulk" of the whole—those who gave it were ordinarily resident in Indian Territory. Finally, an allegation that S. W. Marston, the former Union agent, had written out pro-territorialization propaganda for the full-bloods is easily disposed of: first, it is likely that most of them were illiterate and could not have read anything; secondly, most of their testimony on the Territorialization question expressed their opposition to the idea; and thirdly, Marston actually cooperated with the principal chief of the Cherokee Nation by supplying him with information on the movements of the Patterson committee so that the chief could organize a demonstration against the proposals for Territorial government.[44]

It is true that the committee conducted all its interviews in the Territory in railway towns; but this need be ascribed to nothing more sinister than haste, and there is no way of knowing whether the balance of the testimony would have been altered greatly had Patterson visited such places as Tahlequah, Okmulgee, Chahta Tamaha, and Tishomingo.[45] More damningly, Patterson was financially interested in railroads, and, during his service as chairman of the Senate Committee on Railroads, his political and commercial activities ran in far closer conjunction than was proper.[46] But he was not the whole of the Senate Committee on Territories, and proof of one instance of knavery does not convict a man of general corruption. All in all, when due weight has been allowed for the committee's attachment to the creed of eminent domain, the conclusions set out in the Patterson report seem to have been fairly reached and in the main justified by the general direction of testimony that had been drawn out by careful inquiry.

In January 1879, shortly after Patterson's return from the Indian Territory, the Senate Committee on Territories listened while a Cherokee mixed-blood, Cornelius Boudinot, presented the case for the organization of a Territorial government and a white man, Benjamin Grafton, argued for leaving matters where they stood.

Boudinot maintained that it was plain from all the evidence that life and property were "not as safe in the Indian Territory as elsewhere." In the last seven weeks, he added, there had been at least seven murders there. Desiring nothing less than the creation of a Territorial government, he did not advocate reform of the court system in isolation; but the proposal for court reform was attacked with ferocity by Grafton. Referring to suggestions that United States courts in the Territory should not merely replace or supplement the Fort Smith court, but perhaps even supplant the tribal courts, he declared:

> The real purpose of the effort to establish United States courts over this Territory and to make these Indians citizens of the United States is to force them to abandon their present tribal organizations, and in the end to allot their lands in severalty, so that white men can get possession of them under color of legal title, and thus drive these Indians from their homes and settle the country with white people, in order to build up a local trade for the Missouri, Kansas and Texas Railroad Company, to the end that foreign and domestic bondholders may have their coffers filled with the income from their bonds.

The drive against the tribal governments, Grafton charged, was the product of a conspiracy by "certain railway jobbers and land grabbers" who had "gathered in this our Capital from the money centers of the Old World, and from our own 'Wall Street,' and hover about this building as birds of prey."[47]

Oratorical efflorescence as vivid as this was a commonplace of the

Victorian courtroom, and it may have succeeded in making many a bad case look good, and a good case irresistible. Grafton's appeal here was as direct an address to ignorance and prejudice as the wilder utterances of the Territorializers. The committee, rightly, gave no sign of being swayed by it.

A few weeks later, the House Committee on Territories reported adversely on a bill for the organization of Oklahoma Territory which Benjamin Joseph Franklin (D, Missouri) had introduced in 1877. Franklin's bill, though calling for allotment of the tribal lands, had included a provision for the repeal of the conditional railroad grants.[48]

Early in 1880, while the Committee on the Judiciary was considering a bill to open a federal court in the railway town of Denison, Texas, and to attach the Choctaw and Chickasaw nations to the Northern District of Texas, a Senate resolution was framed to instruct the Department of the Interior to furnish details of applications from railroad corporations for the transfer to them of the lands granted conditionally. The answer to the query was that only the Atlantic and Pacific—which had since foundered, although it was reconstituted later—had demanded such lands and that the demand had been rebuffed. The Denison court bill was then killed by the Judiciary Committee.[49]

Still another House bill to establish the Territory of Oklahoma was laid aside in committee in favor of a Senate bill to install a United States court in the Indian Territory. The Senate bill made no progress either, but its provisions signaled the strategy Congress would deploy more consistently a few years later.

The purpose of Senate Bill 1418 was to place a federal court in the Indian Territory and to utilize it and its officials as the vanguard of unified civil government in the Indian country: once the court had been introduced, preparations would be made for the survey, allotment, and settlement of the tribal lands, the dismantling of the five tribal governments, and the organization of a Territory or State. So while the first twenty-three sections of the Senate bill carried the burden of its immediate object, there were thirteen others devoted to the "other purposes" promised by the preamble.

Sections 24 and 34 provided—after the Five Tribes had signified their assent—for the opening of a land office, to be followed by the survey and partition of the country among the Indians: every member of each tribe, by birth or adoption, male or female, adult or minor, would be allotted a quarter section (160 acres), and the remainder of the land was then to be sold to the United States.

Section 35 would allow any Indian in the Territory, "on compliance with certain requisites," to become a citizen of the United States. Section 36 stated that an Indian who had been granted United States citizenship would not be debarred from his share of the tribal fund.

The earlier sections of the bill proposed making the entire Indian Territory into a single and separate judicial district (thereby confining the Fort Smith regime to the western counties of Arkansas). Besides assuming the duties of the Fort Smith court in criminal cases, the new court would be vested with "jurisdiction of a civil nature" in all suits in which one or more of the participants was a United States citizen where the amount in controversy was not less than $100.

Perhaps the most notable innovation contemplated in the bill was a proposal to award jurisdiction to the United States in any cause, civil or criminal, where the parties concerned were Indians of different tribes. Extradition treaties or formal compacts were in existence between the Choctaws and Chickasaws, the Creeks and Seminoles, the Cherokees, Creeks, and Osages, and the Seminoles and Pottawatomis; but these did not always work well, and there were no formal arrangements whatever between, say, the Cherokees and Choctaws, or where one of those concerned was a member of one of almost any of the "wild" tribes. For example, if a Seminole killed a Kickapoo, or vice versa, neither the United States nor the Seminole Nation could claim jurisdiction. When, despite a favorable report from the House Committee, Senate Bill 1418 failed to proceed, at least one worthwhile reform was lost for several years.[50]

Even if Congress had been interested in this bill, such expansionists as Senator Samuel Maxey (D, Texas) would have been dissatisfied. There was one great hurdle before the bill, and others of a like nature: the proposals for survey, allotment, and Territorial government were not substantive, since nothing could be done without the consent of the tribal governments.

Early in 1882, Maxey gave succinct utterance to his views in the debate on a bill that had no direct connection with political or judicial reform in the Indian Territory but was closely related to the central theme of tribal sovereignty:

> We have got to meet the question whether there is an *imperium in imperio* in this country; whether there is a portion of the territory of the United States around which a Chinese wall may be erected to which the right of eminent domain does not apply.[51]

The matter under discussion was whether the Chickasaw Nation was entitled to prevent the Choctaw Nation from granting a right-of-way to the St. Louis and San Francisco Railway. Maxey was not interested in the legal niceties of the dispute; he objected to the principle that "intercommunication by railway" between one State and another could be forbidden by the Chickasaws, or anyone else. The bill, in which the United States proposed to empower itself to decide this and related questions, matured into a statute on August 2, 1882.[52]

A number of senators who might have been expected to vote against the passage of any bill posing a more overt threat to the governments of the Five Tribes offered no opposition to this measure. Those who did not usually concern themselves with the issue took no interest in it now. Indifference, on this occasion, worked against the tribal governments.

Conversely, however, only a few senators, then and for some years to come, would take sides with the growing Territorialization movement in the House for an out-and-out attack upon tribal autonomy. So, sustained almost as surely by the apathy of some senators as by the sympathy of others, tribal government remained uneasily intact until the end of the decade.

CHAPTER THREE

Federal Law in the Indian Territory, 1866–1883

The western district of Arkansas is a peculiar district.—Congressman James Sener and others, 43rd Cong., 1st sess., House Report 626, June 1, 1874

Anything is preferable to the present system, even an absence of all laws.—Samuel A. Galpin, Report upon the Condition and Management of Certain Indian Agencies in the Indian Territory now under the Supervision of the Orthodox Friends, *1877*

And whereas our citizens are often arrested by deputy marshals for offenses committed against our own laws, committed between our own citizens. . . . Even our homes are not respected by these Argus-eyed officials; if a social glass is given to an old and respected friend, the friend is made a witness to prosecute the friendship which actuated the donor; in fact, if the grasping of power and usurpation of jurisdiction by the district court for the western district of Arkansas be not checked it will not be long before our nationality is swallowed up by it.—Resolution of the Chickasaw legislature to the Secretary of the Interior and then to the President, approved October 17, 1876

In the States and organized Territories, the federal district courts were responsible for the prosecution of statutory offenses within the narrow arc of jurisdiction specifically reserved in the Constitution to the general government. These included the evasion of revenue duty on the manufacture or sale of liquor and tobacco; issuing or circulating counterfeit coinage; forgery of United States Treasury notes or bonds; infringement of the civil rights of any United States citizen; and interference with the operation of the United States postal system, whether by armed robbery of a mail carrier, burglary of a post office, embezzlement of postal funds, stealing (or stealing from) a letter, or sending obscene materials through the post.

The United States courts also held common-law jurisdiction over Government property in any State or Territory and over United States citizens in any unorganized tract of country within the exterior boundaries of the United States of America. The whole of Indian Territory fell within this description.

Thirdly, it was the task of federal courts to punish those who broke the laws enacted for the protection of the American Indian and for the regulation of the Indian country. The most notable of these laws, and those most frequently broken, were the Indian Trade and Intercourse acts.

Both the federal system of law and its administration in the Indian Territory were rotten at their roots. Reform of individual defects in the criminal law was effected tardily, if not grudgingly. Most of the time, most congressmen with any real interest in the Indian Territory wanted either more reform than was politically possible or none at all; either the total suppression of tribal government or an absolute bar on any legislation, irrespective of its merit, that might detract from the national sovereignty of the Five Tribes. When, in the late 1890s, the balance of congressional sympathies had shifted, the politicians could dismantle the five governments, but they never succeeded in making the United States courts as efficient or equitable as they ought to have been, or in turning a bad system of law into a good one.

In the United States courts, death by hanging was the mandatory punishment for murder[1] and for rape.[2] For manslaughter, the *maximum* penalty was three years' imprisonment, to which the judge could, if he was so minded, add the stipulation that the sentence must be served at hard labor, a fine up to $1,000, or both.[3] In 1875 Congress increased the maximum punishment for manslaughter from three years in prison to ten,[4] but not until 1897 did it abolish mandatory capital punishment for murder and rape.[5]

Before the passage of the act of 1897, the disparity between the mandatory penalty for murder (death) and the maximum for manslaughter (three years in prison, later ten) was easily wide enough for a jury in a frontier district to err in the defendant's favor when there was even a shadow of self-defense or some other mitigatory factor. In many cases, this is what happened.

Under common law a jury can bring in a conviction of manslaughter against a defendant indicted for murder if it is not satisfied that "malice aforethought" is present. The trial judge may suggest to the jury that the facts alleged in a case leave no room for a verdict of manslaughter, but the jury is not bound to accept this, because the facts are its preserve: it must decide what they are, and it may view them as it chooses. Much, though, depends on the accuracy, clarity, and fairness with which the trial judge charges the jury on the law, which is his domain.

Common-law concepts in capital cases placed too much trust in the intellect of judges, too much strain on the emotions of jurors, and too much faith in the impartiality of judges and jurors. If for any reason a jury did not wish to convict a defendant of a murder they believed he or she had committed, and where the prosecution had insisted that the defendant must be guilty of murder or guilty of nothing, the jury might still find him or her guilty of manslaughter; but they would be likelier to let the accused walk away.

It was not long before some of the States started to dispense with some of the common-law principles which had been inherited from English law, and adopted a codified body of *statute* law. In 1794, the legislature of the Commonwealth of Pennsylvania passed "An act for the better preventing of crimes and for abolishing the penalty of death in certain cases" under which the crime of murder was divided into two categories. Murder "of the first degree" took in all murder "perpetrated by means of poison or by lying in wait or by any other kind of wilful, deliberate and premeditated killing, or which shall be committed in the perpetration of or an attempt to perpetrate any arson, rape, robbery or burglary" and carried the death penalty. All other cases of murder belonged to the second degree and were punishable by imprisonment.[6]

Other States followed the innovatory example of Pennsylvania. In 1838 Arkansas, at that time a frontier State, enacted legislation almost identical to the Pennsylvania statute, and then went far beyond it in giving statutory definitions to manslaughter and all other felonies besides murder; to justifiable homicide; and to the doctrines of express and implied malice.[7]

Somewhat later, in 1868, Kansas went further still, providing four categories of manslaughter. "Justifiable homicide" was classed as manslaughter in the fourth degree.[8] In Texas the law did not require in a plea of self-defense that the person being attacked had retreated or taken other evasive action before killing his assailant.[9] If this might seem to reflect a desire to accommodate the sudden expediencies of the frontier or Southern traditions of chivalry, the principle did not always hold elsewhere. In Arkansas, for example, death from dueling was classified as murder in the first degree.[10] Further west, in the United States Territory of New Mexico,[11] three degrees of murder were recognized, covering all cases of homicide except those defined as justifiable.

These and other State or Territorial codes, in their regard for local peculiarities of attitude, were expressive of a willingness among legislators to adapt older doctrines to the exigencies of a society in flux, helping it to absorb stresses then absent from the settled States to the East.

Where high crimes were graded by statute, it was always open to a jury to find a smaller degree of guilt than what the prosecution had sought to establish. Even where bad judgment was exercised, the consequences of error were likely to be far less severe than in a case conducted according to common law. A jury might still return a perverse verdict, but it was less likely that a defendant guilty of murder would escape conviction altogether because his or her general character was good, or that an innocent person would be convicted on a capital charge because the individual made a poor impression on the jury. The practice whereby the trial judge, in his "summing up," may comment upon the evidence—although the comment should be balanced by reminders to the jury that the facts are for them to decide on—has often given rise to difficulty, error, and impropriety in the English courts, where it has long obtained. Infallibility in the realm of common law could not reasonably be expected, therefore, of an American jurist, unversed in its proceedings and far removed from the source of its rules and traditions. The easy availability of Sir William Blackstone's popular and supposedly oracular *Commentaries on the Laws of England* was not enough to redress the deficit. Blackstone's four volumes had been published as far back as the 1760s and, for all the lucidity and elegance of the prose style, the scheme of the work is somewhat unscientific and the text sometimes misleading. Nevertheless, prosecutions for murder in the federal courts were governed by common-law principles until well into the twentieth century.

There were federal statutes providing for the indictment and punishment of accessories *after* the fact; but—except in cases of piracy on the high seas—no independent recognition was accorded to the accessory before the fact. In common law the accessory before the fact was equal in guilt to the principal; but, in the words of one of those most qualified to speak on the subject:

> The indictment and trial of accessories before the fact is surrounded with technical embarrassments. . . . The indictment must contain the full and accurate charge against the principal, followed by the technical averments charging the defendant with being an accessory before the fact. It follows as a consequence that the charge against both the principal and accessory

must be proved as stated in the indictment, and that the accessory cannot be tried until the principal has been tried and convicted. If the principal has escaped, the trial of the accessory must be postponed or ultimately abandoned, however strong the proof may be of his guilty participation.[12]

Until 1888 convictions for robbery, burglary, or larceny in the Indian country were punishable by imprisonment for a term of not more than one year. The act of 1888 allowed the judge to award up to fifteen years' imprisonment, a fine of not more than $1,000, or both.[13] Interference with the United States mail or its carriers was, from June 8, 1872, covered by general statute. Conviction for armed robbery of the mails would incur an automatic sentence of life imprisonment with hard labor.[14]

Except for an act of 1862 that made bigamy punishable by a fine up to $500 or up to five years' imprisonment,[15] there were no "immorality laws," as they were termed, until 1887. In that year Congress instituted a scale of imprisonment and fines for anyone convicted of adultery, incest, or fornication wherever federal law applied.[16]

When the Western Judicial District of Arkansas was created in 1851, the district court was given circuit court powers.[17] Although the Justice of the Supreme Court for the Eighth Circuit, which included that district, could sit with, or instead of, the district judge to hear an appeal, he never did; at first the Arkansas court was too far out of the way from the circuit headquarters at St. Louis, and later, when communications were much better, the Justice was too fully occupied with work in Washington to go out on circuit at all.

And so the district judge, as circuit judge, sat in appeal against the judgments of his own court and against rulings delivered by himself. Since, except for a brief period from 1867 to 1868,[18] no appeal could be taken from a federal circuit court to the Supreme Court, the verdict and sentence of the district court at Van Buren or Fort Smith were generally final, unless the prisoner succeeded with his petition to the President for executive clemency.

Fort Smith was not unique among federal district courts in possessing circuit powers; four others shared that distinction—but they rarely had occasion to exercise the common-law jurisdiction which, along with the Indian regulatory provisions, accounted for at least seven-eighths of the judicial business at Fort Smith, and it was only at Fort Smith that trials in capital cases were likely to occur.

In 1889 congressional legislation alleviated on obvious wrong by permitting an appeal to the Supreme Court "upon a writ of error . . . as of right" from a conviction in any federal court on a murder charge. Fort

Smith and other federal district courts with circuit powers were relieved of those powers by the same act.[19]

Judges, marshals, and attorneys for the United States judicial districts were appointed by the President with the advice and consent of the Senate. A President could not always count upon the Senate's acceptance of his nominees, especially when the majority party in that chamber was not the President's; but usually he got his own way at the first attempt.

Only the judge received a substantial fixed remuneration. The district attorney and marshal were paid nominal salaries of $200 or $300, intended to compensate them for time spent on dealing with official correspondence; their real earnings came from fees. Where the judicial district was a State or part of a State, the judge was appointed during good behavior; hence he was almost irremovable, except upon proof of misconduct in office, and then only by impeachment, or on grounds of severe physical or mental disability. District attorneys and marshals were appointed for four-year terms; their commissions could be revoked at pleasure, but in practice premature removal was usually the result of gross malpractice or incapacity.

Where the judicial district was a Territory of the United States, its judge, like the attorney and marshal, was appointed for four years, terminable at pleasure. For these purposes, Indian Territory—when eventually it acquired judicial status—was treated as if it had been a regular organized Territory.

All were political appointees. Unless, as happened on rare occasions, there were overwhelming personal or tactical reasons for choosing someone from the opposing party, the President would naturally select his political allies. Few appointees were politically dormant; most were not only members of the President's party but had obtained some prominence in it. There were always candidates competing for preferment whenever a new district judge, attorney, or marshal was needed.

The district judge could appoint a court clerk; the district attorney could appoint an assistant; and the marshal, by making use of the statute which permitted him to appoint "one or more deputies" without any stated maximum, could dispense patronage liberally. Between them, these three presidental appointees could engage sundry employees and contractors.[20] As, for instance, there was a United States jail at Fort Smith, the court required the services of jailers, a cook, and a physician. Even here, most appointments were decided on a partisan basis. Since there were only eight years (1885–1889, 1893–1897) in the period from 1866 to 1906 when the Executive Mansion was occupied by a Democrat, it followed that the great majority of federal appointees at Fort Smith were Republicans. Throughout that period (except during Reconstruction, when most Democrats were denied the right to vote), the Democratic party controlled the State of Arkansas itself.

None of this implies that the federal system of law would have functioned better had its officers been chosen without regard to political allegiance, for no discernible balance of virtue and ability lay on either side of the party barrier. But if the appointments had been filled on a bipartisan basis, due criticism could not have been countered by charges of partisan bias.

Soon after the Civil War, Henry Clay Caldwell, a long-established resident of Arkansas, was appointed United States judge for the eastern and Western federal districts of the State. Sittings of his court, therefore, alternated between Little Rock and Van Buren, although he spent most of his time at Little Rock.

In March 1870, Logan Holt Roots, a banker and speculator lately arrived from Illinois who had lost little time in getting himself sent to Congress by the attenuated and chiefly Republican electorate, introduced an innocuous bill to authorize holding court in the Eastern District at Helena as well as Little Rock. By February 1871 the Arkansas Senators, Benjamin Rice and Alexander McDonald, had got their hands on the bill and reshaped it.[21]

Their amendment called for the seat of the Western District to be moved from Van Buren to Fort Smith; the transfer of nineteen counties from the Eastern District to the Western District, so that the latter would comprise the Indian Territory and thirty counties of the State; and the appointment of a new judge to take charge of the enlarged Western District. Seventeen of the nineteen counties to be detached from the Eastern District belonged geographically in the Eastern District; one of them, hugging the Mississippi River at the eastern boundary of the State, was Phillips County, whose local government seat was none other than Helena.[22]

On March 3, 1871, by a desperate procedural maneuver and the switched vote of one Senator, the bill went to President Grant for signature. A few hours after Grant had approved the redistricting act, William Story was nominated for the new judgeship. His confirmation by the Senate followed immediately.[23]

William Story had been born in Wisconsin but may have had influential family connections with Massachusetts, where he received his early education. He graduated from the law school of the University of Michigan, went to Arkansas just after the Civil War, and by 1868 was a circuit judge of the State court. He was not quite twenty-eight at the time of his promotion to United States district judge.

The route through which young Story was steered into the federal judgeship may have been devious and remains mysterious. Allegations given currency in Fort Smith by men who had known Story well—that the whole scheme for the redistricting of Arkansas and the elevation of Story had been laid by Senator Alick McDonald to seal the forthcoming wedding of his daughter to Story—cannot be proved. It is on record that McDonald, a banker and merchant from Pennsylvania, had fought hard for the passage of the bill, although the critical amendment had been introduced by his lawyer colleague Senator Ben Rice; that Logan Roots, whose congressional term ended on the day the bill became law, stepped into the United States marshal's office at Fort Smith before the end of that month;[24] and that, about the time he might have been expected to marry the Senator's daughter, William Story made a journey to Minnesota to marry someone who was not the Senator's daughter.[25]

As to the young judge's fitness for high judicial office, it may be remarked that he was endowed with a celerity of thought and suppleness of ethics that would not have put him apart from the rest of the Arkansas carpetbag class.

Before the Civil War the officers of the Van Buren court had little need to enter the Indian country, and during the War years the court had maintained a shadowy existence, notable chiefly for the destruction of its records. In the immediate postwar years the costs of running the district began to mount. Expenses were $6,500 in the fiscal year ended June 30, 1866, but they rose to $17,000, $34,500, and $40,000 for the three years following.[26] These sums were almost treble those of the neighboring Eastern District of Arkansas; but the disparity here and the increased expenditure of the Van Buren court itself could be explained by the court's increased activity. In 1867–1868, 81 warrants were issued from Van Buren, and in 1868–1869, 112 warrants.[27]

At this time supervision of the federal judicial districts was one of the duties of the Secretary of the Interior. Although the Attorney-General was a senior member of the President's cabinet, he was without a department of his own; he, with his assistant and a few clerks, occupied rooms at the Department of the Interior. In June 1870, Congress put an end to this slipshod and ambiguous arrangement by creating a Department of Justice for the Attorney-General, but stopped short of appropriating the funds that would enable the new body to perform effectively.[28] As the new Attorney-General, Amos Akerman, commented at the turn of the calendar year:

[T]he offices of the Department are dispersed in five buildings, some of them at a considerable distance from the others. Until a building sufficient for all of them shall be provided, the purpose of Congress to bring under one direction all the law officers of the Executive Departments will not be thoroughly accomplished.[29]

Almost the last thing Akerman did before quitting office a year later was to remind the House that this situation had not changed.

In spite of this, the new department soon settled down to its responsibilities. Before long the Attorney-General had cause for disquiet over the conduct of affairs in the Western District of Arkansas.[30]

Some time during 1870 the marshal at Van Buren, William Britton, with the eager collusion of some of his deputies, had begun the manufacture of fraudulent accounts. "At the beginning," an investigator noted, the new methods of accounting "were used with caution and the amounts were not large"; "the number of deputy marshals was comparatively small." Judge Caldwell spent too little time at Van Buren to know what was afoot, but the Comptroller of the Treasury and Attorney-General Akerman soon saw that the expenditures claimed by the Van Buren court were now rising too sharply to be explained by the recent increase in its business. Britton was removed from office, ex-Congressman Roots replaced him under the circumstances already described, and the Treasury Department sent a Secret Service man to make inquiries in Van Buren and Fort Smith.[31]

In August 1871, Akerman instructed the district attorney at Fort Smith to institute criminal proceedings against ex-Marshal Britton, Britton's clerk, and a United States "commissioner" (the federal equivalent of a magistrate or probate judge).[32] Charges of forgery were brought, only to be defeated by a combination of irregularities in the selection of the grand jury, perjury, and in all probability the involvement of the district attorney himself in a plot to wreck the case.[33]

The chief source of the extra judicial work Britton and his coconspirators had hoped would serve as camouflage for fraud was the decision of the Missouri, Kansas and Texas Railway (MKT) to avail itself of the provision in the treaties of 1866 for the construction of railroads through Indian Territory.

In the summer of 1870, the tracks of the MKT were pushed southward from Chetopa across the Cherokee Nation. It drew into the Indian country a motley flotsam of laborers, suppliers, and assorted camp followers, with much disorder and a ready market for liquor.[34] By the following spring, the Atlantic and Pacific Railroad (AP), having entered the old Seneca Reservation, in the extreme northeast of the Indian Territory, had met its rival at the new town of Vinita. The AP project ran out of funds when only a single further mile of track had been laid; the MKT continued its southerly way. Muskogee, its terminus late in 1871, soon became noted as the scene of many episodes of violence.[35]

Attempts by the United States marshal to lessen the problems by confiscating the liquor that was their prime stimulus aroused the wrath of railroad executives, whose complaints alarmed the Secretary of the Interior. George Denison, vice president of the MKT, contended that the Fort Smith deputy marshals, in entering freight cars and breaking packages open, were interfering with the railroad's "lawful operations under the charter granted to them by the Government" and "rendering the company liable for the injury done to said freight."[36] Eventually the Attorney-General had to ask the marshal to restrain his deputies:

> I have to request that instructions be given by you to your Deputies not to interfere with any goods whilst in transit, either by the Railway Company or the Transit Company, further than to see that no contraband regulations relating to intercourse with the Indian tribes are not [sic] violated.
>
> It is necessary to the prosecution of the work of building this road through the Indian Country, that the stores and supplies of contractors and subordinates should be allowed to be delivered without interference on the part of your Deputies, and such stores and supplies as are needed should not be interfered with, unless there are good grounds for believing that such supplies are of a contraband character and are being disposed of by the contractors or others to the Indians in violation of law.
>
> This is a matter in which I can give you no specific directions but must leave it, in a great measure, to your own judgment and discretion.[37]

Trouble accompanied the MKT all the way south and across the Red River into Texas. It was with relief that the Creek agent watched the departure of the track crews for the territory of his colleague the Choctaw agent: "The Missouri, Kansas and Texas Railroad, which at the date of my last report was in progress of building, and was bringing in a horde of gamblers and desperadoes, has been completed through the Creek country, and taken along with its front the rowdies and toughs, leaving quiet along its line." Agent T. D. Griffith was equal to the menace. No sooner had the railroad crossed the Canadian River into the Choctaw country than he requested, and was speedily granted, a detachment of infantry to disperse the crowd of roughs who were in attendance.[38]

Arrests, indictments, and trials by the federal authorities were more numerous than they had been before the coming of the railways, but many of the worst offenders escaped punishment. Story would state, quite correctly, that at the term of court for November 1871, thirty-seven persons were indicted for murder. He omitted to add that most of them were indicted in their absence; that five of those accused had been given bail, and had dishonored it; that one who actually stood trial and was convicted of murder was also let out on bond and had forfeited it in return for his liberty,[39] and that, altogether, not one of the thirty-seven indictments for murder had led to the punishment of a murderer.[40]

Expenditures, meanwhile, were soaring. The marshal's disbursements for 1870–1871 had totaled just under $138,000, out of which $43,000 had been spent by Roots during the first three months of his service. For the fiscal year ended June 30, 1872, the cost of running the marshal's office approached $250,000. The court had more to do than before, but as a Government investigator later commented, "these causes [criminal cases] did not create the necessity for the enormous expenditures of money as shown by the accounts of Roots and Britton."[41]

Early in the summer of 1872 there arrived at Fort Smith a young man named Miller, whom Marshal Roots had engaged at $2,000 per year (soon raised to $3,000) to do, as far as could be seen, nothing in particular. Miller's father was the clerk in the office of First Auditor, Treasury Department, whose duty it was to inspect and pass the accounts submitted from the Western District of Arkansas. These accounts went from the desk of Miller, senior, to that of the First Comptroller, but the First Comptroller had much else to do and would approve district accounts for payment after giving them no more than the most cursory attention.[42]

Up to this time, Attorney-General Williams had been worried chiefly by a single category of expense. As he explained:

> A practice has obtained in many of the districts of summoning at each term of the court a large number of witnesses, many of whom are frequently not called upon to testify, and, in many other instances, their testimony, when given, is of such little weight or importance that it does not justify the expenses occasioned by their attendance.
>
> The attention of the marshals and district attorneys and other officers of the courts has frequently been called to this abuse, but apparently without the desired result. This is evidently the case in the western district of Arkansas. In that district the amount advanced to the marshals, during the last fiscal year, reached the large sum of $243809; a very large proportion of which was for witness's fees.[43]

To be precise, $94,526 of this sum represented the outlay on witness fees, compared with some $23,500 from the $138,000 disbursed during the previous year.[44]

At Williams's request, President Grant suspended Marshal Roots from office in June 1872. The man nominated in his place was William Britton, who had preceded Roots in the marshalship and against whom the Department of Justice had tried to secure an indictment for fraud.[45] The reasons for this apparently strange choice were complex, but logical; briefly stated, the Republican party in Arkansas had split into two violently contending factions, and Britton and Roots belonged to opposing cliques, each with sympathizers in Washington.[46]

Several months later, the district attorney at Fort Smith resigned under instructions from the department and was replaced by his former assistant. The new attorney was confirmed in office by the Senate. Britton was rejected but remained in office under presidential warrant, pending the confirmation of another nominee.[47]

Toward the end of 1872 the Attorney-General asked the chief of the Secret Service Division of the Treasury Department to make a second and more searching investigation into affairs at the Fort Smith marshal's office. Early in December an agent, L. B. Whitney, arrived in Fort Smith, under an assumed name and posing as a book salesman.[48]

The subterfuge was in vain. Despite categorical orders to the contrary, Whitney's mail was sent to him direct from Washington, under the official stamp. When it reached the post office at Fort Smith, the postmaster opened and read it and reported its content to those who should have been the last to know. When Whitney, seeing the futility of further efforts at deception, revealed his true identity to the district judge, Story could coolly reply that he had known all about Whitney almost from the day of his appearance in Fort Smith, because "I have a man in Washington who keeps me posted there."[49]

Whitney could not be stopped from collecting a massive quantity of detailed evidence of pecuniary malpractice at the federal court. Bribes had been accepted by the judge and district attorney. Vouchers had been presented to the marshal and approved by the judge for the payment of services rendered by men who did not exist, or did exist but had no knowledge of the transactions with which their names had been connected. Many expeditions to the Indian country had been undertaken solely for the fees and profit on expense claims, the deputies knowing that their prisoners were guilty of the most trivial offenses or nothing. Warrants had been antedated to give the deputies more days against which fees and expenses were chargeable; persons would be arrested without a warrant, and the warrant would be backdated when they arrived in Fort Smith. An arrestee, guilty or not, could sometimes arrange his release by hiring a lawyer recommended by the arresting officer and parting with more than he could afford to pay, perhaps the very horse that had taken him to Fort Smith, because it would have cost him much more to stand trial.[50]

One of these illegalities—antedating arrest warrants—had been sanctioned by Judge Caldwell and Caldwell's predecessors because adherence to the letter of the law would have rendered the court powerless in the Indian Territory. As one Fort Smith lawyer explained:

> [I]t was understood to be the practice of the court that deputy marshals should make arrests of parties without writs in the Indian country, where they saw the offenses committed, or where the evidence was strong of the guilt of the parties, and that the writs should be dated back to the time of the actual arrest of the parties, so that the deputy marshals should get paid for their actual time and actual service. This was based upon the fact that, if the parties were not arrested at the time, before a writ could be obtained they would escape justice, and no protection could be afforded the people of the Indian country.[51]

This was no more than plain sense; but, since the deputy marshals could not be controlled or observed in their every action, its objectives could be served only when the district had a good marshal who would appoint good deputies. Neither prerequisite obtained in the Western Judicial District of Arkansas during the early 1870s.

"We could," vouched the Fort Smith *New Era*, "fill every number of our paper with bloody deeds of the most startling description, committed in a country having no greater population than a good-sized ward in a big city. . . . [T]he worst characters have pretty much their own way, as besides the small United States Marshal's force, there is no restraining power."[52] But a special correspondent for the *New York Times* took a less indulgent view of the Fort Smith deputies than could be expected of a Radical, pro-Reconstruction journal like the *New Era*. According to the New York correspondent, "The United States Marshal at Fort Smith, in Arkansas, seems to be utterly careless what sort of men he sends into the country, so long as they are fighting men. We hear of constant brawls and acts of violence and these men are engaged."[53]

That there was not a great deal of abuse by the deputies of "mileage," the arrangement where an officer charged by the mile for distance traveled in making an arrest and jailing his prisoner, owed less to their forbearance than to the generosity of the estimates, approved by Story, of the minimum number of miles that must be covered in traveling from one specified point to another. A journey to "the extreme end of the Chickasaw Nation" was reckonable at 400, 450, or even 500 miles traveled from Fort Smith, although, as one deputy admitted, "[T]hree hundred miles will take a person to the limits of the Chickasaw Nation."[54] (The maximum distance by crow's flight was just under 250 miles, but mileage fees were computed by "the ordinarily traveled route.")

Since it was ordained by statute that at least one-quarter of the fee payable on a deputy's account was deductible by the marshal for his own use,[55] the more assiduously a deputy served process, the likelier it was that the marshal would employ him again. Britton and Roots retained one-third of a deputy's account. The officers at Fort Smith during the Reconstruction period were by no means the first, or the last, federal employees to misuse a system that left everything to the personal qualities of the marshal and his deputies.

Whitney's most startling discovery is best conveyed in his own words:

> I learned that marshal's checks . . . were being circulated there, in payment of witness fees, juror's fees, etc. When I came there I found those checks in circulation, made the acquaintance of some deputy marshals who had checks issued by the marshal, Mr. Britton. I saw those checks. They (the deputy marshals) claimed that Mr. Britton stated to them there was no money there by which he could pay them, and he issued them with a check. . . .
>
> I found those in circulation there; almost everybody in the town had them—the boarding-house keepers and almost everybody. . . . These certificates that were issued by Mr. Britton were bought up, as a general thing, by Mr. Lanigan, Mr. Scott, and Mr. B. Baer. Mr. Scott was the postmaster. . . . Mr. Lanigan is a merchant there, a man I think of considerable wealth . . . and Mr. Baer, I think, is the President of the First National Bank of Fort Smith. . . .
>
> These checks were selling from twenty to fifty or sixty cents on the dollar. Witnesses and jurors, and all men who held them, were complaining very bitterly—cursing the Government and the court. . . .
>
> Well, these people were buying them up, and it was the impression of the witnesses and men to whom these checks were issued that Mr. Britton, Mr. Scott, Mr. Baer, and Mr. Lanigan had an understanding between them that he should issue the checks, and they buy them up and then divide.[56]

Whitney was told that if Britton was again removed from office, Senator Powell Clayton would do his best to ensure that the new marshal belonged to the same "ring" as Britton. When the detective left Fort Smith at the end of January 1873, he took with him the impression that "the common sentiment there was that the United States district court was a stench in the nostrils of the community."[57]

On March 17, 1873, John Sarber, a lawyer and a former general in the Union army, was nominated for the marshalship in place of Britton. His appointment was confirmed by the Senate next day.[58] Sarber ran the marshal's office on lines similar to those that had precipitated the removal of his predecessors. In August 1873, Whitney resumed his investigations in Fort Smith. With the assistance of a former mayor of the city, Irving

Fuller, he gathered a mass of sworn affidavits. Their lives were threatened and, when their work was finished, they left Fort Smith in secrecy, darkness, and haste.[59]

In February 1874, the House of Representatives directed the newly formed Committee of Expenditures in the Department of Justice "to inquire into the expenses, disbursements, and general management of the western judicial district of Arkansas since its reorganization in 1871." Hearings began on March 18 and continued well into the spring.

Preparations were then made for the impeachment of Judge Story. Story traveled to Washington, and a compromise was struck. On June 16 the House shelved its charges against Story, and when, next day, the judge submitted his resignation in writing the Attorney-General was in a position to inform him at once that it had been accepted by the President.[60]

At the beginning of June 1874, the Expenditures Committee reported to the House with two principal recommendations: "the abolition of the present western district, the annexation of its territory, and the transfer of its business to the eastern district [of Arkansas], and that the whole district, as thus reformed, shall hereafter be known [as] and called the district of Arkansas, with one judge, district attorney, and marshal for that district, instead of the duplicates of these officials"; and a "full and thorough" scrutiny of the administrations of Britton, Roots, and Sarber.[61]

A few days afterward, a resolution of the House directed the Attorney-General to "institute a full and thorough judicial investigation into the character of the allowances that have been paid at the Treasury Department, as well as the claims still due, growing out of expenditures of the marshal's office of the western judicial district of Arkansas since the first day of July, 1870." No more claims were to be paid "until the Department has been satisfied by investigation of their correctness."[62]

On June 24 the Attorney-General appointed Benjamin DuVal special assistant to the United States attorney for the Western District of Arkansas, charged solely to carry out the investigation ordered by the House. DuVal, one of the leading lawyers in Fort Smith, had been one of those who had submitted the charges and specifications upon which Story would have been impeached; but he was also a friend of Logan Roots and would have defended Roots against the Government had the Government not employed him.[63]

DuVal's first duty was to advise the district attorney that his immediate resignation would be welcomed by the Attorney-General. Similar pressure was applied upon Marshal Sarber. William Clayton, a younger brother of Senator Powell Clayton, and James Fagan were appointed district attorney and marshal on the President's temporary commission, pending the recall of Congress; Judge Caldwell returned to the task of holding court in both federal districts of Arkansas.[64]

DuVal withstood insult, threat, and ostracism in Fort Smith. He and an assistant on loan from the Treasury Department examined seventy-four witnesses. Becoming satisfied beyond all doubt that many of the vouchers Britton, Roots, and Sarber had presented to the Treasury for payment were "false, fictitious, and fraudulent," he laid charges against all three, but the grand jury declined to indict any of them. DuVal's recommendation that the Government should now bring a civil suit against Roots was not acted upon.[65]

"I am certain," DuVal reported, "not a tithe of the details of the vast system of frauds has been developed, but which could be exposed in a judicial proceeding."[66] Perhaps that was why no further action was taken; there was no telling where such an inquisition, once mounted, would stop or what the political repercussions might be. The atmosphere about Washington during Grant's second administration was so stiff with corruption that Attorney-General Williams himself was accused of being a party to the Arkansas frauds. The allegation was patently absurd, and was easily refuted; but there were those who had been ready to believe it, not least because there were strong grounds for supposing that Williams had behaved corruptly on certain other matters.[67]

So much for one of the expenditure committee's main recommendations. Their second, that the two districts of Arkansas should be merged, was rejected altogether; but rightly so, because the committee's contention that crime in the Indian Territory was on the decrease was mistaken. Discussion of the issue gave rise to requests for the Government to exercise its option of locating a federal court inside the Territory, but it was decided that the best course lay in finding new and better men for the old structure.

Joseph Bonham Kinsman, of Maine, was the President's first choice for the judicial vacancy at Fort Smith, but his name was withdrawn and replaced by that of Isaac Charles Parker, of Missouri, the former Congressman. Parker was confirmed in office on March 19, 1875, and reached Fort Smith in good time for the opening of the May term of court. He was to live just long enough to see the day twenty-one years later when his court was divested of the last of its jurisdiction over the Indian country.[68]

A review of the work of the Van Buren and Fort Smith courts over a six-year period ending on June 30, 1875, indicates that rather more than 1,300 prisoners were indicted during that time. Nearly as many others had been discharged because the United States commissioner had ruled that there was insufficient evidence to lay before a grand jury or because the grand jury had failed to indict.[69] During William Story's three years at Fort Smith, the annual returns to the Department of Justice received artificial (and illegal) stimulus from the policy devised by Story and the district attorney against those accused of liquor offenses, whereby a single violation could attract two distinct and quite independent charges— breach of the Trade and Intercourse laws, and evasion of Internal Revenue duties. After Story's hurried departure, Judge Caldwell reinstated the principle that excise is not chargeable upon contraband.[70]

Isaac Parker and his district attorney brought to the Fort Smith court far more energy and purpose than it had known hitherto. Six men condemned for murder in Indian Territory were hanged simultaneously at Fort Smith on September 3, 1875, five more on April 21, 1876, and another four on September 8, 1876.[71] The blaze of publicity excited by these events was memorable but might have been misleading: murder trials consumed more of the court's time than others, but most of the cases that came before it related to liquor offenses or larcenies. It was, therefore, even more significant that the court was now making speedy, but just, disposal of the minor cases that comprised the bulk of its docket.

From the cumulative record of the first eight of Parker's twenty-one years at Fort Smith it can be seen that 2,398 criminal and 277 civil cases were heard, with 1,596 of the former resulting in the conviction of the defendant, at a cost of nearly $1.25 million,[72] or some $700 per conviction. There was never a time when the Department of Justice, congressional critics of the system, or both, did not think these costs too high. It was quite as evident that, despite the court's best efforts to make itself respected and feared, crime in the Indian Territory was on the increase. Nor did the substitution of honest and able officials for a pack of scoundrels mean the immediate eradication of all the evils that had flourished under the Story regime.

Parker had not been in Fort Smith two months when he was asked to give his approval to old accounts amounting to $40,000 that had eluded DuVal's investigation.[73] This, and another upsurge in current costs, led Attorney General Edwards Pierrepoint to order another investigation. Parker and one of the Senators for Arkansas went to Washington to argue that the results obtained by the court justified the expense.

Pierrepoint could make nothing substantive from a maze of conflicting evidence, but the suspicions persisted.[74] "It is my duty to operate the laws as I find them, and not question their constitutionality" was Pierrepoint's tart rejoinder to an attempt by Parker to secure the payment of accounts that had been presented improperly; "the manner in which these accounts are to be examined is pointed out by law. They are returned to you."[75]

Another official observer was Samuel Galpin, chief clerk in the Office of Indian Affairs. Galpin had been sent into the Indian Territory late in 1876 to inspect and report to the Commissioner of Indian Affairs on the condition of the agencies that had been established for Plains Indians on land ceded after the Civil War by the Five Tribes. His opinions, and the evidence from which they were formed, are in no way invalidated by the facts that Galpin's superiors had got him out of the office partly to facilitate an investigation into his own conduct and that he was dismissed for improbity shortly after his return to Washington.[76]

If the coming of Judge Parker had wrought a miraculous transformation in the administration of justice throughout the length and breadth of the Indian Territory, Galpin failed to see it. Although he was careful to emphasize that he had not visited Fort Smith itself, and that he had looked at only those parts of the court's jurisdiction remotest from headquarters, the nature and extent of the excesses that came to his notice spoke ill of the ability of the senior officials to select trustworthy subordinates.

The whole system, said Galpin, was "deservedly a byword and a reproach":

> With the insufficient means of communication, the administration of justice from a point so distant as Fort Smith must of necessity lack little of total failure, even when the officers are competent and high-toned. . . . [F]rom the abundance of reports, official and unofficial, which have come under my observation. I believe that many of these deputies should be brought to trial before the court rather than permitted longer to act as officers protected by its authority. . . . If they were brave and upright, and would pursue properly and heartily the multitude of desperadoes who infest the territory in its every part, their zealous use of their authority would find abundant field for personal profit and service to the public. As, however, many of them, passing by, from motives of personal safety, these horse thieves and other outlaws, appear to devote their whole attention and arbitrary power to the arrest and lodgement in Fort Smith of any person, white man or Indian, who is charged, often by perjury, with a petty and technical violation of the Internal Revenue laws, they are no terror to evil-doers or protection to the law-abiding citizen, and are the least valuable members of the body politic.
>
> Indeed, some of the present officers of justice, clothed with the full authority and majesty of the law, are well known as formerly horse thieves.[77]

After identifying one such rascal directly and another obliquely, and recounting the history of one case of flagrant injustice, Galpin commented:

> It is little wonder, then, that with such wretchedly ineffective and corrupt machinery for repressing crime there should be lawlessness beyond mea-

sure. It is safe to assert that the depredations of these professional horse thieves, who make regular trips through the territory between Texas and Kansas, selling in Texas the ponies stolen from Indians on the southward journey, and in Kansas those stolen on the northward, have for the past two years far exceeded the depredations committed by the Indians upon the property of the whites.[78]

Thousands of horses had been stolen from the Kiowas, Comanches, Cheyennes, and Wichitas during 1875 and 1876. Few of the thieves had been taken before the court and convicted, "while the stern and swift punishment meted out for offenses of this character by the unwritten law of the frontier has not been sufficient to check the business." The "plain remedy" would be the division of the Indian Territory into three to five circuits, "each presided over by a competent judge." This would also be of great benefit to "the so called civilized tribes in the eastern portion," notwithstanding their current opposition to such a plan. As an interim measure to mitigate the effect of the continued dilatorinesss that was to be expected of Congress, Galpin recommended that a small force of police should be formed from among the Indians of each reservation and placed under the control of the agent.

Galpin's recommendations echoed views that had been associated with the Interior Department and its satellite, the Indian Office, for several years. His account of what he had seen and heard, adding conviction as well as color to the reports of the individual agents during the intervening period, is persuasive testimony that, despite the energy of the new judge, district attorney, and marshal, the Fort Smith court stood in no higher esteem at the end of 1876 than three years earlier, when Commissioner of Indian Affairs Edward Smith had described its "attempts to administer justice for all the Territory" as "largely a failure, and sometimes worse."[79] Yet the worst of the new evils had been squeezed out, and every effort was being made to eliminate the rest.

The deputy whose iniquities had so aroused Galpin was discharged within a few days of the chief clerk's return to Washington at the beginning of 1877,[80] but the dismissal of a rogue afforded no cure to a chronic problem. When William Nicholson of the Central Superintendency reported to the Commissioner of Indian Affairs that the attachment of the Indian Territory to the Western District of Arkansas was "quite useless to the ends of justice, except in the eastern portions of the Territory,"[81] he was making fair comment.

The court could not keep whiskey peddlers out of the Cheyenne and Arapaho or Osage countries, nor could it scrutinize every action of the few deputies who entered these and other western reservations. It did much better in the eastern half of the Territory—the Five Tribes area—but everywhere its difficulties were insuperable: it had too much to do, in too large a territory, through officers of variable character and quality, upon too slender a body of cohesive criminal law, and against too much economic and constitutional constraint.

An example of the last was the "posse law" of 1858, applicable solely to the Indian country and thought at the time of its enactment to offer sufficient concession to the special problems presented by the Territory. This measure permitted the marshal or deputy marshal to employ up to three persons as *posse comitatus* to assist in the execution of whatever papers he happened to be carrying with him; but from the outset, it was interpreted to mean that he could hire up to three persons for each and every writ. Each "posse" (the term was not a collective noun, although often misused as such outside the Government service) was entitled to "three dollars for each day in lieu of all expenses and services."[82]

Literal application of this law would worsen what was always a difficult problem—the arrest of a fugitive considered unsafe for a lone officer to approach. If the whole force of four men concentrated on catching such an individual, they would probably succeed in getting him, but whether they did or not, other criminals sought by them were likely to have been warned that officers were about and to put themselves out of reach. By working, instead, in ones and twos, the officers might make many more arrests, but they would go in greater hazard of their lives—or be tempted to let the most desperate criminals escape.

Another risk in too rigorous an application of the posse law was that, since an industrious officer could be as much prey to pecuniary temptation as an idler, he might, if denied the opportunity of exercising a judicious creativity in the preparation of his accounts, move to some field of endeavor where he did not have to cheat to secure fair pay.

The liberal interpretation of the statute enabled the marshal's office to counter an epidemic of violent crime, but it lent itself to lucrative abuse of the sort exploited to scandalous proportions during Story's tenure. Congress might have aimed for a compromise by modifying the act of 1858 to allow a deputy marshal to take four, five, or six men with him into the Indian country, or more if the judge or marshal could certify that more were needed, but did next to nothing about the problem until 1895.[83]

Most of the fees payable to the marshal and deputy were determined by an act of February 26, 1853, which remained in force with little change for more than forty years. The officer could claim $2 "for service of any warrant, attachment, summons, capias, or other writ, except execution, venire, or a summons or subpoena for a witness," these items being assessed at different rates. His refundable expenses while trying to effect an arrest could not exceed $2 a day, and for bringing in each prisoner, there was his "mileage," a charge of ten cents a mile "for himself and for each prisoner and necessary guard." Attendance before a United States commissioner and bringing in prisoners or witnesses was worth $2 a day, and there were other occasional duties for which the deputy could charge a fee, but all fees were statutorily subject to the marshal's deduction of one-fourth or more.[84]

Marshals and district attorneys of the United States could live well enough on the fees the statutes allowed them; but there were abundant opportunities for both officers, especially the marshal, to manipulate the regulations to their own profit, and these opportunities were taken in many federal districts at one time or another.[85] In the Western District of Arkansas, although complaints were continually voiced about the expense of running the court and about the bad character of individual officers, corruption as an institution disappeared after the arrival of Parker.[86]

For a year or two Congress helped the reformation along. In January 1877, it undid the gerrymandering act of 1871 by reapportioning the Arkansas counties between the two districts so that the Western District now consisted of nineteen western counties besides "the country lying west of Missouri and Arkansas, known as the Indian Territory." At the same time it allowed the Fort Smith court four annual terms (February, May, August, and November) instead of only two.[87] A month later, on February 27, it repealed the law that had exempted "an Indian in the Indian country" from the operation of U.S. laws against trafficking in "spirituous liquors or wine" when the other parties were all Indians.[88]

While on the face of it this last item of legislation was a curb on tribal sovereignty, the sovereignty here was more theoretical than real. This arose partly from the neglect of the tribal authorities to enforce their own antiliquor laws. Even more significantly, the Fort Smith deputies had often been able to circumvent the immunity afforded to Indians by the old law by recourse to a statute that permitted search for liquor and the confiscation of any property where liquor had been found.[89]

In the spring of 1878, one of Galpin's principal recommendations bore fruit when, responding to the repeated urging of Interior Secretary Carl Schurz, Commissioner of Indian Affairs Ezra Hayt, and a number of agents, Congress provided for the formation of Indian police forces.[90] But Congress could not, or would not, always disgorge the funds requested by the Attorney-General to keep the court in session after the failure of the regular appropriation, forcing its temporary closure on at least three occasions.[91]

One important alteration which did not require Congressional action could have been effected had Parker chosen to use the authority that was already his to appoint United States commissioners in the Indian Territory. A critic, pointing out that more than half the population of the Indian Territory lived west of the MKT Railway, eighty-five miles or more from Fort Smith, thought it Parker's duty to appoint commissioners at Vinita, Fort Gibson, Tahlequah, Muskogee, Eufaula, Okmulgee, McAlester, Atoka, Caddo, and Tishomingo: "This is but simple justice to the complainant, to the witness, and to the prisoner. . . . The fact that justice would be had without such a burdensome expense would prevent crime, by preventing the temptation [for residents] to take life in their own hands that now exists."

Observing that it could cost a man from $50 to $250 to pursue through the courts the thief who had robbed him of a horse worth $40, the writer added: "A shorter way is to pursue, capture and kill the thief and take the risk of detection and imprisonment. We are informed this is not a supposititious case, but has actually occurred."[92]

Judge Parker almost never appointed commissioners in the Territory, and on the very rare occasions that he did, it was with reluctance at the time and regret afterward. His main objection to the location of commissioner's courts in Indian Territory was that, being away from the eye of the district attorney and judge at Fort Smith, they could be neither advised nor supervised: "If commissioners are scattered over the Indian country the annoyance to the people will be much greater than it is by their having to come to Fort Smith, as they will suffer increased annoyance because of frivolous, unnecessary, and improper prosecutions."[93]

Logical and sound as these arguments were, they leave room for a question whether throughout the length and breadth of the Indian Territory there was absolutely no one who could be depended upon to discharge the duties of United States commissioner with capability and fairness. Perhaps Parker, a man of prodigious stamina and no small vanity, merely thought it intolerable that important antejudicial proceedings in his district should be held out of his earshot.

Parker's fondness for jurisdiction as a concept in itself may be seen in the obstinacy with which, at least until the late 1880s, he asserted it as the right of his court to claim from the tribal authorities cases to which adopted or intermarried Indians were party. A habeas corpus hearing would be held, when Parker would review the issues of jurisdiction in such cases. Sometimes he would release the prisoner to the tribal officers; but his admission, on at least one such occasion, that Indian governments were entitled to pronounce upon their own questions of citizenship did not mark an end to these tussles, much less prevent the citizenship issue from remaining in contention between the tribal and federal governments for some years to come. Sometimes in these habeas corpus cases Parker would rule against the tribal authorities. In one such instance, the Reynolds murder case of 1877–78, the Choctaw Nation appealed to the Attorney-General, and won; in another, Parker tried to establish the right of the federal court to try a Choctaw sheriff for the murder of two adopted citizens who, it was said, had been trying to escape.[94]

In other instances the quarrel was between Parker and the Cherokee government. Echoes of the "Going Snake Massacre" of 1872 had not died away when in 1879 the Cherokees refused to surrender a prisoner to the United States, and the federal authorities threatened to send soldiers to help in the service of a writ of habeas corpus and remove the man from the Cherokee national prison by force, if necessary. William Adair, a Cherokee delegate, was keenly aware of the wider implications of an armed collision, and wrote from Washington to advise the principal chief that it was right for the prisoner to have been handed over peaceably, provided it had been done *"under protest"*:

> [A] big fight between our High Sheriff, and the authorities of the United States—may have resulted in the killing of several on both sides—which perhaps would have been greatly to our *prejudice.* . . . If you had *resisted* the authorities of the United States—to the extent of *fighting* (as no doubt you would have been required to do) and had killed several citizens of the United States—the result might have been the passage of the Territorial Bill now pending in Congress.—It is always better to avoid a fight when it can be done consistently.[95]

Protests notwithstanding, interference from Fort Smith in the judicial affairs of the Cherokee Nation, in particular, soon ceased to be a mere nuisance and became a threat. In December 1882, the national council instructed its delegation in Washington

> to call the attention of the government of the United States to the encroachment and abuse of the United States Court at Fort Smith to the unnecessary harassment of our people by its officials and to its assumption of jurisdiction over our adopted citizens in violation of the plain letter of the treaties between the United States and the Cherokee Nation thereby causing confusion and hindering the administration of law and interfering with the Courts and proper officers of the Cherokee Nation.[96]

This remonstrance was presented again two years later, by which time the jurisdictional wrangle between Fort Smith and the Cherokee Nation had been complicated, owing to the intrusions of Kansas "boomers" and others, by the larger issue of sovereignty over the Cherokee Outlet.[97] Only

at the end of the decade, through a combination of Supreme Court decisions and congressional enactments, did the federal courts relinquish all
interest in criminal cases involving Indian citizens by adoption.

Parker's predilection for busying himself and his court with things he
might reasonably have kept away from lends credibility to the comment
of a leading lawyer in Fort Smith that holding court was the judge's "chief
amusement."[98]

The foulness of the air made the courtroom "an abominable place,"
though in Parker's opinion the House of Representatives was much
worse.[99] Worse still was the United States jail in the cellar of the courthouse.

Early in April 1878, a Fort Smith newspaper reported that the jail was
furnishing board and lodging for 78 men: 4 had been convicted during
the February term for murder and were to be hanged in June; the remaining 74 were awaiting the attention of a grand or petit jury. Seven of the
latter had been charged with murder, 11 with assault with intent to kill,
42 with larceny, 11 with liquor offenses, and 1 with rape. A recaptured
convict and a man imprisoned for contempt of court rounded out the
roster.[100] This is a typical inventory of what was described by Attorney-
General Augustus Garland as "the most miserable prison, probably, in the
whole country."

Garland was writing in 1885, when the daily average number of
inmates also was about seventy-eight. This was several times too many for
the two adjacent cellars—55 feet long, 29 feet wide, 7 feet high, poorly
ventilated, and almost without sanitation—jointly "dignified by the title
of the 'United States jail.'"[101]

This dungeon had not been replaced by a cleaner and more commo-
dious structure partly because there were always more demands upon the
House of Representatives for the appropriation of funds than it could
meet and partly because most of those in the Senate and House interested
in taking reform into the Indian country were against anything that
might lengthen the longevity of the Fort Smith court's jurisdiction in the
nations, so delaying the coming of Territorial government.

Even if it is true, as stated by several witnesses before the Patterson
committee, that more than fifty murders had occurred within twenty
miles of Caddo during the last three years and that many of them were
cases for Fort Smith,[102] the evidence overall is that the court was doing
as well as could reasonably be expected in the light of its geographical
location and the regulatory straitjacket on the operations of its field
officers. A total of 821 criminal cases were tried in Fort Smith between
July 1, 1874, and June 30, 1878, 434 of them ending in the conviction of the

defendant.[103] That nearly half the defendants were either acquitted or discharged on the motion of the prosecution should dispose of any accusation that juries at Fort Smith were habitually prejudiced against the accused or that the prosecution strove for a conviction when there were insufficient evidential grounds for expecting it.

A single court situated in the midst of the Territory and employing men no better and no worse than those who served at Fort Smith would have labored under the same difficulties. Places five miles from a new courthouse at Muskogee would have been fifty miles from the old one at Fort Smith, but people living just within the eastern boundary of the Indian country would find the new court fifty miles more distant than the old.

A point as obvious as the last was buried almost out of sight amid the sheaves of convoluted argument exchanged by lawyers and laymen on Capitol Hill and elsewhere for a decade after Patterson's trip to the Territory. Substitution of three or more courts within the borders of the Five Nations, whether introduced on their own or as part of an imposed structure of Territorial government, would have overcome one set of objections and raised a mass of others. At this time not much support could have been mustered in either chamber for any of these plans, and nothing was done.

Congress at least understood that for the policing of the region west of the Five Tribes, a single federal court located among the Five Tribes would be little better than the court at Fort Smith.

Throughout this western tract, the authority of the Fort Smith court was still vestigial. An example of what the Fort Smith officers were failing to do is the complaint of Joseph Hartford, who had charge of the Sac and Fox agency and the neighboring reservations of the Mexican Kickapoo and Potawatomi Indians:

> The neighborhood of those two reservations is infested with a gang of oulaws who locate between the Pottawatomie Reserve and Kickapoo, committing murder and robbery on defenseless citizens of both places; they run off the stock of farmers and when not engaged in this, they are selling whisky. . . . There are over 100 of these lawless characters, well armed with Spencer and Winchester rifles, besides Colt revolvers, and they are a terror for the law-abiding people of the surrounding country. It is hoped that the authorities will deal with these creatures as they deserve.[104]

These ruffians were driven away by a force of soldiers without any assistance from Fort Smith. Action of this kind was covered by the treaties between the tribes and the United States, but it was plain that the civil authority ought to be able to make a better showing in the western half of the Indian country. For the first time, a congressional majority emerged in favor of breaking the jurisdictional monopoly of the Fort Smith court in Indian Territory; but since at first there were two opposing opinions about how this should be done, a compromise had to be thrashed out.

Late in 1881, George Vest introduced a Senate bill for the establishment of a United States court in the Indian country. It got no further than the report stage and was replaced on the agenda by a House bill which, instead of creating a new federal district for the Indian Territory, reparceled the jurisdiction on its western side. Vest, a member of the Senate Committees on Territories and the Judiciary and, for several years past and fifteen years to come, one of the harshest critics of the Fort Smith court and the tribal governments, retaliated by blocking the House bill in the Senate. In time he was induced to withdraw his opposition, and on January 6, 1883, the bill went onto the statute book.[105]

Section 2 of the act annexed to the judicial district of Kansas "all that part of the Indian Territory lying north of the Canadian river and east of Texas and the one hundredth meridian not set apart and occupied by the Cherokee, Creek, and Seminole Indian tribes." All cases arising in the area defined by this section were to be tried at Wichita or Fort Scott. (In general, cases from the Quapaw Agency, the Osage Nation, and the small reservations next to the Osage country would be dealt with at Fort Scott; those from elsewhere in this sector at Wichita.)

Section 3 provided that the remainder of the Indian Territory outside the Five Nations be attached to the Northern District of Texas, which itself had been formed only four years earlier. Cases derived from the district's jurisdiction in Indian Territory were to be tried at Graham, the nearest of its nine court towns to the Red River.[106]

As the officers of the Arkansas court had seldom ventured west of the Five Nations, not much was diverted from the Fort Smith docket by these changes; nor were the Kansas and North Texas courts stretched by their operations in the western reservations.

Nonetheless, as the first legislative abridgment of the jurisdiction of the Western District of Arkansas, and as a measure that was seen by some politicians in Washington as the necessary precursor of more comprehensive reforms, the Wichita, Fort Scott, and Graham courts act of 1883 is a rubric in the political history of the Indian Territory.

In the course of the next dozen years, the Fort Smith court would become more efficient but less adequate: it would do more, and still have more left undone from one year to the next. Its jurisdiction would be curtailed in various ways, but its costs and caseload would grow heavier in response to changes in the Indian Territory which it and the other federal courts in the region could neither control nor contain.

CHAPTER FOUR

Constitutions and Laws
of the Five Nations

*We have our laws, which are good enough if they were
enforced and lived up to; but they are not.—E. H. Colber-
son, an adoptive white Choctaw, to Senator John Patterson,
at McAlester, I.T., November 21, 1878; 45th Cong., 3d sess.,
Senate Report 744, February 11, 1879*

*These tribal governments, within the jurisdiction of the
United States, and yet in a sense politically distinct,—
exercising separate sovereignty and yet dependent upon and
subject to treaties,—are anomalous of course, and in some
respects ridiculous. . . . On the other hand, it is due and
proper to say, these abnormal, rattle-and-straw governments, so far as they reach, are respectably conducted and
effective; and no doubt they have contributed materially to
the tribal peace, safety, and happiness.—Henry King, "The
Indian Country," Century Illustrated Monthly Magazine, August 1885*

Government in the Five Nations, like federal and State
government, was in the hands of elected officials and their appointees.
Unlike the federal and State governments, the Five Nations had no permanent employees. The executive departments of the tribal governments
comprised the principal chief or governor, second or assistant chief, and
treasurer, all elected, and an executive secretary; no scope was offered for
the development of bureaucracy. The executive secretary might be abler
or more articulate than the chief whose appointee he was, or might be
little more than a clerk; in either event communication was direct and
uncluttered. Though the elected legislature could exercise general supervision, this was worth very little when the council was not in session or

when, as happened quite often, a chief chose to run the executive office from home.

The tribal courts—like their obverse, the federal courts acting in the Indian Territory, but to a greater extent—were hampered by the limitations of their criminal jurisdiction. They could determine only those cases where all the parties involved in the crime were Indians. After the act of February 27, 1877, the United States held an overriding jurisdicton over liquor offenses, even where only Indians were concerned.

As the flow of immigration from the United States quickened, the ratio of criminal cases which were the preserve of the federal authorities increased. At the same time, disputes arising from debts or contracts between Indian and United States citizens became commoner. In 1889 and 1890, Congress placed all such cases within the domain of the federal courts, further tilting the balance of jurisdiction away from the tribal system of government; but, until this legislation was enacted, civil controversies between Indian citizens and noncitizens remained private quarrels because the tribal courts, as a rule, would not hear them and the federal courts could not.

Political alignments among Indian full-bloods and mixed-bloods and white adopted or intermarried citizens owed everything to self-interest and nothing to racial distinctions. Most mixed-blood and white citizens were drawn to the "progressive" parties; but so were many of the educated or prosperous minority among the full-blooded or nearly full-blooded Indians. Conversely, a minority of white citizens and mixed-bloods— cattlemen or industrial concessionaries of the tribal governments—were hostile to change: their interests set them against the division of the range into sections or the dissolution of the governments that had granted them trading privileges. These men identified themselves with, and were often prominent in, the conservative parties which the great majority of full-bloods supported.

In the Cherokee Nation, the parties were separated more by questions of personality than political attitudes; there were conservative and progressive elements in all parties. Nowhere was the picture static; in the Choctaw and Chickasaw nations particularly there was a steady increase in the proportion of full-bloods who openly favored progressive policies.

In June 1886, the Senate Committee on Indian Affairs, whose chairman was Henry Laurens Dawes, declared:

> The race aversions between Indians and white people have never strongly implied that either class was degraded by intermarriage with the other. Their aversions have been those that have grown out of national hostilities, intensified by barbarous treatment on both sides during times of war. As

these Indians have advanced in education the white people have sought alliances with them in marriage, until now these five tribes are largely controlled by white men who are respectable. Their loyalty to their adopted country is as apparently earnest and inflexible as that of the Indians of full blood, and they are received into citizenship without exciting the jealousy of the Indians in any marked degree.[1]

Several qualifications should be added to this statement. In the first place, intermarriage, after the tribal removals to Indian Territory, may not have contributed much to the cultural elevation of the nations; as a rule, educated whites would intermarry with educated mixed-bloods, and uneducated whites would intermarry with uneducated mixed-bloods or full-bloods. Nor would the character of the men who controlled the tribes—whether white; nearly white; quarter-blood, half-blood, or full-blood Indian; or black—always accord with respectability's definition of itself. Thirdly, those intermarried whites who were advocates or supporters of tribal self-government on the traditional bases were ruled at least as much by an identity of interest as by an identity of sentiment with the full-bloods.

A complement to the view of the Senate Committee on Indian Affairs was offered two years later by another visitor to the Indian Territory, the daughter of the chairman of that committee:

> It may be better that the red man should work out his problems by himself. His ability to do it, and the progress he will make under favorable circumstances, are provided by the five civilized tribes. The large, unprogressive element, with its laziness and dirt, is no argument against this conclusion. Nor is the admixture of white blood the only enterprising quality in these nations, as is sometimes somewhat superficially charged. Where education and religion and responsibility have joined hands, their pupil has been raised to the extent of his possibility, be he white or red; and when these have been wanting, the white blood has only added crime to stupidity. It is in this last element—the presence or absence of responsibility—that much of the secret lies.[2]

That the uneven conflict between expansionist and centralizing influences in Washington and the separatism of the five tribal governments was not a crude struggle between "red" and "white" values is shown in the constitutional evolution of the Cherokee, Muskogee, Choctaw, and Chickasaw nations. Their constitutions, drawn after the pattern set by the States whose institutions were known to them, implied or envisaged a relationship with the United States similar to what then subsisted between the federal Government and the governments of the individual States. Only the Seminoles devised a constitution that was distinctively their own.

Subjoined to the constitutions were codes of criminal and civil law. If the Cherokee code was less elaborate than that of a State, the Choctaw code less detailed than the Cherokee, the Chickasaw less than the Choctaw, and the Creek simpler still, their spareness commended itself to some. As the journalist and traveler John Beadle remarked of the Creek Nation, "The laws are singularly plain and unambiguous. No space is wasted in definitions, it being taken for granted, apparently, that everybody knows the meaning of such terms as 'steal' and 'murder.'"[3]

Such drollery was not for the lawyer skilled in the practice of common law: the criminal law of the United States, resting mainly on the common law, was similarly without any definition for such terms as "steal" and "murder," and there were times when the meaning of these words was a matter for much argument. But among the laws of the Five Tribes, those of the Cherokees and Choctaws, and perhaps the Chickasaws, represent a clearer and more comprehensive collection than the ragbag of common and statute law that served the United States in criminal prosecutions even after 1890, when a code of sorts was introduced for use in the Indian Territory.

In the Cherokee, Choctaw, Chickasaw, and Muskogee nations, the functions of government were divided between an executive, a judiciary, and a bicameral legislature. Although the chief executive was usually referred to as the governor and addressed as such, only in the Chickasaw Nation was this his official title; elsewhere he was designated principal chief, and the proper style was always observed in formal usage. He was elected by adult male suffrage—for four years in the Cherokee and Muskogee nations, two years in the Choctaw and Chickasaw nations, where no chief executive could serve for more than four years out of six.

Elections for the two branches of the Cherokee national council were held together every alternate year. Members of the upper and lower houses of the Muskogee legislature, the House of Keys and the House of Warriors, sat for four years. There were annual elections for the houses of representatives of the Choctaw and Chickasaw nations, and elections every two years for their senates. General elections were held by the Cherokees, Choctaws, and Chickasaws in August of the appropriate year, and in September by the Creeks.[4]

At the head of the Cherokee judiciary was a supreme court of three, chosen by the national council to hold office for three years.[5] In December 1877, the supreme court was given exclusive jurisdiction "of all cases of manslaughter, and of all cases involving the punishment of death."[6]

There were three judicial circuits in the Cherokee Nation: northern (comprising Delaware, Coo-wee-scoo-wee, Saline, and Tahlequah districts), middle (Going Snake, Flint, Sequoyah, and Illinois), and southern (Canadian).[7] The segregation of Canadian district is explained by the special provisions relating to it incorporated in the Cherokee treaty of 1866.

At first the three circuit judges were chosen by the national council, but after November 1866 they were elected by direct popular vote. Their term of office was four years.[8] Under the act of 1877, which divested them of jurisdiction over the highest crimes, the circuit courts were to hear "all criminal cases, except those of murder and manslaughter, involving directly or indirectly a sum exceeding one hundred dollars" and all civil suits where the issue was title to property, occupancy of the common domain, or an amount of more than $100. It was also the duty of the circuit judges to hear appeals from the district courts, which dealt with lesser criminal and civil cases.[9] The nine district judges and district sheriffs were, likewise, popularly elected, but for two-year terms.[10]

In November 1873, the Cherokee legislature appropriated $6,000 for the construction of a national jail.[11] It was intended that the institution should be ready to receive convicts by November 1, 1874, but it did not open its doors until September 1876. During the interval the national council had provided for the appointment of a "special Sheriff and Deputy for the Town of Tahlequah" and passed "An act relating to the national prison" in forty-seven sections.

This latter measure empowered the principal chief to appoint, for a term coextensive with his own, a high sheriff, who would act as warden, executioner, custodian of the national capitol, "a conservator of the peace, with such general powers as are exercised by sheriffs," marshal of the supreme court, and—superseding the earlier legislation—town marshal of Tahlequah. He could appoint a deputy if he wanted one but would have to pay him out of his own salary of $500 per year.[12] Shortly afterward the high sheriff was authorized to hire guards and a cook, whose salaries would be met by legislative appropriation.[13] By December 1883, when a further act of the council placed the deputy high sheriff on the national payroll, eight guards were on the staff of the prison.[14] There were seldom as many as thirty men on the other side of the bars, and it ought to have been easy for a shift of two or three guards to hold them, but escapes were frequent.

Homicide was divided into four categories in the Cherokee criminal code: murder, manslaughter in the first and second degrees, and "excusable" or "justifiable" killing. Death by hanging was the penalty for murder; a conviction for manslaughter carried a term of two to ten or one to five years in the national prison, according to degree.[15] Assault with intent to kill or rob was punishable by three to five years in prison; the offenses of burglary, robbery, and larceny were subdivided into nine categories of crime and punishment, imprisonment for the offender being accompanied by a fine in six of the nine grades.[16] Rape was to be penalized by a term of ten to fifteen years' imprisonment; or by hanging, if the victim was less than twelve years old.[17] Accessories before or after the fact were in most circumstances treated as principals.[18] Corporal punishment for theft and other offenses was abolished in 1875[19] when a new code was adopted,[20] although the national prison had not yet been built.

The supreme court of the Choctaw Nation was an appellate body only, formed by one judge from each of the three organized districts (Moshulatubbee, Apukshunnubbee, and Pushmataha), appointed for four years by the two houses of the general council in joint session. Original jurisdiction over all felonies, all contractual disputes, and all other actions and suits where the matter at issue exceeded $50 in value belonged to three circuit courts, whose boundaries were identical with those of the districts and were informally often known as the district courts. These circuit judges were elected quadriennially by the registered voters of their districts.

Each district was divided into counties, each with a sheriff and a judge elected to serve for two years. It was the duty of the county judge to conduct the preliminary examination in all criminal cases and to rule on the lesser civil issues.[21] An act of November 4, 1886, abolished circuits for the courts of higher original jurisdiction. Each district was thereafter to have a single court town for hearing proceedings arising from felonies and major controversies. The term "district court" now became the official appellation for these tribunals.[22]

District chiefs and district light-horse men (one for each of the sixteen counties of the nation) were retained in the Choctaw constitution of 1859, but the gravitation of executive authority from the districts toward the principal chief was signaled by an act of October 29, 1860, creating a force of six national light-horse men, who would be his appointees and would be under his "exclusive direction and control."

In 1877 the scale of salaries for the leading members of the executive and judicial hierarchies was the same as that laid down in 1860: principal chief, $1,000; national light-horse, $200 for the captain, $150 for each trooper; supreme court judges, circuit judges, and national attorney, $400; district chief, $250; district (county) light-horse man, $150; county judge, $100; and sheriff, $75. The sheriff and certain other officers, salaried and unsalaried, were also allowed fees.[23]

Murder and manslaughter were defined in the Choctaw criminal code. The death penalty was imposed upon conviction for the graver offense; the lesser carried one hundred lashes.[24] Rape, at its first commission, called for one hundred lashes; a second conviction made the offense capital.[25] Armed robbery, actual or attempted, would also bring "one hundred stripes"; where property was stolen, the offender would have to make restitution to his victim.[26] Grand larceny—the theft of property valued at $25 or more—was worth "one hundred lashes well laid on the bare back"; if the property happened to be a horse, a second offense of the same kind would incur the death penalty. For petty larceny, the court could award any number of lashes up to one hundred.[27]

Parties to incestuous marriage were to receive for their first violation of the consanguity laws "one hundred lashes, well laid on, on their bare backs"; for a repetition of the offense, the portion was doubled, although administered over a period of two days. In either instance, a fine of $200 could be substituted, or added, at the court's discretion.[28]

Thirty-nine lashes were given for arson, and compensation exacted for the victims.[29] Perjury merited a fine of $5 to $100 or five to thirty-nine lashes, according to the inclination of the court.[30]

All sentences were executed by the county sheriff or at his direction; he was paid $5 for the execution of a death warrant and $2 for every whipping administered under order of the court.[31]

There were only four counties in the Chickasaw Nation—Pickens, Pontotoc, Tishomingo, and Panola—each constituting a judicial district. Together, the four counties formed a single circuit, whose court had jurisdiction of all criminal cases and all civil claims where the amount in controversy was at least $100; minor civil suits were the preserve of the county courts. There was one district attorney for the whole nation who also acted as attorney general. The sheriff of each county was to be assisted by "a sufficient number of constables" whose powers were the same as his.

The three judges of the Chickasaw supreme court—whose function, like that of the Choctaw Nation, was solely appellate—and those of the circuit court were chosen by the legislature for a four-year term; all the other officials were elected by popular vote for two years. A sheriff could not hold office for more than four years out of six.[32] In 1876 the legislature restricted the number of constables to one for each county.[33] At about the same time it gave the governor the right to mobilize a militia "whenever he may deem it necessary for the welfare and protection of the Chickasaw Nation," its constituent companies to consist of not fewer than twenty-five but not more than sixty citizens each.[34] Later two constables were allowed for each county. They, like the sheriff, were paid a salary of $400 per year.[35]

Murder in the first degree and treason were capital crimes; murder in the second degree (killing another "with premeditated malice" but not wilfully) made the perpetrator liable for one to five years "in the dungeon of the national jail." Accessories were treated as principals in all cases of murder, treason, and robbery.[36]

Robbery, for the first offender, entailed fourfold punishment: restoration of the goods stolen or their value; a fine of up to $100; thirty-nine lashes "with a good hickory switch"; and up to six months' imprisonment with hard labor. A second conviction for robbery would require the guilty party besides repaying the victim to meet a fine up to $500, receive one hundred lashes, and serve a prison sentence of up to one year. A third conviction made it a capital offense.[37] Burglars were to be given thirty-nine lashes and to make double restitution of the property stolen.[38]

Chickasaw law was hard on perjurers: the penalty was one hundred lashes "on the bare back, well laid on by the sheriff or constable," accompanied by a fine of $10 to $500.[39] Any person convicted of the introduction or sale of ardent spirits was fined, for the first offense $10 or $25, and $40 or $50 for any further transgression;[40] after the act of February 27, 1877, he or she could in addition, or as an alternative, face prosecution by the United States for the same infringement, even if no citizen was connected with the illegal transaction. Drawing or leveling a deadly weapon wilfully and maliciously was "a high misdemeanor" for which a fine of from $25 to $50 was to be imposed by the county judge.[41]

In the Creek or Muskogee Nation, the senior tribunal of law, known as the "supreme court" and the "high court," was composed of "five competent recognized citizens . . . who have attained the age of 25."[42] They were appointed for four years by vote of the national council to adjudicate all civil cases where the amount in dispute exceeded $100.[43] This supreme court was without criminal jurisdiction and had no appellate duties; there was no provision for appeal in the Creek laws except direct to the principal chief for clemency in criminal cases.[44]

When the six districts of the Muskogee Nation were established, they were designated Coweta(h), Arkansas, North Fork, Muskogee, Deep Fork, and Wewoka[45]; but in 1877 Arkansas district became Muskogee district, the old Muskogee district was restyled Okmulgee, and North Fork district took the name Eufaula.[46] Each district had a judge, chosen by the national council; a prosecuting attorney, chosen by the principal chief and confirmed by the national council, and a light-horse company of five, including a captain, elected by the voters of the district. All these offices were vacated at two-year intervals.[47] Civil cases in which the value of the thing at issue was no more than $100, and all criminal cases, came before the district court. Emoluments were not lavish: the judges of the supreme court were paid $3 per day while in session and 20 cents per mile for necessary travel; the district judges, an annual salary of $200; and the light-horse men, including the captain, $125 each. No salary was reserved for the prosecuting attorney; his remuneration was determined by the number of convictions he secured.[48]

Murder in the Muskogee Nation was killing a person "willfully and unlawfully" or "while engaged in an unlawful act," and it was a capital crime. An aider and abettor was equal in guilt with the principal.[49] Killing in self-defense was lawful.[50] Theft by force or by stealth was punishable by 50 lashes for the first offense, 100 for the second, and death for the third.[51] Rape was punished by 50 lashes for a first offense, death for a second; arson, by enforced restitution and 100 lashes; incestuous marriage by 50 lashes; resistance to officers by 25 to 100 lashes.[52] Perjurers were given 50 lashes, disqualified for life from public office, and "debarred from being considered a valuable witness in any of the courts of this nation." If false testimony brought pecuniary loss to the wronged party, the perjurer had to pay the sufferer double; if it brought the victim bodily harm at the hands of the court, the false swearer was to be punished in the same way.[53]

No code of laws for the Seminole Nation was ever published and no manuscript record other than the revised code of 1903 is known. In 1885, for the benefit of members of the Senate Committee on Indian Affairs, Holputta-che, second chief of the Seminole Nation, summed up the main features of what was, in the opinion of Anna Dawes, "perhaps the most nearly pure democracy we have on the continent."[54]

> [W]hen an individual kills another they convict him and kill him, and when a person is convicted of having stolen property they whip him on the bare back, and give him fifty lashes for the first offense, sixty-five lashes for the second offense, and eighty-five for the third offense, and then kill him for the fourth offense. When it is understood that some one has stolen property the chief issues a writ for his arrest and places it in the hands of the light horse company, who make such an arrest, and when he is taken the chief calls the entire nation together to try the case. He calls all the male members together. They meet in council and they have what is of the nature of a judicial committee, at any rate it is a committee of five members, who draft and formulate the laws; they draft a law to answer the case, and it comes before the council in writing . . . and the entire body act upon the law which has been drafted.
>
> They [the Seminoles] are divided into little towns, and each one of those towns is entitled to three members of the general council, and they are the persons who vote on the ratification of the laws.[55]

For some years the Muskogee criminal code was followed in most cases other than those of homicide,[56] but in time an individual body of law evolved from the statutes enacted at intervals by the Seminole general council. Complexities were absent, though not all were as concise as a law passed in January 1894 to deal with disturbers of the peace: the offender was required to pay an immediate fine of $25 or, upon failure to pay, to receive an equally summary punishment of twenty-five lashes.[57] Civil suits seldom reached the general council; usually they were "settled by arbitration, the governor acting as general peacemaker and paternal advisor."[58]

A revised code was promulgated in December 1902 and January 1903 after Congress had reduced the powers of the Seminole court. It is probable that this code was, in great part, a collation of laws passed earlier and still current.[59] One noteworthy alteration was that the death penalty was no longer demanded for a fourth conviction of theft or rape; instead, the criminal was treated as a first offender, and allotted fifty lashes.[60]

There were fourteen "towns" or "bands" (including two for ex-slaves) who elected their own chiefs every fourth year on the first Tuesday in April. They and two subchiefs from each town formed the membership of the general council. Candidates for the position of principal chief were nominated by a national convention, the delegates to which were chosen by town vote on the first Tuesday in April of an election year. The principal chief and second chief were elected by direct popular vote on the first Wednesday of the following June and began their four years in office on the first Monday in July.[61]

The light-horse company consisted of a captain, whose salary was $500 per year; a lieutenant, who received $450; and eight privates, who were paid $300 each.[62]

Criminal and unresolved civil cases were placed before the general council by the band representatives, who in their towns acted as justices of the peace and administrators of estates. Anyone dissatisfied with the management of an estate could petition the general council for the appointment of new administrators in place of the town chief and subchiefs.[63]

Shooting was the prescribed form for the infliction of capital punishment among the Creeks,[64] Seminoles, and, except for a period of eight years from 1859, the Choctaws;[65] hanging was the mode of execution in the Cherokee and Chickasaw nations, the only ones with national prisons.[66] County jails were built in the Choctaw Nation during the mid-1880s, but none of the other tribes ever made provision for county or district jails.[67]

Among the executive powers of the Creek principal chief was granting a reprieve or pardon to a condemned criminal.[68] The Cherokee chief could, with the advice and consent of an executive council of three, pardon "persons convicted of murder, manslaughter, or other high crimes."[69] No power of pardon was attached to the governor's role elsewhere until the Seminoles extended it to their principal chief about 1900; before that, he could do no more than refer a case back to the general council for retrial.[70] The principal chief of the Choctaw Nation was permitted to suspend the execution of sentence; and if he suspended it "sine die," that could be tantamount to a pardon.[71]

Such was the material of the institutional foundations of the Five Nations. The legal apparatus was on the whole a sturdy though unfinished model, on which much more could be built, but did it work? Many residents of the Indian Territory—citizens of various classes and noncitizen whites and blacks, thought that it did not, and said so.

"There is," remarked a Cherokee mixed-blood, "a want of moral sanction from the law"; its officers were "pretty slack sometimes" in enforcing their writ.[72] A white man whose home was in the Choctaw Nation described the laws as "a dead letter." The Indian laws, he added, "look very nice in the books, but that is as far as they get."[73] "Choctaw law," commented a church missionary, "is too weak to protect Indians."[74] And when a wealthy Creek stated that within a year there had been some two dozen murder trials in the Muskogee Nation of which but two had ended with the conviction of the defendant, his interlocutor was skeptical: he believed that there had been more murders and fewer arrests than the witness had accounted for.[75]

Many Creek full-bloods, explained a leading mixed-blood, distrusted the courts; they yearned for the plain, peremptory ways of the past, when law had been dispensed by the towns of the tribe.[76] He did not say it, but this was the sentiment which helped to keep alive the old rivalry between "upper" and "lower" towns that bedeviled the Muskogee Nation and perhaps broke it as a unitary force.

Samuel Sixkiller, the Cherokee captain of the Union Agency Indian Police, agreed with Senator John Tyler Morgan (D, Alabama) that it was "common practice" for both tribal and federal officers "to pass by . . . pistol fights and gun fights, unless somebody is either killed or badly shot."[77]

Most of these assertions, admissions, or expressions of opinion, and many others like them, occur in testimony before one or the other of two congressional committees in 1885. None of the spokesmen cited here were full-bloods, and it might be objected that they were not typical members of their tribes or that their views and attitudes were unrepresentative; but their criticisms are significant because they were voiced to some of the men in the forefront of the campaign to force political or judicial reform upon the Five Tribes when that campaign was beginning to run strongly, and because the testimony was published and widely cited. Its value as evidence may be tested against material drawn from other sources.

The Administration
of Justice
by the Five Nations

The indictment against Overton Love, County Judge of Pickens County, was taken up. The attorneys for the defendant . . . made a motion to quash the indictment, "because" said they, it contained two counts. One charging with misdemeanor in office; the other involving the rights of property. The attorney pro tem, Benjⁿ Kemp, for the Nation, coincided with them in opinion; and pronounced a eulogium, in his way, on Judge Love's former character. "Sic transit gloria mundi!"—Charles P. H. Percy, attorney general of the Chickasaw Nation, Tishomingo, January 17, 1870, report on January term of the District Court of Panola County, Records of the Chickasaw Nation

I have called on you according to law, but since you seem to be ignorant of the law, I will ask you to get some one to read Article III, Section 3 of the law governing Dist. Courts and Dist. officers. . . . I want you to comply with the law and send me your whole Light Horse Co., at once. As I am in actual need of them here.—R. R. Bruner, judge, Okmulgee district, to H. C. Stidham, judge, Muskogee district, May 29, 1895, Records of the Muskogee Nation, Light Horse, Doc. 32101

No appraisal of how well the tribal systems of law were applied can be valid unless account is taken of the civil disturbances that from time to time racked the tribal governments. During the twenty years after the signing of the Reconstruction treaties, insurrection erupted in the Muskogee Nation on three occasions, and the Cherokee Nation was dogged by recurrent factional violence that was at least partly political in character and origin. Later, the Choctaw and Chickasaw nations, too, were plagued with political vendettas; but, while these difficulties sprang mainly from a division in attitudes toward proposals for reform, the earlier feuding was the product of past differences.

Trouble arose in the Muskogee Nation soon after the Civil War from the dissatisfaction of a small but aggressive force of pro-Union full-bloods with the treaty of 1866. They felt, with justification, that insufficient recognition had been given to their loyalty to the Union; more questionably, they maintained that the peace terms had been too generous to the Confederate Creeks, enabling the latter to regain control of the tribal government a year later.[1]

Sands, the leader of the dissidents, charged the rival party with electoral fraud and the expropriation of money that belonged to the northern Creeks. At first the majority of "loyal Creeks" were out of sympathy with Sands, whose adherents were held to be "the most ignorant and superstitious members of the tribe, with no licence to speak for the thousands of the loyal Indians."[2] In time, the insurgents gained at least covert support from most Union Creeks, and the government was unable to suppress the rebellion.

Agent J. W. Dunn reported in July 1869 that there had been more murders within the last year "than in all the years since the close of the war" but added that "it is not considered proper for the United States to interfere, unless the Creeks find it impossible to enforce the laws and apply to the United States for protection."[3] Dunn's superintendent disagreed. In his submission, "the Creek authorities should be furnished with a force sufficient to put down insubordination or insurrection."[4] In the autumn of 1871, after Sands and his three hundred followers had disrupted a meeting of the national council, Chief Checote raised a corps of special light-horse. Only then, and with the help of the Creek agent, were effective measures taken against the malcontents. Even then, the rising was not beaten down; it merely subsided because of the death of its leader.[5]

Although brief and bloodless, the Lochar Harjo uprising of 1876–1877 deepened the chasm between Upper and Lower townsmen and between Union and Confederate partisans. Lochar Harjo, a Lower Creek who had fought on the Union side, and a very able man, was elected principal chief in 1875, but a majority in each house of the legislature belonged to the other party, and in December 1876, Harjo was removed from office, having been impeached for illegal partisanship in the allocation of offices. He and his supporters were ready to take arms against the government, but a combination of diplomacy and special light-horse effected a peaceful resolution of the dispute.[6]

In July 1882, the old animosities flared up again after a "Northern" horse thief was released by his friends from the custody of the captain of light-horse for Wewoka district, a "Southern" man. Several men, including the captain, were killed in the melee or after it, the two sides sharing the casualties. Some of the criminals were arrested; others were joined by former allies of Sands and Lochar Harjo, now led by Isparhecher, an unlettered full-blood—another of the minority of Lower Creeks who had served on the Union side during the Civil War. The upshot was the "Green Peach War."

For the third time, the principal chief invoked his emergency powers to call up a special light-horse force, and in February 1883 Isparhecher took refuge in the Sac and Fox reservation. In August of that year, through the mediation of the Board of Indian Commissioners, an agreement was concluded between the two parties. Isparhecher and his followers were given amnesty; the Union agent was to arbitrate on all disputes arising from the disorder; the national light-horse was to be abolished or reformed; members of both parties were to help to ensure the honest conduct of the next election; and United States soldiers were to be stationed at Okmulgee "to maintain peace and assist the civil officers in the enforcement of law and order" for as long as their colonel and the agent judged necessary.[7]

Little blood has been shed in the Green Peach War; but, just as the very occurrence of the outbreak had again exposed the organic weakness of the Muskogee Nation, so the manner of its cure did not speak well for the ability of the nation to handle serious disorder within its borders.

Despite extreme bitterness between the Ross (or Northern) and Adair (Southern) parties, intensified by the angry reaction of the Adair men to the terms accepted in 1866 by the Northern delegation to Washington, the Civil War was not carried into the peace in the Cherokee Nation. Instead, the Ross party split soon after the death of its leader in 1866. Many of the Union full-bloods, including the Pins but headed by a mixed-blood, Lewis Downing, threw in with the former Confederates, building an alliance upon their common opposition to the treaty of 1866. William Potter Ross, a nephew of John, led the rival aggregation, which called itself the National party.

Tribal accession to the treaty of 1866 had sealed the fissure opened by the treaty of 1835; but in doing so, had created a new breach. Yet now the opposing parties were almost united in their hostility to land allotment and Territorialization, for these proposals were supported only by some in the Southern wing of the Downing party. When a number of Southern Cherokees who agreed with the plan to sectionalize and Territorialize the country were run out of the nation or killed, there was no general wish to see the aggressors arrested and punished.[8]

In November 1874, the bitterness of the rivalry between William Ross, the principal chief, and Downing turned into street warfare when armed followers of both men congregated in Tahlequah. After two drunken Ross partisans had murdered one of their enemies, a shooting affray occurred between the two private armies, and a number of men were wounded. No official action was taken against the two killers.[9]

Talk of civil war in the Cherokee Nation was revived at the turn of the year when two men were killed and two others, deputy sheriffs, wounded; but whiskey and personal animosities had more to do with this episode than the opposing political affiliations of the two sets of participants.[10]

When Principal Chief Dennis Bushyhead, with the connivance of the Cherokee national council, declined to make way for the apparent winner of the election of August 1887, it required only a brief, though determined, show of force to evict him. Bushyhead's retreat from office may or may not have been statesmanlike, but it was certainly discreet; the armed supporters of Joel Mayes, the candidate of the rival Downing party, were more numerous and better deployed than his. This collision of ambitions did not prevent Bushyhead, as tribal delegate, from working smoothly alongside Mayes to thwart the passage of a Territorial bill.[11]

An extended series of troubles whose background was, in part, of a political character, developed from the settlement among the Cherokees of the Delawares. In 1867, the Delawares, like the Cherokees a tribe with a strong admixture of white ancestry, sold their lands in Kansas, dissolved their national government, and purchased allotments in the Coowee- scoowee and Delaware districts of the Cherokee Nation. Tension was fomented by the Delawares' belief that the land they had bought was of poor quality, and the displeasure of the Cherokees at the presence in their midst of a self-sufficient people who farmed their land according to the sectional principle.[12]

Blood was spilt between the two for the first time in August 1870 when a Delaware killed a Cherokee in self-defense. The law demanded that the killer should be tried in a Cherokee court if at all; but, as the district was inhabited mainly by Delawares, most of those summoned for jury service were members of that tribe. The father of the dead youth, convinced that his son had been murdered and that the Delaware jurors would vote to excuse the defendant solely because be was a Delaware, tried to have the case transferred to the United States court at Van Buren on the insufficient ground that the mother of the deceased was a United States citizen. Finally he resorted to blood vengeance. Others entered the feud from both sides of the tribal line.[13]

On Tuesday, August 5, 1873, while the general election was in progress, a group of Cherokees tried to kill a Delaware at the polls. The district sheriff and his deputies assumed the role of spectators. No one was killed on that occasion, but in the course of the feud at least four Delaware and four Cherokee lives were taken. Those who stood trial for murder were beneficiaries of an impartiality of a kind; none on either side was executed.[14]

Throughout the Cherokee Nation there was a general reluctance among district sheriffs to make arrests for homicide, among prosecuting attorneys to press charges for murder where arrests were made, and among jurors to convict in a prosecution for murder. A dozen murders were committed in or near the town of Tahlequah between 1868 and 1878, within the tribal jurisdiction, and only one case was pursued all the way to the conviction of the murderer. The same period was said to have produced at least thirty-three murders in Illinois district, all apparently matters for the Cherokee courts.[15]

Toward the end of the era of tribal self-government, the Holdenville *Times* reviewed the cases of homicide that had occurred in Illinois district since the close of the Civil War. It found that 53 Cherokees by blood, 1 white adoptee, and 11 black citizens had died violently in that district during the thirty-two years. Only three murderers, all freedmen, had been hanged. Cases known to be in the federal jurisdiction were excluded from this reckoning, but "several" homicides in this category were known to have occurred. "Illinois district," added the writer, "is only forty miles long and twenty wide."[16] He might also have chosen to point out that its citizen population numbered about 2,300—roughly 1,700 Indians by blood, 100 or so adopted whites, and some 500 blacks.[17]

In his report for the year 1894–1895 the attorney general of the Cherokee Nation, presenting details of the murder cases he had prosecuted in a period of nine months, called it "a chapter of blood that is appalling when we consider that but about 30,000 persons are amenable to Cherokee law." He had appeared in twelve murder trials; a thirteenth had had to be continued because of his inability to be in two places at the same time; and four other cases were pending. Four defendants had been acquitted; two had secured verdicts of accidental killing; two had mistrials; three had been convicted of manslaughter and sent to prison; and only one had been found guilty as charged and hanged.[18]

Removal of homicide cases from the purview of the district courts in

1877 had meant that murderers would be prosecuted with far greater
energy than before, but it had not made the typical Cherokee jury any less
loth to find them guilty of a capital offense. Only a few murderers had
been hanged by the district authorities before 1875,[19] when it was provided that all executions should be performed at the national prison by the
high sheriff.[20] A full-blood known as Dirt Seller became, on October 15,
1877, the first man to be hanged there.[21] Spade Sunshine, also a full-blood,
became only the fifth almost ten years later.[22] Altogether, just fifteen men
had been hanged at the national prison when the Cherokee courts were
terminated in 1898.[23]

Reprieves from the death sentence were granted by the principal chief
and executive council. Commutation was to a term of imprisonment,
usually ten years or less.

After February 1877 the Cherokee authorities were disinclined to initiate prosecutions for the introduction or sale of alcoholic drinks; the United
States had accorded itself priority of jurisdiction in that field and was
allowed every opportunity to make the most of it. Liquor circulated freely
in the Cherokee Nation and throughout the Indian Territory, federal and
tribal statutes notwithstanding; its ready availability was at least as well
known to some of the tribal legislators as the rest of the population.[24]

Little was seen in the Cherokee Nation of organized livestock theft
until the 1890s,[25] but larceny of horses or cattle on a smaller scale was
always common, and the district officers were not zealous in dealing with
criminals guilty of theft or other lesser felonies. There were rarely as
many as forty men at a time in the zebra-striped uniform of the Cherokee
national prison; eighteen to twenty seems to have been the average number of inmates. Among the prisoners there would always be several who
had been convicted of murder or manslaughter and several others serving
short sentences for misdemeanors committed in the town of Tahlequah.
The small number of thieves within the prison walls bore only a remote
relationship to the amount of property that Cherokees were stealing from
other Cherokees.[26]

Although the criminal statutes of the other four nations provided for
the death penalty after a criminal had received a set number of convictions
for any one of certain felonies (as did those of the Cherokees until November 1875), these laws were almost never allowed to run their full course.
The principal chief of the Muskogee Nation made copious use of his
pardoning power to extricate habitual criminals from the death penalty
for a third conviction for theft.[27] The Choctaw and Chickasaw governors
had no pardoning power, and it may be that instead of being prosecuted
through the courts the most persistent thieves were dealt with by their

neighbors. As we have seen, four convictions were required by the Seminoles before they executed a thief (or a rapist). They maintained that they had rarely needed to whip a thief as often as thrice and had never had to execute one.[28]

Napoleon Ainsworth, a mixed-blood Choctaw lawyer, told the Dawes committee in May 1885 that at the most recent term of court in his (Moshulatubbee, or First) judicial district only two defendants out of forty had been acquitted. He did not say how many miscreants had escaped indictment or arrest.[29] About a year later, the grand jury of the same district found no bill of indictment against sixteen of seventeen alleged murderers. The case against the seventeenth was dismissed a year after that.[30]

At the August 1885 term of the third (Pushmataha) district court, only a handful of the fifty-eight defendants were acquitted; but more than half of the rest did not stand trial, preferring to plead guilty to adultery or a misdemeanor and be fined. One man was acquitted of murder. One prosecution for murder was abandoned because the defendant had died, and another withdrawn, probably because the case was outside the jurisdiction of the Choctaw courts. Two murderers were convicted: one was shot after his appeal had been rejected by the supreme court; the verdict against the other was reversed.[31]

The judges of the Choctaw supreme court seem to have carried out their duties with fairness and good sense. Most of their work was in the civil field; only about 70 criminal cases came to them upon appeals granted by the circuit courts of the three districts from 1866 to 1898. Thirty-eight of these were appeals against convictions for murder. The supreme court affirmed 18 of the convictions, reversed 10, and remanded 9 to the lower court for a new trial; the disposition of 1 case is uncertain.[32] In each case their reasoning was embedded in a few terse and elliptical sentences:

> [T]he proceedings of the Circuit Court held in Kiamitia County [were] correct and the law of evidence well handled, and the Judgement of said court strictly in compliance with the law. Therefore the Judgement of the lower court is hereby affirmed and ordered to be carried out.[33]

> The points in the Bill of Exceptions [were] duly considered and weighed in all of its bearing. The Court is of the opinion that the crime [was] wilfull and premeditated in taking the life of Lewis Parver in violation of law. Therefore the decision of the lower court is affirmed.[34]

And where the defense had based its appeal on the use of translated testimony and an assertion that a conviction had been secured without the evidence to warrant it, the reasons advanced by the defendant's counsel were declared, after a short commentary on the circuit court proceedings, to be "not sufficient in law for reversal of the decisions of the lower court. Therefore the decision of the lower court is affirmed."[35]

But only a minute proportion of the serious crime in the Choctaw Nation within Choctaw jurisdiction was ever compressed into supreme court proceedings; much of it never got as far as the examining judge of the county. A note of weary resignation can be detected in reports like the one in an Atoka newspaper that, after the latest foul and gratuitous murder, no attempt had been made to capture the killers, even though their tracks were clear in the snow.[36]

Such crimes, even excluding those to which U.S. citizens were party, were almost legion; many, if not all, were reported by one or more of the newspapers published in the Indian Territory, at Fort Smith, in North Texas, or by the special correspondents for the St. Louis press.

In the summer of 1893, officials of the United States court were so incensed at the repeated failure of the Choctaw authorities to make even a token investigation into the murders of two full-bloods that a deputy marshal was sent to look into the case. In due course he presented the Choctaw sheriff with two prisoners. After a perfunctory examination in county court, the suspects were released. The prevailing sentiment among local Indians was one of anger at the United States officers for presuming to meddle in Choctaw affairs.[37]

Some of those to be executed by the Choctaw authorities were spared by negligence or intervention. At least twice in the 1890s Principal Chief Wilson Jones exercised powers denied him by the constitution to procure through his use of national light-horse the freedom of murderers just before they were to be shot. No effort was made to recapture the men, who were obliged only not to live openly at their old homes. One of them, who was wanted on other charges by the United States, was killed by a deputy marshal.[38]

For a time, anyone sentenced to be whipped in Moshulatubbee district was allowed to wear a shirt for the occasion. Some took the opportunity to dress well for the ceremony. Ainsworth spoke of a case "where a man was tried for petty larceny who had five or six shirts on; this fellow knew he was going to get it."[39] More generally, though, these punishments were carried out to the last letter of the law. Women, unless they were in an advanced state of pregnancy, were treated the same as the men.[40]

In the main, the courts of the Choctaw Nation were attentive to lesser lawbreaking and diligent in punishing it, but inclined to stand aside from the prosecution of those guilty of the higher offenses. Most of the men who were lawfully shot by the Choctaw authorities had murdered close kinfolk, in most cases with great brutality. Other homicides were usually reserved for informal redress. Political murder came within this category. This attitude was not confined to the more obstinate and ignorant full-bloods. Dick Locke, a prominent white Choctaw and a man of some education, had this to say about the arrest and conviction of nine men who had assassinated four of their political opponents: "The men are guilty of murder, but not in the first degree. . . . [T]hese people should not be shot. They killed; it was like all political feuds—the quickest man comes out on top. . . . A certain element was planning to exterminate them, but they happened to get there first."[41] Few, it seems, had heeded the advice tendered so earnestly by Allen Wright shortly after the Civil War "to rely upon the strong arm of the nation."[42]

John Mashburn, an intermarried Chickasaw who had served as a judge in Panola county, said in his old age, in 1927, that the penalty for conviction of a capital crime in the Chickasaw Nation was death by shooting. It was in fact death by hanging; but the extreme rarity with which it was exacted, as much as the passage of thirty years since the demise of the Chickasaw courts, makes this lapse of memory no cause for wonderment.[43]

Several murderers were executed in the Chickasaw Nation during the 1870s. In April 1877, as though to underwrite the certainty of punishment, the presiding judge sentenced a murderer "to be hung by the neck until dead—dead—dead";[44] but most trials for murder ended in acquittal, and most convictions were reversed. Saffron Dyer, a full-blood who was hanged in the Chickasaw prison in 1885, appears to have been the last man to suffer capital punishment according to Chickasaw law.[45] Many murders were officially ignored. No action was taken against a man who almost killed his son in a street battle, or against the son when, fully recovered, he murdered the father a year later, or against the man who murdered the son at the same spot a few years after that.[46]

After a Chickasaw had been shot dead from the roadside by another member of the tribe, whose identity was known to all, a newspaper correspondent in Gainesville, Texas, commented: "Both parties being Indians no arrest has been made, nor is there likely to be [any], as the Chickasaw courts scarcely ever punish one of their people for crime."[47] This, although overstated, was still too near the truth to be dismissed as just another item of malicious propaganda from yet another enemy of tribal government.

By the late 1880s, when there was a widening rift between most Chickasaw full-bloods, on one side, and most mixed-blood and white citizens, it was likely that, where only full-bloods were concerned, any conflict in court between the rules of jurisprudence and tribal tradition was likely to be resolved in favor of the latter. In 1887 a man charged with two cold-blooded murders sought to excuse himself from one of them on the ground that the victim had been a witch. He was indicted only for the other.[48]

Although the criminal docket of the Chickasaw circuit court was never heavy, cattle and horse thieves were punished with some regularity between 1868 and 1880. In January 1868, for example, two thieves were each given thirty-nine lashes, fined $50, and sent to prison for one month. But by the later 1880s, very few criminal cases of any description were coming before the Chickasaw courts.[49]

The right of any citizen to be armed when traveling was recognized for many years by all five tribes; but violent crime among both citizens and noncitizens was so common in the Chickasaw Nation that in September 1884 the legislature prohibited carrying "any revolver or any pocket pistol of any kind" by any private citizen except when helping commissioned officers or in pursuit of horse thieves. The Union agent was asked to remove any noncitizen who flouted the new law; citizens could be fined from $25 to $100. So few citizens were ever brought into court under the new law that there are no grounds for supposing that the long catalogue of murders and woundings by firearms, covering the last fourteen years of tribal self-government, would have been even lengthier without this act.[50]

Pleasant Porter, one of the most articulate Muskogees and perhaps the most thoughtful, agreed with a suggestion put forward by Senator Morgan that the division of jurisdiction between the courts of the nation and those of the United States was "detrimental to the moral power of the Creek government" because the inability of the Muskogee authorities to act against United States citizens who had broken the tribal laws encouraged lawbreaking among the Creeks themselves. He added in support of this theory that a Creek officer would "find considerable difficulty in arresting a person charged with crime, but a United States marshal can arrest anybody"—meaning, doubtless, that although the Creek officer could arrest a white man who had broken the law of the Muskogee Nation, the arrest would then involve the officer in the nuisance of dealing with officials of the federal court or the Union agency.[51]

This was a real problem, and it afflicted all five nations, but it was not a precipitant of lawlessness among the Indians themselves. The main source of the inadequacies of the Muskogee courts lay in the political fragility of the Muskogee Nation. An indication of the barely suppressed turmoil in several districts of the nation, even during periods of surface tranquillity, was the frequency with which district light-horse men re-signed or were suspended from office by the principal chief in response to a request from the judge of the district. Often such requests were accompanied by a petition, and sometimes there would be a counterpetition. Usually most of the names on a paper from one side can be recognized as those of Creek full-bloods, and most of those on the opposing document can be identified as belonging (or presumed to belong) to whites, mixed-bloods, and ex-slaves. No doubt there were instances when both the officer and his critics were motivated by partisanship; but some of the officers who were removed or suspended were guilty beyond question of bribe taking or other forms of misconduct.

A light-horse man of Muskogee district, whose removal had been sought because he had shown signs of being intoxicated while confiscating "wiskey" from other people, explained that the offense had occurred on Christmas Day, when he believed himself free to have a good time. He volunteered the defense that "I was not to [sic] drunk to know any thing and I was in proper mine [sic] during the time." The captain and two members of the North Fork district light-horse resigned "on account of the troubles in which we are now involved," five months after Chief Harjo had declined to act on a petition for their removal. William Durant, proffering his resignation from the captaincy of Muskogee district because "the Presiding Judge and myself cannot agree," declared, "I have performed my duty satisfactory to all my people irrespect to Race or Collor [sic]."

Principal Chief Ward Coachman was petitioned from Arkansas district to take action against the whole light-horse company because they "violate they oath and laws by talkin [taking] bribe and leting prisoners get away." Lambert Scott, captain of Deep Fork district, was suspended for "informing persons against whom the Pros Atty had charges of their liability to legal prosecution." Daniel Miller was suspended from the captaincy of Coweta district for "allowing witnesses to mix with prisoners and disobedience to the Judge's orders &c." These charges drew a blast of counteraccusation from Miller, and the lives of the judge, prosecuting attorney, and light-horse captain of Okmulgee district were menaced by two light-horse privates.[52] Numerous incidents of a comparable nature are on record.

Though, in general, erring or negligent officers could be replaced without difficulty, a recurrent fault is not nullified by machinery to effect a temporary local cure. It is plain enough that, during the last thirty years or so of Muskogee self-government, the district companies of elected light-horse were, on the whole, not much good. But the failings of the light-horse were not so much a cause as a symptom of the decline in respect among the Creeks for the laws of their nation. The fault lay near the center of the laws themselves, with the principal chief's right to issue a pardon to a convicted criminal and the government's failure to repeal an ostensibly harsh penal measure that had become nugatory through non-enforcement.

In the spring of 1891, the Union agent announced that if in future the Creeks attempted to execute a felon upon a third conviction for theft, he would ask the United States court to serve a writ of habeas corpus, on the theory that the penalty for this class of offense fell within the Constitutional prohibition of cruel and unusual punishment.[53] Up to that time, however, neither the Interior nor the Justice Department had shown any inclination to tamper with the operation of the courts of the Five Nations where there was no dispute over jurisdiction. Not one of the thieves pardoned during the 1870s, 1880s, and early 1890s owed the extension of his or her life to the threat of federal intervention. In 1897, a few months before the abolition of the Creek courts, the United States did prevent the Muskogee authorities from carrying out several executions; but, even then, a higher federal court ruled that the interference was unlawful.[54]

James McHenry, judge of Coweta district, believed that a thief named Douglas Murrell deserved capital punishment and that he had been saved from execution once before, "but no statement can be found in our defective Court reports"; still, he asked the principal chief to pardon Murrell and another thief. He was seconded by the clerk of the court, who thought that Murrell should be excused "as he is a young man first, has a family, good family connections among our colored citizens and many sympathizing friends." Chief Checote granted the pardons.[55] In Coweta district, ex-slaves and their descendants greatly outnumbered "Indians by blood," and, in the Muskogee Nation overall, they represented about one-third of the citizen population. With most other voters confirmed in their allegiance, the outcome of a general election could be determined by the "freedman vote."[56]

Another thief was pardoned because he was, at the time of the third conviction, still only "about fourteen years old." Eliza Cates was pardoned "on account of the small values of the articles stolen and being a woman"; two men were pardoned because they had already received 150 and 225 lashes, respectively, for accumulated offenses, had suffered greatly, were family men, had paid damages, and "promise to do better."[57] As far as the records show, no appeal for relief from the death penalty for theft was ever denied.

Appeals for clemency from murderers were granted with almost the same regularity. Five men were executed for the murder of two light-horse men in 1882, but eight others were pardoned later when Checote heeded their pleas that "the high state of public feeling and prejudice which ranged against them in the district" made it "hardly possible to obtain a fair and impartial trial."[58] It appears that no death sentence was carried out in the Muskogee Nation after the late 1880s.[59]

Seven "freedmen" were sentenced to be shot in Wewoka district in the spring of 1891. One had been convicted of a third larceny offense; the other six were habitual criminals whose murder of two special light-horse men near the Muskogee-Seminole border had inflamed feeling among the local full-bloods. A force of special light-horse was d.   to assist in the executions, but Principal Chief Legus Perryman arranged for the seven to escape before the arrival of the firing party. The Paris, Texas, *News* described the fiasco as "a well-laid scheme" to avert an armed collision between ex-slaves and full-bloods.[60] No documentary record can be found of Perryman's actions or the reasoning behind them. The chief, a black Creek, may have believed that, if the shootings were carried out, the ex-slave colony in Wewoka district would erupt, whereas, if the sentences were quashed, there would be indignation among the full-blood majority, but nothing more. The seven vanished, and there were no violent repercussions.

A continuing problem for the Creeks was the railroad town of Muskogee. After the transient army of laborers, contractors, and supernumeraries around whom the railhead settlement had sprung up moved south, the nucleus of a permanent town remained. Whites, Creek ex-slaves, blacks from the United States, and some Cherokee mixed-bloods, but hardly any Creeks by blood, composed the population of Muskogee. Some were respectable traders and laborers; others were social parasites. As an entrepôt for the illicit trade in liquor, the place was a continual source of annoyance for federal and tribal authorities. In the autumn of 1876, Union agent Marston asked Chief Harjo for "a brief and explicit statement . . . in regard to the administration of the laws of the Nation."

"Allow me again," he went on, "to call your attention to the *public nuisance* of Muskogee—women selling whiskey and making mad men of your citizens. . . . If these sellers of whiskey were U.S. citizens I could and would put a stop to their hellish traffic, but they are Indians, and your law only is applicable to them, & it is your duty just as much to protect licensed traders from harm by them as it is my duty to protect indians from harm by U.S. citizens." But the Indians, here, were Cherokees, not Creeks.[61] Still, although these difficulties were not of the Creeks' making, the failure of the Creek authorities to attempt to apply a remedy to such of the ills of Muskogee as were within the legal remit of the nation made them worse.

Several months later Congress enacted the measure under which liquor offenses involving only Indians were returned to federal jurisdiction,[62] but Muskogee remained a troublesome town. A deadly feud broke out between local blacks—most but not all of them Creek citizens—and visiting Cherokee mixed-bloods. The Cherokees accused the blacks of being thieves, as some were; the blacks accused the white, or nearly white, Cherokees of being actuated by nothing but racial hatred—an exaggerated charge but probably not altogether without foundation.[63]

Frederick Severs, a white Creek trader, complained to Chief Checote in 1880 that "our *quiet little town*" of Okmulgee was well on the way to acquiring "as bad a name as *Muskokee,*" with turbulent and obscene behavior a nightly occurrence: "Please notify your Light Horse to be more vigilant and spill all cider or anything that will intoxicate but I learn one of the Light Horsemen Billy Bruner—was very drunk in Town yesterday shooting his pistol around Town."[64]

Soon after this, the national council passed laws of the sort that might, to the great benefit of tribal sovereignty, have been put in force at least five years earlier. An act to ban the sale of "extract of Jamaica ginger or any kind of bitters containing alcohol, within one mile of the M.K.&T. Rail Road, except for medicinal purposes" was approved in October 1880.[65] Its purpose was to prevent the sale or consumption of certain beverages not expressly barred by the Intercourse Acts. Another statute, enacted during the same session of the council, declared keeping a room for gambling and the use of gaming devices to be misdemeanors.[66] This legislation entered territory unknown to federal law, since gaming was not an offense under common law or statute. The Creek courts could not punish a white or black noncitizen for violating these laws, but they could report him to the Union agent. Drinking and gambling were not exiled from the streets of Muskogee but, during the 1880s, as the town grew as a center for the staider forms of commerce, it shed much of its bad reputation.

Although the compactness of the Seminole Nation enabled the town chiefs and light-horse to keep a close watch on any potential troublemaker, its disadvantages from their point of view were greater. Criminals traveling between the Muskogee Nation, on the east and north, and the Chickasaw Nation, on the south, or the Potawatomi reservation on the west, could quickly cross the Seminole country and pause just long enough among the Seminoles to seize horses or cattle.[67]

During 1885 the Seminoles lost much stock to "cow-boys" employed on the leased cattle ranges of the Potawotomi reservation and to other thieves. On May 1 of that year, a gang of these men, heavily armed, openly drove away some sixty head in the presence of most of the Seminole owners.[68] Principal Chief John Jumper raised a force of fifty special policemen, or light-horse, to guard the western boundary of the nation; and his emissary, John F. Brown, secured from the federal authorities an assurance that any whites caught stealing from the Seminoles, and resisting arrest by Seminole officers, could be killed without prosecution for murder by the federal court.[69]

There was so little crime among the Seminoles in the early postwar years that the speed with which a local lawbreaker could put himself beyond the bounds of Seminole jurisdiction was rarely an impediment to the enforcement of the law; in September 1871, for example, the Seminole agent reported that within the past twelvemonth, only two crimes had occurred. A thief had been caught and punished, but a murderer had eluded capture.[70] By the early 1880s matters had changed for the worse. For a time, the Seminoles were disposed to display leniency to convicted thieves, but in November 1886, not long after John Brown had succeeded Jumper as principal chief, it was announced that no more pardons for larceny would be forthcoming.[71]

Murder was uncommon in the Seminole Nation; but the Seminoles, unlike their Creek neighbors, always carried out the death sentence. Two murderers were executed together in June 1887,[72] and in October 1896 three were put to death within four days—making, it was unreliably reported, eight executions for the year to date.[73] At about this time, a woman in the Muskogee Nation was given eighty lashes for adultery.[74]

Relations between the Seminole and Muskogee chiefs were nearly always cordial, even though, despite common origins and similarity of language, there was a good deal of ill-feeling between their peoples. Tension was high during the early 1880s when some of the Creeks carried their political feuding into the Seminole country, "disarming our men and shooting around generally among the Seminoles." Chief Jumper asked Checote "to have such disorderly proceedings stopped," adding: "The Seminoles are not well informed about your troubles and some of them might resist and make the trouble worse."[75]

The scope for friction between the governments of the two tribes over questions of criminal extradition was restricted (though, as it proved, not removed) by the fourteenth article of the treaty of August 28, 1856 between the United States and the Muskogee and Seminole nations: "Any person duly charged with a criminal offense against the laws of either the Creek or Seminole tribe, and escaping into the jurisdiction of the other, shall be promptly surrendered upon the demand of the proper authority of the tribe within whose jurisdiction the offense shall be alleged to have been committed."[76]

All the surviving evidence shows the Seminoles to have been almost always punctilious in complying with their obligation to yield up Seminole or Creek fugitives from Creek justice. But most of the requisition orders between the Seminoles and Creeks came from the Seminole side.[77] Sometimes the Muskogee authorities made prompt arrest and delivery of individuals wanted by the Seminoles. Sometimes they had difficulty or took their time in finding the wanted person. On other occasions the Seminole demands were met tardily, grudgingly, or not at all through the operation of technical pretexts which, out of political considerations, the Muskogee chief was obliged to advance, seemingly against his sounder judgment or better instinct.

One set of objections hung on the fallacious argument that the extradition provision of 1856 was invalidated by the resettlement of the Seminoles, under the treaty of 1866, on territory forcibly vacated by the Creeks. The documentary origins of this contention can be traced to a demand— thinly disguised as a petition—from Coweta district, in which Chief Coachman was asked to desist from having Creek citizens

> arrested by your arbitrary edict and upon demand made by the chief of the Seminole people . . . thus making your office perform the function of a high sheriff's office to a people who are resident upon our domain simply by sufferance and who have *only* a *temporary* conceded right of the exercise of jurisdiction, upon *their own people* and who have *no authority* whatever over the citizens of the Muskogee Nation, whether charged with crime committed in the section of the country where they are now permitted to reside—or in any other section of our Nation.

The "petition," most of whose signatories were ex-slaves, concluded with a threat, scarcely veiled, of unpleasant consequences if Coachman did not "suspend" the transfer of Muskogee citizens to the Seminole Nation.[78]

Coachman put this paper before the national council and asked them to consider its merits and those of the Creek-Seminole "compact."[79] A letter to Principal Chief John Chupco of the Seminole Nation drew a reasoned expatiation upon the provisions of the treaties relating to the extradition issue.[80] It is evident that both Coachman and Checote, who returned to office as Coachman's successor, sympathized with the arguments of the Seminoles and did their best to comply with requisition orders as far as political or practical constraints permitted. Nevertheless, the dispute was far from over, and within a short time a second front of controversy had opened up between the two tribes.

Many Creeks were convinced all along that, when the lands allocated to the Seminoles under the treaties of 1866 were being surveyed, a narrow strip of country belonging to the Wewoka district of the Muskogee Nation was placed by mistake inside the Seminole boundaries. These claims were resisted by the Seminoles, whose national capital, also called Wewoka, lay within the disputed tract. During the 1870s the Secretary of the Interior intervened to calm matters down, but the quarrel was revived at the end of the decade.[81] On May 4, 1880, with the Creeks demanding a second and more careful survey of the area ceded for the Seminoles in 1866, Chupco reviewed the issue and its implications:

> That we are unfortunately located, by the authority of and express direction of the United States, upon lands rightfully belonging to your Nation is no fault of ours. . . . [I]f the Seminoles *have no jurisdiction* the Creeks are *prohibited* from exercising any. . . .
>
> To wait till the boundaries are properly located and the lines of our permanent location are marked out before depredators and escaping criminals can be reached and brought to answer for the willfull [*sic*] crimes committed by them would offer a *Premium* to plunder and robbery hitherto unknown in the history of our Country.
>
> . . . With assurance of my profound regard and the Friendship and Brotherhood of myself and people for you and yours now
>
> Evermore—I am Truly Yours[82]

The disagreement was still alive in 1895 when the Seminole principal chief had to call upon the support of the Union agency to secure the delivery of a Seminole who had committed murder in the border strip and had been arrested and charged by the Creeks. Agent Dewit M. Wisdom sent a United States Indian policeman to collect the prisoner.[83] Shortly afterward the boundary question was settled by the Department of the Interior in favor of the Seminoles.[84]

Extradition arrangements between the Choctaws and Chickasaws were governed by the sixth article of their treaty with the United States of March 4, 1856: "Any person duly charged with a criminal offense against the laws of either the Choctaw or the Chickasaw tribe, and escaping into the jurisdiction of the other, shall be promptly surrendered upon the demand of the proper authorities of the tribe within whose jurisdiction the offense shall be alleged to have been committed."[85]

Where a person charged with a criminal offense in either nation had fled to the other, it was necessary only for a writ to be placed in the hands of the authorities of the nation in which he had taken refuge. When a fugitive from the Choctaw courts had been arrested in the Chickasaw Nation, the Choctaws would send an agent to fetch him back, and he would be handed over without ado unless there was doubt about the agent's credentials or identity.[86] The same procedure was adopted after a

Chickasaw fugitive had been arrested in the Choctaw Nation.[87] A Choctaw guilty of a crime in the Chickasaw Nation and captured there could be tried as though he were a Chickasaw, and vice versa.

On July 3, 1843, an "International Compact" between the Cherokees, Creeks, and Osages was concluded at Tahlequah; it was ratified by the assemblies of all three tribes later that year. Section 5 of the Compact provided for the extradition of criminals from one to another of the signatory nations, an important stipulation being that orders of requisition must be "accompanied by reasonable proof of guilt." During the 1870s and early 1880s the principal chiefs of the Muskogee Nation repeatedly failed to supply these proofs when issuing requisitions on the Cherokee governments, and the Cherokees as consistently demanded either a sworn statement against the accused or a copy of the bill of indictment. The agreement also provided that "if a citizen of one [nation] commits wilfull [sic] murder or other crime within the limits of another Nation, parties to the compacts . . . he shall be subject to the same treatment as if he were a citizen of that Nation."[88]

Although the chief executives of both nations tried to keep faith with the spirit and letter of the Compact, the problem created by the killing near Muskogee of a Cherokee citizen in a brush with black Creeks was made intractable by a dispute whether the fatal shooting had occurred on the Cherokee or the Creek side of the boundary marker. Union agent John Tufts, when asked to arbitrate, declined to do so, preferring that the Indians should settle the matter among themselves; he agreed, however, to adjudicate if there was deadlock on the "Native Commission" appointed by the two tribes jointly to investigate the affair. The Commission found for the Cherokees, and two black Creeks were extradited, tried, convicted, and sentenced to be hanged. Chief Bushyhead, satisfied that the men had not received a fair trial, obtained a reprieve for them and secured their release.[89] This case was only one bloodied link in a chain of violent incidents between Creek ex-slaves and Cherokee mixed-bloods which strained but did not upset the friendly relationship between the two governments.[90]

Edith Smith, a Cherokee schoolteacher in the Coweta district of the Creek Nation, felt impelled to take her dismay at the slow course of justice to the head of the Creek government:

> In my last communication from Judge McHenry, he said the wheels of the law ground *slowly,* but I would certainly get the horse in time. I wrote to him to recover his *value,* if he was purposely detained away from home— which I am told is the *fact,* and that *either* the horse, or property to cover his value might be placed in the hands of Dr Williams at Muskogee until I

could be notified, and get it. . . . I have waited with patience for the *law* to take its course, but I have come to the conclusion that your Judges and light-horsemen are *either very* slow, or else they do not care to work for me, being a citizen of the Cherokee Nation, but I have given years of the best labor I could give for the benefit of your people, and it seems strange I cannot receive common justice.[91]

Nothing was done until Miss Smith complained to a former Cherokee principal chief—and a friend of Checote's—William Ross. Finally, in December 1881, nearly a year after the horse had been stolen, Checote noted that the matter had been "attended to."[92]

The general principles of the International Compact of 1843 were reaffirmed by representatives of the Five Tribes at North Fork, Creek Nation, in November 1859; the Choctaws and Chickasaws, as mentioned, had not participated in the earlier agreement. Chief Wright was apprised of the limitations of the judicial provisions of the new arrangement when, in the winter of 1868, he sought the extradition from the Cherokee Nation of two Cherokees who had been charged with horse theft in the Choctaw Nation. James Vann, assistant and acting principal chief of the Cherokee Nation, replied that his desire to comply with the request ran contrary to, and was outweighed by, the nature of his responsibilities to his own people.

> For while I willingly acknowledge all the obligations of the compact to be binding alike upon all who were parties to it, I can not lose sight of the fact that it has not made provision for the preliminary steps to be taken to give out on requisition on demand for the apprehension and delivery of persons accused of committing offenses against the person or property of citizens [of] another Nation, other than the one to which the accused belongs to [*sic*]. This then is left open and has to be arranged between the parties, before the terms of the compact can be complied with; for the compact takes away no constitutional right secured to either the Choctaw or the Cherokee, by the Constitution of their respective countries.

Furthermore:

> Your present demand is a writ that does not bear *test* in a legal sense. It does not sufficiently set forth facts so as to form on such case for action so as to enable the accused to meet the charge, or enable them to secure compulsory process for obtaining witnesses, but, worse than all, it lacks the essential of not bearing the evidence of being supported by oath or affirmation as our laws require.[93]

In June 1870, a Reciprocity Compact was concluded between the Cherokee, Muskogee, Seminole, and Osage nations.[94] Its importance was mostly symbolic: the older agreement between the Creeks and Seminoles was unaffected, and so was the 1843 Compact binding the Cherokees, Creeks, and Osages. It could have compelled extradition between the

Seminoles and the Cherokees or Osages, but no evidence has been found that it was ever needed. When a Muskogee principal chief alluded to the document in a letter to his Seminole counterpart, the latter had to plead ignorance.[95]

A Supplemental Compact was approved by representatives of the Cherokee and Muskogee nations in October 1884. Besides reaffirming the provisions of the original Compact of 1843, it incorporated a temporary suspension of Muskogee laws for the seizure and confiscation of Cherokee property in that nation, furnished remedies for the recovery of debt and enforcement of contracts where the parties belonged to different nations, and left it to the individual legislatures to "regulate by law, the time, manner, and conditions upon which the citizens of the other Nation may be allowed to reside temporarily within its limits." Both legislatures ratified the agreement; later the Osages, too, subscribed to it.[96]

Less than eighteen months later, at an Indian International Conference held at Eufaula, a new and comprehensive compact was drawn up in fourteen sections. It was ratified by the signatory nations at different times in 1886 and 1887. Now, for the first time, the Cherokees, Choctaws, Chickasaws, Creeks, and Seminoles were all associated with one another and with some of the western tribes in a formal instrument of diplomacy.[97]

Before the promulgation of this Amended Compact, the occasional requests for extradition between the Cherokees, Creeks, or Seminoles on one side and the Choctaws or Chickasaws on the other lacked any definitive basis or form. They rested on nothing firmer than a friendly understanding, and were sometimes conducted like those between the Choctaws and Chickasaws, or the Creeks and Seminoles, sometimes with the prior transmission of proofs as was required for the service of the requisition orders between the Cherokees and Creeks. When the Creeks wanted the Choctaws to detain and surrender "refugees from justice" for crimes committed during the upheavals of 1882–1883, their principal chief asked only for the "name of the agent who is authorized to receive these parties" at "whatever place you may specify at the line of the nation."[98]

On the other hand, when the Choctaws wanted a petty thief who had moved to the Creek country, a copy of the indictment was demanded. Principal Chief Edmund McCurtain deemed it "unnecessary" to submit the indictment, "which is in the Choctaw Language," and sent Checote "the substance of the indictment in English."[99] Two years later, seeking the extradition of five Creek citizens from the Chickasaw Nation, the Muskogee principal chief enclosed descriptions of the men and the information that they had been indicted, but not the indictment itself.[100]

In 1886 the Starr gang, a band of Cherokee mixed-bloods and whites, made several raids on the Choctaw side of the Canadian River. Chief McCurtain, instead of dealing directly with the Cherokee governor, asked the Union agent to inform him of the facts and to obtain the cooperation of the Cherokee authorities. Chief Bushyhead instructed the sheriff of Canadian district to work with the Choctaw officers. Presently the Cherokee sheriff arrested one of the Starrs, but could not prevent his rescue by the rest of the gang two days later.[101]

Perhaps the best illustration of the value of the Union agency in coordinating the efforts of several governments to eradicate a problem common to all is provided by agent Dew Wisdom's negotiations with the Cherokee and Creek principal chiefs and the leading officials of two federal courts in the autumn of 1894. Several bands of outlaws, composed of whites, Cherokee mixed-bloods, and black Creeks, but known collectively to all who read newspapers as "the Cook gang," had committed armed robberies and murders between early July and late October. By November their exploits, real and alleged, and the actual and supposed inadequacies of the law enforcement officers opposed to them, were filling whole columns of Eastern newspapers and were being pointed to by congressmen as proof of the rottenness of the tribal government and the federal judicial system in the Indian Territory.

Agent Wisdom obtained from Judge Parker, at Fort Smith, an assurance that, "in case any Cherokee or any other Indian or citizen should kill an outlaw, or any person supposed to be one, or *acting with* outlaws, that such person so killing would receive *ample protection*."[102] On November 5, 1894, the Muskogee principal chief approved an act of council which "directed the Judges of each district to order the L. H. Company to assist the officers of the United States in capturing or exterminating the bands of outlaws" and authorized the light-horse captains "to deputize as many citizens as may be necessary to carry out the purposes of this act."[103] Within a few months these gangs and their offshoots and imitators had been dispatched or dispersed.[104]

"This assurance is positive," Wisdom had declared to Chief Harris. The emphasis was needed, for the relations between the officers of the federal courts and those of the Five Tribes—the Cherokee Nation in particular—were often no smoother through the 1880s and early 1890s than they had been at the time of the Going Snake fight in 1872. A notable case was that of Sheriff W. E. Sanders of Cooweescoowee district, which arose in 1888. After he and his men had killed an outlaw from Texas, Sanders had to extricate himself from a murder charge at Fort Smith. The dead man had not been indicted for crime anywhere in the

Indian Territory (though his connection with one case of robbery and murder seems to have been established later), and he was not even a claimant for Cherokee citizenship.[105]

If the Cherokee authorities had been served with a writ of requisition from the governor of Texas concerning any of the outlaw's many crimes in that state, the Cherokee sheriff might have been handled less roughly by the federal authorities. Such a document had been put in the hands of the Muskogee principal chief by the governor of Texas for a much-noted horse thief, William Posey. Chief Coachman issued a proclamation, and within two months Posey, who had been in the Indian Territory un-molested for more than a year before the service of requisition, was killed by three light-horse men. Union agent Marston, after an investigation, reported that "all is satisfactory," but advised Coachman "to retain the Governor's requisition paper in the files of your office."[106]

Posse service with the light-horse did not save a Creek citizen named Charles Gibson from a serious run-in with the federal authorities in March 1886. Several associated parties of Creeks and Choctaws in pursuit of a gang of cattle thieves killed one of them, a United States citizen. Later Gibson, from Eufaula district, and James King, a Choctaw, were jailed at Fort Smith. In due course, after "great inconvenience, hardship, disgrace, and loss of money in lawyer's fees," they were released. King's losses, amounting to $500, were reimbursed by the Choctaw government; Gibson, after a very long delay, petitioned the Muskogee national council for $450 and got it.[107] Conflicts between the United States courts and tribal law officers became much commoner during the late 1880s and early 1890s, and there were times when the federal courts seem to have been more concerned with jurisdiction as an end in itself than with the ends of justice.

Part of the explanation for the many homicides that occurred within the ambit of the tribal courts but were not pursued to the conviction of the guilty parties, even if they were investigated, may lie in a subterranean survival of the older custom of clan vengeance. But it would be fanciful to see, in the predilection for redress by violence exhibited by many Indian citizens with little or no Indian blood, evidence of the tenacity of a specifically tribal tradition. Indeed, the inability of constitutional provisions and legal process to rid the Five Tribes of this proclivity for settling disputes through shedding a rival's blood demonstrates that tribal society in Indian Territory was anything but unique. Its norms and standards in this regard were similar to those observed in—to take a few examples without straying from either the northern hemisphere or the nineteenth century—Corsica, Calabria, the larger Italian islands, parts of the Balkans, West Virginia, Texas (especially), and many other southern and western areas of the United States itself.

The governments and courts of the Five Tribes in Indian Territory had many failings. Extenuation of the failings comes from the very circumstances that caused the extinction of the courts and governments. It is that the noncitizens who lived among the Indians under the ramshackle system of law administered with only fitful efficiency from federal courts located outside Indian Territory, were at least as inclined as the Indians to resolve their quarrels by direct and drastic methods.

CHAPTER SIX

Industry, Immigration, and Tribal Sovereignty, 1866–1886

But can this magnificent domain of fifty millions of acres be kept sealed for the solution of the slow progress of Indian civilization? Candor compels a negative answer. Already the Missouri, Kansas, and Texas Railway is building its line through the Territory, bisecting it from north to south. The breath of the engine will be the inspiration of a new life;—it will let in a flood-tide of civilization that nothing can resist. . . . The rubicon was passed when the locomotive crossed the southern boundary of Kansas.—Milton W. Reynolds, "The Indian Territory," The Western Monthly, *November 1870*

Within the past six years the Indian's sentiments have undergone a radical change respecting railroads. He now hauls to the station on the line his pecans, pork, corn, and cotton, and his surplus game, receives a liberal sum of money in exchange, and goes home satisfied that the railroad is a friendly institution.—Theodora R. Jenness, "The Indian Territory," The Atlantic Monthly, *April 1879*

Dissolution of the governments of the Five Tribes, and the subsequent organization of a single State government for the whole Indian Territory, was imposed from Washington, but it would not have come about as it did, or when it did, without political support from within the tribes. Similarly, the flow of capital and labor from the States to the Indian country was induced by inner, besides being driven by outer, forces. Statehood was not created by economic transformation; but economic considerations provided the issue that did most to divide tribal politics into traditionalist and progressive camps.

Agrarian expansion—large-scale ranching or farming—depended upon the exploitation of the traditional system of land ownership in common and the exclusion of homesteaders. Industrial expansion—mining, railroad construction, forestry, and their dependent substructure of banking, merchandising, and real estate dealing in the new unofficial "towns"— threatened the older system and those committed to it. But tribal particularists were not always opposed to industrial development; for example, Choctaw governments of all persuasions involved themselves in the mining and timber industries, thus remaining at least partially in control of them and deriving considerable revenues. There were also many Indian politicians—John F. Brown of the Seminoles and Pleasant Porter of the Creeks perhaps the most prominent among them—who upheld tribal sovereignty in public while quietly gaining from their investments in private industrial corporations.[1]

After a pause of eight years, the program of railroad building was resumed during 1881–1882 when the grandly named Saint Louis and San Francisco ("Frisco") Railway, which had acquired the construction rights formerly held by the bankrupt Atlantic and Pacific, put down sixty-five miles of track from Vinita to Tulsa, just inside the Muskogee Nation. In 1885 the line was extended three miles, across the Arkansas River to Red Fork; and the next year a further ten miles was opened for traffic between Red Fork and Sapulpa for use during the cattle-shipping season only. This, and the continued southwesterly construction of the line—which was not put in hand until the later 1890s—exhausted the obligations shouldered by the tribes under the railway provisions of the Treaties of 1866; thereafter, the admission of railroads into the nations seemed a question wholly for the tribal governments.[2]

There was one complication. Under a provision of the Choctaw-Chickasaw treaty of 1855, restated in 1866, all the land occupied by the two tribes belonged to them jointly; hence, neither government could offer a charter to a railway company without the consent of the other. Much would depend on whether the two governments were in political affinity at the critical time; if they fell out over the issue, it was to be expected that the United States Government would step in as arbiter and that, whatever the outcome, the bill would be paid by all Five Nations in lost sovereignty. At any rate, this is what happened during the construction of a third railroad line.

This next phase of railway building in Indian Territory began with a plan to lay the tracks of another division of the Frisco across the north-western corner of Arkansas toward the town of Paris, in northeast Texas. It evolved through a clash between the Choctaw governor and the speaker of his national house of representatives, disagreement between the Choctaw and Chickasaw governments, and bestowal by Congress of constitutional approbation to the doubtful and slippery doctrine of eminent domain.[3]

Jackson McCurtain, a Progressive full-blood, was principal chief of the Choctaw Nation in 1881. He wanted the Frisco to be granted a right-of-way through the nation; but the speaker of the house, Benjamin Smallwood, tried to thwart the passage of the requisite bill by voting against it twice, first to produce a tie and then to break the tie. McCurtain, having satisfied himself that the speaker's double vote was unconstitutional, approved the bill anyway, only to be confronted by Governor Frank Overton of the Chickasaw Nation. Overton, a range cattleman with very little Chickasaw blood, was the leader of the "Pullback" conservative party of the Chickasaw Nation and set himself strenuously against the proposals. At no point would the track be as near as fifty miles to the eastern boundary of the Chickasaw country, but Overton's opposition was based on the land-ownership clauses of the treaty of 1855. He was supported by the National (conservative) party of the Choctaw Nation, and the complaint was referred to Washington.[4]

Congressional approval was needed before a railway could take a right-of-way in the Indian Territory; but the Senate, aided by the quarrel between Indian conservatives and progressives, went far beyond this by drafting and passing a bill of its own. Under the act that followed, far less land was reserved for the railway than had been offered by the Choctaw government, and for this reduced concession the company had to pay $3,000 annually to the Choctaw and Chickasaw governments instead of the $2,000 first asked by the Choctaws.[5]

In securing for two national governments terms better than those to which one of the governments had agreed and intervening at the lawful request of the other government—whose head was one of the most vigorous and acerbic critics of federal interference ever to emerge from tribal politics—Congress had asserted a right to force its own terms upon the nations. Eminent domain had been established as a dogma that could attract the force of law whenever a majority in each legislative chamber in Washington thought proper.

This new division of the Frisco line was built during 1886–1887 on a meandering course through the Choctaw Nation to Paris, Texas, and two other important routes were constructed almost concurrently with this: the Kansas and Arkansas Valley, across the Cherokee Nation between

Coffeyville, Kansas, and Van Buren, Arkansas, and the Gulf, Colorado and Santa Fe (a division of the Atchison, Topeka and Santa Fe), which cut through the Cherokee Outlet, Unassigned Creek and Seminole lands, and Chickasaw Nation to Gainesville, Texas, and on to Galveston.[6]

These railways, and others that came later, brought a handful of noncitizens—railroad and express company employees and the dependants of those who were married—to each new station and speeded the development of the infant extractive industries. They also beneficial to the beef cattle industry of the Indian Territory, but much of their freight and passenger traffic passed all the way through. It is hard to see them as presenting an actual threat to the security of the tribal governments; nor, despite the dread their coming had inspired in many full-bloods, can it be argued with conviction that they changed the nature of tribal society.

Perhaps the most important consequence of the expansion of the railroad system in the Indian Territory was the extension of the powers of the federal courts at Fort Smith, Wichita, Fort Scott, and Graham. Hitherto the United States courts had had no civil jurisdiction in Indian Territory except in cases where constitutional questions were at issue, but in July 1884 Congress enacted legislation enabling any Indian nation or tribe, or any individual living in the Indian Territory, to sue or be sued by each of two railroads to which it was granting a right-of-way through the Territory.[7] The United courts for the Northern District of Texas, Western District of Arkansas, and District of Kansas were given concurrent jurisdiction in all such controversies; any of them could be used for litigation in any case arising in the Indian Territory.

Coal was mined in the Choctaw Nation under license from the Choctaw and Chickasaw governments from 1866 onward by several intermarried white citizens, most notably James McAlester, D. M. Hailey, and Robert Ream, who were joined shortly afterwards by a number of Choctaw mixed-bloods. Ream was a civil engineer; Hailey a physician and druggist; McAlester became a wealthy merchant and one of the two leading cattlemen in the Choctaw Nation.[8]

In 1871 a tribal royalty was placed on all mining operations in the Choctaw Nation. Less than six months later the Choctaw supreme court ruled that the royalties act was "not in accordance with the Choctaw constitution or the 1866 Choctaw-Chickasaw treaty with the United States and therefore unconstitutional." A second royalties act, passed in 1873, was rejected by the supreme court on October 8, 1875. On October 26 the general council passed a royalties act for the third time, and the principal chief, Coleman Cole, asked Secretary of the Interior Zachary Chandler to approve an interim order preventing the Osage mine from removing lumber or coal from the nation until the royalties question had been settled. After the general superintendent of the Missouri, Kansas and Texas Railway had interceded with predictions of calamities that would ensue from an enforcement of the ban, Chandler found grounds for exempting the Osage company from its provisions.

In the summer of 1877, Governor Cole ordered the national and county light-horse to arrest McAlester, Ream, and two of their mixed-blood associates, with the apparent intention of having them shot for treason in leasing their holdings to noncitizens. The four escaped, or were allowed to escape, three leaving the Indian Territory for a while. About a month later they returned briefly, when attempts were made to agree upon a truce, but they were not able to reestablish themselves until Cole's departure from office in 1878.[9] Cole had had no legal authority to issue the writ for the arrest of the three, but apologists could always plead in extenuation of his assumption of unconstitutional powers that he was acting for the higher public good: "[H]e believed the necessity of the case was such that the duty to guard, as Chief Executive, the Nation's rights, gave the office of Supreme Chief the power he had exercised, without any grant thereof being needed."[10]

By 1885 McAlester and the other mine owners in the Choctaw Nation were employing eight hundred men "from all parts of the globe—Americans, Italians, English, and Swedes"—and, McAlester avouched, "intoxicating drinks are kept out." The arrangement then in force was that the Choctaw Nation leased the mines to the private developers but that all contracts had to be approved by both the Commissioner of Indian Affairs and the Secretary of the Interior.[11] This proviso placed a limitation upon the national sovereignty of the Choctaws, but it fell far short of allowing the federal Government the means to apply an economic or political stranglehold.

A greater threat to the Choctaw Nation was the unlicensed noncitizen labor the industry drew to the mines at McAlester, Krebs, Lehigh, Atoka, Savanna, and Coalgate. The tribal government allowed the miners to enter the country license-free, on the principle that they could always (in theory) be removed if need be. The mining settlements attracted saloon keepers, gamblers, and prostitutes, who were neither licensed nor sanctioned by the government, but whose presence was tolerated; and there was a large trade in alcoholic spirits and other potions which, though hardly intoxicants, certainly contained alcohol.[12] Few Indians would work at the mines, and the Choctaw government seems to have neglected the mining camps as studiously as the Creeks avoided Muskogee. The presence in the nation of so many people who were outside its jurisdiction, and among whom perfect peace could not have been expected to prevail, invited the attention of the United States authorities and helped to hasten the day when the court at Fort Smith would be supplemented by one in the Indian Territory.

Even more damaging to tribal cohesion was the breach among the Choctaws opened by development of the mines. The conflict between the conservatives, like Cole, and the progressives, such as Isaac Garvin, Cole's successor as principal chief, is evidence that tribal sponsorship of industrial expansion was not synonymous with support for Territorialization and allotment since Garvin no less than Cole stood against these demands; yet discord over the one issue tended to inhibit unity on the other.[13]

There were three facets to the fortunes of the range cattle industry in Indian Territory during this period.

The first was the granting of grazing rights to ranchers on such western reservations as the Cheyenne and Arapahoe, and Kiowa-Comanche-Wichita, or, away to the northeast, in the Osage Nation, Quapaw Agency, and various of the small reservations bordering upon the Osage country. Since only the Osage lands were patented to the tribe, and not even the Osages were on terms with the federal Government comparable with those subsisting between Washington and the Five Tribes, sovereignty was not at issue. Anyway, these grazing agreements were attacked with vehemence and in the end with success by politicians and promoters who paraded under the banner of antimonopolism while aiming only to accomplish the sectionalization and settlement of the whole Territory.[14]

The second was the free ranging of cattle on the unoccupied lands known as the Cherokee Outlet (or "Strip") and the Unassigned Lands of the Creek and Seminole nations.

By the early 1880s it was clear that the federal Government would not be resettling any more "friendly Indians" on the territory ceded for that purpose by the Cherokees, Creeks, and Seminoles under the treaties of 1866. Title to the empty portion of the Outlet apparently resided with the Cherokee Nation, and with the Creeks and Seminoles in the Unassigned Lands of the original reservations.

It was prime cattle country, and in the Outlet, as on the home reservations of the Five Nations, the tribal governments attempted to collect a levy on cattle grazed or driven (sometimes with much loitering along the way) by noncitizens. Early in 1877 a case was taken to the Fort Smith court and was decided against the Cherokee Nation after Judge Parker had charged the jury in these terms:

The fact of a man being in the Indian country without a permit is no excuse for seizing his property. Neither the Indian Sheriff nor any other officers of the Indian country can seize or remove him or his property. If a citizen of the United States is in the Indian country without permission, as intruder, the authorities can report the fact to President Grant, who is backed by all the military power of the United States, and he can send soldiers to put him out. The Indians are protected against intruders by a power much more potent than their own, which will vindicate their rights whenever invoked.[15]

Parker realized that in practice there was little that all the President's horses and all the President's men could do about the intruder problem. Writing privately at about the same time as the Cherokee grazing-tax case was determined by his court, he remarked: "There is but one way to remove intruders. . . . An intruder so removed may return at once to the reservation. He then becomes liable to a fine of $1,000, but the intruder cannot be imprisoned in satisfaction of that judgment, and must be set at liberty."[16]

But in 1878 the Senate Committee on the Judiciary stated that the Cherokee Nation was entitled to levy a grazing tax in the Outlet. This had the effect of setting aside the verdict in the Fort Smith case and establishing that the Five Tribes were not without a remedy for intruders with livestock. Such a tax was imposed by the national council a year later; when many of the cattlemen refused to pay up, the Union agent was called upon to evict them.

Later, in 1882, the Department of the Interior took the view that building fences and cabins by cattlemen in the Outlet amounted to unlawful settlement, and in March 1883 this view congealed into official policy. Shortly before then, however, the cattlemen had formed themselves into the Cherokee Strip Live Stock Association. In May of that year this new body concluded a five-year lease with the Cherokee Nation for an annual consideration of $100,000, payable half-yearly in advance. What had, in the past, been seen by the cattlemen as confiscatory and by the Cherokees as a mixture of deterrent against trespass on the home reservation, advance charge against damage caused by trespassing cattle, and casual income, now became a fiscal quid pro quo, apparently safe from federal interference, which would enable both parties to realize some of the potential of a rich natural asset.

In 1880 the name Oklahoma, which had been proposed in 1866 for the organized Territory projected for the whole Indian Territory, was applied for the first time to the Unassigned Creek and Seminole lands.[17] During 1884 the hopeful colonizers who wanted these lands for themselves had adopted this usage and put it into general circulation.

Pressure for these Unassigned Lands to be thrown open had become intense in much of the Middle West, especially Kansas and Missouri. Late in 1883, Senator James David Walker (D, Arkansas) offered a resolution "that the Secretary of the Interior be directed to furnish copies of all documents and correspondence in his office relating as to leases of lands in the Indian Territory to citizens of the United States for cattle-grazing and other purposes." Acceptance of this resolution led to three years of intermittent but often fierce debate, interspersed with visits to the Indian Territory during recess by House and Senate committees.[18]

The imminence of a change of Government policy was signaled when Attorney-General Garland rendered an opinion that there was no legal basis for the leasing of land by reservation Indians. President Grover Cleveland gave orders for the removal of all stock held unlawfully on the reservations and repeated instructions given earlier for the vacation by cattlemen of the Unassigned, or Oklahoma, lands. His orders were executed, but in the Unassigned Lands they were purposely executed without a great deal of haste or thoroughness; the cattlemen never having claimed any right to be there in the first place, the Government considered that there was no point to be made.[19]

Protestations by ranchers and their friends that the Oklahoma lands had been emptied of cattle were dampened when one observer reported that "not less than sixty thousand (60,000) head of cattle [were] held in Oklahoma as their own grazing grounds" in March 1886. One corroborative witness reckoned that, while there must have been 50,000 head at least, the more probable total was double that figure. These cattle and their herders, it was noted, had no more right to be in the Oklahoma country than would-be farmers from Kansas; yet the soldiers who so firmly ejected the tillers of the soil were making no more than a feeble pretense of driving away the cattle outfits.[20]

William Springer (D, Illinois), as dedicated a self-seeker as could be found in the House of Representatives during his twenty years in it, labored sedulously for years to secure Congressional acceptance of legislation to create a Territorial government and delivered many strident speeches on the subject, but the prize for rabble-rousing and prejudicial hyperbole belongs to Springer's predecessor as chairman of the House Committee on the Territories, William David Hill (D, Ohio). Drawing professedly from the voluminous testimony gathered in the Indian Territory by the Holman and Dawes committees and recently published, Hill declaimed:

> [W]e have a feudal system there equal in its barbarism to that of the Middle Ages. If the Democratic party have any mission at all in this country it is to legislate for the interest of the masses of the people against

the few. If there is class legislation on the statute-books it ought to be repealed. If there are monopolies they ought to be abolished.

. . . Let us wage eternal war on all these monopolies in every shape. . . . The resistless energy and enterprise of the American people have spanned all the great mountains and united the Atlantic and Pacific by bands of iron and steel. The same energy and enterprise will not forever permit this vast area of fertile country to be turned over to monopolists and worthless savages.

The people will get the facts, and the dark shadow which now hovers over this garden of the great valley will be dispelled in the industry of thousands of happy farmers, and another bright star added to our glorious constellation in the Federal galaxy.[21]

One does not have to approve of monopolies or class legislation, decry the feats that spanned a continent, or allow the senses to capitulate to the jocund vision of a myriad Nestors cheerfully tilling "the great valley" to understand that these were really three different faces of the "resistless energy and enterprise of the American people." The cattle industry was not monopolistic, although it was beginning to tend toward that direction, and the description "worthless savages" fitted very few Indians apart from some of the criminals. The great offense of cattlemen and Indians was to be the few who stood between the land and the landless masses.

Hill's views, with some slight differences in emphasis, were shared by nearly all politicians in the Middle West without regard to party. Isaac Struble (R, Iowa) almost matched Hill for inflammatory bombast:

The imperative necessity of preserving the cattlemen in his unlawful possessions, the outlaw in his immunity from justice, the Indian agent in his field for speculation, and the Indian in his mental and moral degradation, by a further continuance of the present anomalous and outrageous condition of affairs in the Indian Territory has been portrayed in vivid colors until we are almost led to believe that Anglo-Saxon progress has reached an obstacle which it cannot surmount, and that the civilization of the revolver and bowie-knife is the only civilization possible to that benighted region.[22]

This, again, was a compound of exaggeration and untruth intershot with flashes of quasiimperialism. Furthermore, no such lurid picture of conditions in the Indian Territory had ever been flaunted as an object for exaltation. But the great awkwardness about leasing the Cherokee Outlet and sectors of United States Indian reservations to cattlemen was, for politicians like these, that it had so much good sense to commend it.

Indians on United States reservations gained not only revenue but relief from unauthorized cattle because trespassers would be turned away by the lessees; the grass, which was "belly-deep to horses," would, if unused, merely be burned. Even so, the Government did force the leaseholding cattlemen to leave the reservations.[23] The Government could not order the removal of cattle from the Cherokee Outlet until it had purchased the title from the Cherokee Nation or found a way of weakening that title. As long as the pastures were populated by Cherokee Strip Live Stock Association cattle, there would be no cheap sale to the Government; hence no influx of homesteaders by townsmen to menace the nation's institutions and domicile from across the threshold. Far from endangering Cherokee sovereignty, therefore, the use of the grasslands of the Outlet as pasture for range cattle shielded that sovereignty.[24]

Neither the Creeks nor the Seminoles ever asserted a sovereignty over the Unassigned Lands analogous, through the negotiation of leasing arrangements with cattlemen, to that exercised by the Cherokees over the Outlet. The strongest evidence that the presence even of trespassing cattle was a hindrance to the plans of the homestead and Territorialization lobbies and correspondingly beneficial to tribal sovereignty was the political pressure exerted to have the herds removed from what Congressman William Warner (R, Missouri) in 1888 would call "the Botany Bay of the United States."[25]

Ranching in the homelands of the Five Nations was the third aspect of the range cattle industry in the Indian Territory. In its purest form, the communal system of land use lent itself readily to ranching. The individual enjoyed the sole right of access within an area one quarter mile from his home fence, but he could use as much of the common domain as he needed, provided that no one else had established a prior right by using it before him.

From time to time the tribal governments enacted laws to prevent individual ownership of very large herds. Such legislation as that adopted by the Choctaws, Chickasaws, and Creeks to restrict pasturage to one square mile, or 640 acres, and by the Cherokees to limit it to 500 acres (later increased to 1,000 acres), was invoked against trail drivers from Texas, who would sometimes "squat" with their herds upon a large expanse of the country, and enforced through the federal courts. Many Indian citizens, though, flouted these laws. Later, in the Muskogee Nation, cattlemen devised elaborate networks of fictitious leases to circumvent the regulations. Here and elsewhere a well-placed bribe could be a serviceable substitute for stratagem.[26]

Some idea of the extent to which, before the Civil War, the tribal economies depended upon beef cattle raising may be gathered from the report that at least 300,000 head valued at $4 million were lost during the War.[27] In 1885 the Holman committee was told that only about twenty Creeks owned as many as 200 head apiece, with only some half dozen of those owning 1,000 or more; in the Choctaw Nation there were just two very large pastures, one "ten miles through," the other "eight miles through." A Cherokee cattleman informed the Dawes committee that the biggest herd owned by a citizen numbered about 5,000 head; the second largest, 2,000. Dennis Bushyhead, the Cherokee principal chief, testified before Holman that "some" citizens owned 6,000 or 7,000 head each, although there were not more than 150,000 head in the nation (excluding the Outlet). There were then about 4,500 families of Cherokee citizenship.[28]

Allegations submitted to the Patterson committee in 1878 connected such prominent Cherokee politicians and ranchers as William Rogers and William Adair with the Chickasaw governor, Frank Overton, and others as members of an "Indian ring" committed to maintaining the tribal status quo to serve their personal interests. Corroboration is lacking, but there is no reason for disbelieving it out of hand. Men like these had more in common with one another than with the poorer members of their nations.[29]

Commissioner of Indian Affairs John Atkins, a firm but fair-minded proponent of the allotment of tribal lands, was appalled by what he saw on a visit to the Muskogee Nation in 1885. "Already the rich and choice lands are appropriated by those most enterprising and self seeking . . . cultivating farms exceeding 1000 acres in extent [and entitled to] nearly 1000 more by excluding all others from the use or occupancy of a quarter of a mile in width all round the tract fenced. What a baronial estate!" At one such establishment, Atkins found that the de facto owner was employing "laborers hired among his own race—perhaps his own kith and kin—at $16 per month," living in huts or cabins "without a month's provisions ahead for themselves and families"; "[t]hey owned, of course, their tribal interest in the land, but the proceeds of the valuable crops which were raised by their labor swelled the plethoric pockets of the proprietor."

This he described as "a condition of semi-slavery" existing in each of the "five civilized nations" and growing directly out of holding lands in common. Later he learned that an expanse of "rich valley land" eight times the size of the one he had first seen was in the hands of one man, while another held four thousand acres. He had been informed by "very intelligent resident citizens" that day laborers, together with those who cultivated less than five acres for themselves, comprised "one-sixth of all Cherokees, and one fourth of all Choctaws, Chickasaws, and Creeks; and an even larger ratio among the Seminoles." If these were "the sacred rights secured by treaty, . . . the United States are pledged to uphold and maintain a stupendous land monopoly and aristocracy that finds no parallel in this country except in two or three localities in the far West."[30]

The greatest social and economic threat to the tribal governments was one imported by the Indians themselves, or by some of them—licensed white labor from "the States." A thickening stream, eventually a flood, of farm and ranch hands, mechanics, artisans, and other laborers—along with a few merchants and professional men—were permitted to bring their families into the nations upon payment of a fee to the appropriate tribal government.

For proof that the likely consequences of the license policy were understood from the time of its inception, there is no need to look further than the countermeasures adopted by the conservative parties when they were in office during the later 1870s. When Frank Overton was reelected governor of the Chickasaw Nation in 1876, one of his first actions was to frame and secure the passage of legislation raising the annual license fee from twenty five cents to $25.[31] Similar measures were adopted by the Choctaw Nation at about the same time, including laws that raised the fee for the marriage of a white man to a Choctaw woman first to $25, then to $100.[32] In November 1876 the Muskogee chief, Lochar Harjo, approved a law that set the permit fee at $1 per month or fraction of a month and required of the citizen a bond of $25 for each noncitizen in his hire.[33]

The Choctaw law was devised to inhibit immigration and, no less, intermarriage between bachelor permit holders and Indians; it was a conservative measure, intended to restrict the number and influence of intermarried citizens and curb the use of immigrant labor for the expansion of individual landholdings. A third, nonpartisan reason for this legislation was the difficulty in ejecting those who stayed on after their permits had expired. The official mechanism was cumbersome. G. W. Ingalls, the first Union agent, had been asked by the Choctaw government to remove at least 750 intruders and had removed none of them.[34]

There were three objects to the Chickasaw permit law: to raise revenue; to discourage Chickasaws from hiring men of poor quality; and to stimulate a drive against intruders. S. W. Marston, the new agent, was concerned by the "disturbance" arising from the presence of "irresponsible" intruders but felt himself powerless to institute the "vigorous measures" he recommended, and did nothing. The Chickasaws decided to act on their own.[35]

Marston complained, mistakenly, that the permit law ought to have been submitted for his prior approval and that its provisions violated the terms of the Choctaw-Chickasaw treaty of 1866. He declared it void. The Choctaw principal chief then asked Commissioner John Quincy Smith to dismiss Marston. Smith advised the Secretary of the Interior that, though Marson's action had not been "fully warranted," there was "no reason to suppose that it was due to anything further than erroneous judgment upon a question of law." The Secretary, in a letter to Chief Cole, confirmed that Marston had been at fault.[36]

Overton, meanwhile, summoned the militia and proceeded to collect the tax. Those without an employer, or whose employer would not pay up, were escorted to the national boundary. Removal by this means was illegal, but effective. Although some of the permit holders prepared to resist the militia, no clash of arms occurred. In his annual message for 1877, Overton stated with satisfaction that the result had justified the means, "for many thousands of dollars have been added to the treasury that could have been reached in no other way, and very many trifling and suspicious characters have been driven from the country."[37]

Complaints to Marston about Overton's method of collecting the tax renewed the earlier dispute; this time, although the Commissioner of Indian Affairs upheld the Chickasaw Nation, Interior Secretary Schurz overruled him and demanded of Overton that "further action under the Permit Law . . . must cease."[38] Overton complied, but petitioned the Senate, whose Judiciary Committee was instructed to inquire into the matter.[39] The upshot was that the nations continued to regulate the permit tax to their own requirements but had to depend upon the United States to remove those for whom no tax had been paid.[40]

In 1877 the Cherokees, in contrast to the Chickasaws, Creeks, and Choctaws, repealed the permit law, thereby allowing the unrestricted entry of white labor. Late in 1878 the national council abruptly reversed this policy by laying a monthly tax of $25 on the employment of any white laborer, mechanics excepted. The penalty for noncompliance was $100 and one year in the national prison. Critics, in an allusion to the aversion of most full-bloods to the cultivation of crops, called this "breech-clout legislation": strict enforcement of the law, they maintained, would cause "ninety per cent. of the improved land of the nation" to lie idle.[41]

Then, in 1885, Congressman John Rogers (D, Arkansas) advanced the argument that the tribal governments' imposition of high license fees was "in direct contravention" of the "spirit" of the treaties of 1866, which, as he said, provided for the admission of certain categories of white employee. The congressman's ire had been aroused by an act of the Choctaw Nation, approved on November 2, 1882, which placed a tax of $16.50 upon "every lawyer, doctor, carpenter, wagonmaker, blacksmith, wheelwright, millwright, tailor, shoemaker, miller, machinist, sawyer, tanner, clerk, teamster, or any other artisan or non-citizen," and stipulated a fine of $50 to

$100 for any citizen who broke the law by failing to pay the levy.[42] But Rogers was doing scarcely more than following the tracks well trodden by Schurz, Marston, Overton, and Cole in the late 1870s. Article 43 of the Choctaw-Chickasaw treaty of 1866 neither required the nations to admit an unlimited number of noncitizens nor prohibited a tax upon those employing noncitizens.

The Choctaws went further in 1885, instituting an absolute embargo upon the employment of noncitizens as herdsmen. Here the objective was to forestall the transfer by stealth of great swathes of the tribal domain to open-range ranching. A glance at any issue of the Atoka *Indian Champion,* the weekly organ of the cattle interests of the Choctaw and Chickasaw nations, with its reproductions of hundreds of company brands from all five nations, furnishes persuasive evidence of the rapid growth of the range cattle industry at this time, in the Choctaw country and elsewhere. The ban was removed in 1887.[43]

By engaging a white man as a tenant, laborer, or herder, and paying his license fee, an Indian could expand his holdings simply because two men could use more land than one; or he could go into partnership, sub rosa, with the permit holder; or, if he lacked energy or ambition, he could invite the licensee to do all the work in return for a share of the profits. Similar principles obtained where an Indian hired more than one laborer. Alternatively, cattlemen from Texas or elsewhere could control large areas of rangeland by arranging for their employees to receive licenses.

In 1877 agent Marston compiled a set of statistics for the population of the Five Tribes, classifying the tribal membership into "Indians by blood," "White Indians by marriage" (or "by adoption"), and "Black Indians by treaty," and further dividing the "Indians by blood" into full-blood and mixed-blood. His findings may be summarized as in table I.

Neither the Choctaws nor the Chickasaws had admitted their ex-slaves, and Marston's information on these "emancipated negroes" was imprecise. It was estimated that there were 4,000 in the Choctaw Nation and 2,300 in the Chickasaw Nation, but these figures may have concealed many recent arrivals ineligible for tribal citizenship.

A total of 327 white United States citizens were living among the Five Tribes as federal employees or licensees, but Marston was unable to learn how many whites were resident under permits issued by the tribal governments, except that there were 35 in the Seminole Nation and 250 in Sequoyah, one of the nine districts of the Cherokee Nation. Data from other sources placed the total number of white residents, excluding those who were tribal members, at 6,200, 1,200 of whom were railroad employees.

Table I. The Five Tribes Classified by Race

	Cherokees	Choctaws	Chickasaws	Creeks	Seminoles
Full-bloods	8,800	8,700	3,100	10,500	1,903
Mixed-bloods	6,000	6,000	2,500	1,200	33
Black citizens	3,500	—	—	2,500	506
White citizens	700	1,300	200	60	1
	19,000	16,000	5,800	14,260	2,443

Source: Patterson Report, vol. 3, 111–14.

On this reckoning, the population of the Five Nations was approximately 70,000, including 57,500 citizens, 33,000 full-blood Indians.[44]

Noncitizens were usually ignored by the census takers of the Five Tribes.[45] In 1880 it was estimated that there were from 17,000 to 20,000 United States citizens, "being either negroes or white residents" (including 6,000 squatters), in a total population of 74,000. Three years later the Union agent, John Tufts, judged that there were 16,000 whites in the Territory under license from the Indian governments and 3,000 under license from the United States Government. In 1885 his successor, Robert Owen, put their respective numbers at 17,000 and 3,000, but added that there were also 5,000 people who had been denied citizenship by the various tribes, 3,000 or 4,000 wilful intruders, and some 1,500 "emigrants, visitors, [and] pleasure seekers."[46]

At that time the citizen population of the Five Tribes stood at about 63,000, inclusive of adopted ex-slaves and adopted or intermarried whites. Therefore, nearly one-third of the populace owed no allegiance to any tribal government, were beyond the reach or protection of civil law, and would incur the attention of the federal authorities for any criminal act committed by or against them. They represented a growing hindrance to the autonomy of the Five Tribes—the intruders, whom the Indians could not legally remove, doubly so.

Although the intruders were an encumbrance to tribal sovereignty, the problem does not appear to have been exploited by the United States to embarrass the governments of the Five Nations. On the contrary: during the 1880s the Union agents were far more disposed to remove squatters than Ingalls and Marston had been. Agent Tufts condemned the intruders "as a class . . . unfit to be in the Indian country" and asked for the adoption of measures that would rid the Indians of their presence.[47] Agent Owen, several years later, suggested that intruders who had been removed should face trial and imprisonment if they again attempted to settle in the Indian Territory without leave.[48]

The threat posed to tribal self-government by the permit holders and

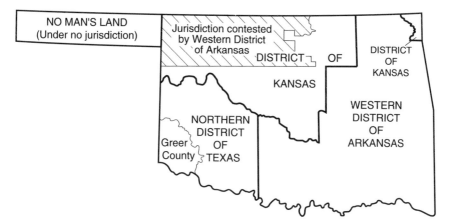

MAP 1. FEDERAL JUDICIAL DISTRICTS IN INDIAN TERRITORY, JANUARY 6, 1883–
FEBRUARY 28, 1889

Under the Courts Act of January 6, 1883, the whole of the Indian Territory not occupied by the Five Tribes was removed from the U.S. Western Judicial District of Arkansas and awarded to the District of Kansas and the Northern District of Texas. The main course of the Canadian River separated the two districts within the borders of Indian Territory. The court towns, for Indian Territory cases, were Wichita and Fort Scott, Kansas, and Graham, Texas.

In his capacity as judge for the Eighth Circuit of the United States, Judge Parker of the Western District of Arkansas ruled that the unassigned portion of the Cherokee Outlet was still, in the legal construction of the term, "occupied by" the Cherokee Nation. This opinion placed the tract beyond the jurisdiction of the Kansas district and within his own. Parker's attitude to this issue may have been one of the reasons behind the decision of Congress in 1889 to strip his court of its circuit powers.

The seven small tribal reservations that comprised the Quapaw Agency at the northeastern corner of the Cherokee Nation were a part of the District of Kansas from January 6, 1883, to May 2, 1890, and again from May 3, 1892, to September 1, 1896. Cases arising there were usually dealt with at Fort Scott.

other United States citizens lawfully resident in Indian Territory, although clearly visible by the early 1880s, became deadly only at the end of that decade. This was partly because by then there were so many more of them; but at least as important were the judicial reforms of 1889 and 1890 which among much else, brought United States citizens living in Indian Territory and the processes of civil law within the reach of one another. Contracts between Indian and United States citizens, hitherto unenforceable from either side, were now protected by federal law. At the same time, a wedge was forced between the governmental institutions of the Five Nations and their own citizens.

Economic development, with its associated demographic adjustments, was, therefore, more a magnet for administrative realignment than the motor of great political change. Suppression of the Five Tribes governments was urged on by outside commercial interests and hastened from Washington by the increasing number of legislators and officials who listened to them. But there was a far greater response to the demands of prospective homesteaders, to the imperial visions conjured among the restless or aggressive elements in American society by the rejuvenated spirit of Manifest Destiny, and most of all to the allure of territorial expansion and social advancement through conferment of a pattern of government that was distinctively American. The conversion of any block of territory in the United States into a Territory of the United States might owe much to economic and social conditions; but in the end it was an exercise in constitutionalism, accomplished by men who were, for the most part, lawyers by profession or training, among whom legislative questions were settled legalistically.

CHAPTER SEVEN

Congressional Intervention and Judicial Conflict, 1878–1886

From the best information in the possession of the committee it would seem that justice is fairly administered by the local [tribal] courts, and the Territory will compare favorably in the administration of law and in the preservation of public peace with the Territories of the Union organized under the acts of Congress.

There would be less necessity for this legislation still if the United States would observe its treaties, and see to it that its own citizens respected the law.—Minority Report on HR 5634, House Report 755, pt. 2, 46th Cong., 2d sess., April 10, 1880

A bill was introduced into Congress, as its title imports, "to establish a United States Court in the Indian Territory, and for other purposes . . ." an insidious measure that may well deceive our friends from its plausible fairness, is the transfer of the United States court from Ft Smith Arkansas to Muscogee Indian Territory.—D. H. Ross and R. M. Wolfe, Cherokee Delegates to the Congress of the United States, February 13, 1882, Records of the Cherokee Nation, Federal Relations

The growth of federal influence among the Five Tribes through the Indian bureau of the Department of the Interior seemed to have been checked on May 27, 1878, by a single sentence in the Indian Appropriation Act for the year ending June 30, 1879. An amendment inserted by the Appropriations Committee of the House and resisted by the Senate only as far as the conference stage provided: "The Union agency in the Indian Territory is hereby abolished, and the duties heretofore devolving upon said agency are transferred to the office of the Commissioner of Indian Affairs."[1]

Not long after his service at Muskogee had been terminated by the operation of this act, former agent Marston was approached by an Indian who had sought his removal yet still valued his counsel. He was asked for advice on what to do about the habitually trespassing cow of a neighbor and found a good answer: "Oh, drive her all the way to Washington."[2]

Closure of the Union agency seemed to ensure that the Five Tribes country and its governments would not be affected by another provision of the Indian Appropriation Act for 1878–79. Under this paragraph, funds were made available to the agencies for "the services of not exceeding four hundred and thirty privates at five dollars per month each, of Indian police, to be employed in maintaining order and prohibiting illegal traffic in liquor in the several Indian reservations." By the beginning of November, and despite the low pay ($8 a month for an officer, $5 for a private), the experiment appeared to be succeeding on twenty-two of the thirty agencies where it had been tried. Several of these forces had been established in those areas of the Indian Territory where they were most needed, such as the Osage Nation and the Cheyenne-Arapaho and Kiowa-Comanche-Wichita agencies.[3] Congress did not increase the pay, but made a greater sum available so that the agents could recruit more men.[4]

But in February 1879, Congress reinstated the Union agency for 1879–80.[5] It would remain in existence until Oklahoma became a State.

Shortly after his arrival at Muskogee the new Union agent, John Tufts, recruited an Indian police force. He was delighted with the performance of these men. "The police system is good," he wrote in 1881, "and . . . while it costs the Indian Department something to keep the police on duty, the government has saved much more than their cost to the Departments of War and Justice."[6] He meant that some of the work carried out by the Union agency police would otherwise have been done more expensively by soldiers or deputy marshals.

A year later Tufts declared that his police "do not interfere with the officers of the nations in any way, hence there is no clash of authority with officers of the nations. All work in harmony, the police arresting those only over whom the Indian authorities have no jurisdiction, and delivering them to the United States marshals." The police were, he averred, "approved of by the best men of the nations. The thieves, whisky peddlers, desperadoes, and their paid attorneys have used every means to have the police abolished, but their efforts have only made the friends of law and order more determined to keep them on duty."[7]

These statements lacked a good deal of what was notoriously the truth, unless Tufts meant that the Cherokee and Creek governments—those with which the Union agency, because of its location, was most closely in contact—excluded the best men of the nations. From the beginning, the authorities of the Five Tribes were resentful and distrustful of a scheme which, as they maintained, had not been designed to apply to their half of Indian Territory. The attachment of a force of police to the Union agency could be justified only if their use led to a reduction in the liquor traffic and the systematic removal of intruders, and gave no embarrassment to the tribal officers. None of these criteria were satisfied by the officers enrolled by Tufts.

Since the Union agency police were all citizens of the Five Nations, the tribal courts had jurisdiction over any offense committed by or upon them, provided that the other parties were also citizens. This in itself could aggravate an existing problem where one or more of the parties belonged to a nation different from that in which the incident had taken place. Usually jurisdiction would be taken by the latter, but the question always depended upon the exact terms of the relationship between the tribes.

Early in January 1882 a well-connected young Cherokee named Ross Cunningham became the third man to be killed within a few weeks by members of the Union agency police under circumstances suggestive of murder. Cunningham, who was drunk, was shot dead in Muskogee by another Cherokee, an off-duty agency policeman, after a dispute at a brothel run by a white intruder couple. Tufts dismissed the man, who was then escorted to the railway station by some of his colleagues so that he could make his escape. He was later arrested but again escaped, and never faced trial before the Creek authorities, who held jurisdiction in the case.

Inquiry developed the fact that at least some of the agency police stationed at Muskogee, when not about their official duty, acted as a kind of town constabulary. Their service in this capacity was paid for by various traders, some of them intruders and some of them continually in breach of the good order that the police were supposed to maintain. In one of a series of letters to the Commissioner of Indian Affairs, the Cherokee delegates leveled the charge that the keepers of the brothel Cunningham had visited seemed "to be under the special protection of the police."

There were, as the delegates noted, no statutes defining the duties of the Indian police beyond a single phrase contained in an annual appropriation act. The Indian agent had, in their words, "certain functions only

... without the slightest pretext for setting himself up as a judicial officer save in cases expressly defined," and the police force was "only his creature." Above all, wrote the delegates,

> we object to . . . the interpolation of this indian police into our judicial system. It never was designed by the law of the United States for the five nations. . . . It is sure to lead to conflict and abuse.
>
> If the agent will remove all intruders and reduce the unnecessary number of whites licensed by law to stay in the country we will guarantee peace, law and order.

Cunningham, they conceded, was quarrelsome when drunk; but they went on to attribute his drunkenness to the quashing of a Presidential ban upon the sale of liquor at the military post of Fort Gibson. The prohibition had been relaxed to permit the post sutler to sell "light wine" to military personnel, as a result of which he had been selling whiskey to anyone who wanted to buy it.[8]

Some of the fault for the unhappy situation at Muskogee lay with the continuing failure of the Creek authorities to make any provision for policing the town. They seem consistently to have shunned the place as an alien enclave, an unwanted railway settlement, altogether beyond the pale of Creek law and society.[9] This attitude, although understandable enough, was a poor face to put on their sovereignty. Residents of Muskogee, apart from a number of ex-slaves, were out of the reach of the tribal courts; but they were under the nose of the Union agent. If the Creek government had placed a competent official in the town of Muskogee, they would probably have succeeded in having intruders and miscreants removed, not least because of the ease with which the agent could have been reported to Washington for failure to act.

Several months after the Cunningham affair, a spotlight was thrown on the failure of Congress to enable legal proceedings to be instituted when the parties were members of different tribes and at least one of them was not a member of one of the Five Tribes.

In September 1882, Robert Poisal, a half-blood Arapaho, was murdered in the Potawatomi–Absentee Shawnee reservation, between the Creek Nation and the Unassigned Lands. His assassin, a Creek named Johnson Foster, was captured by Seminole light-horse men and handed over to the military authorities at Fort Reno. Some of the Arapahos were so enraged that the United States Attorney-General, in response to a request from the Interior Department, asked District Attorney Clayton to institute a prosecution for murder in the Fort Smith court. Clayton told the Attorney-General that this would be a waste of time because the United States court was without jurisdiction. "The fact that these two

Indians belong to different tribes makes no difference," Clayton added, "because the statute is general, covering all the tribes."

Hiram Price, the Commissioner of Indian Affairs, argued that the case was excepted from the general law by a clause in the 1867 treaty between the United States and the Cheyenne and Arapaho Indians. Painstakingly, but firmly, the Solicitor-General showed that Price's contention was of no substance; but he did suggest that a hopeless prosecution might "effectively call the attention of Congress to the general subject, which indeed seems to require further legislative consideration."

Foster, the murderer, could not be tried by the Creeks because the crime had taken place outside the Muskogee Nation and had been committed against a member of a tribe with whom the Creeks had no formal or informal arrangement for extradition; and he could not be tried by the Potawatomi, the Absentee Shawnees, or the Arapahos because they lacked courts of justice. In the end, the Government was able to hold Foster on the strength of old charges of horse stealing and introducing liquor. In June 1883, he was conducted to Fort Smith by a deputy marshal, who was given a military escort and needed it to ward off an attempt by Arapahos to lynch the prisoner. A few weeks later the Assistant Attorney-General instructed the attorney for the District of Kansas to initiate a prosecution for murder even though, at the time the offense was committed, this court had no jurisdiction in the Indian Territory. It was left to the culprit himself to resolve both his own immediate difficulties and the jurisdictional quandary of the United States by murdering a United States citizen—the deputy who was taking him to Kansas—and escaping. He was never recaptured.[10]

Despite the discomfiture of the federal judicial system by the Poisal case and the obvious possibility of a recurrence, Congress waited until 1890 to award jurisdiction to the federal courts in all crimes and civil controversies where the persons concerned were members of different tribes or nations, including the Five Tribes.[11]

Congress was only a little less tardy in enacting a law to meet the interests of Indian citizens employed by the United States in work that was sometimes dangerous, often resented by most other Indians, and almost always ill paid. The excesses of some policemen at the Union agency have been noted, but on the whole the Indian police of the Indian Territory had given good service. From the inception of the policy, and in report after report, year in, year out, complaints about the puny sums paid out to the Indian policemen were relayed from the agents to the Commissioner, from the Commissioner to the Secretary of the Interior, from the

Secretary to the President, finally to find expression in the President's message to Congress. In 1884, Commissioner Price wrote:

> I cannot conscientiously perform my duty nor do justice to this meritorious body of men without again calling attention to their meager salary, and urging that a more liberal compensation be paid to them. This office requires that they shall be men of unquestioned energy, courage, and self-command; be in vigorous bodily health; be good horsemen, and good shots with rifle and pistol.[12]

When Congress heeded these pleas, it did so without erring on the side of generosity. On July 1, 1885, the pay of the officers was raised from $8 to $10 per month, and that of the privates from $5 to $8.[13]

An amendment offered to the Indian Appropriation bill early in 1885 proposed that "murder, manslaughter, rape, assault with intent to kill, aggravated assault and battery, arson, burglary, and larceny, within any Territory of the United States, and either within or without an Indian reservation" should be "subject therefor to the laws of such Territory relating to said crimes." In bringing the amendment, Representative Byron Cutcheon (R, Michigan) proffered the customary excuse for legislation introduced as a rider to an appropriation bill—that he would not have resorted to such methods had he seen the least chance of the measure becoming law by the more conventional route.[14]

These proposals would not extend to the Indian Territory, which was not an organized Territory with a Territorial code of laws. A Texas Democrat, James Throckmorton, attempted to tack onto the bill a further amendment to grant the Fort Smith court "civil jurisdiction over the five civilized tribes of the Indian Territory in cases of debt on contract or torts committed upon the personal property of any person either in or out of said Territory."[15] Throckmorton's amendment was struck out in the Senate, but most of the original rider was retained and entered the statutes on March 3, 1885, with the rest of the Indian Appropriation Act. The offense of "aggravated assault with battery" was excluded from the final draft of the Serious Crimes Act, or Indian Crimes Act as Section 9 of the Appropriation Act came to be called.[16]

Section 8 of the same act empowered President Cleveland "to open negotiations with the Creeks, Seminoles, and Cherokees for the purpose of opening to settlement under the homestead laws the unassigned lands ceded by them respectively to the United States by the several treaties of August 11th, 1866, March 21st, 1866, and July 19th, 1866."[17] The wording of the section implied recognition by Congress that the Cherokee Outlet and the Unassigned Lands formerly occupied by the Creeks and Seminoles had been ceded conditionally, besides confirming that the Government had abandoned the policy of resettling these tracts with "friendly Indians" (or ex-slaves, in the former Creek and Seminole lands) from outside the Territory—the policy for whose furtherance, and no other reason, the Cherokee, Creek, and Seminole lands had been ceded. In June of that year the Indian International Council declared with hardly a dissenting voice that the projected negotiations would be "incompatible with the rights, interests and future security of the Indian Territory" and recommended that the tribal governments should not enter into them. The Creeks wanted to go further. At a meeting with Seminole leaders that September their representatives proposed an approach to the federal Government for the recovery of the tribal title to the Oklahoma lands; but, the Seminole party being absolutely "non-committal on the subject," the matter could not be taken forward. The Creeks, probably, would have leased their portion of the lands to cattlemen. But Principal Chief Brown, of the Seminoles, was always disinclined to bargain with the range-cattle interests in his home nation, and for this, or whatever other reason, preferred the status quo in the Oklahoma country.[18]

President Cleveland was in no hurry to begin negotiations with the Indians on a matter which, plainly, they saw as not negotiable. He went no further than to issue orders for the removal of ranchers' cattle, their herders, and the persons and property of homesteaders from the Un-assigned Lands. Supporters of the homestead movement later complained that these orders were executed far more energetically against the farmers than against the cattlemen and their stock.

Since Cleveland had no authority to act against the Cherokee Strip Live Stock Association, even if he had wished to, Congress decided to proceed on its own initiative. The inquiry which the Senate Committee on Indian Affairs under Chairman Henry Laurens Dawes (R, Massachusetts) conducted into the "Condition of the Indians in the Indian Territory and Other Reservations" was the outcome of three separate resolutions. The first, passed on June 11, 1884, instructed the Committee, principally, "to inquire into the condition of the several tribes and bands of Indians in the Indian Territory, the tenure by which the lands in the several reservations in said Territory are now held, and the character of their actual occupation and use." The second, on December 3, 1884, instructed it to investigate "leases of land in the Indian Territory or Indian reservations for grazing and other purposes . . . and the persons, corporations, or associations named therein as lessees" and to inquire into the circumstances under which the coal leases were made, the means by which they were obtained, and whether they were "conducive to the welfare of the Indians in said Territory or Indian reservations." The third, dated February 23, 1885, when the first stage of the inquiry (into leases) was still incomplete, authorized it to continue its investigation during the next recess.[19] Since another part of the Committee's brief was to inquire into "the need, if any, of legislation" for the Indian Territory, the way was open for an exhaustive survey of every aspect of government in the Indian country.

At about the same time, a House Committee was being assembled to undertake a comprehensive review of Indian policy in the West. William Holman (D, Indiana)—called, among other things, "the watchdog of the Treasury," "the hayseed statesman," and "The Great Objector"—was allotted the chairmanship of the Special (or Select) Committee appointed on March 4, 1885, "to inquire into the expenditure of public moneys in the Indian service and the Yellowstone Park, and certain other matters connected therewith."[20] Holman, whose managerial and parliamentary skill was obscured from some by his idiosyncrasies of manner and unpolished exterior, had twenty years of congressional experience behind him and was one of the House's spokesmen on Indian affairs, public lands, and Government expenditures.

Although the Holman Committee's terms of reference were wide, its efforts would be concentrated upon the collation of evidence on the conditions prevailing on the western reservations and among the Five Tribes, and on the feasibility of a resumption of the policy of removing Western tribes to Indian Territory.

The objectives of the two committees were complementary. Endorsement by Holman of a withdrawal from the resettlement policy would clear the path for the consideration of an alternative policy proposed by Dawes, and adverse findings by Dawes on the Cherokees' leasing the Outlet would facilitate an assault from the House upon the Cherokee government and the Five Nations as a whole. Both committees would be soliciting testimony on the efficacy of the court systems, federal and tribal. If the courts were shown to be inadequate, Congress could turn to the option, available since 1866, of using judicial reform as a pressure point.

A subcommittee of the Senate Committee on Indian Affairs arrived in the Indian Territory in the third week of May 1885. Besides the chairman of the committee, the visiting members were John Ingalls (R, Kansas), Samuel Maxey (D, Texas), John Tyler Morgan (D, Alabama), and James Jones (D, Arkansas).

Henry Dawes was about halfway through the second of his three consecutive terms in the Senate. He was well noted as "the friend of the Indian," devoted to a policy of doing for the Indian what he believed to be the best for the Indian; and it was his steady conviction that at the heart of that policy should be the allotment of the tribal lands in severalty. He held with as much consistency that the terms of the Government's treaties with the Five Tribes should be maintained strictly, so that allotment of their domain should proceed only with their agreement. Dawes was a reasonable man in his way, a genuine believer in his expressed conviction that Indians who objected to land allotment were unreasonable in their opposition to it. Since, in his settled opinion, their disagreement was wrongheaded, it was the duty of the United States Government to pursue negotiations with as much vigor and persistence as might be needed to induce the tribal governments to acknowledge the superiority of the arguments for allotment and to conclude an honorable pact with the United States on that basis.

Ingalls, renowned as an orator, rabidly anti-Southern in many public pronouncements even twenty years after the Civil War, was remarkable among Western politicians, and especially among Kansas politicians, as a fervent spokesman for the sovereignty of the Five Tribes. He had a financial interest in the operations of the Cherokee Strip Live Stock Association; but that in itself no more presupposes corruption than the fact that such enemies of tribal government as George Vest and Bishop Perkins had been employed as attorneys by the Missouri, Kansas and Texas Railway.

Morgan, though a staunch upholder of States' rights, was not one of those Southern politicians who found in the issue of tribal autonomy a cause analogous to that of the freedom of State governments from federal interference. His sectional loyalties were secondary to an absolute conviction in the supremacy of the United States Constitution and America's imperial destiny.

Jones and Maxey articulated, and shared, the prevailing sectional attitudes of the Democratic legislatures that had sent them to Washington. Jones was set against any lessening of the jurisdiction of the Fort Smith court; Maxey strove to reduce that jurisdiction by having some of it transferred to the Eastern District of Texas, with his hometown, Paris, getting the courthouse. Possession of a flourishing courthouse was an important matter for the politically active classes of such towns—bankers, property speculators, hotel keepers, saloon men, but above all for the multitude of restless, ambitious lawyers, always too many for the opportunities. All five members of the Senate subcommittee were lawyers—little to be wondered at, for among the occupants of the seventy-six seats of the upper chamber during this period, only a dozen or so came from outside the legal profession.

Dawes and his colleagues spent little more than a fortnight in the

Indian Territory or in towns that abutted it, but in that short time copious testimony was taken at Muskogee, Fort Gibson, Tahlequah, Eufaula, McAlester, Caddo, Denison, and Fort Smith. Views and information were submitted on allotment, territorialization, railroads, the federal and tribal courts, the rights of freedmen, education, and the leasing of tribal lands for mining and grazing.[21] At the end of it all, the Committee came down solidly against premature homesteading of the Oklahoma lands:

> [T]he Committee . . . unite in the conclusion that the United States have no right to dispose of the ownership in the soil of that ceded tract without further agreement with these tribes [Creek and Seminole], except for the purpose of settling other friendly Indians upon those lands.[22]

On the larger issue of whether, or how far, tribal government should be superseded by federal institutions, Morgan's imprint, touched only lightly by the views of Dawes and Ingalls, is clearest:

> The supreme law exists in and pervades the Indian country, but in these areas our political power has no support of the judicial authority through which it can be applied to these important subjects. . . .
>
> Their governments should be recognized as being in every way lawful as far as they do not violate the constitution of the United States, and should continue under their own control.
>
> It would neither be wise or [sic] just to supplant the present governing power of these tribes by forcing upon them a new body of voters, or their methods of government by substituting in place of them Territorial governments responsible directly to Congress. . . . Such a course would violate our treaties with them. But the security of their property rights, of their rightful control over their tribal lands, of the rights of individuals to protection against any power exercised by the local governments that would violate the liberties secured by the Constitution of the United States alike to all the people, demand that the supreme judicial authority of the United States should be extended over and enforced amongst these civilized tribes.[23]

It was then (and it remained) Morgan's hope that the United States Supreme Court would become the final arbiter of decisions that were still disputable after they had been dealt with by the tribal courts of last resort.

Much attention was given to the administration of the lower reaches of federal law. In a compromise that had been fashioned to accommodate views as disparate as those of Maxey and Jones while giving due weight to the statements offered by most Indians (not quite "every Indian," as asserted in the report) in support of establishing a federal court in the Indian Territory, the committee recommended that the Western District of Arkansas should be split into two divisions, with a new court town in the Indian country becoming the headquarters of the westerly division.

A suggestion that "enlightened Indians" should be placed on federal juries as "the first distinct recognition of their capacity to exert the duties of citizenship in the United States" could have originated with either Dawes or Morgan. Another, that the Supreme Court should be amenable to appeals from the federal district court at Fort Smith, could have come from any of the members or all of them.[24]

Most of the program of the House Select Committee was carried out during the summer recess, when Holman and his party inspected the Northern agencies (with a short official excursion to Yellowstone Park) and those in upper Arizona and New Mexico. In October 1885, the committee reassembled. Holman and his associates visited the San Carlos Reservation in Arizona, interviewed General George Crook in Albuquerque, and concluded their grand tour in the Indian Territory, dispersing at Muskogee on November 8.

During their week at the Union agency the members of the committee met some of "the chiefs and other headman" of the Five Tribes, when "some matters not directly pertinent to the subjects of inquiry with which the committee was charged, incidentally arose, especially as to the dividing among the Indians in those nations of our [*sic*] lands in severalty and as to settlement of Oklahoma [Unassigned Lands] by the whites, and the policy of settling Indians on that portion of the Territory."[25]

There was disagreement among the five members of the committee about what advice should be given on policy toward the Indian Territory. Holman and his two fellow Democrats, while strongly opposing any resumption of the policy of transplanting Indians to the Territory—their argument was that the strength of tribal attachments to their own localities should be respected—recommended that those who had already been resettled in the western part of the Territory should be moved on into the Unassigned Lands ("Oklahoma lands") and that the areas thus vacated should then be made available to homesteaders.[26] The two Republicans demanded "a radical change," urging that the sooner this was effected, the better everyone, including the Indians, would be served: the Indian Territory, "even imperfectly developed," could provide homes for 3 million people. Their opinion was that the "reservation system, not only in the Indian Territory but throughout the United States, should be cut up . . . at the roots" through a policy of allotment in severalty. Where the majority were merely critical of the leasing by the Cherokees and others of "vast pasture fields" as "not tending to the civilization of the Indians" and a threat to "the peace of the country," the two Republicans described the cattlemen in the Outlet as "trespassers" and called for their ejection.[27]

Thus, though the collective view of the Dawes committee was that reform should be introduced into the Indian Territory gradually, discreetly, and circumspectly, the sense of the message from the Holman committee was that the House should seek an early solution to the problem. It was in the House, therefore, that further efforts were made to create a unified Territory by a single piece of legislation.

Three bills to organize a Territory of Oklahoma were introduced early in the life of the Forty-ninth Congress. The third of these (HR 7217) was reported favorably and debated lengthily in the House before being withdrawn by the chairman of the House Committee on the Territories, William David Hill (D, Ohio). This was a curious hodgepodge, providing for the whole of the Indian Territory outside the Five Tribes to be joined with the Neutral Strip ("Public Land Strip" or "No Man's Land") and organized into Oklahoma Territory. Although the bill did not encroach upon the homelands and institutions of the the Five Tribes, Hill and his allies declared that soon the nations would welcome the idea of incorporation into the new Territory.

To assist the process of amalgamation, the very name "Indian Territory" would vanish from the map: the whole area, including the section occupied by the Five Nations, would be known as Oklahoma. As to the administration of federal law, the majority report of the Territories Committee condemned the courts at Fort Smith, Wichita, Fort Scott, and Graham as a source of "enormous expense" and a failure. As in the Harlan bill of 1865 and all its many successors, three new federal courts in the Five Tribes country were envisaged.

For the rest, Hill and his allies roundly dismissed as "untenable" the arguments used to justify leasing tribal lands for pasture. The obvious, and fatal, flaw in the bill was its supposition that the Indian tribes who occupied or held title to much of the country intended for inclusion in the proposed Territory would give, retrospectively, the consent that was required before the project could be realized. If such consent were withheld, the United States would acquire a Territory consisting of No Man's Land.[28]

The strength of the opposition to the bill may be gauged from the fact that no fewer than five members of the House Committee on the Territories had signed a minority report sharply critical of the bill and the reasoning upon which some of its underlying assumptions had been based. In particular, the contention that the grazing leases in the Cherokee Outlet were invalid was met by a painstaking rebuttal.[29]

A quite different but equally formidable set of arguments for the Cherokee claim to sovereignty over the Outlet had been presented shortly before this in a court of law. After a clerk of the Union agency, Connell

Rogers, had been indicted at Wichita, Kansas, for arson committed in the Outlet upon the encampment of unlawful settlers, the question arose whether under the Courts Act of January 6, 1883, jurisdiction resided at Wichita or at Fort Smith. If the Outlet was, in law, a part of the Cherokee Nation, the case was a matter for Fort Smith since, as far as the operation of United States law was concerned, the Five Nations were wholly within the Western District of Arkansas.

Isaac Parker, when called upon as circuit judge to consider questions affecting the jurisdiction of his own district court, usually found in its favor. His judgment in the Rogers case ran true to form; but in this particular instance it was also an affirmation of Cherokee sovereignty. Fort Smith owed its jurisdiction in the Outlet, Parker explained, wholly to the Cherokee Nation's title there.[30] Although soon afterwards Justice David Brewer of the Eighth Circuit of the United States Supreme Court held in a similar case that the Outlet lay within the jurisdiction of the Kansas court, he did so in terms that did not altogether contradict Parker on the question of title. Thus the issue whether the Cherokees "occupied" the Outlet remained unresolved.[31]

After the collapse of the Hill bill, there was further recourse to the sporadic policy of asserting the primacy of the federal government through jurisdictional reforms. In the first and perhaps most notable of these items of remedial legislation—the repair of a serious weakness in the Indian Crimes Act of 1885—Congress was responding to the force of events that might never have occurred but for the carelessness, and ignorance, of those who had drafted the bill and secured its passage through Congress. The act, placing Indian employees of the federal government in United States Territories within the jurisdiction of the United States courts, did not reach the Indian Territory, although it appears that some of its sponsors had intended that it should and that many people who ought to have known better believed for a while that it did. Because of this neglect, the United States Indian police in Indian Territory could be neither prosecuted nor protected by the federal courts. In particular, the Union agency police—a more respected and far better managed force now, but no better liked than before by many Five Tribes citizens—suffered through being subject to the tribal courts, since the operation of the system was likely to reflect a popular bias against the police.

Congress did adopt legislation similar to the Indian Crimes Act for express application in Indian Territory, but only after it had been presented with proof of its earlier oversight. One evening in September 1886 some of a party of whites and Cherokee mixed-bloods, on a riotous visit to Muskogee, opened fire on several Union agency police, wounding Captain Samuel Sixkiller. Those of the revelers who were Indians certainly knew that, in shooting at Indian policemen, they were breaking no federal law; presumably they must have known too that they were breaking the laws of the Creek Nation, and felt confident that they had nothing to fear on that score.

They did not know that Sixkiller and one of his men held additional commissions as deputy United States marshals and were on this account protected by a federal law passed in 1871. Two of the offenders were caught and punished; but, had none of the Indian officers been deputy marshals, the worst that could have befallen the attackers was arrest by Cherokee officers, extradition to the Creek Nation, a fine for carrying deadly weapons in a public place, and, possibly, being sued for mayhem.[32]

On Christmas Eve of the same year, Sixkiller was murdered in Muskogee by two Cherokee mixed-bloods. One of the murderers was later killed by a deputy United States marshal. The other was arrested in the Cherokee Nation by deputy marshals; passed to the Cherokee authorities, for extradition to the Creek Nation, after a habeas corpus hearing at Fort Smith; handed over to the Creeks; enabled to escape by what the Union agent, with some generosity toward the Creek officials, described as "gross negligence"; recaptured in the Cherokee Nation; again extradited; and again allowed to get away.[33]

Early in the new year, when the sense of outrage at the murder was still strong, Representative John Rogers (D, Arkansas) submitted an amendment to the current Indian appropriation bill. On March 2, 1887, after three minor additions to it had been accepted, the Rogers amendment became law:

> [I]mmediately upon and after the passage of this act any Indian committing against the person of any Indian policeman appointed under the laws of the United States, or any Indian United States deputy marshal while lawfully engaged in the execution of any United States process, or lawfully engaged in any other duty imposed upon such policeman or marshal by the laws of the United States any of the following crimes, namely, murder, manslaughter, or assault with intent to kill within the Indian Territory, shall be subject to the laws of the United States relating to such crime, and shall be tried in the district court of the United States exercising criminal jurisdiction where said offense was committed.[34]

Soon after this, a jury at Fort Smith returned a verdict which furnished a salutary reminder that a transfer of jurisdiction afforded no guarantee of a just outcome. Thomas Knight, lieutenant of the Union agency police, and two Texas Rangers, were looking for stolen cattle in the Chickasaw Nation when they came upon a well-known thief and desperado, a white man named Albert St. John. They tried to arrest him and, when he made violent resistance, killed him. Although it was shown that they had acted in self-defense, a jury at Fort Smith seems to have been more impressed with the argument that they had no formal authority to arrest St. John. All three were found guilty of manslaughter. Judge Parker (humanely but illegally) suspended the sentence on Knight and his companions, and President Cleveland pardoned them.

The case should not have proceeded beyond an examination before the United States commissioner.[35] Knight had been indicted in October 1886, some four months before the enactment of the Rogers amendment, but the prior existence of legislation such as this might not have helped in this particular case. Within its own terms of reference it was a just and reasonable piece of lawmaking; but it could be seen, too, as a component of a legislative strategy. One who regarded it in that light was the unnamed "officer of the Government located at the Five Agencies [Union agency]" whose views in a purportedly private letter to Congressman Rogers the congressman at once made public.[36] The letter closed:

> The United States must not release their grasp in this Territory. To remand it to Indian rule is to consign this fair land to anarchy, red ruin, and utter woe, or, as Tennyson puts it in his last poem, "Cosmos, Chaos! Chaos, Cosmos!."[37]

CHAPTER EIGHT

A Double Thrust
at Tribal Sovereignty

I know . . . that at this time there is a large manifest interest among the Indians for having a court held within their Territory. . . . [D]o let us have a court amongst these people, and let them feel that after all they have some interest in the United States and some right of participation in our Government through the courts.—John Tyler Morgan, Democratic Senator from Alabama, in Senate debate on the Vest court bill (S. 270) February 9, 1889, Congressional Record, 20:1715

Perkins, Springer, Mansur, Struble, Peters, Baker, all of you Oklahoma champions—you are a mixture of politics but a unit on Oklahoma. We love you all and you shall find a place in our family prayers for ever and ever.—Guthrie, Oklahoma State Capital, March 15, 1890

Numerous bills relating to the Indian Territory were introduced in the House of Representatives during the early weeks of 1888, many of them from the Committee on the Judiciary. Most were blocked or dropped in committee, but several that were converted into law increased the authority and ambitions of the federal courts and were the direct precursors of the radical reforms that laid the foundations of Territorial government in the western half of the Indian country and quasi government by the United States courts in the eastern half.

When Hill's bill was abandoned in December 1886, twenty years of intermittent pressure to bring Indian Territory under the political control of the United States had come to naught. Even so, and despite the coolness of the Senate toward this policy, efforts to displace the tribal governments by a single legislative sledgehammer blow were continued under Hill's successor as chairman of the House Committee on the Territories, William Springer.

The alternative line of attack, the one that Congress as a whole chose to adopt, was concentrated upon two sectors: first, the residual sovereignty of the Creeks and Seminoles over the Unassigned (Oklahoma) Lands; and second, the unexploited inability of the tribal governments to oppose the establishment of United States courts in their territory.

The exact shape of some of the legislation that emerged from Congress was determined less by the declamatory rhetoric or expository logic of parliamentary exchange than the more informal processes of the interchamber Committees of Conference, from which extramural influences of the worldlier sort were not always barred. Still, the record of the public debate in Congress is important as a compendium of the larger arguments being pursued among the political classes and in the press of the country at large.

In some sections of the United States there was little or no interest in the Indian Territory or in legislation to alter its status. Many members of Congress shared this indifference, but several of those most active in the debate over the political future of the Indian Territory were from States whose voters and legislatures were wholly unconcerned by the question. The burden of the debate during this period was assumed by about a dozen Senators and perhaps seventeen members of the House. Several were from New England, one from Colorado; the rest were from the Middle West or Texas and the Southern States.

House of Representatives

Charles Baker	(R, New York)
George Barnes	(D, Georgia)
James Buchanan	(R, New Jersey)
David Culberson	(D, Texas)
Silas Hare	(D, Texas)
Charles Hooker	(D, Mississippi)
Thomas McRae	(D, Arkansas)
Charles Mansur	(D, Missouri)
Bishop Perkins	(R, Kansas)
Samuel Peters	(R, Kansas)
John Rogers	(D, Arkansas)
William Springer	(D, Illinois)
Thomas Stockdale	(D, Mississippi)
Isaac Struble	(R, Iowa)
Charles Turner	(D, New York)
William Warner	(R, Missouri)
Joseph Washington	(D, Tennessee)

Senate

James Berry	(D, Arkansas)
Matthew Butler	(D, South Carolina)
Richard Coke	(D, Texas)
Henry Dawes	(R, Massachusetts)
George Edmunds	(R, Vermont)
John Ingalls	(R, Kansas)
James Jones	(D, Arkansas)
John Morgan	(D, Alabama)
Orville Platt	(R, Connecticut)
Preston Plumb	(R, Kansas)
John Reagan	(D, Texas)
Henry Teller	(R, Colorado)
George Vest	(D, Missouri)

These men were divided not by party but by sectional or local interests in most instances, principle or prejudice in others. Sometimes sectional and local interests were at odds with each other. Among the Southern Democrats, the members from Arkansas and Texas were concerned primarily with the courts issue; since their guiding purpose was to uphold the virtues and necessity of the Fort Smith and Paris courts, they were against the proposals for Territorial government. If Territorial government could not be excluded altogether, they wanted it to be confined for as long as possible to the western half of the Indian country. Several of the other Southerners—Butler, Barnes, and Hooker—were uncompromising defenders of tribal rights; another, Morgan, was an enlightened expansionist; yet another, Washington, a crude expansionist; and one, Stockdale, virulently antagonistic to the governments of the Five Tribes and Indians in general.

The Easterners were as divided as the Southerners. Platt—at this time—and Buchanan were cautious expansionists: they urged the early settlement of, and introduction of Territorial government to, the Unassigned (Oklahoma) Lands but held that nothing further should be done without the clear and unforced consent of the Five Tribes' governments.

Dawes, unlike Platt, did not disagree with the establishment of federal courts in the Indian Territory; like Platt, he hoped for the gradual, voluntary surrender of the tribal governments to sustained persuasion. But his contribution to the discussion, at least before the Senate in open session, suggests that his first preoccupation lay with the maintenance of his position as the leading Republican expert and spokesman on all aspects of the Indian Question. As the architect of the General Allotment Act, often called the Dawes Act, of 1887, which had provided for the allotment in severalty of almost all the land occupied by Indian tribes outside the Indian Territory,[1] he intended, and expected, to be well to the fore in any debate on the future of the Five Tribes.

George Edmunds, as a constitutional lawyer, was to the Senate what Culberson was to the House. He was also leader of the Republican party in the upper chamber. He spoke cogently on the courts issue and pressed hard for the creation of a United States court in the Indian Territory with plenary jurisdiction over United States citizens—a stance that put him in opposition to Dawes, who thought that the outside courts should keep some of their jurisdiction.

From the Republican side of the House, Charles Baker of New York spoke as forcefully as anyone for any measure that would hasten the Indian Territory toward Statehood. Across the aisle, Charles Turner, also of New York, a gifted young orator with what proved to be a very brief congressional career before him, spiritedly defended the rights of the Five Tribes governments.

Henry Teller, the only one of the senators or representatives from the new Western States to evince much interest in the Indian Territory, argued for the amalgamation of the Neutral Strip and the Unassigned Lands into a United States Territory. Beyond this, he professed to be able to reconcile the two not very compatible notions that Congress could not seize the Outlet but that Congress must insist upon acquiring this and other Indian lands. Annexation, he explained, must be preceded by the payment of a fair market price.

The Middle Westerners, almost without exception, were aggressive advocates of any policy that would open up the whole Indian Territory to settlement and commercial development. Only John Ingalls and George Vest, two very diferent men from very different backgrounds, were partial exceptions. Vest followed a course peculiarly his own. His enthusiasm for the creation of a Territorial government for the Indian country, and the rapid and inexpensive purchase of the Outlet, was outmatched by a propensity for setting himself against a majority of his own party. Vest was ex-Confederate, free silver, and anti-imperialist; his stand on the Oklahoma issue seems to have been caused by an antipathy for the Fort Smith court so violent that it is impossible not to conclude that he cherished a deep and personal loathing for the judge of that court. Isaac Parker had begun his political career in Missouri as a Democrat.

The Fiftieth Congress, and the first session of the Fifty-first, produced legislation that was critically important to the history of political change in the Indian Territory. It would be well, therefore, to precede a review of the legislative program with a note on its salient features.

First, there was an attempt by William Springer to push through a bill (HR 1277) similar to Hill's Oklahoma bill, which had been withdrawn in December, 1886. When the Springer bill foundered on the shoals of House procedure, its author assembled another (HR 10614) that was almost a replica of the earlier one. This was passed by the House but squeezed out of the Senate timetable. Some of its provisions were written into later bills.

After the Springer bills came an ostensibly modest set of proposals which, having attracted a series of amendments, took final shape as the most significant addition to the statute book affecting the Five Tribes since the ratification of the treaties of 1866. This act established a United States court in the Indian Territory, though at the outset that court enjoyed only limited civil and criminal jurisdiction. At the same time, the judicial boundaries of the outside courts were redrawn, resulting in a further diminution of the Western District of Arkansas. The Muskogee bill, as it was usually called, was introduced by Culberson in January 1888 and became law on March 1, 1889.[2]

Next, and even more important, was a rider on the Indian appropriation bill for the fiscal year ended June 30, 1890. It was conceived early in 1889 when representatives of both the traditionalist and progressive parties in the Muskogee Nation, abruptly diverging from the common policy agreed at the Indian International Council, decided to invite the United States Government to buy out the tribe's interest in the lands ceded in 1866. A few weeks later their change of attitude was matched by the Seminoles, thus placing the unassigned area in the lap of the United States. The rider to the appropriation bill promised that the Unassigned Lands (the Oklahoma lands) would be opened for homesteading under the terms of a presidential proclamation; it made no provision for the establishment of a civil government.[3] The bill was signed on March 2, 1889; the proclamation followed before the end of that month, and the lands were opened on April 22.

Just over a year later came the omnibus measure popularly, but inadequately, known as "the Oklahoma Act." It conferred Territorial status upon the Oklahoma lands, together with the former Neutral or Public Land Strip; invested the new Territory with a provisional government and the apparatus to create its own pattern of local self-rule; placed all the reservations occupied by so-called "non-Civilized" Indians, except the Quapaw Agency, within its boundaries and therefore under the jurisdiction of the newly established Territorial and United States district courts for Oklahoma; awarded the Oklahoma courts jurisdiction over federal cases arising in the unassigned portion of the Cherokee Outlet; adopted from the statutes of Arkansas something like a coherent body of criminal and civil law for application by the federal courts in what now remained of Indian Territory; widened the criminal jurisdiction of the Muskogee court greatly, inside its diminished district, without relieving the Fort Smith and Paris courts of their jurisdiction over the higher felonies; vested the Muskogee court with the power to hear all civil cases originating in Indian Territory in which United States citizens were concerned; made all criminal and civil cases involving Indians of different tribes or nations in Indian Territory an issue for the United States courts; and permitted any member of any tribe or nation in Indian Territory to apply to the federal court for United States citizenship without any loss of tribal rights and privileges. All this, and more, became law on May 2, 1890.[4]

Passage of the General Allotment Act on February 3, 1887, prefigured the renewal of attempts to implement comparable policies in Indian Territory. It followed as a matter of course, therefore, that the House Committee on the Territories, under Springer's chairmanship, should resume the policy toward Indian Territory that it had adhered to ever since the end of the Civil War; accordingly, proposals for comprehensive reform were once again put before the lower chamber. In the end, like their predecessors, the Springer bills came to nothing while others far less ambitious, introduced at about the same time, ensured the eventual success of the graduated approach preferred by the judicial committees of the two chambers and the Senate generally.

Among the miscellany of bills introduced in the House in January 1888 and subsequently buried or rejected in committee, one asked for a right-of-way to be granted to a railroad, two were concerned with the charges levied on freight shipments through Indian Territory, one was aimed at raising the salary of the federal judge at Fort Smith, and five proposed, collectively, to award further civil and criminal jurisdiction to the United States courts.[5]

Another bill, presented from the Judicial Committee by John Rogers, passed swiftly into law, remedying one of the worst flaws in United States criminal law. Except where United States mail or other Government property was involved, robbery, burglary, and larceny in the Indian country, although separate offenses in common law, carried the same penalty: a fine of $1,000, not more than one year's imprisonment, or both. Since the fine could not usually be collected, the only punishment for armed robbery committed without physical violence was a prison term of one year or less.[6]

After Rogers's bill had reached the statutes, robbery, burglary, and certain kinds of larceny, including horse theft, were all punishable by up to fifteen years' imprisonment, although it remained within the judge's discretion to substitute, or add, a fine.[7] Once again Congress was reacting to events rather than anticipating them: horse stealing was becoming commoner and was being carried out on a larger scale than before, a white man had recently received the maximum prison sentence of one year for armed robbery of the Creek national treasury at Okmulgee, and train robbers had visited Indian Territory for the first time in December 1887, less than a fortnight before the introduction of the bill.[8]

An evil of long standing, aggravated by the use of the Territory as a haven by men who had committed mail robbery and other crimes in Texas during 1887, was palliated by an act of June 4, 1888. Under the new law, the United States marshal of any district could enter the Indian Territory to arrest a fugitive from a federal writ. This measure was introduced by Culberson, but it was Rogers who took it through the House. The operation of this law, said Rogers, would "relieve the Indians of grossly demoralizing influences and grievous annoyances." So it would; but it would also enhance federal influence in Indian Territory.[9]

Shortly afterward, on June 9, the last of the many bills introduced by Rogers became law. It enlarged the protection offered by the act of March 2, 1887, to Indian officers in the federal service so that it covered *posse comitati* and guards in the employ of the United States Government. Assault, assault and battery, and obstruction by threats or violence were added to the offenses answerable to the United States courts if committed by any Indian citizen against another who was working for, or temporarily acting for, the United States courts or Indian agents or had been so employed at any time in the past.[10]

This last proviso was intended to shield such Indians from revenge for their actions during past Government service; but it was also an encumbrance upon the jurisdiction of the tribal courts because crimes committed against persons in this category would sometimes be quite unconnected with their one-time official actions. Indeed, the whole act violated the terms of the treaties of 1866, which reserved for the Five Tribes the right to try their own citizens in cases where only their own citizens were concerned. In practice, the federal courts sometimes recognized and yielded to this principle by turning over the defendant to tribal custody, though only after a certain amount of wrangling.

Culberson's court bill was introduced on January 4, 1888.[11] His object had been no more than the transfer of federal jurisdiction in the Choctaw and Chickasaw nations from the Western District of Arkansas to a new division, to be created by the bill itself, of the Eastern District of Texas.

The town of Paris, in Lamar county, which had recently become the southern terminus of a branch of the St. Louis and San Francisco Railway, was visualized as the headquarters of the new divisional court.

The Culberson bill passed the House on March 22, 1888. On April 16, George Vest, as chairman of the Senate Committee on the Judiciary, introduced "an amendment by way of substitute" to strike out all but the enacting clause of the House bill and insert in its stead a bill to establish in the Indian Territory a United States court with full jurisdiction over all issues of federal law, thereby relegating the federal courts at Fort Smith, Wichita, Fort Scott, and Graham to cases within the boundaries of the States in which these towns were situated. The House bill, meanwhile, retained its place on the calendar, but it and the Senate substitute disappeared from view until February 1889.[12]

The resistance mounted by the Five Tribes to the congressional reform program of 1888 was feeble. Three of the nations sent no delegates to Washington, and the Chickasaw Nation sent only one, G. W. Harkins. The Cherokee Nation was represented by a delegation of four, but their defense, as may be seen from their report to the national council at the end of the year, was founded in the wildest fantasy: "The Delegation soon ascertained that the Oklahoma Bill had been framed and introduced to enable one or more Railway Company [sic] to realize land grants through the 'Territory', and under the pressure of the Boomer and border state interest which has been so long demanding the opening of the Territory to white settlement."[13]

There is no dispute about the force of the pressure from "Boomer and border state interest." None were more aware of it and more responsive to it than a little group of congressmen from the Middle West, whose leader at that time was Springer. But the delegation's pigheaded reiteration of the oft-refuted assertion that the Territorial bills were a device for the railroads to exploit land grants was nullified by the very text of the bill they were opposing, since one of its provisions specifically declared forfeit all the land grants that Congress had previously offered. The delegates had seen this, of course, and reacted by standing reason on its head:

> These bills may reasonably be construed as part of the programme then formed [in 1866], and indicates the pressure of a mighty railroad interest which the Indians will have to continue to combat or be themselves overcome.
>
> This is so in the face of the provision on both bills repealing the said grants and pretending to annul the contracts made under them by such repeal.
>
> If the grants were valid and money borrowed under them the action of our party cannot invalidate them. If not valid no repeal is required.[14]

Here was a pretty example of inverted logic, for in reality, once the grants had been repealed, any question of their earlier validity became irrelevant. In fact, there was no such question: the grants had been conditional, and the railroads had failed to meet the conditions. It was to reassure the more suspicious and ignorant of the full-blood Cherokees that a provision to repeal the railroad grants was written into the bill, but George E. Sanders, S. W. Gray, W. P. Boudinot, and L. B. Bell may not have wanted the least educated of their fellow Cherokees to be reassured. Railways and other corporate bodies stood to gain much from the opening of the Unassigned Lands or the Cherokee Outlet, or from anything that would bring settlers to the Indian country; but instead of exercising their minds on this, the Cherokee delegates exhumed and rattled the skeleton of the land-grants scare of the 1870s.

Nor does it seem to have occurred to the delegates that, as far as the governments of the Five Tribes were concerned, the most objectionable features of the Springer bill were at the heart of it. The United States Government proposed in effect to annex land first and negotiate its purchase afterward. These faults were dissected by George Barnes and another Southern congressman, William Elliott (D, South Carolina), in a minority report dissenting from Springer and the other members of the House Territories Committee.[15]

In the spring of 1888 the Springer bill became inextricably locked in the procedural mechanism of the House. Springer resolved the impasse by reintroducing the measure, with a few small changes, as a new bill (HR 10614). In this form, the bill passed the House on February 1, 1889, by a vote of 147 to 102, with 75 abstentions. On February 5, it was referred to the Senate Committee on Territories.[16]

By this time the Cherokee Nation had in Dennis Bushyhead and Colonel Harris a delegation far more capable, intelligent, and resourceful than the quartet that had been sent to Washington in 1888. Their instructions on the courts issue, like those given to their predecessors,[17] were simple: if and when it became plain that Congress meant to create a court inside Indian Territory, the delegates were to press for its location at Fort Gibson. Evidently they must have caught the ear of Senator Berry, for when the courts bill came before the Senate, he urged the case for Fort Gibson, although without supporting it with an amendment.[18]

What had happened to the courts bill in the Senate was that Senator Jones of Arkansas, to Vest's very apparent anger, had introduced, on February 8, 1889, a second substitute, intended to supersede both Culberson's original and Vest's substitute. Jones's bill would preserve the main corpus of the Culberson House bill, but allowed for the establishment of a

United States court with jurisdiction in lesser cases over the whole Indian Territory. The court envisaged by Jones would handle all civil cases in which United States citizens resident in Indian Territory were party "when the whole of the thing in controversy or damages or money claimed shall amount to $100" and all criminal offenses against United States law except those punishable by death or imprisonment at hard labor. Responsibility for dealing with felonies would therefore rest with the authorities at Fort Smith, Graham, Wichita, Fort Scott, or Paris.

In drafting his bill, Jones sought to rectify the worst defects of the United States criminal law: murder was divided into two degrees; the criminality of an "accessory before the fact" was given a definition; and specific penalties were set for such offenses as attempted armed robbery, embezzlement, kidnapping, altering brands on livestock owned by others, obstructing railroad track, and various social misdemeanors.[19]

The Jones bill was, then, mindful of the interests of the electors of western Arkansas, placatory to the friends of the original Culberson bill, attentive to the demands for an overhaul of United States criminal law, and heedful of the arguments of all but the most relentless enemies of the "outside courts." In some of the senator's words:

> The evil sought to be remedied by this bill is the practical denial of justice at Fort Smith on account of that court being overrun with business. From the beginning to the end of the year the jail is all the time full of people who are brought from the Indian country to that town for trial.
>
> If the bill proposed by the Judiciary Committee should be enacted into law there would simply be a transfer of this court from Fort Smith to Muscogee in the Indian Territory, and there would be no lightening of the work, no lessening of the number of cases to be tried in that court below the number now tried at Fort Smith; but, on the contrary, if I understand the full purport of the bill, the number of cases will be larger to be tried in the newly-established court in the Indian country than is now tried at Fort Smith. . . .
>
> Establish this court of comparatively limited jurisdiction at first; let that be tried, and then in the course of a few years, if it shall appear to Congress and to the people that this court is able to enforce the law in all cases . . . it will be well enough then to invest the court with complete and entire jurisdiction.[20]

James Berry, the other senator from Arkansas, found a second line of argument for Fort Smith's retention of at least partial jurisdiction over serious crimes. Congress had recently appropriated $100,000 for the construction of a new courthouse at Fort Smith and another $50,000 to pay for a new federal jail there. Muskogee, as the senator averred, had neither courthouse nor jail; but neither had Fort Gibson.[21]

George Edmunds commented caustically on the Culberson bill and on the Courts Act of 1883. The Culberson bill was "an intensification of the existing law of extraditing everybody who did anything supposed to be an offense," and the 1883 act "was a bill of centrifugal jurisdiction, whirling them [the prisoners] around and dropping them into one State or the other as the case might be." Such measures as these, he believed,

> tend undoubtedly to increase the attendance of people at the court in the State of Kansas where these offenses are to be tried, and to enhance the value of hotel property there on account of there being more visitors. It would have the same effect, I suspect, at Paris [Graham], Texas, in the State of Texas, which was another place of revolving jurisdiction, to whip out a lot of people to that country, and a still heavier effect in whirling them down to the Arkansas River, where Fort Smith is situated.

"The interests of justice in the Indian Territory could best be served," he added, "by carrying the visible and practical administration of justice in the form of a court of the United States into the heart of the Territory, whose witnesses are near by and where impartiality would be certainly quite as likely to be exercised as in those cases of real extradition for trial."[22]

Some of these arguments were pushed further by John Tyler Morgan, whose clarity of vision and sureness of purpose were always evident. Morgan, unlike Edmunds, found something to say for the Culberson bill; the more courts, the stronger the chances of lessening the hardship and expense of defendants on bail or witnesses by travel between home and the place of trial. But Culberson's plan, opined Morgan, did not go nearly far enough: "That does not do any good; that does not meet the evil; that does not introduce the court into the Territory where it ought to be."

Morgan much preferred the Vest bill, because it provided for a United States court to be sited at Muskogee with plenary federal jurisdiction throughout Indian Territory. If the Vest bill could not be passed, he was "willing to fall back upon" the Jones bill, which would give partial jurisdiction to a court at Muskogee, "because I want to make a start upon it." He was in no doubt about what he wanted to see after that start had been made:

> As to the locality, it is one merely of convenience in the first place; and in the second place, it is to the effect that is produced by the holding of a court within that Territory upon the civilization of the Indians, and the further effect also of placing within that Territory in an active way the exercise by the United States Government of its power and jurisdiction over these people. We have got, sooner or later, to incorporate them into this Union either as a State or a Territorial government, and this is a step

in the right direction. It is the first step to take, that of establishing courts there for the administration of justice.[23]

One further alternative was never considered. At any time after the United States had concluded its treaties with the Creeks and Seminoles in 1866, a federal courthouse could have been placed in the Unassigned Lands; once the Atchison, Topeka and Santa Fe Railway had been opened for service, a good argument could have been made for siting it there. As yet, there was no town along the railway, for, though an attempt was being made to give the name Oklahoma City to Oklahoma Station,[24] its resident population numbered fewer than a dozen. But if a court had been installed there, it would have been followed by as much of a town as was needed to support its officers. In the meantime, both Purcell and Paul's Valley, in the Chickasaw Nation, were near enough and populous enough to supply jurors. Oklahoma City would have been within easy reach of about as many residents of the Indian Territory as could conveniently travel to Muskogee. Finally, the choice of Oklahoma City as court town, without seeming to cast a shadow over the actual sovereignty of any of the Five Tribes, would surely have given the United States the kind of leverage that must have induced the Creeks and Seminoles to sell land they could never use. By 1889, as it happened, they were thinking of selling it anyway.

Early in January 1889, in expectation of the passage of the Oklahoma bill (HR 10614), a Creek delegation consisting of Pleasant Porter, David Hodge, and Isparhecher traveled to Washington for discussions with Secretary of the Interior William Vilas. On January 19, in consideration of $2,280,857.10, the Creek delegation agreed to convey to the United States the "absolute cession and grant" of all the territory the Muskogee Nation had conditionally yielded to the United States in 1866, including those parts now occupied by other Indian tribes.[25]

The presence in this Creek delegation of men as keenly opposed to one another as Porter and Isparhecher, and the Muskogee national council's prompt ratification of the agreement, suggest that the tribe was more united on this issue than on any other in its history. There was a dissident group whose leaders threatened to kill the whole delegation, but it never came out into the open and soon subsided into silence.[26]

Not much could be done about the Creek cession unless the Seminoles agreed to relinquish their title to the adjacent land, but it was already known that they would. They met Vilas for formal negotiations in mid-February, and a bargain was struck for nearly $2 million. On February 19 the President transmitted the Seminole proposal to the Senate.[27]

Very soon after their arrival in Washington that month the delegates

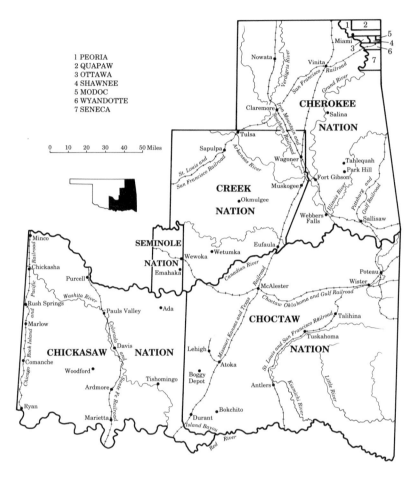

1 PEORIA
2 QUAPAW
3 OTTAWA
4 SHAWNEE
5 MODOC
6 WYANDOTTE
7 SENECA

MAP 2. THE FIVE NATIONS AND QUAPAW AGENCY, 1889 *(Reproduced from W. David Baird and Danney Goble,* The Story of Oklahoma *(Norman: University of Oklahoma Press, 1994), 277)*

of the Cherokee Nation were told that Springer's Oklahoma bill had been reported favorably by the Senate Committee on Territories and that "a very decided majority of the members of the Senate" would support it at the vote. On February 24 they engaged special counsel and wired Principal Chief Joel Mayes to join them in Washington, explaining their actions in a letter of the same date:

> We have sent for you by telegraph in order to get your advice and assistance in order that we . . . may devise plans by which we can defeat the Oklahoma Bill for a United States Territorial Government.
>
> Now . . . we deem it for the best interest of the Cherokees that legal

counsel be employed and we have therefore made a contract with C. C. Clements and W. S. Peabody, with the understanding that we pay them as follows, provided the said bill should be defeated, viz: They, Clements and Peabody, make a charge of fifteen thousand dollars for such service; but we agree to pay them immediately after the Bill is defeated the sum of $2,500.00 and then will pay them $2,500.00 more at the meeting of the Cherokee National Council on the first Monday in November, 1889. We will further urge upon the Council the importance of paying them the balance of $10,000.00 but if the Council should refuse to pay this balance, this obligation shall be of no further force and effect.[28]

A copy of this letter was passed to Clements and Peabody. It seems most improbable that even a bare majority in the Senate would have supported the Springer bill, but the question was never put to the test. On February 25, 1889, the day after the Cherokee delegates had hired the two Washington lawyers, a perfunctory attempt to bring the bill before the Senate was turned aside, and it disappeared from view. The Fiftieth Congress closed on March 4, and on April 1 the Cherokee Nation paid Clements and Peabody $2,500 for their services. A further payment of $500 followed later.[29]

Vest's amendment to the Culberson courts bill was agreed to by the Senate after its rejection of Jones's amendment, and a committee of conference was duly appointed to strike some sort of deal with the House. The Speaker appointed the House conferees three days later, on February 12, 1889. On February 26, the day after the demise of the Springer bill, the two sets of conferees emerged with their compromise. They had in effect assembled a new bill from components of the Culberson and Vest bills, the Jones amendment, and original provisions of their own. Both branches of Congress accepted these proposals, and on March 1, 1889, the composite bill was approved by President Cleveland.[30]

From that date the adjudication of minor crimes and all civil disputes over $100 or more would be the responsibility of the new United States district court for the Indian Territory at Muskogee. Jurisdiction over major crimes in the lower part of the Choctaw Nation, the Chickasaw Nation, the Neutral Strip (No Man's Land), and that portion of the Indian Territory formerly attached to the Northern District of Texas now belonged to the newly created fourth division of the Eastern District of Texas, with headquarters at Paris.

Serious crimes in the Cherokee, Muskogee, and Seminole nations and the upper part of the Choctaw Nation remained the preserve of the Western District of Arkansas. The district of Kansas retained jurisdiction over serious crimes committed within the Cherokee Outlet, the Oklahoma district, and the rest of the area allocated to it in 1883—except the

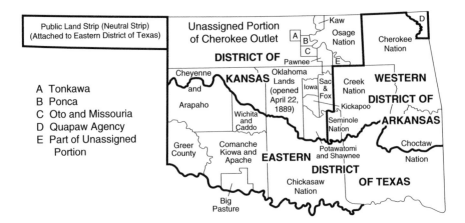

MAP 3. FEDERAL JUDICIAL DISTRICTS IN INDIAN TERRITORY, MARCH 1, 1889–MAY 1, 1890

Both the Courts Act ("Muskogee Act") of March 1, 1889, and Sections 13 and 15 of the Indian Appropriation Act of March 2, 1889, were the product of political compromise. They represented the most that the expansionist and homestead elements on Capitol Hill and elsewhere could get through Congress at that time.

The more radical advocates of courts reform had wanted the abolition of the exercise of federal jurisdiction within Indian Territory by courts located outside it. Their object was to create a new federal court, based in Indian Territory, with the power to determine all criminal and civil causes in which U.S. citizens were concerned.

Congress duly established a federal court at Muskogee, but restricted its remit to civil disputes involving $100 or more, and minor crimes; responsibility for the prosecution and trial of serious offenders remained with courts situated in Kansas, Arkansas, and Texas.

The area covered by the Wichita court was unaltered. The Fort Smith court was relieved of its jurisdiction in the Chickasaw Nation and more than two-thirds of the Choctaw Nation. These portions of Indian Territory, along with the tract previously policed by the Graham division of the Northern District of Texas, were allocated to the new Paris division of the Eastern District of Texas. (See text accompanying Map 4 for details.)

An important feature of the Courts Act of 1889 was its definition of the boundaries of Indian Territory. As a result, the Public Land Strip ceased to be No Man's Land; it now lay within the jurisdiction of the Paris and Muskogee courts.

Meanwhile, first the Creeks and then the Seminoles had agreed to sell to the United States their residual title to the lands they had conditionally ceded in 1866. Sections 13 and 15 of the Indian Appropriation Act of March 2, 1889, provided for the release of the unassigned (Oklahoma) part of the Creek and Seminole cession for homesteading and settlement. The opening of this small central tract of Indian Territory fell far short of the demands of the Territorialization and homestead lobbies; but together with the installation of the federal court at Muskogee, it brought their goals much nearer.

No governmental or judicial apparatus was reserved for the Oklahoma lands after the opening of April 22, 1889. Public order was maintained by deputy marshals of the Wichita and Muskogee courts, the army, and an ad hoc scheme of local government. The federal courts were greatly overextended: the Muskogee court was unable to serve the whole of Indian Territory, nor could the Paris court deal effectively with serious crimes committed in the Public Land Strip or on the western reservations that had been the jurisdictional preserve of the Graham court. It was, however, recognized on all sides that this position was not intended to obtain for very long.

During this period, the Fairchild Commission (popularly known as the Cherokee Commission) was negotiating for the purchase of the Cherokee Outlet and areas occupied by smaller tribes west of the ninety-sixth meridian, so that the lands could be opened for settlement. Congress and the Harrison administration were awaiting the outcome of these negotiations before conferring Territorial status upon Oklahoma. When, late in 1889, it was seen that the Fairchild Commission was making no progress, a bill was prepared in terms which presupposed the eventual success of the negotiations. These provisions were incorporated in the Organic Act, popularly but misleadingly called the Oklahoma Act, approved by President Harrison on May 2, 1890.

After the passage of the Organic Act, the expression "Indian Territory" covered, for practical and judicial purposes, only the Quapaw Agency and the country actually inhabited by the Five Tribes and under the political control of their governments.

The measure provided a temporary government by the name Territory of Oklahoma for all the lands relinquished by the Creeks and Seminoles, added the Public Land Strip (thereafter called the Oklahoma Panhandle), and attached the Cherokee Outlet for judicial purposes.

Besides this, the act greatly strengthened the authority of the Muskogee court, thereby promoting the influence of a system of law enforcement administered by the federal Government. The Muskogee court was given the power to determine probate and the duty of administering a substantial body of civil law drawn from the State code of Arkansas. The Arkansas criminal code, wherever it did not conflict with federal law, was adopted in its entirety and applied by the U.S. courts at Fort Smith, Paris, and Muskogee, with the two former retaining the higher jurisdiction throughout the Five Nations.

Another very important clause in the act enabled citizens of the Five Nations to acquire U.S. citizenship without forfeiture of their tribal rights.

Anomaly and paradox continued to stalk the language of the legislators and the effects of their actions. In the Quapaw Agency (but nowhere else) the Muskogee court held jurisdiction in cases of higher as well lower crime from May 2, 1890, to May 3, 1892, when Congress created a third division of the U.S. Judicial District of Kansas with headquarters at Fort Scott.

In requiring the Fort Scott court to prosecute "all [federal] crimes . . . defined as infamous . . . of which the courts in Kansas have heretofore had jurisdiction" in the Quapaw Agency, the lawmakers ignored the fact that the Kansas courts had had no such jurisdiction for two years.

The structure of criminal and civil law which Congress had bestowed upon Indian Territory was a Babel of common law, U.S. statute law, and Arkansas State law. Its obscurities and contradictions led to many disputes among the three or four federal courts, and between them and the courts and governments of the Five Tribes. The general effect of the reforms of 1890 was a concerted demand from interested parties in both Oklahoma Territory and Indian Territory for more reform, with the aim of securing the liquidation of the tribal courts and governments and the formation of a single State. The appointment of the Dawes Commission and the Courts Act of March 1, 1895, were the first notable results of that agitation.

small Quapaw Agency, which gained the distinction,[31] perhaps by acci-
dent, of being the only part of the Indian Territory where the Muskogee
court held jurisdiction in all criminal matters, major or minor.

There were other important provisions in the act: "all laws having the
effect to prevent the Cherokee, Choctaw, Creek, Chickasaw and Seminole
Nations . . . from lawfully entering leases or contracts for mining coal for
a period not exceeding ten years" were repealed, and several modifications
proposed by Senator Jones were grafted onto the United States criminal
law (but not those for which the need was greatest—the division of murder into two defined categories and statutory recognition of the accessory
before the fact).[32]

The Northern District of Texas lost all jurisdiction in the Indian
Territory, although its marshal and district attorney foolishly tried to exercise it in retrospect over crimes that had occurred in No Man's Land
before March 1, 1889.[33]

So, at last, twenty-three years after the Reconstruction treaties had
been proclaimed, the United States could lay the cornerstone for a courthouse in Indian Territory. Muskogee at this time had about 1,200 inhabitants, most of them United States citizens. The Creeks in whose midst the
town was situated were better disposed than the Cherokees toward the
prospect of a federal court in their country, which may be why the United
States Government had ruled out any idea of locating it at Fort Gibson.
Travel to Muskogee from most parts of the Chickasaw Nation and the
remoter sections of the Choctaw Nation was awkward; but the town was,
by the norms of the time and place, within comfortable reach elsewhere.
Nearly all the settlements in the Indian Territory lay along one or other of
the railways, the MK&T especially, and much of the court's work would
be provided by them.

On the day that he signed the Muskogee bill into law, March 1, 1889,
President Cleveland also approved a bill embodying the Government's
agreement with the Muskogee Nation for its surrender of all title to
the lands ceded in 1866. With the Springer bill blocked by the Senate, a
bill had to be drafted specially and rushed through Congress to seal the
agreement.[34]

Since the Seminole agreement had not yet been ratified by the council
of the nation, the two transactions could not be combined in a single bill.
Instead, provision for the Seminole purchase was included in the Indian
appropriation bill (HR 12578), and several related—but not financial—
amendments were tacked on. If these amendments had been presented
in a bill of their own in the closing days of the session, they would have
excited enough opposition to stifle them several times over. For this rea-

son, use was made of the widely condemned but widely practiced device of a rider on a financial bill to slip a piece of general legislation through Congress. Thus the proposal to pay the Seminole Nation $1,912,942.02 "for all the right, title, interest, and claim which said nation of Indians may have" (from its conditional cession of 1866) met little opposition.

Nor was any obstacle put in the way of the amendments that came next, introduced by Samuel Peel (D, Arkansas) in the last days of February. These declared the lands sold by the Creeks and Seminoles a part of the public domain, to be reserved for settlement under the terms of a presidential proclamation, and authorized the President to appoint three commissioners, "not more than two of whom shall be members of the same political party," to negotiate with the Cherokees for the Outlet. On March 2, 1889, about forty-eight hours before Cleveland was succeeded in office by Benjamin Harrison, the bill received the presidential assent.[35]

Ratification by the Seminole council of the Washington agreement followed a fortnight later. On March 23 Harrison issued a proclamation setting out the conditions under which the Oklahoma district, the only vacant portion of the Creek and Seminole cession, would be opened to homesteaders at noon on April 22.[36] Owing to the failure of the latest Territorial bill, the newly settled district would be without any official form of local government; there would be only the United States courts for Kansas and Indian Territory, whose jurisdiction after the opening would be exactly as it had been before, supplemented by soldiers from Fort Reno whose orders were to prevent or quell any civil disorder.

At the appointed moment, cavalry trumpets and firearms signaled the start of "Harrison's Horse Race" from various points along the perimeter of the Unassigned Lands. Simultaneously, in the heart of the district, thousands of men, mainly members or employees of Kansas townsite companies, crawled out of freight cars or swarmed out of the long grass by the railroad tracks to scoop the real prizes—the most promising town lots in Guthrie and Oklahoma City. Some, who had been appointed deputy United States marshals or to other official positions, had only to step off the railroad right-of-way to claim their quarter sections.[37] As one participant remarked, "The imbecile policy of the government in the manner of opening the new Territory [sic] for settlement invited just this sort of enterprise."[38] But the central problem stemmed from the failure of Congress to frame Section 13 of the Indian Appropriation Act in the plain and unambiguous language that is the enemy of litigation.

Section 13 did not state that any person inside the district at the moment it was opened was barred from acquiring land under the homestead or townsite laws. It debarred anyone who should "enter upon and occupy" any part of the tract before the stated date. Many lawyers' fees were to be earned in disputes growing from different constructions of that phrase.

"Perhaps Oklahoma City did not have as many as Guthrie, for it was not a land office town," observed one settler, "but there must have been more than a hundred lawyers in Oklahoma City in a week after the opening. Most of these fellows claimed to be expert land office lawyers . . . they would furnish the evidence and win the claim for you for a little additional consideration."[39] It was not always as simple as that; one celebrated case was unresolved until 1909.[40] Still, the point about the profusion of lawyers was well made. Even three months later, when the population was smaller than it had been in the first days of the settlement, Guthrie had 115 in a population of 9,347.[41]

By nightfall on April 22, the Oklahoma district contained between 50,000 and 60,000 people. Guthrie had roughly 10,000;[42] Oklahoma City, perhaps as many. Less fancied sites such as Lisbon (Kingfisher), El Reno, Norman, Lexington, and Stillwater had each attracted several thousand. Much fraud had accompanied the land rush, but hardly any violence and no bloodshed. Most of the garish yarns that packed the telegraphic columns of distant newspapers for a week or so after the Run were untrue.

Gambling violated no federal law, and gaming dens sprang up in abundance; but for a while those who frequented them behaved well. Dependable evidence of this comes from a letter written by United States Marshal William Jones of the Kansas court to his wife. The letter was written at Guthrie a week after the opening.

> There is over 50 gambling houses. The town only one week old and claims 15,000 inhabitants. . . . There has not been a single man killed in the territory [district] since I came down. I never saw a community more orderly with the exception of the gambling houses and they are orderly although they are poor deluded fools who patronize them. No people are more orderly than these people, and I am disgusted with the newspapers that are continually reporting such sensational lies. There is not one word of truth in what they say regarding the lawlessness.[43]

At first, the antiliquor statutes were enforced rigorously by the deputy marshals and soldiers. Later, the laws operated to the partial satisfaction of all; saloons and barrooms were banned, but no one who wanted a drink experienced much difficulty in getting one. Reports of liquor being confiscated or discovered were commonplace, but it is obvious that a great deal more was not confiscated or discovered. At Guthrie, for example, there was the Woodbine, "a hotel on corner of Harrison and Railroad avenue, which is run on the broad plan of anything you order even to soda pop and a fair damsel."[44]

Both Guthrie and Oklahoma City were quick to adopt ad hoc systems of town government. A lively rivalry subsisted between the four contiguous municipalities that constituted Guthrie. In Oklahoma City a quasi-political contest was fought, with much bitterness on both sides, by the "Seminoles" (nicknamed after the Seminole Town and Improvement Company) and the "Kickapoos" (after the tribe of local Indians least receptive to the ways of civilization, but also, supposedly, because they "kicked" against their opponents' arrogation of authority).

Plans for local government had been devised by the "Seminoles," whose candidates were then elected to every office. From the beginning, their authority was given de facto recognition by General Wesley Merritt, commanding officer of the Department of the Missouri, and accordingly the provost marshal from Fort Reno, Captain Daniel Stiles. Besides closing down the gambling dens from time to time, helping the new town policemen to enforce a ban on "soliciting openly on the street," and assisting the deputy United States marshals to regulate the antiliquor laws, Stiles gave general backing to the town government. Fresh council elections were called after the "Seminole" proposals for a city charter had been rejected by popular vote. Stiles was accused, perhaps unjustly, of siding with the "Seminoles" when he ordered his men to break up a crowd at the polling place. Most of the offices, including that of mayor, fell to the "Kickapoos" anyway.[45]

There was very little violence in any of the new settlements during their early months; less, perhaps, than in many Eastern communities of comparable size. No one was slain in Guthrie until August 6, 1889, when a physician shot and killed another man in a dispute over a land claim; and he was acquitted on grounds of self-defense.[46] Several men died violently in Oklahoma City and Kingfisher in the same period, and in Oklahoma City there was a single simulacrum of the frontier-town desperado in the person of the "boy murderer," Clyde Mattox—"sallow, frail, keen, determined, and polished like cold steel."[47] Young Mattox's career as criminal, escaper, and convict excited innumerable newspaper stories without being anything like enough to sustain portrayal of Oklahoma City as a typically gory Western boom town. A little later on the newly settled country was plagued by robber gangs,[48] but these men were the profiteers, not the products, of a society in flux.

It is difficult to establish but easy to visualize a connection between the Muskogee bill and the proclamation to open the Unassigned Lands. Vest's amendment to the Culberson bill had been introduced on April 16,

1888, nine months before the Creeks had agreed to sell their interest in the cession of 1866, and the issue thereafter, or as much of it as was for the public ear, related to how much jurisdiction was to be awarded to the projected court. But by the time Vest's bill was given to the floor of the Senate, it was February 8,[49] and everyone in the Capitol with any interest in the subject must have known that the Seminole Nation's relinquishment of its residual title would soon follow, clearing the way for a series of land openings. The imminent eruption of scores of thousands of United States citizens in a district hitherto almost devoid of lawful inhabitants without a scrap of civil law to accommodate the differences inherent in the evolution of a governable society must have worked on the minds of the conference committee on the courts bill and impelled them toward the conclusion of an agreement.

James Shackelford, a Republican from Kentucky, was appointed as the first district judge of the new federal court and took up his duties at Muskogee early in April 1889.[50] His first court term was short, from early June until the Fourth of July and lightening the criminal and civil dockets by only 24 and 90 cases, respectively. But already the necessity for such a court and the inadequacy of the court after Congress had provided it had been demonstrated: at the adjournment, 230 cases had not been disposed of, and "a great many more" had yet to be filed.[51]

When the court went into session again, early in September, the criminal docket was so large that the civil cases were "all put out of sight" until it had been worked through. By the middle of the month, the "little coop of a jail" had forty-six inmates.[52] By June 30, 1890, a further 284 criminal and 194 civil cases had been wiped off the slate, yet despite Shackelford's efficiency and dispatch, several hundred items in each category had not been reached.[53] It is impossible to say how many of these cases originated in the Oklahoma district and how many in the remainder of the Indian Territory, but with the passage of a little time crime in Oklahoma became commoner. Judge Cassius Foster of the Wichita court had 43 murder cases before him at the beginning of the September term, 1890, most of them derived from murders committed in the Oklahoma district during the nine months or so prior to May 2 of that year. At that time the population of the district had settled at just over 61,000; so even when allowance is made for uncaught murderers and killings where self-defense had been established at the first hearing, the statistics do not postulate a society that was light on the trigger, given the circumstances.[54]

Once the Unassigned Lands had been populated, a Territorial government could not be far away. Congress was showered with petitions and memorials from the more politically minded of the settlers, but an answer had to be found to the question of how great an area could be placed under the Territorial system. A speaking tour in September 1889 by Springer, Perkins, and most of the other leading promoters of Territorial government elicited renewed agitation from their supporters not merely in Guthrie and Oklahoma City but Sapulpa, Muskogee, Vinita, and the Chickasaw Nation.[55]

Much would hinge upon the speed with which the Fairchild Commission—the so-called Cherokee Commission—provided for by Section 14 of the Indian Appropriation Act of March 2, 1889, could fulfill their brief. The commissioners were charged with the task of persuading the Cherokees and other Indians "owning or claiming lands lying west of the ninety-sixth degree of longitude in the Indian Territory" to cede to the United States "all their title, claim, or interest of every kind or character in and to said lands" for the consideration of $1.25 per acre.[56]

The three commissioners arrived in the Cherokee Nation in July 1889 as the Cherokee government was negotiating with members of the Cherokee Strip Live Stock Association for an agreement that would allow the cattlemen a further fifteen years' use of the Outlet for a total of $6.6 million, payable in annual installments. This sum was not much smaller than what the commission was authorized to offer the Cherokees for a final surrender of title.

Principal Chief Joel Mayes was inimical to the commission and dismissive of their offer. The commissioners, strongly supported by Secretary of the Interior John Noble, wanted President Harrison to issue an order for the clearance of cattle from the Outlet,[57] but the Chief Executive temporized. Harrison had still not acted on December 9, 1889, when Orville Platt, chairman of the Senate Committee on the Territories, introduced a new Oklahoma bill, or even on February 5, when the Platt bill was taken up for debate.[58]

It was, explained Platt, a bill whose objectives were tightly circumscribed:

> There are a great many questions which have been suggested with relation to the Territory which is to be established in Oklahoma or in the Indian Territory, and this bill is simply the ordinary bill which is to be passed for the organization of a Territorial government applicable only to the land which is now open to settlement.
>
> Many of the questions came before the Committee on Territories, and we felt that if we went outside of providing the ordinary Territorial government for that portion of the country which has been declared open to settlement, we should get into infinite discussion, and that the first thing it was best to do was to pass such a bill as we have reported here and then take up these other questions.[59]

Opposition to the limited nature of the proposed bill was led by Plumb, Vest, and Eugene Hale (R, Maine). Hale maintained that the "paraphernalia of an entire Territorial government" for the Oklahoma district as it then stood should be withheld unless it was "most affirmatively and distinctly stated" in the bill that the area "covered by this Territorial scheme" would be greatly expanded. Otherwise, he argued, the inhabitants of the newly made Territory would resist any attempt to weaken their autonomy and political influence through amalgamation.[60]

Plumb renewed the suggestion that the Neutral Strip should be included in Oklahoma Territory, affecting to be intent only upon securing the well-being of the few thousand men and women who had moved into the area:

> I say the condition of things existing in No Man's Land today is a scandal on the legislation of this Government. It is not a Botany Bay. . . . The people who have gone there to make homes are just as honest, just as sensible and level-headed people as can be found in the world; but the misfortune is that every man who steals a steer in Texas and wishes to escape from the jurisdiction of the courts there runs over to this region.[61]

In cold fact, the worst criminal conflict that ever occurred in No-Man's-Land was an all-Kansas affair. On July 26, 1888, the heavily armed representatives of two towns in Stevens County in southwest Kansas, engaged in a struggle over which was to become established as the seat of local government, were stalking one another in the Neutral Strip when one party allowed itself to be surprised by its quarry. Four men, including the sheriff of Stevens County, were murdered.[62] Nearly three months later, Attorney-General Garland wrongly instructed the United States district attorney for the Northern District of Texas that No-Man's-Land lay within the jurisdiction of that court, commenting that "it is not to be tolerated that the lawlessness resulting in so many alleged murders should be disregarded."[63] The prosecution failed, and a hugely expensive attempt to claim retrospective jurisdiction for the Paris, Texas, court, was carried all the way to the United States Supreme Court before it crumbled.[64]

But even this period, before No-Man's-Land was brought by statute into the Paris division of the Eastern District of Texas, knew only a few isolated cases of murder among those actually living in the Neutral Strip. Many years afterward a sometime resident explained why; few of the settlers owned anything to be killed for, and there was a general recognition that

> the absence of restraining statutes gave the settlers, and officers from the states, a free hand in the capture and removal of those who had broken

state laws. Statutes frequently hamper the officer in his struggle with the outlaw while statutes never restrain the outlaw. But in No Man's Land, the officer was as free from legal restraint as the outlaw always makes himself.[65]

In a speech that was sometimes muddled and sometimes downright dishonest, Plumb exaggerated the extent to which the Neutral Strip had afforded sanctuary for fugitives and appeared to doubt whether the Paris court really had jurisdiction, even after March 1, 1889. He was, however, fully justified in drawing attention to the remoteness of Paris from No Man's Land: "[I]t is 900 miles by the way people have to travel."[66]

On the other hand, this narrow rectangle was at no point less than 125 miles west of the Oklahoma district, and it was absurd to suggest that these two altogether dissimilar segments of land could be combined under a Territorial government unless the Outlet, which separated them, was included. ·

Plumb nevertheless simulated unconcern over what was to become of the Outlet, predicting only that "prior to the adjournment of this Congress we shall have possession of and title to that Outlet." He blandly ignored the fact, well known to him, that the creation of a Territorial government involved considerations far weightier than the greater convenience of a journey of 125 miles to federal court than one of 900 miles, not least because, once Territorial government had been installed, the significance of the federal court would be much diminished. The Senate did not mind; it agreed to the amendment.[67]

Authority was imparted to Plumb's prophecy about the Outlet, and credibility removed from his disclaimer of interest, by his political proximity to Secretary Noble and the two Republicans on the Cherokee Commission. Promptly upon the acceptance of his amendment, he put down another, under which the United States courts for Oklahoma Territory would assume jurisdiction over federal offenses committed in the Outlet. The proposal was defeated, but it would be resuscitated later in the House.[68] Less than a week later, on February 17, 1890, President Harrison proclaimed that no more livestock could be driven into the Outlet and that any already there must be removed no later than October 1.[69]

When the House began its debate on the Oklahoma bill, also on February 17, it had been rewritten by the House Committee on the Territories, whose chairman was now Isaac Struble. It was really a substitute bill, retaining only the prefix of the original, S.895. In it the two main features of earlier, unsuccessful Oklahoma bills reappeared: the new Territory would comprise the entire Indian country, other than the Five Nations but including the Outlet; and for the administration of United

States laws, the Five Nations area would be apportioned between three courts with full jurisdiction and based in the nations.

Among the innovatory proposals of the redrawn bill was a set of provisions which would graft upon the United States law for application within the Indian Territory only most of the misdemeanors and lesser felonies punishable under the statutes of the State of Arkansas and forty-six chapters of the Arkansas civil code. The felonies included larceny, seduction, extortion, kidnapping, and embezzlement; among the misdemeanors were libel and slander, abduction, assault and battery, horse racing, obscenity, and breaking the sabbath. Attachment, civil rights, divorce, landlord and tenant, marriages, and wills and testaments were among the civil matters to be adopted from the Arkansas code.[70]

The House's substitute was strenuously opposed by George Barnes, who pointed out that it differed from the Senate bill "not merely in language and phraseology, but also in policy," proposing as it did "not merely to form a Territory out of lands to which we hold title but also out of lands to which we may hereafter acquire title." "As long as the land is in dispute the government which you create over it is a government *in nubibus*. . . . [Y]ou erect your superstructure without laying a basis upon which your superstructure shall rest, and therefore the superstructure ought to fall."[71]

Quite so, but the redrafting of the bill did not proclaim any change of policy. The House's latest proposals were as consistent with the aims of its territorial expansionists ever since 1865 as the Senate bill was consonant with the prevailing temper of the upper chamber during that period. Silas Hare, a Democrat from Texas, introduced a memorial from William Byrd, governor of the Chickasaw Nation, protesting against the courts provision of the bill.[72] Byrd said that from its inception the court at Muskogee had been looked upon by the Chickasaws "with great distrust and misgiving." It was "a radical innovation" for which they were not ready, and there was a "want of a sufficient number of competent and impartial jurymen in the Indian Territory."

In the opinion of the Chickasaws, or at least their governor:

[T]he jurisdiction now conferred on the Paris division of the eastern district of Texas, on the district court of the western district of Arkansas, at Fort Smith, and the district court of Kansas, at Wichita, is satisfactory and in all respects better than the conferring of such jurisdiction would be on any United States court that could be organized in the Indian Territory. Jurymen in those courts are intelligent and impartial, they are disinterested, and in every sense and for every reason, until our people are better prepared, these courts should be left undisturbed. . . .

The time may come when by the direction of their people they may voluntarily consent to a Territorial or State government; but that time is not now, and your memorialist appeals to the sense of justice and fair dealing of your honorable bodies not to bring the mighty power of the Government of the United States down on a peaceable, confiding, and defenseless people by the establishment of a Territorial or State government or courts within their borders, which are but one part of the machinery of such governments. It is but the beginning of the end, and the end is the annihilation of the Indian tribes in the Indian Territory.[73]

Hare asserted that the Muskogee court, although overburdened at first, now had too little to do and cost too much. Any theory that, with the excitement and social dislocation of the Oklahoma Run already a matter of history, the need for such a court had receded, would be shown by events to be spectacularly wrong. But both Hare's speech and Byrd's memorial were too charged with political self-interest to be worthy of respect.

Behind Hare were the lawyers, bankers, and merchants who ran the local Democratic party and were anxious to preserve for northeast Texas the perquisites flowing from the Paris court's jurisdiction in the Indian Territory. Byrd, like Frank Overton before him, was a Chickasaw cattleman with very little Indian blood whose use of large tracts of common land encouraged him to align himself with the Pullback party, which consisted of conservative full-bloods and a few mixed-bloods with everything to gain from continuation of the status quo. Byrd's credentials as spokesman for his people were dubious in the extreme; his election to the governorship in 1888 had been secured by sharp practice or worse.[74]

Another Southern Democrat, Charles Hooker, attacked the courts provisions of the Oklahoma bill with passion and precision.[75] He saw that the adoption of the Arkansas statutes by the Indian Territory federal courts anticipated and would hasten the abolition of the tribal courts without hindering their operation. The yoking of these proposals with a bill to convert Oklahoma district into a United States Territory indicated a design to supplant the five tribal governments: "You are endeavoring to make the laws of the State of Arkansas, under the judicial system you propose to establish in the Indian Territory, the laws by which the laws of the Indians themselves are to be adjudicated."

Hooker recalled that he had not opposed the legislation enabling the Creeks and Seminoles to complete the sale of their lands; the Indians were, he had thought, "the best judges of their own interests." Even so,

I have doubted the policy on the part of the Indians to sell lands to the Government of the United States which should enable it to establish a Territorial form of Government, to be occupied by white people, and, subsequently, to be a State occupied by white people. Because . . . it would furnish a leverage by which you might eventually extinguish the title of these people to all their lands.[76]

As for the plan to place the Cherokee Outlet within the jurisdiction of the federal courts in Oklahoma Territory, "I do not look with much favor upon such a proposition as that, nor do I like this idea of taking other people's property for 'judicial purposes.'"[77]

Another opponent of the bill, Charles Turner, commented scathingly on the closing lines of one of its later sections under which "any member or citizen of any Indian tribe or nation in the Indian Territory" was to be allowed "to invoke the aid" of the United States courts therein "for the protection of his person and property, as though he was a citizen of the United States":

> I am not a lawyer or the son of a lawyer, nor does it seem to me that it requires any remarkable legal lore to see that this provision at once abrogates every particle of power in the Indian courts, for any man who finds himself convicted by the judgment of an Indian court can under the provision at once become, so far as this matter is concerned, a citizen of the United States. There no longer exists any constitutional tribunal having authority to enforce the laws which the local legislature or the congress of the several Indian nations may make. Their power to make laws remains in form, but there has been taken from their hands the power to enforce such laws.

Turner's remarks on the "extraordinary legislation" by which a form of government was to be provided by the United States for the Outlet were even more corrosive: "There was a time when a great deal was said about 'taxation without representation.' This is worse than that: that is, in my judgment, the absolute confiscation of the property of people without representation on this floor." In his opinion, "[T]he Senate bill covers all the ground that we ought now to cover."[78]

The extreme position among the reformers was occupied by such men as Henry Morey (R, Ohio), who maintained that even the House's substitute bill did not go nearly far enough:

> I shall be prepared to unite in any effort that may be made on this floor to strike out the anomalous, un-American, and unrepublican provisions of this bill, which the jurisdiction of extra-territorial courts is extended for the punishment of crimes and offenses committed within this Territory, and shall favor the extension of the jurisdiction of the Territorial courts created for the Territory of Oklahoma over the entire Indian Territory. . . .
>
> The Indian Territory as it now exists is a well-defined part of our country, with a public history pertaining to the whole Territory. It is advantageously situated to become a great and powerful State, and I urge

my objection to any temporary expedient of legislation which may tend to permanently divide this magnificent country by Territorial lines. This bill does so divide it. . . .

In my judgment it will tend to the permanent division of the Indian Territory.[79]

Both Morey and an ally from the Democratic side, Joseph Washington of Tennessee, inveighed against the courts at Fort Smith and Paris— "What a feast for lawyers, bailiffs, jurors, and those who usually assist in the administration of justice!"—"A useless extravagance which ought not to be longer indulged."[80]

Beneath the hyperbole was a layer of fact; but much of the rage was synthetic or applicable to a different set of premises. Obviously, if the Indian Territory was divided into three judicial districts, each with its own battalion of appointees and a large body of extra criminal law to enforce besides more work in the civil field, the bill to the United States Treasury would be heavier yet. Did men like Morey and Washington believe that most congressmen, or their taxpaying constituents, would regard the expenditure as money well spent? The truth was that the Ohio Republican, the Tennessee Democrat, and those who agreed with them objected to the Fort Smith and Paris courts chiefly because the continuing connection between those courts and the Five Tribes country impeded their hopes of bringing the whole Indian Territory into a single State or organized Territory.

For all the exclamatory verbiage they could not have believed, as Morey professed, that the formation of Oklahoma Territory in the western half of the Indian country and the maintenance of some kind of separate jurisdictional structure in the eastern half would throw up a permanent barrier between the two. It was, after all, crystal clear that the Oklahoma bill was intended to expedite the reverse. But for men like Morey, and Bishop Perkins of Kansas, beside whom William Springer and Isaac Struble were models of moderation, the day after tomorrow meant the future indefinite.

On March 13, 1890, the House substitute for the Senate bill was passed, after minor amendments, 140–25. Upon an unopposed motion by Perkins, it was retitled "A bill to organize the Territory of Oklahoma, to establish courts in the Indian Territory, and for other purposes."[81] The Senate rejected the bill as redrafted by the House in its entirety and appointed Platt, Shelby Cullom (R, Illinois), and James Jones as its conferees.[82] This was on March 18. Next day the House insisted on its amendments, and Struble, Perkins, and Springer were named as conferees.[83]

On March 25, Principal Chief Mayes and delegate Bushyhead, in Washington, wrote to Peabody and Clements. The letter itself seems to have been lost or destroyed, but it informed the attorneys that "another Oklahoma Bill had passed the House of Representatives, which included within that Territory over six million (6,000,000) acres of Cherokee lands; and that, while they [Mayes and Bushyhead] did not feel authorized to make a contract for any stated price, they believed the Cherokee Nation would pay a very liberal fee, if we would have that portion of the Bill eliminated which took the Cherokee outlet into the Oklahoma territory."[84]

Peabody and Clements had received only $3,000 of the $15,000 the Cherokees had agreed to pay for their earlier intervention; but only the first $2,500 of this sum could be deemed a strictly contractual liability, apparently. It is a fair surmise that the attorneys realized, first, that in a renewal of the association with Cherokee politicians lay their best hope of collecting the rest of what they may have regarded as a debt of honor, and secondly that if the Cherokee Nation's lucrative arrangement with the Cherokee Strip Live Stock Association could remain in force, the nation would be in a position to reward them handsomely for preserving its sovereignty over the Outlet. A letter written by Mayes three days later confirms that the Cherokees gave no specific undertaking while hinting heavily at the prospect of a generous settlement:

> I will personally make a friendly request of you, not in the capacity of a delegate authorized by the National Council, to use your influence to defeat these provisions in said Bill. I make this request not with a view of binding myself or the Nation to pay you an Attorney fee in the matter, but on account of the friendship you have shown and services rendered to our people in the past on similar occasions.
>
> Now if you can successfully defeat these provisions in this Bill and you can show to the Cherokee people that your services have been valuable in this respect I feel assured the Cherokees will act liberal towards you, but that matter will be left with the National Council.[85]

Later, with negotiations between the Cherokee government and the Cherokee Commission approaching a climax, the attorneys reminded Mayes, "We were successful in this undertaking and in having other changes made, as suggested by you at that time. No compensation has been received for these services."[86]

When the members of the Committee of Conference found themselves deadlocked over the Oklahoma bill, they did not, as was customary, report to their respective houses on the differences between them. Instead, they drafted a compromise bill, with a strong recommendation for its acceptance. Much of the new bill followed the outline of the House amendment, but the Senate conferees insisted upon several alterations. Thus, the existing judicial district would be split into three divisions rather than the three distinct districts that had been proposed within identical boundaries. The formal complaints of delegations from the Five Tribes were met by the insertion of amendments "specifically guarding the rights of those nations under their treaties with the United States." In particular, the Cherokee Outlet would not be included even nominally within the political boundaries of Oklahoma Territory, although it would be attached to it for federal judicial purposes.

A clause to enable any citizen of the Five Tribes to choose to be tried in or conduct a suit in a United States rather than a tribal court was not deleted; but on the whole there was far less immediate damage to Indian sovereignty and self-government than had seemed probable.[87] Either, then, Peabody and Clements had persuaded a wavering senator on the Conference Committee to hold the line against the three House conferees, or (much likelier) at least one of the House conferees had been induced by these silver-tongued attorneys to temper his reformist zeal.

Nonetheless, only half a withdrawal had been made on the question of the Outlet. By insisting that the Oklahoma courts, Territorial and federal, should take jurisdiction over the area, the House conferees showed their conviction that the Outlet would soon be merged with Oklahoma politically as well as judicially. Yet the Cherokee Nation's sovereignty had not been wrested away; the Cherokee government retained the power of negotiation with the United States, and even sale under duress was better than seizure.

Although both chambers accepted the conference report, the Senate did so only after further lengthy debate and a vote—50 yeas, 5 nays, and 29 absentees. George Vest, one of the five dissenters, chaffed at the chequered character of the new measure: "The whole bill all the way through seems to have been put in by parcels, as Desdemona listened to Othello's story of his military exploits and dangers by flood and hell. It seems as if everybody who came along with a suggestion got it into this bill."[88]

Indeed so much had got into the forty-four sections of the bill that it was only after President Harrison had appended his signature that someone noticed an error in the wording of one of the boundary clauses, the effect of which was to donate a large slice of the State of Texas to the Territory of Oklahoma. The bill was recovered from Harrison, corrected, sent back to him, and became law on May 2, 1890.[89]

For a plain exposition of its significance as a document of policy, we need not look beyond the published views of the chairman of the House Committee on Territories. Speaking of the "language in the bill providing that the boundaries of Oklahoma Territory may be changed at any time and additions made to it, and that disposition of the Territory otherwise may be made by Congress," he proffered this explanation: "That language is in harmony with the united sentiment of the conferees of both bodies, that under no circumstances, in so far as present action can go, shall there be two States erected within what is now known as the Indian Territory."[90]

In the Senate, Matthew Butler of South Carolina, another of the five who opposed the adoption of the conference report, turned critically to one of the motive forces of that policy.

> [W]hen we yield to clamor—for that is what it is—from the outside we are too apt to go astray. We experienced precisely the same thing in the last Congress when there were a lot of boomers camping along the border, demanding to cross into Oklahoma. I myself was told as a member of the Committee on Treasuries that if I did not yield certain points there would be war upon the border. . . . We yielded then and we are yielding now to an unreasoning and unreasonable clamor from the outside made by people who are anxious to get these public lands.[91]

Land hunger and land greed were certainly at the root of much of the agitation, although executive and congressional action in relation to the Indian Territory during the late 1880s and early 1890s, while often seemingly in direct response to popular pressure, may have been mainly the product of political imperialism in which the defeat and abolition of the tribal governments was partly an end in itself and partly the means to other ends. Satisfaction of popular material demands was one of these. Consolidation of the Union in preparation for a more strenuous part on the world stage may have been another. Nor should one overlook the propensity of government to extend its reach by the growing weight of its expanding career bureaucracy.

Further momentum was imparted by the pressure upon American society which built up during the last third of the nineteenth century through heavy and decreasingly homogeneous immigration from Europe. Immigration and industrialization were accompanied by, and may have caused, a partial displacement of the native-born population. Industrialization, again, and the centralizing tendencies of a proliferating federal Executive had made great inroads upon Jefferson's America. The opening of Oklahoma and the semipopulated tribal lands of the Indian Territory would at once offer a revival ground for Jeffersonian values, serve the exigencies created by the social and economic imperatives of the day, and provide an outlet for the aggrandizing spirit that was beginning to pervade the public mood. The Five Nations were not united—in themselves or together—in the face of the gathering forces at their gates; but those forces did not mind one way or the other.

Although only congressional legislation could surmount or set aside the barrier of tribal sovereignty, agencies created by the legislature for the service of the Executive increasingly assisted the process by supplying Congress with unblocking mechanisms. The Cherokee Commission had been discharging its brief with assiduity. In May and June 1890, the Iowas, Sacs and Foxes, Potawatomis, and Absentee Shawnees, who between them occupied most of the "assigned" portion of the Creek and Seminole cession of 1866 and relinquishment of 1889, agreed to terms for the sale of the lands surplus to tribal requirements after allotment of a quarter section to every Indian man, woman, and child. When these lands were opened by the Run of September 22, 1891, they at once became an administrative part of Oklahoma.[92] In October 1890 a similar agreement was concluded with the Cheyenne and Arapaho tribes; their lands were opened by the Run on April 19, 1892.[93]

The Cherokee Outlet remained. Harrison's order that all cattle were to be driven out of the Outlet by October 1, 1890, had been modified by another, extending the deadline to December 1. Even this was not obeyed by all; many owners could find no alternative range for their stock, and winter was closing in. Robbed of the right to negotiate a further lease with the Cherokee Strip Live Stock Association, the Cherokee Nation levied and tried to collect a tax on the cattle.

On December 19, 1891, the Cherokee Nation, having turned down an offer of some $8.3 million, undertook to grant cession and relinquishment for $8,595,736.12. The national council ratified the agreement on January 4, 1892, and the deed of relinquishment was executed on May 17, 1893. All the former Cherokee lands between the ninety-sixth and one-hundredth meridians now lay at the disposal of the Government.[94]

During that summer a crowd of some 100,000 accumulated along the borders of the Outlet. By the middle of September, they were assembled at three points in Oklahoma Territory and six in Kansas. Amid even greater tension and excitement than had been produced by the Oklahoma Run of 1889, the Outlet was opened on September 16.[95] In the dash and scramble for claims, ugly and violent scenes were far commoner than they had been in the earlier land openings. The hardships endured by the homesteaders through a torrid summer, and desperation wrought by the depression which had broken during the first days of spring that year, may account for some of this.

Proclamations and military patrols notwithstanding, cattle and cow-boys had remained in numbers until a few weeks before the date set for the Run.[96]

Oklahoma Territory, as constituted by the act of May 2, 1890, consisted of seven organized counties apportioned between three federal and Terri-torial judicial districts, together with almost all the unallotted Indian lands other than the Five Nations. Those unallotted lands, although included within Oklahoma Territory, could not at first contribute to its government or be administered as part of it except in a judicial sense. Judicial attach-ment to Oklahoma Territory of the unassigned portion of the Cherokee Outlet placed the latter on a par with them for day-to-day purposes.

Two new counties were formed, and four of the original counties were extended, after the Run of September 22, 1891; six were added and two enlarged when the Cheyenne-Arapaho reservation was opened in 1892. Seven more counties were brought into Oklahoma Territory by the opening of the Outlet, raising the total number to twenty-two, and neces-sitating a judicial reorganization. By an act of December 21, 1893, the Territory was divided into five districts and provision made for the ap-pointment of two additional judges.[97]

By now, within five years of the opening of "Old Oklahoma," the only areas assigned to the new Territory that had yet to be drawn fully into its formal organization were the Osage Nation, where the growing mixed-blood element strove for recognition as "the sixth civilized tribe"; the two remaining great reservations to the west (Comanche, Kiowa, and Apache; Wichita and Caddo); and four smaller reservations elsewhere (Ponca; Kaw, or Kansa; Oto and Missouria; and Kickapoo). There was also the unresolved question of Greer County, the title to which had been in dis-pute between Texas and the United States for some years. Indian Terri-tory, therefore, now comprised only the tiny reservations of the Quapaw Agency, which were policed by the United States court at Fort Scott, Kan-sas, and the lands of the Five Tribes.

The judges in Oklahoma Territory were still required to conduct both Territorial and federal proceedings in each county of their districts. Years later, one of them, Andrew Bierer, remarked upon the "memorable fact" that in the period from April 22, 1889 to May 2, 1890, when there had been nothing more than a makeshift quasi-legal form of local govern-ment—supplemented by the federal courts and the military authorities, whose powers were very limited—"there was less crime and less distur-bance than . . . at any period since."[98] The deterioration was rapid. Before long, the courts of the new United States Territory were congested and their judges exhausted.

CHAPTER NINE

Problems of Government and Jurisdiction, 1886–1893

In the matter of government it may be truthfully said that the residents of this agency are surfeited. . . . Yet with all this it is patent to the close observer that there are proportionately little enforcement of law and a greater need for an improved judicial system.—Leo E. Bennett, Report of Union Agency to the Commissioner of Indian Affairs, September 1890, Annual Report of the Secretary of the Interior, *1890.*

We venture to say that the McAlester court is one too many in the Choctaw Nation. . . . Do away with Paris and Fort Smith jurisdiction and you will do away with justice and equity as far as the Red man is concerned.—Letter from "A Citizen," in Atoka, Choctaw Nation, Indian Citizen, *March 10, 1892.*

The U.S. court at Fort Smith claims jurisdiction as far south as Tushkahoma, while that at Paris claims jurisdiction as far north as the top of Winding Stair mountain, thus overlapping each other a distance of twenty miles.— Lehigh, Choctaw Nation, Leader, *in Fort Smith, Arkansas,* Elevator, *June 2, 1893.*

Robert Owen, United States agent for the Five Tribes, wrote in September, 1886, that "the Indian courts, though as a rule . . . not well conducted" were "growing more respectable under the strong educational forces at work."[1]

A year later, without seeking to juxtapose cause and effect, he noted that "the number of United States citizens is steadily increasing in the agency under the Indian permit law" and that "the United States district court for the western district of Arkansas has more business than it can possibly attend to": "[M]any cases I would have otherwise presented for the protection of this agency have been passed by because of their minor character when compared to more important criminal matters, and the present embarrassment of the court in the multitude of important cases to hear." And this despite there being "few courts . . . where business is conducted with more celerity or greater fairness, due largely to the very superior ability and high character of Hon. Isaac C. Parker."[2]

The statistics provide the most graphic testimony to the magnitude of Parker's task. They depict a battle that was slowly being lost. At the end of the fiscal year on June 30, 1883, 517 criminal cases had been terminated, and only 41 were still pending. Over the next twelve months the number of cases terminated rose to 580, leaving 63 incomplete. During the fiscal year 1884–85, 582 cases were dealt with, but 87 had to be carried over. On June 30, 1886, no fewer than 724 further cases had been disposed of, but as many as 122 remained outstanding. The annual expenditure of the court had increased from $160,000 for the fiscal year 1882–83 to $250,000 for 1885–86.[3]

In February 1887, the district ran out of money and, with no special appropriation forthcoming from Congress, Parker was forced to close down the court until July.[4] That year only 350 cases were terminated and, since many deputy marshals left the service because of the closure, fewer criminals were arrested. Even so, 146 cases were pending at the end of June.[5] In 1887–88, 552 prosecutions were terminated, leaving 113 still on the books at the end of June; the cost to the Government that year was $276,000.[6]

This takes no account of the civil work of the court, which consisted almost wholly of lawsuits from the western counties of Arkansas or simple forfeiture hearings for goods confiscated as a result of liquor, unlicensed-trading, or tobacco prosecutions, or the criminal cases arising in the western half of Indian Territory, which were now handled by the districts of Kansas and Northern Texas. Jurisdiction in the Indian country brought some 30 to 40 criminal cases a year to the Graham, Texas, court, and 50 or 60 to the court at Wichita, Kansas, adding about $10,000 and $15,000 to their respective annual costs.[7]

A total of 590 cases were finished at Fort Smith during 1888–89, with 148 still on hand at the end of the year. Although, after the Courts Act of March 1, 1889, the Fort Smith court was concerned only with the more serious offenses committed in a reduced section of Indian Territory, as many as 781 criminal cases were terminated during 1889–90, with 111 still on file on June 30.[8] By the end of 1890–91, the Muskogee court had been overrun: 1,076 criminal cases had been tried, but 417 were yet to be cleared, along with 808 out of the 825 civil suits in which the United States was a party and 797 out of the 1,461 private suits filed during the year.[9] The new federal court at Paris, Texas, was only getting into its stride during 1889–90, when about 300 cases originating in the Indian Territory were placed on the docket. The tally for 1890–91 was almost double that figure.[10]

While these courts may have comported fully with Owen's criterion for a "well conducted" system, their ever-growing caseload does not suggest that "strong educational forces" were making the courts' work easier or its results more enduring. Though the "respectable" United States courts were surer in the punishment of crime than those of the Five Tribes, they were no more successful in preventing it.

In the Chickasaw and Choctaw nations the electoral contests of the later 1880s were, even more than the ones of former years, a struggle between those who wished to promote the "strong educational forces" endorsed by the Indian Office, and those set on excluding them or reining them back. Both sides resorted to illegal means in that struggle. The result of the Chickasaw general election of August 1888 was reversed by legislative chicanery, rectified by insurrection, and resolved in favor of the wrong man after he had appealed to the Department of the Interior. Several years of political and judicial deterioration in the Choctaw Nation were brought to an anarchic and blood-spattered climax in the early 1890s with progressive and conservative elements about equal in their disregard for the values the "educational forces" were aiming to inculcate.

Reference has been made to the Cherokee election of 1887, when the candidate for principal chief who won at the polls was translated into office only by the superior deployment of armed supporters. Both leaders were intelligent, capable, and educated—the possessors of qualities by no means necessarily of a piece with scrupulous integrity in the management of public affairs.[11]

In the Muskogee Nation the old enmities smoldered on. Any chance for a progression to political harmony vanished with an enactment of the national council in the autumn of 1892 that placed much of the homeland at the disposal of cattle syndicates.

Only in the Seminole Nation were there no serious political difficulties. In 1885 John F. Brown succeeded his father-in-law, John Jumper, as principal chief. Thereafter, until the turn of the century, the nation was ruled by a small clique consisting of the principal chief, his brother Andrew Jackson Brown, other members of the Brown family, and two or

three Seminole full-bloods. The governmental records kept by the Seminole Nation have been lost (believed destroyed), but it is evident that the
nation was run almost like a family concern by the Browns, who owned
stores at Wewoka and Sasakwa.[12]

One informed though not unprejudiced portrayal of the political and
social problems afflicting the Indian country is contained in a memorial
prepared in July 1888 and presented to the Senate during the debate on
the Vest court bill:

> I assume you are informed and know the true situation and recent acts
> of hostile strife and contention officially reported to the Interior Depart-
> ment, which warrants the assertion that all the five civilized tribes or
> nations in the Indian Territory are in a state of subdued insurrection and
> rebellion, caused by individual and party feuds, growing out of the con-
> tinual agitation and the unsettled question of sectionizing and allotting in
> severalty these lands, and which threatens to disintegrate their present
> governmental existence in the near future. . . .
>
> It is a local political issue in all these nations or tribes. One party,
> favoring and advocating allotment and lands in severalty, raises the stan-
> dard of the progressive party; the other party, opposing this, is called the
> full blood or national party.
>
> . . . The large and wealthy land-holders, who have thousands of acres
> fenced and under control for the benefit and profit of the pasturage,
> barring out annual cultivation and homestead occupancy and improve-
> ments, joined with the lawless and desperado class—and such are numer-
> ous—and support the 'full blood' or non progressive party. . . .
>
> These contests occur at each and every election held in these respective
> nations or tribes and increase each time in hostility, and which now have
> grown to such a magnitude that those tribes or nations are not capable or
> able to peaceably dispose of their difficulties in a lawful manner and
> amicably settle their national or tribal contentions. . . .
>
> Up to 1880 these nations or tribes of Indians were the most contented,
> progressive, and happy class of Indians of any west of the Missouri
> River. . . . Now they are, in their civil and political condition, directly the
> opposite, and as a people or a community the most contentious, disor-
> ganized, rebellious, refractory, and fractious of any and all people inhabit-
> ing the United States. . . .
>
> In addition, there are now nearly 1000 miles of railroad constructed and
> in operation within the territorial boundary, and numbers of incorporated
> companies located and doing business in the Territory. There are mining,
> insurance, lumbering, stock raising, and grazing companies, with no law
> to control their acts or to furnish a remedy or redress a wrong in any civil
> transaction growing out of the prosecution and progress of their business,
> or protect the Indians against the infringement of their rights.[13]

Charles Brownell, the memorialist, then ran the rule over the white
noncitizen population of the Indian Territory, whether there unlawfully,

by permit of the tribal governments, or under United States license. Those noncitizens who stood with the Progressives he identified as "the better class, and law abiding residents"; those who allied themselves with the "full-blood party" he stigmatized as the "lawless and desperado class." In truth, there were members of both classes on each side of the dispute—some Indians, some not.

Despite the bias and overgeneralization, Brownell's memorial included an accurate conspectus for one approaching crisis.

William Guy, a Progressive, succeeded to the governorship of the Chickasaw Nation in 1886 after a very close election, but the opposing Pullback party formed the majority in the legislature. Although the legislature altered the constitution by disfranchising the intermarried white citizens, most of whom were partisans of Guy, the incumbent seemed to have secured reelection in 1888. The Pullbacks in the legislature, however, used their majority to reject the polling returns from the area where support for Guy was strongest, so putting in their candidate, William Byrd. A band of Guy's supporters led by Sam Paul descended upon the national capitol at Tishomingo, expelled Byrd, and installed Guy as governor. Byrd, the avowed enemy of federal interference, appealed to the Union agent. The issue went to William Vilas, the Secretary of the Interior, who found grounds for Byrd's reinstatement.[14]

These events were magnified by the press, whose prophecies of pitched battle came close to incitement. The unadorned facts were damning enough, but not so demeaning as to cause tribal government as an institution to compare too badly with the brand of democracy practiced in many other parts of America. Electoral malpractice, if not pandemic and continuous, occurred in many cities and sections of the United States at many times. The electoral troubles of 1888 were the outgrowth of twenty years of political tension in the Chickasaw Nation, and they poisoned the atmosphere for the future, but armed conflict had not quite broken out, as it had in the contemporaneous political feuding between two pairs of towns in western Kansas—Woodsdale and Hugotown, Ingalls and Cimarron. The turmoils of the Kansas county-seat disputes commanded acres of coverage in the regional and local press, but they were not seen as evidence that Kansas was unfit for Statehood.

In the Muskogee Nation, where the structure of tribal self-government was the most fragile, the conventional operation of parliamentary democracy damaged Creek national sovereignty as badly as a further bout of internecine armed strife might have done. On November 2, 1892, Principal Chief Legus Perryman approved a law which, repealing earlier legislation to restrict pasturage, allowed "every citizen or company of citizens . . . the right to build pastures larger than one mile square along the border of this nation by securing the consent of the citizens who may be residing within such proposed enclosure, or who may be residing within one half mile outside and from such enclosure." There was a proviso that "such pastures to be hereafter built, shall not be of greater width from the border than ten miles." Anyone intending to enclose an expanse of that size was required to enter into a written contract with the principal chief and to pay an annual tax of five cents on every acre enclosed. Once the pasture had been enclosed, no citizen could "make a claim or any improvement whatever" inside that area without the consent of the contractor. The law was to be in force for six years and was renewable thereafter.[15]

As a scheme to raise revenue for the national treasury, the Creek contract pasture law was comparable with the Cherokees' lease of their Outlet to an association of cattlemen, but there was no true parallel: the Outlet was barred by treaty to settlement by Cherokee citizens, whereas the Okmulgee government had empowered its chief executive to sign away the common domain of the home reservation, the consent clause notwithstanding. Dew Wisdom, the Union agent, was fiercely critical of the measure:

> I know of no law more shrewdly devised to foster and support a monopoly, and I know of no monopoly that more insidiously undermines the rights of the common Creek citizen, than this Creek pasture law. It has made the small farmer and the small herdsman homeless in his own country, excluded him from the common heritage, deprived him of a natural and legal right that he never should have surrendered, and has installed over him the despotism of alien corporations, who wax fat off his grass, which they obtain at the grossly inadequate price of 5 cents per acre. . . . It is true that the lease, in the first place, is granted to an Indian, but it is also true that in the second place it is sublet or subleased to a white man or noncitizen.[16]

Even less of comfort to the Creek government was the charge, leveled here by Wisdom and in Congress by other critics of the contract pasture law, that in curtailing the rights of Creek citizens to the use of the land that was their common heritage the Muskogee Nation had breached the terms of the treaty of 1856. Under Article 15 of that treaty:

> So far as may be compatible with the Constitution of the United States, and the laws made in pursuance thereof, regulating trade and intercourse with the Indian tribes, the Creeks and Seminoles shall be secured in the unrestricted right of self-government, and full jurisdiction over persons and property within their reservation limits.[17]

The submission was that the contract pasture law was contrary to the Constitution of the United States.

As if that were not enough, there was sworn testimony from one of the lessees, a citizen of the Creek Nation, that contracts were sealed by direct cash payment into the private fund of Principal Chief Legus Perryman and that Perryman encouraged the applicants to bid against one another, pocketing the moneys advanced by the highest bidder. Certain testimony educed in a civil suit between two ranching partnerships, heard before the United States court at Muskogee, was laid before Congress:

MR [N. B.] MAXEY: I will ask yourself if you had to pay anything to get this lease.

A. [Witness] This lease No. 1?

Q. Yes, sir.

A. Well, I intrusted them $300 before they would even write the lease for me.

Q. Was that the chief?

A. Well, there was nobody there but the chief and me. He sent his clerk in another room to write the contract and he said if I would intrust them $300 he would go to work and write the lease and I took him in as a partner.

Q. When he wanted you to go and see [James] Parkinson and see if he would give you more, he wanted to raise his interest?

A. He wanted to raise his interest.

Q. Said he could get more from other parties?

A. That is what he said.

Q. Did his private secretary tell you how much Willison & Weldon had offered him?

A. His private secretary told me they had offered $500.[18]

Protestations by the Indian governments, their delegations, and their defenders against any action by the United States that was contrary to the "solemn obligations" guaranteed by treaty did not sit comfortably beside such legislation as the Creek contract pasture law, the Chickasaw confiscation law, the leasing of large tracts of the Cherokee public domain,[19] or the mistreatment by the Choctaw authorities of tribal members who had availed themselves of the newly granted right to United States citizenship.[20]

Nor were impassioned pleas for the inviolability of tribal sovereignty compatible with the policy, followed in the late 1880s and early 1890s by all but the Seminoles, of permitting white settlement on a massive scale.

Intruders of the several different sorts were present in force, but they were heavily outnumbered by white United States citizens who were living in the Indian Territory with official sanction.

Enumerators for the United States census of 1890 found more than 29,000 white noncitizens in the Cherokee Nation in a total population of 56,000. In the Choctaw Nation some 28,000 inhabitants out of 44,000 were white noncitizens; in the Chickasaw Nation, 48,000 out of 57,000. The Muskogee Nation had 3,000 out of 18,000; the Seminole Nation, only 100 or so out of 2,700 residents. All told, 178,000 people were living in the Five Nations when the census was taken, including 109,000 white noncitizens.[21]

Agent Bennett estimated in September 1892 that the noncitizen whites numbered 130,000 in a total population of 200,000.[22] His successor, Wisdom, writing a year later, placed the noncitizen population at 150,000 and predicted a rapid rise during the remainder of 1893 and for 1894.

> The population of the Indian Territory who are United States citizens exceeds that of ten States and Territories, and it would seem that the time has gone by when the people should be denied rights which are regarded, under the Constitution and laws of the country, as fundamental, and which are respected everywhere else.[23]

Most of the newcomers flocked to the so-called cities or towns where in addition to the trade, professional, or residential license fees payable to the tribal government by all, the lot holders paid rent to the Indian holders of the occupancy titles. Sometimes the original Indian owners sold out to noncitizens but retained nominal title to safeguard themselves from prosecution under tribal law.[24]

Similar circumventions were becoming common practice in the Cherokee farmlands and the range country of the Creek Nation. The hazards of this were pointed out by Principal Chief Joel Mayes in his message to the Cherokee national council in November 1890:

> You should teach the people that every one has an equal interest in this our common country, and when they properly understand and fully appreciate this great family government and estate, they will know that a few citizens can not fence up and own the entire country. . . .
>
> The way in which this monopoly is greatly carried on is by our citizens entering into pretended leases of the land to noncitizens for a number of years, which is plain violation of the laws of this nation. The citizen, as a general thing, has never invested a dollar in this transaction. I am also informed that a land office business is being carried on between noncitizens in buying and selling these leases.
>
> You can at once see the great evil and danger that will be entailed on the country by this unscrupulous action of our own citizens.[25]

Mayes told the legislators that they would be justified in "resorting to extreme measures to relieve our country of this curse"; but nothing was done because the leading opponents of leasing could not countenance, in public, the obvious corrective: allotment of the tribal lands in severalty. In consequence of this, the smaller ranchers and farmers, mainly white adoptees and the poorer mixed-bloods, were squeezed between monopolists, who were mostly mixed-bloods and whites, and the tribal legislators, most of whom were full-bloods or dependent upon the support of the full-bloods, who generally used least land but did not wish the communal system to be disturbed.

The rising agitation in Congress against the weakness or culpability of the tribal governments in permitting their citizens to be deprived of the use of their own soil cannot all be dismissed as incipient Populism or opportunistic speciousness decked out as humanity. Nor was the argument that the tribal governments had broken their treaty obligations by allowing the common land to be leased or enclosed merely an exercise in Congressional legalese to prepare the way for a policy of punitive expediency. Concern may have been felt as well as expressed.

Many of the problems faced by government in the Indian Territory during these years grew out of conflicting claims of jurisdiction. Throughout, from the end of the Civil War to the closure of the Indian courts, disputes over the citizenship of a fugitive or a defendant were a continual source of conflict between the tribal and federal authorities. It was only in August 1886 that a ruling by the United States Supreme Court confirmed the right of the Cherokee Nation to determine who were its citizens.[26] Even then, the Department of the Interior declined to extend the principle of this decision to those who had claimed citizenship before August 11, 1886. The implications were threefold: the Fort Smith court could still intervene in Cherokee cases where one or more of the parties had been admitted into citizenship before that date; the Union agent need not execute removal orders directed at those whose unsuccessful claims had predated the Supreme Court ruling; and the Cherokees' denial of citizenship to, and the Interior Department's refusal to act against, these claimants meant that the Cherokees' sovereignty was threatened by the presence of a large block of rootless people who were, willy-nilly, within the criminal jurisdiction of the United States. In December 1886, therefore, the national council passed an act, approved by the principal chief on December 8, providing for the appointment of a commission to deal with all applications for citizenship.

The federal court at Fort Smith lost jurisdiction it had never sought when, on May 21, 1883, the Choctaw Nation at last adopted its ex-slaves under Articles III and IV of the Choctaw-Chickasaw treaty of 1866. But in the Chickasaw Nation the ex-slaves were restored to United States citizenship against the express will of the United States. An adoption act had been approved by the progressive governor, Cyrus Harris, on January 10, 1873, but in October 1876 the legislature repudiated it. A further act of the Chickasaw legislature, approved on October 22, 1885, implicitly repealed the freedmen adoption act of 1873 and was used a decade later to secure the release of an ex-slave who had been charged with murder by the Chickasaw authorities. No great pressure was brought upon the Chickasaw Nation to comply with the adoption articles of the treaty of 1866; the question was left for the Dawes Commission to determine in the last years of the century.[27] In 1890 there were some 3,800 blacks in the Chickasaw Nation, including a few who had married into the tribe, and only about 3,100 Chickasaws by blood.[28]

Other legislation on the citizenship issue was enacted by the Choctaw and Chickasaw councils, either to serve immediate personal or party interests or to ensure that political control stayed in the hands of those who were Indians by blood. Always the result was a weakening of tribal sovereignty.

A law of the Choctaw Nation passed in 1886 decreed that thereafter no claimant would be admitted to citizenship without proof of a quantum of at least one-eighth Choctaw blood, the admixture to be white and Indian.[29] This act was designed partly to inhibit any influx of Mississippi Choctaws, whose Indian ancestors had accepted United States citizenship rather than participate in the removal to Indian Territory; but its more direct cause was the appearance in the nation of several hundred members of two families called Glenn and Tucker, all claiming citizenship on the strength of their descent from a Choctaw half-blood, Abigail Rogers, born in 1760.[30] Neither the claimants nor their claim would go away.

In the end the dispute was settled against the Glenn-Tucker parties; until then, they hung on in the Choctaw Nation, voteless and unwelcome, yet another group of aliens subject only to federal law. The Chickasaw disenfranchisement act of April 8, 1887, under which adopted and intermarried members of the tribe were deprived of their citizenship, helped the Pullback candidate to win the next gubernatorial election and his party to retain control of the legislature. It also added a large, malcontent, and potentially insurgent element to the noncitizen population.[31]

Edmund McCurtain, a former principal chief of the Choctaws, failed to recognize in the Muskogee court legislation of 1890 a comprehensive danger to the system of tribal government. In a letter to Leo Bennett written shortly after the general election of 1890—a campaign that, although notable for its bitterness, was merely the precursor of much worse—McCurtain found fault not with the Muskogee act as such, but with two of its specific provisions, including the one that allowed members of the tribes to apply for United States citizenship.

We have just passed through an exciting political struggle, and now that it is over, the people are all settled down as before the election, and there is no hard feelings existing between the members of the two parties.

The people generally are satisfied with the present system of government, with however the exception of the new United States court established in the Territory. There are many parts of the law that are objectionable, and particularly that part which allows Indians to take out citizenship papers and become citizens of the United States. As a rule the only parties availing themselves of this section of the law are those who have violated our laws and take the oath of allegiance to the United States to escape the penalty of their crime. I know of some cases of persons applying for [United States] citizenship who have committed murder, others for theft and violation of lease law, etc. . . .

I would suggest that the law be amended so as to designate what courts shall have jurisdiction over crimes committed by Indians previous to their becoming citizens of the United States.

Another objectionable feature of the new court is the collection law. The whites have all the advantage of the Indians in this law. They can make any kind of an unjust claim against an Indian, and drag him up before the court and ruin him. But when a white man owes an Indian they cannot collect unless he is worth $500 (as that amount is exempted from executors). The class of whites that come to this country never have any property and never accumulate anything while here, and when they get in debt to us we have no way of collecting it.[32]

McCurtain's contention that the only Choctaws with an interest in taking United States citizenship were criminals was a good deal less than the truth, and it had been demonstrated often enough that a criminal did not need to be a United States citizen to escape the attentions of the Choctaw authorities. His assertion that the election of 1890 had left no legacy of ill feeling was similarly remote from the facts.

Agent Bennett was not short of criticisms and suggestions. "Under the present arrangement," he wrote, "conflicts of jurisdiction have arisen that are a disgrace to the judicial system of the [United States] government":

This very complicated condition tends to leave hundreds of cases for which there appears to be no remedy. . . . I am advised . . . that there are no penalties under the United States law for the following crimes: forgery, swindling, embezzlement, seduction, disposing of mortgaged property, assault with intent to rape, burglary in the daytime, fraudulent disposition of property.

The latter assertion was no longer valid. The deficiency had just been repaired by section 33 of the Omnibus ("Oklahoma") Act, whereby the laws of Arkansas were extended to Indian Territory for the trial and punishment of these and other offenses.

As was, perhaps, no less than was to be expected, Bennett found that the Muskogee court's capacities as a civil tribunal compared badly with the informal system that had preceded it, when "this agency adjusted all such matters by acting as an arbitrator," charging no fee. The big difference between the two methods, on which Bennett had nothing to say, was that the agent's rulings had not been legally binding.

Since, however, the Muskogee court was now a fixture, Bennett had advice about how it might be made more effective.

> One provision of the present court bill [act] that is unwise and unjust is that barring the United States court from jurisdiction in controversies between citizens of the same nation. I would recommend its repeal or that it be so amended as to permit any citizen to elect for himself whether or not he will bring the suit in the United States court. As at present provided adopted citizens of some of the Nations are constrained in the protection of their property to return to the old "shot-gun policy" which prevailed before the court was established. The court ought to be able to protect all our people alike—which it is not—for in some Nations the adopted citizen is not allowed to sue, although often made defendant. I speak from experience and personal observation.[33]

But before and after the introduction of the Muskogee court, and regardless of the availability of the tribal courts, men of all types and degrees of citizenship were inclined to resolve their controversies by doing violence to their opponents. Bennett, like Owen, overrated the "civilizing" capabilities of the courts of law and the Union agent.

Bennett's remarks on the disabilities of adopted citizens were in general true of the Creeks and Seminoles. The treaties between the United States and these two nations contained no provision to exempt adopted citizens from the jurisdiction of the federal courts, and after 1866 adopted Creeks or Seminoles retained United States citizenship.[34] All this was well known to Bennett, who had lived in the Muskogee Nation for years as physician and newspaperman; it may not have been known to the Easterners who read his reports.

Edmund McCurtain's views on dual citizenship were shared by a majority of the Choctaw general council. On October 25, 1890, the new Progressive governor, Wilson Jones, approved an act by which "any member of the Choctaw tribe of Indians, whether by blood, adoption, or marriage," who had taken the oath of allegiance to the United States was disqualified from all public office, disfranchised, and barred from jury service.[35] When Fritz Sittel, a wealthy intermarried Choctaw who had taken out United States citizenship papers, sued another Choctaw over property valued at $50,000, the jurors ignored the charge of the judge, put aside the facts, found against Sittel, and awarded damages of $4,000 to his opponent.[36] The United States Government could do nothing for him.

In contrast, the federal Government did interpose its authority between the two feuding parties during the Choctaw troubles of 1892 and 1893. These troubles began with a fiercely contested gubernatorial election in the summer of 1892 in which the Progressive candidate was adjudged by the council, with its Progressive majority, to have defeated Jacob Jackson, leader of the National party. Amid the charges and countercharges of electoral fraud both sides began preparations to take their dispute outdoors. A month after the election four Progressive officeholders were murdered in Gaines County, in the north-central part of the nation. Leo Bennett, as Union agent, was permitted to mediate and obtained the surrender of seventeen men who admitted to having participated in the murders.

The National partisans then disbanded, as they had promised to do, but the Progressives reneged on their agreement and tried to pluck the prisoners from the custody of the Union Agency Indian police. Bennett, with twenty men against two hundred, then read out the Indian Officers Act of June 9, 1888, and assured the mob that "while they might forcibly take the prisoners, it would only be at the loss of lives upon both sides, and even then they would have to answer for the deed before the United States courts which, I had no doubt would take pleasure in breaking their necks."[37]

Hostilities were suspended, and one of the prisoners—a Chickasaw ex-slave and therefore not answerable to the Choctaw authorities—was sent to Fort Smith. The other sixteen were placed in the custody of the sheriff of Gaines County. Both the Progressive forces and the remustered supporters of the National party then disbanded. Bennett, fearing that the worst was yet to come, "as both parties believe they are right in the matter . . . and are willing to fight and die for their belief if necessary," asked for military assistance and was given a troop of cavalry. Nothing further happened until February 1893, when the sixteen prisoners who were awaiting trial applied unsuccessfully to the Department of the Interior for Government pressure upon the tribal authorities to present their case in court or release the defendants on bail.

Soon after this, another of the Jackson party was rescued from a national light-horse man en route to the county jail. Chief Jones then took advantage of laws passed during the 1880s that allowed the principal chief to call out a force of militia during an emergency. There was one armed clash in which several men were wounded but none killed. Once again the excitement subsided after the Secretary of War had placed a detachment of soldiers at Bennett's disposal.

In June, nine of the sixteen defendants were convicted of murder and sentenced to death. Intercession by the Interior Department eventually brought about the release of eight of the nine, who were allowed to leave for the Chickasaw Nation. Jones, upon being asked whether he had the power to pardon the men, answered in the negative—but he could, and did, request the judiciary to suspend the sentences. Silan Lewis, the ninth man, was executed in November 1894 by the sheriff of Gaines County.[38]

So much for an episode that was of great service to enemies of tribal particularism. Both sides in the Choctaw dispute had, in all probability, tried to steal the election. The party in control of the general council, having investigated the returns and found that they placed the opposition candidate at the head of the government, had pronounced for its man. The leaders of the frustrated National party, the voice of tribal self-sufficiency, had encouraged interference from Washington. The Progressive partisans had shown such interference to be morally if not legally justified. The principal chief, like the Ross party in the Cherokee Nation during the 1840s, had misused the national light-horse and militia. United States cavalry and United States Indian Police—the latter a body whose very existence was resented by most other Indians—had twice been summoned to prevent a bloody disintegration of order and government. And the Department of the Interior, however worthy its motive, had crossed the limit of constitutional propriety in its sustained and almost wholly successful efforts to nullify the operation of the Choctaw courts.

A complex issue on which the federal courts of Fort Smith, Paris, and Muskogee were often in conflict between themselves or the Interior Department hinged upon how much alcohol was needed for a liquid to be classified as an intoxicant. In June 1887, Attorney-General Garland advised the district attorney at Fort Smith that a substance called Hoxie Nerve Food should be included in the interdict.[39] A compound known as Choctaw beer, containing a little alcohol and a lot of water, with an admixture of other ingredients—barley, berries, hops, and tobacco—which was the staple beverage of the mining camps and other white settlements of the Choctaw and Chickasaw nations, was banned by an act of the Choctaw council in 1886;[40] but its use by United States citizens was a subject that divided legal opinion.

Vendors of Choctaw beer were much heartened by a decision of the Fort Smith court that it was not an offense to manufacture the stuff, but controversy was further stirred in July 1889 when agent Bennett, exercising his general powers, raided the Choctaw mining town of Lehigh, where he found, "like the Queen of Sheba when she visited King Solomon, 'the half had not been told'. . . . his own officers had been conspiring with shame, crime, immorality, vice and all other things subversive of law, order and the well-being of society."[41]

In other eyes, though, Bennett had acted with an arbitrary arrogance that evoked comparisons with the behavior of revenue officers during the last decade of colonial rule. The manufacture of beer was not, after all, an illicit process.

> [W]hen he comes with other officers of the law and virtually takes the law in his own hands, and becomes a law breaker himself, it is time the citizens of Uncle Sam had something to say . . . what right or what authority has Indian Agent Bennett got for going into people's houses, breaking their barrels and spilling their beer, breaking their measures, kettles and pots, and, I am informed, in one instance spilling the flour on the floor . . . they forcibly broke open houses when the owners were out, and searched through trunks and broke open valises. It was in the name of the law it was done, but without any process of law whatever.[42]

The writer of this letter and others engaged in the beer business soon found that Judge Parker's dispensation for the manufacture of beer did not extend to its sale. This distinction was applied at Fort Smith to the discomfiture of several beer vendors during 1890, but people carried on making, selling, and drinking beer.[43]

In the meantime, the beer question had become caught up in the convoluted controversy over the jurisdiction of the Muskogee court in relation to the courts at Fort Smith and Paris and the jurisdiction of the Union agent in relation to all of them. A cause célèbre arose late in 1889. Just before Christmas, Bennett decided to close down the gambling houses in Ardmore. As was his right, he borrowed two deputy marshals to assist the agency police in this work. Quite legitimately, but perhaps tactlessly, he obtained this help from Fort Smith instead of applying to the new federal court at Paris, within whose jurisdiction the Chickasaw Nation was included.

On December 23 the agent's men disarmed the gamblers, seized their gaming paraphernalia and furniture, piled it in the street, and burned it. One of the gamblers then went before the Paris court and swore out a complaint against the two Fort Smith deputies and Captain Charles Leflore of the Union Agency police, alleging larceny. The legal issue was whether the Indian Police, or anyone seconded to the force, held jurisdiction over noncitizens in the Indian Territory. In ruling that the three had a case to answer, the United States commissioner prevented the police from performing many of their duties until April, when the charges were dismissed.

Leflore complained to agent Bennett, Bennett to Commissioner of Indian Affairs Thomas Morgan, and Morgan to Secretary of the Interior John Noble, who discussed the matter with Attorney-General William Miller. The Attorney-General then directed Judge David Bryant of the Paris court and Judge Shackelford of the Muskogee court to cooperate with the Union agent and Indian Police and instruct their subordinates to do the same. A rebuke was delivered to the United States commissioner at Paris.[44]

One effect of this imbroglio was to dispel the argument that some provisions of the act of May 2, 1890, such as those which put misdemeanors in Indian Territory within the reach of the federal court at Muskogee, would leave little or nothing of the agent's very broad statutory right, and duty, to employ the Indian police "in maintaining order and prohibiting illegal traffic in liquor." In theory, then, there would be maximum coordination and minimum friction by order of the Secretary of the Interior and the Attorney-General.

In July 1891, Judge Bryant ruled that Julius Kahn, a vendor of "pale malt" or "malt tonic," whose ingredients included an alcoholic content of one and five-eighths per centum, had no case to answer. Kahn had been prosecuted under Section 2139, U.S. Revised Statutes, which forbade the introduction of ardent spirits, and Bryant's decision had the effect of a declaration that malt liquors were not spirituous or vinous. In Fort Smith the ruling was described as "nonsensical"; in Muskogee, agent Bennett, with the approbation and support of Secretary Noble, announced that he would use Section 2140 to close down the beer saloons. Section 2140 entitled the Indian agent to search for liquor and confiscate it.[45]

Armed with this section, the Indian police shut forty-one beer saloons in the Chickasaw Nation and all the "hard cider joints" besides, seizing not only the goods in the houses but the houses themselves. The proprietors were taken before Judge Shackelford, but the district attorney dismissed the cases because, as he saw it, jurisdiction in these particular circumstances lay not with Muskogee but with the Paris court. A few days later, Shackelford ruled in a test case that beer was "a spirituous liquor." Secretary Noble and Attorney General Miller had by now parted company. Noble stood solidly behind Bennett's attack upon the beer trade, and Miller insisted that the Interior Department should respect the judgments of the Paris court.[46]

After the failure of the prosecutions at Muskogee, beer saloons were opened "in every village in the agency, almost without exception." The Commissioner of Indian Affairs supported Bennett in the revocation of the licenses of traders engaged in the beer trade, but would not consent to the removal of unlicensed traders from the Indian country.[47]

In the light of Shackelford's decision that Choctaw beer was an intoxicant and that prosecutions for its sale could be brought by his court, Bennett resumed his drive against the saloons. Judge Bryant then made it known that if Bennett's men molested any licensed dealer, they would be arrested by Paris deputies and prosecuted; if any beer was confiscated, the charge against the United States Indian Police would be robbery. A month later, when Bennett, disregarding the warning, once again set the Indian police upon lager dealers in the Chickasaw Nation, the United States marshal of the Paris court instructed his deputies to arrest the policemen for acting upon the agent's orders.[48]

Some six weeks later, in March 1892, cooperation between Bennett and the United States marshal at Muskogee resulted in the closure of all the dives in Lehigh and the arrest of their proprietors. The object under scrutiny was a brand of malt tonic called "extra fine"; and the effect of the prosecution is best summed up by the newspaper correspondent who noted in June that "pale liquor has supplanted the lemon stands at Muskogee."[49]

Judge Parker, whose interpretation of the law often differed from Judge Bryant's, encouraged the prosecution of beer vendors in that part of the Choctaw Nation left within his jurisdiction and, when a case came before him, charged the Fort Smith jury that beer was included within the prohibition of spiritous liquors. Shortly afterward, Congress came in on the side of Bennett and Parker. An act of July 23, 1892, ordained that "ale, beer, wine, or intoxicating liquors of whatever kind" were to rank with "ardent spirits" as goods that could not be sold or otherwise disposed of in the Indian Territory. Yet the new act, an amendment to Section 2139 of the Revised Statutes, did not forbid the *manufacture* of ale or beer.[50]

Jurisdictional confusion and conflict between the Fort Smith, Paris, and Muskogee courts marked the seven years of their coexistence in Indian Territory. L. L. Stowe, foreman of a grand jury at Ardmore, included this example in his report to Shackelford:

> The anomaly of the people and its courts are [*sic*] without parallel.
> Note for instance the jurisdiction of this and the United States district court at Paris, exercising in some cases concurrent jurisdiction, and in other cases the jurisdiction is conflicting and irreconcilable. Only a few days since an individual stood charged in this court by indictment for

larceny, and upon that day, the day upon which his case was set for trial, a deputy United States marshal for the Paris court, ignoring the court's jurisdiction, arrested the accused, and without giving him an opportunity to make bond, speedily transported him to and lodged him in the United States jail at Paris for a lesser crime, to wit, introducing.

Result: the bond of accused was forfeited and his trial for larceny delayed if not wholly defeated.[51]

This particular situation could have come about only because the Paris officer was holding an older warrant and had a will to serve it. Although the case was unimportant in itself, it offers a good illustration of how annoyance, injustice, and expense could arise from the operation of a system intended to produce the opposite effects.

Relations between the different courts were further strained when the official behavior, or unofficial misbehavior, of deputy marshals belonging to one court led to their appearance in a rival court. The upshot of a visit by three Muskogee deputies to "a negro dance on the Canadian river" was a trip to Paris, Texas, in the custody of three deputies of the latter court. Some of the male dancers had objected to the presence of the deputies, whose response had been to shoot into the crowd. Assault to kill in the Chickasaw Nation was a matter for the Paris judge when United States citizens were concerned.[52]

More serious and tortuous was the Wash Bruner case of 1892, which arose after the pursuit of a band of black horse thieves through the Chickasaw and Seminole nations had culminated in an affray at Bruner Town, an ex-slave settlement straddling the Seminole and Creek border. A local man was killed in the melee, and the officers, deputy marshals of the Paris court, captured and jailed several of the gang. But the killing had occurred in country under the jurisdiction of the Fort Smith court, which proceeded to institute a prosecution against the Paris officers. All five deputies were discharged by the United States commissioner at their preliminary examination after evidence on their behalf, and against the gang, had been given by the second chief of the Seminole Nation. Means were then found at Fort Smith to reopen the affair. Four of the deputies went on trial before Parker in June 1893 and were acquitted.[53]

In September 1892, Bennett delivered himself of a detailed critique on the intrinsic defects of the new judicial pattern, their influence upon his position, and their effect as an obstacle to the progress of the Indian Territory to Statehood. After reviewing the powers of the courts at Muskogee, Paris, and Fort Smith and the "active part" his agency had always taken "in the suppression of the liquor traffic, gambling, intrusion, and kindred evils," he wrote in part:

Controversies often arise over which none of the above-mentioned courts can or will assume jurisdiction, owing to an apparent conflict of authority, and this agency and its officers have at times been hindered in the discharge of official duties by the action of these courts. Indian courts have been balked in the enforcement of their laws against their own citizens. Indian executive officers have been forced to defend damage suits brought in the United States court by non-citizens who have connived with individual citizens to escape the operations of Indian laws; and again the conflicts of opinions and the diversity in the rulings of the several United States courts upon questions of law have proven to be not only a serious annoyance but a positive injury, notably so in the matter of the introduction and sale of lager beer within the limits of this agency.

A few of these entanglements, in my opinion, exist without cause. Many more would not exist were the exclusive original jurisdiction, both civil and criminal, vested in one United States court for the Indian Territory; and to this end Congress ought to take early action. Yet perfection in the judicial system can not be reached until the rights and privileges of all citizens and non-citizens are protected by a common law to which all are alike amenable. This will only be when the Indians recognize in Statehood the highest form of self-government attainable by a civilized and enlightened people; when they discard the idea that the Federal Government is a foreign power, to which their interests cannot be intrusted without a surrender of the right of self-government guaranteed in their treaties, when they throw off their yoke of guardianship which they have long since outgrown; and in the halls of State and of Congress, through their own representatives, take a part in the enactment of the law governing their interests. . . .

Although these Indian nations claim to be independent, with rights and powers of self-government which can not be interfered with by the United States, their frequent appeals to the Federal Government for protection and assistance in enforcing their own laws is an acknowledgment of their dependency as subjects of the United States Government.[54]

Probably no single aspect of the administration of the law in Indian Territory, except for the fee system of payment, was the source of as much controversy as that which enveloped the questions of whether United States commissioners should be located in the Territory and, if so, what their powers should be. The United States commissioner—to reiterate—was the federal equivalent of the probate or examining judge (or magistrate) of the State courts. As such, his chief function was to determine whether the evidence presented at a preliminary examination was sufficient, prima facie, for the case to be referred to a federal grand jury, whose duty it was to decide whether an indictment should be returned.

It soon became evident that such officials were needed in the Indian Territory to moderate the cost of running the court from Fort Smith and to relieve the onus placed upon the accused and the witnesses who, under the existing arrangements, were forced to travel to Fort Smith for a hearing that might well end with the discharge of all concerned. This argument had a natural corollary: the further the commissioner's office from the courthouse, the harder it was for the judge and district attorney to keep him under supervision. During Story's judgeship a commissioner was appointed at Boggy Depot in the Choctaw Nation and another at Fort Gibson in the Cherokee Nation. Their activities aggravated the problems their appointment had been intended to alleviate: many trifling or false charges were brought to enable those involved (including sometimes the accused) to swindle the Government on fees and expenses.[55]

Judge Parker was always opposed to the use of such commissioners in the Indian Territory. In the first fifteen years of his service, he appointed only two "as an experiment." One was removed in 1879 at the request of the Choctaw delegation because of his efforts to win local support for schemes to sectionize land.[56] Later, in August 1885, the former Union agent and sometime congressman John Tufts was appointed to serve as commissioner at Muskogee. In June 1887, however, he was disqualified on a technicality raised by the First Comptroller of the Treasury.[57] Robert Owen, Tufts's successor at the Union Agency, spoke warmly of the new commissioner,[58] but his approbation was not echoed by Parker. In the judge's opinion, "[F]rom the standpoint of a fair and proper enforcement of the law, the experiment was a failure."

Parker and his district attorney, William Clayton, gave Attorney-General Miller several reasons for their antagonism to any proposal for the reintroduction into the Indian Territory of commissioners for Fort Smith. Joseph Wilson, district attorney at Paris, took the opposite view: five commissioners had been placed in Indian Territory shortly after the Eastern District of Texas was extended into it.[59] Miller, having commented that there was "much to be said on each side of this question," concluded with this advice to the president of the Senate:

> The only remedy, in my judgment, is to bring the courts having jurisdiction of all kinds of offenses in the Indian Territory closer to the people.
> . . . I have no doubt that it would be greatly to the public advantage, as well as for the convenience of the people, that the court in the Indian Territory should have jurisdiction not only of misdemeanors, but all minor felonies.[60]

Miller's cryptic dissent from Parker's opinion was freed from ambiguity in his annual report for 1890, when he repeated with heightened emphasis his recommendation for the sort of reform that would be unwelcome at Fort Smith and Paris alike.[61]

By that time, the federal court at Muskogee had become enwrapped in a legal conundrum of its own on the use of United States commissioners, which took shape and substance from doubts about the nature of the powers and duties reserved for these officials under the act of May 2, 1890. The adoption of so many Arkansas statutes and so much of the Arkansas procedure led to the supposition that the nine commissioners in the Indian Territory would, like their equivalent in the State of Arkansas, have the authority to make final disposition of misdemeanor cases. Several of the congressional lawyers most closely engaged in securing the passage of the bill thought as much; but their opinion was not shared by Judge Shackelford, and the commissioners of the Indian Territory remained, for a time, no more than examining magistrates.

Delegation to commissioners of the power to try the lesser criminal cases would save money and reduce the pressure on the district court and its officials. But there were two objections. It was notorious that commissioners in many federal districts, sometimes acting in concert with deputy marshals, had built up their income by permitting or even encouraging frivolous or baseless prosecutions. Moreover, a commissioner's earnings, being derived from fees, could soon outstrip the salary of the district judge. Extension of the commissioners' powers would broaden the scope for the proliferation of both evils; but it ought, also, to ensure greater care in the selection of appointees.

Early in Cleveland's second administration the new Attorney-General, Richard Olney, invited the incoming judge and district attorney of the Muskogee court to reexamine the law. If in their opinion it would not allow the commissioners to try misdemeanor cases, they were to say whether it should be changed.

One good argument for a change in the law was implicit in the delay of six months that ensued before a slackening of court work left District Attorney Clifford Jackson enough time to answer Olney's queries. Jackson's reply, in substance, was that although he and the judge, Charles Stuart, were sure that the commissioners were not entitled to try misdemeanors, they believed that "investing commissioners with powers to finally hear misdemeanor cases would be a great satisfaction to the people of the Territory." The whole question, he admitted, was "a most perplexing one": "I do not know whether I have made this matter as explicit as you desire, but I have tried to make it as clear as I can."

In a second letter to Olney, Jackson suggested a wide range of reforms. If misdemeanors were to be disposed of by the commissioners, the United States ought to be represented by counsel. This would necessitate the appointment of nine new assistants to District Attorney Jackson, one for each commissioner's court. Moreover, said Jackson, all—commissioners, deputy marshals, assistant district attorneys, and the district attorney—should be paid by salary instead of fees:

> With these changes over the present system, I am satisfied that the expense of prosecutions in this Territory would be materially reduced, and the people better satisfied with the manner of trying cases. . . .
>
> Of course there is a vast and steady increase of our population, and the necessary expense of prosecution of crime in our court is increasing all the while.[62]

Olney had a mind of his own about the fee system. In asking Congress for its "summary abolition" he was recommending a reform that "had received the earnest advocacy of every Attorney-General for the last twenty years," although none had spoken as forcefully as he. Olney was scandalized by "what may fairly be characterized as the maladministration of justice in the Indian Territory" and demanded legislation to end the "wastefulness" and "inefficiency" of the outside courts by creating more federal courts in the Territory and giving them full jurisdiction, or fuller than that which the Muskogee court then possessed.[63]

Congress was already moving toward the last phase of its relationship with the governments of the Five Civilized Tribes. In the last hours of the Harrison administration, legislation was adopted to provide for the appointment of a commission of three to negotiate with the Five Tribes for the extinguishment of their title to the lands held by them.

The debate that preceded the enactment of this measure was shaped by criticism of the courts structure of the Indian Territory. In introducing the joint resolution that bore the seed of the Dawes Commission Act, George Vest, "Missouri's Little Giant," delivered the wildest of his several philippics on "the existing order of things in what is known as the Indian Territory":

> The farce of administering justice there is a blot and a stain upon the judicial system of the United States. . . . A more miserable farce was never perpetrated under any civilized code than that which now obtains as to the five civilized tribes in the Indian country. . . . Each of these outside courts in Arkansas and Texas costs the people of the United States more today than the federal court for the southern district of New York. . . . No such monstrosity has ever been known in judicial annals. It is a system of organized plunder. . . . The costs are piled mountain high and paid out of the tax money of the people of the United States. . . . If [the Fort Smith hangman] had lived in the Dark Ages . . . he would have been entitled to a knighthood, for I believe it was the usage in those ancient days when the executioner had struck off the heads of so many belted knights or earls to make him a member of that illustrious order . . . and when this man has

made it an even hundred human lives that have been sacrificed to this Moloch of our jurisprudence, why not make him one of the capitalists and favored classes of this great country?[64]

Vest condemned the court at Fort Smith as "a slaughter house" yet berated its deputy marshals for "hunting up petty offenders in order to get the costs" instead of meeting the genuine outlaws "pistol to pistol." This last accusation was stupendously untrue: in recent years many deputies had been killed by desperadoes, and many more desperadoes had been killed by deputies. Not all his allegations were as spurious. He made effective use, up to a point, of a letter from a cousin of the Cherokee principal chief, Joel Mayes, which, although laced with imagery as extravagant as Vest's, put a sounder case than the senator's for further congressional action in Indian Territory.

> Outside capital has been gradually pouring into that country, to be invested in cattle, until they have monopolized the entire range. This is effected through that class of citizens who are termed half-breeds (a half-breed is one who is partly white; many who have only a sixty-fourth part of Indian blood are termed half-breeds), and principally through this class of citizens they manage to introduce their capital and evade tax laws and other laws. . . . There are many white men also in this country who have married into these tribes who are also engaged in this illegal speculation. These people are the "Wall Street" of the Territory.

These men, the writer continued, manipulated the Cherokee legislature by persuading the "ignorant full-bloods" that if they consented to a change, the land would fall into the hands of white noncitizens or be swallowed up by railroad grants, thereby inflaming their minds against those citizens, "perhaps a majority of the entire community," who desired a program of allotment. So much was true. Thereafter, hyperbole took wing:

> The law and order of that country is a howling farce, with no moral stamina to back it up. The country is one grand asylum for all the criminals who choose to accept it as a safe retreat. The federal court at Fort Smith, with all of its regiment of low-flung marshals, reeks with filth. . . . The six shooter and bell spur are ornaments that command universal respect.

Vest's correspondent then surpassed even this picturesque nonsense with an allegation that Judge Parker, upon the interposition of a priest, had freed a robber on payment of a one-dollar fine.[65] This mischievous anecdote may have been inspired by the well-known fact that Parker's wife was a Roman Catholic. There is not a scrap of evidence that the judge's conduct of his court was any more influenced by his wife's Catholicism than by her conviction that she was Pocahontas reborn.[66]

After the senators from Arkansas had defended Parker's personal character and the general character of the Indian Territory's inhabitants, Orville Platt contributed a speech so far removed in tone and tenor from the moderation of his comments on the Oklahoma bill that his later espousal of imperialism does not seem surprising:

> I regret that one of the most important political governmental questions in our whole history should be seemingly obscured by a discussion which has arisen with reference to the condition of certain courts. The real question which should interest the American people is the question of whether we can longer endure five separate, independent, sovereign, and almost wholly foreign governments within the boundaries of the United States.
>
> The joint resolution itself . . . scarcely touches the great question which should interest us most, because it does not in terms look at all to the wiping out of those governments, if I may be pardoned the expression. It looks simply to the matter of allotting the lands in severalty in the Indian Territory and the sale of those which are not allotted.[67]

Platt's contention that immigration from the United States had destroyed the rationale of tribal government in the Indian Territory, together with the fact that most of the newcomers had entered the Territory with the permission of the Indians, supplied the material for his argument that the Five Tribes governments had annulled the conditions under which the country had been set apart for them; ergo, "the time has come when these governments must be abandoned."[68]

The Senate at large was not ready to throttle the tribal governments at a leap. Most senators still preferred a policy whereby the structure of tribal government could be dismembered in stages. Even Bishop Perkins of Kansas, a newcomer to the Senate, did not find it too difficult to come to terms with this way of thinking.[69] Although, he urged, "we should resort to more heroic measures and provide for statehood for the Indian Territory," the first step, to be taken "at the earliest opportunity," should be "to give to this court organized in the Indian Territory full and exclusive jurisdiction of all offenses committed within that Territory":

> I am in favor of organizing Oklahoma Territory and the Indian Territory into a great state, admitting it into the Union either as an Indian State or otherwise. I do not care what the name may be. . . . If this can not be done then we must . . . organize Territorial governments in the Indian Territory, increase the powers of the courts existing there, and by lawful methods give protection to life and property in that country.[70]

Vest's resolution was left on the table of the Senate on January 4, 1893, but on March 1 its provisions reemerged as an amendment to the Indian appropriation bill. Two days later the bill became one of the last acts of Congress approved by Benjamin Harrison.[71]

Grover Cleveland's second administration was eight months old before, complying with the Section 16 of the Indian Appropriation Act, he put forward the names of Henry Dawes, who had retired from the Senate; Meredith Kidd of Indiana; and Archibald McKennon of Arkansas as commissioners to negotiate with the Five Tribes "for the purpose of the extinguishment of the national or tribal title to any lands within that Territory now held" by them. The nominations were confirmed immediately by the Senate, and the three made ready to take up their duties in the Indian Territory at the turn of the year.[72] The Commission to the Five Civilized Tribes, soon to be known far and wide as the Dawes Commission, was now in being.

During the four years since the passage of the Muskogee act, the federal courts had tried hard to contain the rising inflow of prisoners and process. Their failure was made to look worse by their own increasing demands upon the Treasury. In its first full year, 1889–90, the Muskogee court had spent $98,000 clearing 478 cases. The broadening of its criminal and civil jurisdiction under the act of May 2, 1890, gave it much more to do and, at the close of the year on June 30, 1891, it had disposed of well over 1,000 criminal and more than 600 civil cases; but its costs had risen to $165,000, and over 400 criminal and 1,600 civil cases were on the waiting list. A year later its account stood at 1,252 criminal cases and 646 civil suits terminated at a cost of $240,000, and on July 1, 1893, after a twelvemonth in which 1,588 criminal and 1,117 civil cases had been removed from the dockets, a total of 1,702 prosecutions still pending was poor compensation for a reduction in expenditure to $225,000.[73]

At Fort Smith there was no sign of the intended diminution of labor or expense. During the four years to July 1, 1893, the court decided 3,644 criminal cases and 104 civil suits in which the United States had an interest and ran up a total bill of more than $1 million. The disbursements for 1892–93, when 1,155 criminal cases were closed, came eventually to $288,000.[74]

During the same period of four years, the Eastern District of Texas completed 1,160 criminal prosecutions for an outlay of just over $1 million—almost as much as it had cost the Fort Smith court to get through more than thrice as many. Some two-thirds of these Texas cases, and about four-fifths of the cost, belonged to the Paris division and were derived almost wholly from its jurisdiction in the Indian Territory. A total of 345 criminal cases were pending on June 30, 1893—again, three times as many as were awaiting attention at Fort Smith.[75]

All told, therefore, more than 4,000 criminal cases from Indian Territory were settled by the Fort Smith and Paris courts between July 1, 1889,
and June 30, 1893, at a cost to the United States of $1.7 million. Addition of
the 6,841 civil and minor criminal cases that went through the Muskogee
court and the $731,000 required for its upkeep produces a grand total of
11,000 cases of all classes and overall expenditure of nearly $2.5 million.
This amount was more than one-eighth of the cost of all the federal
judicial districts in the United States; and, while the other districts—
possessing none of the general criminal jurisdiction exercised by the
Fort Smith, Paris, and Muskogee courts or the civil functions of the last-
named—were made much cheaper by these circumstances, the distinction
was not dwelt upon or even recognized by critics of the conduct of
judicial affairs in the Indian Territory.

One piece of legislation whose provisions were enforced none too
diligently by deputy marshals in the Indian Territory was the Sexual
Offenses Act of March 3, 1887.[76] Though directed mainly at polygamists
in Utah Territory, it had the secondary effect of making adultery and
fornication felonious offenses if committed by United States citizens in
Indian Territory. Both offenses were punishable by imprisonment. The
first was prosecuted from time to time; the second, rarely. Later, though,
after the adoption of the Arkansas criminal statutes in 1890, the newly
added "morality" laws appear to have been enforced with greater tenacity.

The deputies were not always of exemplary deportment. One, proceeding to Fort Smith with a group of prisoners, broke his journey at
Purcell, Chickasaw Nation, for a little illicit entertainment. With a party
of friends, all drunk and firing their revolvers, he "went to a house of bad
repute." After the "disorderly" conduct of the revelers had led to their
ejectment, the deputy was shot dead by another rowdy. The assailant was
hunted down and killed.[77]

A little later, three well-known officers of the Paris court visited the
office of the editor of the Gainesville, Texas, *Evening Register,* "knocking
him down and kicking his head and face in a most brutal manner." In a
story about one of the trio, the editor had adduced a connection between
the officer's frequent journeys through Gainesville and a married woman
of that town. All three deputies were heavily fined for aggravated assault,[78] but they remained in the employ of the marshal's office and made
many arrests, sometimes in the face of great physical danger.

A convention which met at Fort Smith in January 1889 to discuss the
probable results of an opening of the Oklahoma district was told that, by
the best estimates, 300 people had been murdered in the Indian Territory
during 1888.[79] Even if the true figure was only half that, a great many

murderers must have been uncaught, even unidentified. The multiple death sentences pronounced by Judge Parker and executed on the gallows at Fort Smith—for example, 6 men received sentence on February 2, 1889; 4 men and a woman on April 29 that year; and 6 men were hanged on January 16, 1890, after 3 others who were to have joined them had been granted commutation or respite—seem numerically unimpressive in comparison.[80]

Although most of the defendants who came before Parker were liquor traffickers, horse thieves, and other larcenists, it was his conduct of capital cases that excited most notice. Much of the ensuing controversy was caused by his isolation from, and virtual independence of, the designated circuit judge on the Supreme Court bench because of his dual role as district and circuit judge. Since, in practice, persons convicted at Fort Smith had no appeal except to executive clemency, a great deal depended on whether defendants could secure a fair trial in Parker's court. Jurors hearing a murder trial in the federal court at Fort Smith were allowed little scope by either the judge or the district attorney for finding a verdict of manslaughter when it was put to them plainly that if the defendant was guilty of anything, he was guilty of murder. Where, as in the case of George Brashears, a jury went its own way to the extent of bringing in a verdict of murder where there was ample room for manslaughter, Parker and the district attorney would encourage an application for leniency and give it their full support.[81] Where, as occasionally happened, a jury returned a conviction for manslaughter or an acquittal when in the judge's view the facts would justify nothing less than a conviction for murder, he would turn the full force of his feelings upon the jurors before letting them go.[82]

It was held against Parker that his charges to juries were far too long and that this lengthiness in itself amounted to unfairness because it burdened the minds of the jurors with far more than they needed to know or to think about. Worse than this, his diffusiveness led him into avoidable error in the definition of such common-law concepts as "malice aforethought" and "constructive flight."[83]

For these and related reasons, many death sentences were commuted by the Executive. An application for pardon or commutation was first examined by an official at the Department of Justice, the Clerk of Pardons (later known as the Pardon Attorney), whose task it was to select the most important and most deserving cases and pass them to the Attorney-General. The Attorney-General or one of his assistants would study the clerk's report and, in the gravest or most difficult cases, the accompanying papers. Exceptionally, the Attorney-General himself would examine the transcript of a trial, or extracts from it, before making his recommendation to the President. Usually the President would accept his Attorney-General's advice; instances occurred, notably when Cleveland occupied the Chief Executive's chair, when he would work his own way through the case papers before making up his mind.[84]

The procedure was the same in noncapital cases, except that all applications had to be accompanied by the recommendation of the sentencing judge and the prosecuting attorney or their successors in office. It is probable that all the real work on these lesser cases was done by the Pardon Attorney and, where there were problems, an Assistant Attorney-General. Often there were two considerations: the merits of the case and the importance of those who supported the application.

On balance, justice may have gained rather than suffered because these officials were unfamiliar with conditions in the Indian Territory; had not seen or heard the witnesses, defendants, judge, jurors, or spectators; and had not felt the atmosphere of the courtroom. It is evident that the Fort Smith court knew days when forensic processes were thrown out of true by the strength of its judge's personality. There was every need for a corrective factor.

An important consideration here was the quality of the Attorney-General. Among those who held the post between 1866 and 1906 only two, Alphonso Taft and Joseph McKenna, were inadequate. Neither held office for as long as a year. Most of the others were men of high intellect, much learning, and great administrative ability: Charles Devens (1877–1881), Benjamin Brewster (1882–1885), William Miller (1889–1893), Richard Olney (1893–1895), Judson Harmon (1895–1897), and John Griggs (1898–1901). The principal duties of the Attorney-General were to consider questions of law referred to him by other branches of the Executive; to prosecute specific cases placed before him by the President; to negotiate with congressional and other political leaders on questions of expenditure, patronage, and judicial reform; and to run his department. In his technical capacity he was concerned mostly with constitutional, civil, and corporative law: he would have very little time to scrutinize the niceties of a criminal trial from one of his districts, but occasionally, if the case was important enough or even interesting enough, he would make time to do so. Very few of the Attorneys-General had prior practical experience in the field of criminal law. Later it would be argued by Parker and others that this made them and the Assistant Attorneys-General unfit to speak upon matters of criminal law. This was nonsense. If Richard Olney never argued a case before a court in his career, it did not make him any less one of the finest legal minds of the day.[85]

It has been maintained that Parker was careless with the law, unversed in its finer points. Reference to some of his charges to grand and petit juries and to his pronouncements out of court affords convincing evidence—at any rate, to a layman—that he was deeply read in the law but evinced a keener regard for what he felt to be the spirit of the law than what he knew to be its letter.[86] This is true even when allowance is made for the fact that, in criminal trials conducted in the federal courts under common law, the judge was always much freer to comment upon the evidence than in comparable cases before a State court. The Attorneys-General and their principal aides seem to have been well aware of the distinction; but they also believed that Parker was inclined to make too much of it. Sometimes they were right, sometimes wrong. The same may be said of Parker's tendency to stress their total lack of practical experience in this branch of the law while extending little credit to their learning and intelligence.

Something surer and more flexible than presidential clemency was required to put a curb on the judge's arbitrary influence. It was one of Parker's admirers from the Democratic side, Senator Jones of Arkansas, who introduced a bill to abolish the court's circuit powers in all cases and to provide for a writ of error to be taken automatically from the district court to the Supreme Court after a conviction for a capital felony. Besides this, a new federal circuit court would be set up to hear appeals against convictions at Fort Smith on lesser charges. George Vest, supporting the bill, declared that "for years men have been executed without any right to ask the judgment of the Supreme Court of the United States whether it be judicial murder or not."

The bill was sent to President Cleveland just before the end of the session; but Cleveland's confidence in Parker was unshaken, and by leaving the bill unsigned at the adjournment he was able to frustrate a measure of which he disapproved.[87] Congress was not to be denied. Early in the new session, on December 18, 1888, Jones introduced another bill, identical with the first except in the date for its operation. Cleveland again declined to provide his signature; but since the legislature would still be in session at the end of the ten days prescribed by the Constitution for the approval or rejection of a bill laid before the President, it was an empty gesture. The bill became law on February 6, 1889, and went into effect on May 1.[88]

Almost the first successful applicants to the Supreme Court were two of the worst desperadoes ever to face judgment at Fort Smith. A new trial was ordered and ended in their being found guilty of manslaughter only. There were few such reversals before 1894, and the friction between

Parker and the superior body, which grew in intensity as the interventions of the Supreme Court became more frequent, might have been obviated if a congressional majority could have been summoned to enact into law the Attorney-General's annual request, regularly echoed in the presidential message, for the division of the crime of murder into degrees.

The new law made no difference to the Paris court since it had never possessed circuit powers. There the problem, from the viewpoint of those who believed that laws should be either enforced or repealed, was the notorious reluctance of a Texas jury to convict for murder if the circumstances of the killing even hinted at self-defense. Combined figures for the years 1890, 1891, and 1892 show that 169 persons were charged with murder and 108 indicted; but of the 108, only 1 was found guilty of murder and 8 of manslaughter. There were no executions at Paris until 1894. But the courts of Texas, and the Five Tribes, were not alone in their unwillingness in inflict the death penalty upon murderers. During those same three years a total of 16,987 murders were reported throughout the United States, but only 332 lawful executions were performed. There were 557 lynchings during the same period.[89]

Relations between the federal and tribal courts were no less contentious in the 1880s and early 1890s than during the 1870s; yet at Fort Smith there was a greater willingness to hand over Cherokee or Choctaw prisoners to their national authorities if the latter claimed jurisdiction under the terms of the treaties of 1866.[90] Judge Bryant at Paris went much further. In June 1890, he declared that he could take no jurisdiction in any case where all the parties were Choctaws, intermarried or not, even if one of them had served as an officer of the United States court or as an Indian policeman. This amounted to an opinion that the Indian Officers Act of 1888 was unconstitutional.[91] A year later, this principle was confirmed by the Supreme Court in *ex parte Mayfield,* a decision that put a halt to citizenship controversies as a factor affecting criminal jurisdiction.[92]

In at least two instances Cherokee cases were taken to Fort Smith through the operation of the provisions of the treaty of 1866 which permitted one of the parties to have the proceedings removed to the federal court when a resident of Canadian district was involved. The vexatious properties of this strange and anomalous law were demonstrated by John Drew, who, after being sentenced by the Canadian district court to five years in the national prison, applied to Parker for a writ of habeas corpus and was granted bail pending the hearing. Parker allowed both the writ and the consequent motion for a new trial, to be held at Fort Smith. Drew took occasion to extend the period covered by his bail but was tried in his absence, convicted, and sentenced, as before (and as the statute dictated) to five years' imprisonment. To the relief of the Cherokees who had gone bail for him, Drew surrendered a few days later.[93]

A far worse threat to the independence of the judiciaries of the Five Nations materialized from the renewed searching by lawyers for pretexts to invalidate the verdicts of the Indian courts by asking the United States Supreme Court to rule that the tribal proceedings had been in some way contrary to the provisions of the Constitution. Three such instances occurred early in 1893, all of them in the Cherokee Nation, and in each case the Cherokee system of justice, so often in the past justly censured for its failings, had secured the result the facts merited.

In *Talton,* the defendant was convicted of a brutal murder and sentenced to death. His lawyers then embarked on a series of maneuvers that delayed the operation of the law for a further three years. It was suggested at first that the victim's service as a federal officer would give jurisdiction to the Fort Smith court, but that ground had been cut away by the *Mayfield* decision. Talton's lawyers, however, obtained a writ of habeas corpus from Fort Smith and argued that their client, who was white-skinned, was a United States citizen. When this failed, they contended that the recently enacted Cherokee statute governing the composition of grand juries violated the Constitution of the United States. The Supreme Court disagreed and after several further postponements Talton was hanged. Nevertheless, the Cherokee government, by acquiescing in these procedures, had conceded the judicial primacy of the United States.[94]

A similar case occurred in October 1893 when the judge at Muskogee, Charles Stuart, issued a writ of habeas corpus in favor of two men due to be hanged the next day at the Cherokee national prison. It was argued for one man, a white adopted citizen, that he had not fully complied with the intermarriage law, for the other that he had been indicted under the allegedly "unconstitutional" grand jury law, and for both that their constitutional rights had been breached by irregularities in the conduct of their trials. Once again all pleas failed, but it is apparent that the intellectual and political basis of tribal sovereignty had diminished to the point where it could be thrown into the balance against the necks of a pair of murderers.[95]

CHAPTER TEN

Judicial Reform and the End of Tribal Self-Government, 1894–1899

Of course we desire full jurisdiction. . . . If the people of this country were permitted to have all classes of crime tried here by their own courts and juries, it would not only greatly reduce the public expenditure necessary to run these courts, but it would tend to encourage and elevate our people, and prepare them for the graver duties of citizenship when they shall be entrusted with the right of self-government.—Charles B. Stuart, U.S. district judge, Muskogee, Indian Territory, to Richard Olney, Annual Report of the Attorney General, *1894*

If the end of government and the administration of justice is the protection of the life and liberty and property of the citizen, then the governments and courts of the [Indian] nations are a failure, for they afford that protection to neither.—"[Second Annual] Report of the commission appointed to negotiate with the Five Civilized Tribes of Indians," 54th Cong., 1st sess., S. Doc. 12 (November 18, 1895, printed December 5, 1895)

Nearly three years passed before the Dawes Commission succeeded in opening full negotiations with the tribal governments. During that interval Congress introduced further courts into Indian Territory, arming them with plenary jurisdiction over all criminal and civil cases except those that were the preserve of the tribal courts.

Transfer of jurisdiction from the tribal to the federal courts for all civil actions begun, or criminal offenses committed, after the end of 1897 was the next step. It was accompanied by a measure subordinating the tribal governments to the Executive branch of the United States Government. Abolition of the tribal courts followed a year later, in June 1898, as part of the Curtis Act, which also provided for the allotment of the tribal lands within the next eight years and the maintenance of the facade of tribal government for the same time. Subsequently three of the Five Nations were allowed to retain courts of law for the duration of tribal government, but their jurisdiction was confined mainly to minor matters.

The three members of the Dawes Commission arrived in the Territory in January 1894 to hold exploratory talks with representatives of the Five Tribes. Almost at once "grievous complaints . . . regarding the administration of justice" came to their ears. Meredith Kidd gave his spare time "to an examination of the real situation here" and, a few weeks later, exhibiting early signs of the bluntness that would cost him his position the following year, condemned the courts at Fort Smith, Paris, and Muskogee in a letter to Senator David Turpie of Indiana:

> Each of these courts have [sic] a brood of deputy marshals who traverse this country, arrest citizens for slight offenses, carry them sometimes 100 or 200 miles, take them before a commissioner, and have them bound over to appear at one of the courts. There are nine U.S. Commissioners whose sole duty is to hold preliminary examinations, and place defendants under bond for their appearance at one of these courts.
>
> . . . [G]reat energy is displayed in bringing the most trifling causes before them, such causes often costing the Government from $50 to $100, and oppressing the people by carrying them great distances for examination. . . .
>
> . . . [C]ommissioners receive from the Government from $22,000 to $25,000 per year. The vast amount of these trifling causes finding their way to the [Indian] Territorial court so increases the business of the court that the clerk is receiving from the Government from $22,000 to $25,000 per year. . . .
>
> The whole thing is patchwork, the result of an attempt to improve things by additional legislation.
>
> It is a waste of time to attempt to improve it by further amendment, and [it] ought to be cut up root and branch.

Kidd estimated that if the Muskogee court was given jurisdiction over all federal cases in Indian Territory, some twenty-five United States commissioners appointed and empowered to try all minor cases, civil and criminal, and a salaried deputy marshal attached to each commissioner's court, the cost of maintaining the judiciary in Indian Territory would be cut by more than three-quarters. These changes would, he believed, eliminate a system more oppressive than "anything this side of Russia." He had praise for all three judges and for District Attorney Jackson ("a most estimable officer"), but the judicial arrangements overall were "a disgrace to civilization." The jails, wrote Kidd, "remind one of the prison pens beside the great road to the Siberian mines."[1]

Early in April three members of the Senate Select Committee on the Five Civilized Tribes—Henry Teller, Orville Platt, and William Roach (D, North Dakota)—followed the Dawes Commission to Muskogee, spending not quite ten days there: long enough to confirm the ideas they had started out with.

> This section of country was set apart to the Indian with the avowed purpose of maintaining an Indian community beyond and away from the influence of white people. We stipulated that they should have unrestricted self-government and full jurisdiction over persons and property within their respective limits, and that we would protect them against intrusion of white people, and that we would not incorporate them in a political organization without their consent. Every treaty, from 1828 to and including the treaty of 1866 was based on this idea of exclusion of the Indians from the whites and non-participation by the whites in their political and industrial affairs. We made it possible for the Indians of that section of country to maintain their tribal relations and their Indian polity, laws, and civilization if they wished to do so. And, if now, the isolation and exclusiveness sought to be given to them by our solemn treaties is destroyed, and they are overrun by a population of strangers five times in number to their own, it is not the fault of the Government of the United States, but comes from their own acts in admitting whites to citizenship under their laws and by inviting white people to come within their jurisdiction, to become traders, farmers, and to follow professional pursuits.[2]

Evidently it had not occurred to the select subcommittee that the "Indian polity, laws and civilization" the Five Tribes had taken to the Indian Territory had been acquired through "the influence of white people" and that four of the five had admitted whites to citizenship long before the removals. They seem also to have overlooked the provisions in the treaties of 1866 relating to the admission of United States citizens under license and the construction of railways inside the Indian Territory, neither of which suggests any determination by Congress to exclude whites or their influence.

The select committee's observations and recommendations on the courts system were more soundly based and better argued. They were similar to those of Meredith Kidd, Attorney-General Olney, and District Attorney Jackson. "The present system," they concluded, "is intolerable."

At the end of that month Teller, as chairman of the Senate Committee on the Judiciary, presented a memorial from five members of the South

McAlester bar. Their criticisms, though very like Meredith Kidd's in substance, were set out in far greater detail. The burden of their message was that, even with its jurisdictional limitations, and despite having a judge, Charles Stuart, who was "an unusually thrusting one," the Muskogee court was submerged beneath its caseload:

> When it is stated that at the January term, 1894, of the court in this, the second division, the docket showed 589 criminal and 260 civil cases . . . and that the docket in this division is the smallest of any of the three, you can form a conception of the magnitude of the task imposed upon one judge.[3]

On July 2, 1894, partly in response to actual need, partly to satisfy the clamor he and his colleagues had helped to promote, Teller introduced a bill, S.2173, to amend the acts of March 1, 1889, and May 2, 1890, and "to provide for the redistributing of the Indian Territory for judicial purposes, for an additional judge and more United States commissioners, and to prescribe the jurisdiction, duties, and authority of such judges and commissioners, and for other purposes."[3] Later Teller brought in an amendment carrying a proviso that reserved to the Indian courts "jurisdiction in civil and criminal cases arising in the country in which members of the nation by nativity or adoption shall be the only parties." It is significant, and indicative of the intent of the drafters, that there was no such proviso in the original.[4]

The reason for this signal omission was that the original contained two provisions for the transfer of criminal and civil proceedings from tribal to federal courts. "There will be no more farcical proceedings in the Indian courts . . . when the Teller bill gets through," averred one Washington press correspondent;[5] but both proposals were withdrawn after much lobbying by the Cherokee delegation,[6] including a printed memorandum addressed to Teller. Before entering into a closely reasoned argument on the implications of the two offending provisions, the writer remarked:

> I am keenly sensible of my weakness, or rather the infinite disadvantages I am required to encounter . . . because of the popular sentiment that has recently acquired the force of the Gulf stream, and insists that Indian governments of Indian Territory must be abolished and a territorial government erected instead.[7]

The Teller courts bill was passed by the Senate without discussion. It was not taken up by the House until the following January, a month after the publication of the first annual report of the Dawes Commission, whose official tour of the Indian Territory had coincided with a crime rush that lent itself readily to sensational treatment by the press and received it.

On October 24 Secretary of the Interior Hoke Smith, when asked what should be done "to prevent permanently the lawlessness and reign of terror that now exists in the Indian Territory," replied: "Abrogate the treaties, abolish the tribal relations, establish a territorial government and extend the jurisdiction of the United States over the whole territory."[8] Smith's views were opposed by his colleagues in Cleveland's cabinet and the President himself, but they typified those of the rising free-silver wing of the Democratic party, and were shared by a growing number of senior Republicans.

The "reign of terror" was nothing worse than a serious outbreak of armed robbery in the Cherokee, Creek, and Choctaw nations during and throughout the second half of 1894, the worst of several such irruptions in the Indian Territory between 1887 and the late 1890s. Some three or four really dangerous men and perhaps thirty loutish youths and ne'er-do-wells were the culprits. A band known as the Cook gang, responsible for about a third of the armed robberies in the region during that period of five or six months, was credited with nearly all of them by the press.

A long sequence of highway robberies, interspersed with several murders in the furtherance of robbery, was presented in the press as an upheaval of anarchy. A newspaper in north Texas proclaimed, *TERRORISM RAMPANT: An Unprecedented Carnival of Crime,*[9] but the style of such journals as the *New York Times* and New York *Herald* was no less mettlesome.[10]

Officialdom in the Indian Territory was as infected as much of the newspaper industry with a craving to promote a general alarum from a localized crime wave. A letter to the Cherokee principal chief from one experienced and esteemed Government employee, Union agent Dew Wisdom, closed with these lines of irradiant fatuity:

> As the Roman once said: "Carthage must be destroyed." (The Latin of it is, Carthago delenda est) so I say the "Cook gang must be destroyed," and it is the burning issue of the hour, and no other motto ought to be inscribed upon our mingled banners.[11]

But "the burning issue of the hour" had betaken itself to Texas several days before that letter was written, there to be quenched very quickly. Methodical and coolheaded investigation in the Indian Territory itself had been inhibited by the verbal intemperance of newspapermen, officials, and propagandists.

It was to be expected that the Dawes Commission would comment on the outbreak of crime. Their report was finished on November 20, 1894, at the height of the hysteria, and transmitted the febrility that had surrounded its preparation. The commissioners may have been impressionable; or they may have been unscrupulous in their exploitation of evidence that might assist the verdict they had mentally formed even before their arrival in Indian Territory. Their purpose, after all, was to move Indian Territory closer to Statehood. One editor saw the question in these terms:

> The outlawry and reported deeds of desperate men in the Indian territory is doing more to advance the cause of statehood every day that the Dawes Commission have done during their stay. With all due respect to them and their honest efforts, we have no hesitancy in saying that the Dawes Commission have been helped more by recent outbreaks of lawlessness than by any other means.[12]

Dawes, Kidd, and McKennon cannot be acquitted of malevolence without being convicted of stupidity.[13] Even if it had been true that the tribal courts were "helpless and paralized [sic]," that violence, robbery, and murder were "almost of daily occurrence," and that "no effective measures of restraint or punishment [were] put forth to suppress crime," these three statements formed no circumstantial chain, since much of the murder and violence, and nearly all the armed robbery, was outside the jurisdiction of the tribal courts, even when the criminals were Indians. As it happened, a fair number of the miscreants were Indian citizens, mostly Cherokee mixed-bloods and Creek blacks, but at least half were white noncitizens.

It was a matter of record that railroad trains passing through the Indian Territory had been "stopped and their passengers robbed within a few miles of populous towns."[14] But since the later 1880s, crimes of this nature had been common not merely in the western States and Territories but throughout the South and Middle West, including the home States of Commissioners Kidd and McKennon. During the mid-1890s there were a number of train robberies scarcely beyond the suburbs of St. Louis, yet the newspapers of that city continued to denounce the Indian Territory for its lawlessness.[15] Banditry and murder were commoner in the Indian Territory than elsewhere in rural America at this time, but not nearly to the extent implied by the Dawes Commission.

The commissioners damaged their credibility still further by repeating an assertion that, in the Cherokee Nation alone, as many as fifty-three people had been murdered during September and the first twenty-four days of October 1894. Isaac Parker put the total at about eight, four of which were federal cases. Parker's figure was too low; but the total of fifty-three was far too high.[16]

The local newspapers recognized that most of the brigandage was outside tribal jurisdiction and, having identified the federal authorities as their target, attacked them at times with a vigor close to ferocity.

Elsewhere in the report there was justification for much of the harshness of the commissioners' criticism. "Corruption of the grossest kind" permeated the whole process of government, as they charged; but even here the true picture was not as bleak as that drawn by the Dawes Commission. A few months later, for example, the council of the Muskogee Nation, the frailest political unit among the Five Tribes, summoned the vitality to secure the impeachment and removal of Principal Chief Legus Perryman for his part in a scheme to defraud the national treasury.[17]

It was also true that almost 1.25 million acres—well over one-third of the tribal domain—in the Muskogee Nation had been appropriated by sixty-one citizens for pasturage and cultivation. The commissioners might have added that, in the Cherokee Nation, 140,000 acres were to all intents and purposes owned by twenty-three individuals.[18] But there were only a few large cattle ranges in the Chickasaw Nation, and none of even middling size in the Seminole Nation after the recent removal of the few one-mile enclosures.[19] In the Choctaw Nation at this time there were only two very large pastures—one in effect owned (though of course Choctaw law could not acknowledge this) by Wilson Jones, the merchant and politician, the other by J. J. McAlester, the merchant, mining magnate, and U.S. marshal.

The problems with the tribal estate in the Chickasaw, Seminole, and Choctaw nations were indeed of a different order—different from those of the Cherokee and Creek lands and different from one another. In the Chickasaw Nation much of the land was being farmed by tenant farmers, mostly from Texas. The Seminole Nation was, politically and economically, the fief of the Brown family, though the Dawes Commission omitted to say so. As to the Choctaw Nation,

> [V]ast and rich deposits of coal of incalculable value have been appropriated by the few, to the exclusion of the rest of the tribe. . . . Large and valuable plants for mining coal have been established by capitalists under leases by which, together with "discoverer's claims" authorized by the tribal governments, these coal lands are covered, and under the workings of which the rightful owners are being despoiled of this valuable property with very little or no profit to them.[20]

At the turn of the year a delegation from the Five Tribes was sent to Washington to oppose "any adverse action on the part of Congress which might spring from the unfavorable report of the Dawes Commission." "The report," stated a newspaperman in Washington, "has stirred up a hornets' nest in the five nations": "It is regarded as the most dangerous attack yet made upon their autonomy as nations, and the delegates are all on the rampage about it."[21]

Fears expressed by Colonel Harris, the Cherokee principal chief, who was leading the delegation, that distribution of the tribal lands in severalty would lead to land monopoly, ring hollow against the fact that the monopolies already held a large segment of the Cherokee Nation and a much larger piece of the Muskogee Nation. For the Muskogee Nation, a rancher, lawyer, and politician, Albert McKellop, assailing the Dawes Commission for having overstated the frequency of highway robberies and other crimes in the Indian Territory, exaggerated the extent of the exaggeration. He asserted that the United States could be justified in the annulment of the treaties concluded with the Five Tribes only if "they [the United States] can show that they are doing it for self-preservation" but did not add that his name appeared near the top of the list of sixty-one companies, partnerships, or individuals controlling well over 1 million acres of the Creek domain in violation of those same treaties.[22]

A day or two later Judge Parker appeared in Washington. He was in the middle of a prolonged dispute with the Supreme Court and was resisting an attempt by that tribunal to "discipline" him. Parker visited the Department of Justice and, accepting an invitation to dine with President Cleveland, took the opportunity of advising the Chief Executive what he thought needed to be done in the Indian Territory.[23]

Parker's journey to Washington may have been prompted mainly by rumors that certain congressmen were planning to amend the pending Teller bill by stripping the Fort Smith and Paris courts of all jurisdiction in Indian Territory. Congressmen who had always preferred this course would have demanded it anyway; but their hand had been greatly strengthened by the fury of the verbal assaults directed at the Fort Smith deputies for their failure to make an early end of the outlaw gangs that had been so lively in 1894. When political enemies of James McAlester, the marshal of the Muskogee court, attacked him on that ground, he and his friends turned the tables by retorting that his role could only be a subordinate one; as serious crimes were outside the jurisdiction of the Muskogee court, the Fort Smith officers took the lead in all matters concerning them. Further impetus for court reform came from the publication of the Dawes Commission report. Dawes aimed for the abolition of tribal government, but if that object was not at once attainable, its advocates in Congress could, as before, press for court reform to take them nearer their goal.

Parker testified before the House Committee on the Judiciary on

January 10, pleading the virtues of the tribal governments and those of the federal courts at Fort Smith, Paris, and Muskogee. His testimony provoked a bitter letter from a spectator, a white resident of Indian Territory. The letter was addressed to Attorney-General Olney but found its way from the Department of Justice to an Arkansas congressman, Thomas McRae, who introduced it into the House debate on the Teller bill:

> Before the committee meeting in question Judge Parker denied that there exists a necessity for a change in the judicial status of the Indian Territory. . . . In his specious and cursory defense of existing institutions and conditions in that country Judge Parker had nothing to say of the outlaw reign of terror which has for some months disgraced his jurisdiction. . . .
>
> Deputy marshal rule does not conserve good citizenship under a home jurisdiction; under a foreign jurisdiction it is vicious and odious. The people of the Indian Territory are treated as subjects of a conquered province. . . . They are smarting under the manifest and manifold wrongs of the present iniquitous system. . . .
>
> We mistrust and fear the deputy marshal almost to the degree that we do the outlaw. The distinction between the two is in many instances a very fine one. . . .
>
> The conscience of the people of the Indian Territory has become as paralyzed as are their hands in the remedying of this evil. . . .
>
> . . . Why is their prayer not heard? I suspect that it is because we are political orphans, unrepresented and disfranchised. Not so with the towns of Paris, Tex., and Fort Smith, Ark., The interests of their lawyers, stores, hotels, and saloons are protected; and at what a cost to 250,000 American citizens whose liberties are bartered to pay them tribute.
>
> . . . The foreign courts of high jurisdiction [Paris, Fort Smith] and the home court of petty jurisdiction [Muskogee] have united, through their congressional watchdogs, in seeing to it that we get nothing more. Herod and Pilate, having crucified a helpless Christ, will divide his raiment amicably.
>
> Judge Parker puts his bare assertions anent Indian Territory conditions against the exhaustive official report of the Dawes Commission. The latter has expressed the truth, but not half the truth. Judge Parker may have been talking for his job, like many another patriot who comes to Washington.[24]

Perhaps the writer's powers of reason had been numbed by the fiery splendor of his imagery. Those who were "unrepresented and disfranchised" were in that position as a result of an act of free will on their part. While most of them had entered the Indian Territory with the consent, even the encouragement, of Indian citizens, they had come in the knowledge that they were forfeiting all formal political rights, just as they were releasing themselves from the obligation to pay local, State, or federal taxes. Did they now hope to be granted representation in Washington without taxation? But the real point is that representation in Washington could not come without State or Territorial government, either of which would mean the imposition of taxes upon all, Indian citizens and noncitizens.

No doubt Isaac Parker had been "talking for his job," and there was truth in criticisms elsewhere in the letter of the deputy marshals of the Fort Smith, Paris, and Muskogee courts, though the taunt that these men were "swaggering bullies . . . so handy with their guns when there is no danger and so venal in the working up of cases" was unjust. Some deputies were brutal, and some dishonest, but very few were cowardly. Recklessness in a deputy was neither an individual nor an official virtue, but where prudence was not an option many officers showed extreme bravery, when given the chance.

McRae and another Arkansas Democrat, Sebastian Little, were the principal adversaries of the bill. Their argument was that, if it became law, it would retard the progress of the Indian country toward Territorial or State government by leaving untouched the jurisdiction of the Fort Smith court. Yet neither they nor anyone else brought in an amendment to curtail the powers of the courts at Fort Smith and Paris. There was one important alteration: the bill as accepted by the House provided for the division of Indian Territory into three judicial districts instead of two. Only ninety-two members were in attendance when the vote was taken.[25]

On the following day, January 15, 1895, when the Indian appropriation bill for 1895–96 was before the House, Little delivered a massive oration on "the condition of affairs that now exists in the Indian Territory." After allowance has been made for the overblown rhetoric, its portrayal of tribal politics, supported by the evidence of several recent financial scandals, remains a powerful presentation of one side of the question.

Little's attempt to prove, by giving a public reading of newspaper accounts of numerous individual crimes committed by Indian citizens and noncitizens in the Indian Territory, that there was a general disregard for law and order among the people living in the Five Tribes country, may also have been effective in delivery, but it is unpersuasive in print. Newspapers do not record the ordinary events of ordinary lives on an ordinary day; normality does not make news. Even the fact that in the Fort Smith court alone there had been 860 convictions during 1894, nearly all from the Indian country, did not make the Indian Territory "[t]he very glen of criminal miasma, the fumes and the poison from which are not only penetrating the best blood of that country, but [whose] contaminating influence is extending into the adjoining States."

Little was fiercely scornful of the tribal delegates, some of whom may have deserved the censure, though perhaps not the venom that charged it:

These men come here clothed with authority to represent their tribal governments with the money they have so wantonly filched from the pockets of the poor and uneducated natives. . . .

In their talk about the poor Indians these delegates, with their pity, their tears, and their sorrow, remind one of the story of the crocodile, which runs as follows:

There was a crocodile lay on the banks of the Nile; He screamed and cried and exclaimed, "My heart, my heart, oh it doth break out of the pity for the little fishes I ate."

[Laughter]

. . . They say, "Let us alone for a little while longer; for a few years, until we eat up the wealth and prosperity of that country." I say, strike off their hands and restore that country to the people to whom it belongs naturally, so that every man, every woman, and every child living there of native blood shall have an equal, equitable, and just proportion of the country.[26]

The Teller courts bill had been with the Committee of Conference for just over a week when, on January 22, Senator John Tyler Morgan introduced a new courts bill in the guise of an amendment to the Indian appropriation bill for 1895–96. Morgan's amendment, like the House's amendment to the Teller bill, called for judicial districts to be formed in Indian Territory, each with its own judge, attorney, and marshal and each to have full jurisdiction over all criminal and civil cases in which United States citizens were concerned. Its objective in the longer run was, as Morgan later explained, "gradually to get rid of the Indian courts."[27] In specific terms, the amendment demanded removal of all criminal and nearly all civil jurisdiction from the tribal courts two years after its passage into law, besides the immediate abolition of the outside federal courts.

Harris and the rest of the Cherokee delegation learned, or discerned, that this amendment was intended to anticipate the Teller bill, which was still locked in the conference committee, or to supersede it there. Early in February 1895 they wrote to the President with their objections to the amendment. Their grounds for complaint: first, it violated the treaty of 1866 by proposing to interfere with the Cherokees' right to try their own citizens; second, it would indirectly nullify all the other treaty undertakings and demoralize the Indians by depriving them of the assurance that they were the "masters of their own property"; third, federal courts with powers to try *all* cases would be foreign tribunals to full-bloods who could understand neither the English language nor laws and practices not their own; fourth, such a "radical" change so instantly instituted would mark a break with the "fair and equitable" manner in which (they wrote) the United States had always dealt with the Five Tribes.[28]

Several days later, Harris and another delegate wrote frankly to one of their friends in the Senate, William Vilas (D, Wisconsin), asking him to "urge Senate Bill 2173 to a successful termination." This, the Teller bill, "having passed through regular parliamentary channels," would "meet all the demands for the faithful execution of law in the Indian Territory."

> On the other hand the Morgan Amendment to HR 8479 [the Indian appropriation bill], is being pushed in such a peculiar way as to make the impression that discussion and examination by Judiciary Committees were unnecessary.
> From the manner in which this amendment is being rail-roaded, the conclusion is inevitable that the advocates of the measure would disregard the usual parliamentary procedure, as well as prevent the possibility of executive interference by the exercise of veto power.[29]

President Cleveland, they knew, could not easily veto an Indian appropriation bill, no matter how much he wanted to protect the Five Tribes from violations of the treaties of 1866 and to preserve the presence in Indian Territory of the Fort Smith and Paris courts.

Delegates and representatives of the Creek, Choctaw, and Chickasaw nations joined the Cherokees in a letter to the three members of the Senate Committee on the Indian appropriation bill, elaborating upon the arguments the Cherokee delegates had put to the President. The joint letter ended:

> [T]here is and has been great complaint at the immense costs of the United States Courts in our country, as now created.
> We submit that, if this amendment should become a law, and the Federal jurisdiction extended over everybody and everything, the expense will be very much greater.[30]

"The fight for and against the Morgan amendment to the Indian appropriation bill has commenced in earnest," a Washington correspondent reported on February 6. Rumor had it that "Senator Jones of Arkansas is behind the Morgan amendment, as the Alabama man has no real interest in the matter, though the Arkansas congressmen are all favorable to opening up the territory to the whites."[31] It may have been impolitic for Jones to put himself at the head of a call for legislation that would involve the abolition of the Fort Smith court's jurisdiction in Indian Territory, yet the proposal to do away with the tribal courts gave expression to one of Morgan's pet themes—the absolute power of Congress "through the assistance of the President" in "all matters relating to human government" within the boundaries of the United States. In 1892 he had introduced a bill to allow the United States Supreme Court to hear appeals from the highest courts of the Five Tribes, only to have it rejected by the House of Representatives.[32]

On February 8 the Senate conferees on the Teller bill recommended nonconcurrence of the House amendments. Vilas, Teller, and Platt were to represent the Senate at the conference with the House that could be expected to follow.[33]

Congressman David Culberson was the main obstacle to the Morgan amendment. He had announced that he would not "give up the jurisdiction the Paris court has in the Indian territory if he can help it" and would "fight the amendment at every step through the Senate and house, and then . . . fight it if it passes before the President himself." Culberson had already declined to yield to the Morgan amendment in return for a fifteen-month extension of the Paris court's jurisdiction in Indian Territory. By February 6, he was considering, ostensibly without enthusiasm, an offer for the extension to be lengthened from fifteen months to eighteen. There was conjecture that President Cleveland might carry his opposition to the Morgan amendment to the point of refusing his assent to the Indian appropriation bill, and it became known that Morgan's supporters hoped to circumvent this eventuality by incorporating the provisions of the amendment in the Teller bill while the latter lay before the conference committee.[34] It was the purpose of Culberson and the other House conferees to frustrate this scheme altogether or drive a hard bargain.

The next phase of the proceedings was later sketched with theatrical brio by a member of the Cherokee delegation:

> Around this bill [the Morgan amendment] and insisting on its passage were the lobbyists from Arkansas, Oklahoma, and Indian Territory. For a while it seemed to be moving with the force of a cyclone. All of its friends were exultant, and predicted its passage. Of course, our delegation was doing all that was in their power to avert the monstrous stroke which was aimed at the very heart of our nation. We sent in our protests to the committee having the bill under consideration, expostulating against its passage, while we, as opportunity offered, spoke personally to members in reference to the bill.[35]

A press correspondent reported on February 11 that the Morgan bill "seems to be wandering around in space":

> I asked Senator Teller today if this amendment was liable to be attached to his bill and he replied that he did not know. Inquiry from Senator Jones, who seems to be the moving spirit behind the Morgan amendment, elicited the information that the Morgan amendment was now a bill in itself. He said that the committee [on appropriations] has concluded that it was better that the amendment should be detached from the Indian appropriation bill and should be offered to the senate on its own merits. The appropriations committee has the right of way on their measure, and when the appropriation bill came to them it would be temporarily laid

aside that the court bill of Mr. Morgan should be considered. If the latter passed, then when the regular Indian appropriation bill came up the court bill would be attached to it as an amendment.

He went on to say that in the House "the only hearty antagonisms will have been removed by the concessions made to Mr. Culberson and a few more men who are interested in the Paris and Fort Smith courts." He also reiterated the thought that the bill might be vetoed if Cleveland saw the proposal to expunge the Indian courts as a violation of the treaties, and pointed out that if the Morgan bill ran into difficulties in the Senate, "it can be attached to the Teller bill in conference."

This anonymous but well-briefed newspaperman was able to assert that although the House conferees on the Teller bill would not be appointed until the following day, they would "favor the Morgan bill."[36]

Next day, February 12, Culberson moved that the House further insist upon its amendments to the Teller bill. He, Joseph Bailey (D, Texas), and George Ray (R, New York) were appointed as the House side of the forthcoming conference committee.[37]

Morgan resubmitted his amendment to the Senate "with some slight change of verbiage" on February 22, the day after the Indian appropriation bill had been reported back to the chamber without his original set of proposals. After a lengthy address by Morgan, and certain procedural complications, the amendment was ruled out of order as "general legislation on an appropriation bill."[38] At that juncture, "the Teller bill, at last released from the side track in which it had been for some time held, presumably to make way for the passage of the Morgan bill, came moving on."[39]

The defeat of the "Morgan scheme" was hailed by the Cherokee delegation as "a happy deliverance of our country from immediate overthrow." Unlike many of their predecessors, the delegates of 1895 did not see that any act of Congress to consolidate institutions of the federal Government within the borders of the Indian Territory would bring the tribal governments a long step closer to extinguishment by the United States. They even believed, or professed to believe, that "the vast amount of judicial machinery put in operation in our country by the Teller law" would prove that "there can be no necessity for the nations of a territorial government," there being, according to them, no possibility of a Territorial government being introduced without tribal consent.[40]

The courts bill that emerged from the conference committee on February 25 was in effect a new measure—a hybrid fashioned from the Senate bill, the House amendment, some of the less radical features of the Morgan bill, and various provisions welded in to pacify Culberson and other allies of the Fort Smith and Paris system. By the end of the month, the conference report had been accepted by both branches of Congress, and on March 1, 1895, it received the presidential signature.[41]

All but one of the eleven sections of the act would apply from the date of its passage. The exception was Section 9, which stipulated that the courts at Paris, Fort Smith, and Fort Scott were to retain their jurisdiction in Indian Territory until September 1, 1896, when the three new district courts would assume responsibility for all criminal cases originating in the Indian country except for those belonging to the Indian courts. There was a further qualification: the outside courts would continue to hold jurisdiction in cases that had arisen before the date of the transfer, even if no writ had been issued. During the eighteen months between the approval of the act and the assumption of full jurisdiction, the three new courts would exercise the same powers as the previous court at Muskogee.

Muskogee now became the headquarters of the Northern District of Indian Territory, which was composed of the Creek, Seminole, and Cherokee nations and the Quapaw Agency; Vinita, Miami, and Tahlequah were the other court towns.

The headquarters of the Central District, which consisted of the Choctaw Nation, was South McAlester. The other court towns were Atoka, Antlers, and Cameron.

Ardmore (the headquarters), Purcell, Ryan, and Chickasha were the court towns for the Southern District, which comprised the Chickasaw Nation.

Charles Stuart and James McAlester, judge and marshal at Muskogee, were transferred to the Central District, at South McAlester. District Attorney Jackson would remain at Muskogee. Two new judges, marshals, and district attorneys were to be appointed, all for four-year terms terminable at pleasure, as with comparable appointments in organized United States Territories.

Each marshal could appoint up to four deputies. If "specially authorized" by the district judge, that number could be increased without set limit. For the first time, the deputy marshal would be a salaried officer. These were the regular deputies. Temporary or "special" deputies could be appointed "in case of emergency," their pay and expenses to be calculated on the same basis as the salaried officers'.

Each of the district judges was to appoint up to six United States commissioners, and one constable would be appointed for each commissioner's court, all to be paid by salary. The commissioners were authorized to try civil cases where the disputed sum was no more than $100

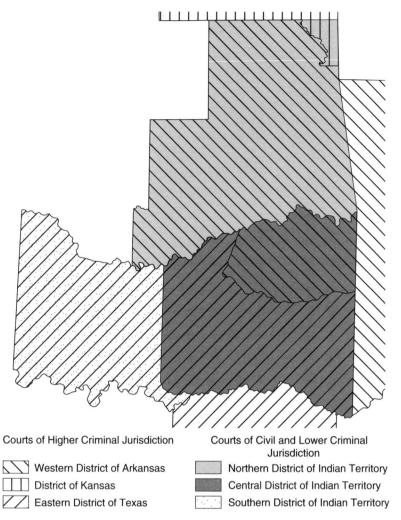

Courts of Higher Criminal Jurisdiction

| | Western District of Arkansas |

| | District of Kansas |

| | Eastern District of Texas |

Courts of Civil and Lower Criminal Jurisdiction

| | Northern District of Indian Territory |

| | Central District of Indian Territory |

| | Southern District of Indian Territory |

MAP 4. FEDERAL JUDICIAL DISTRICTS IN INDIAN TERRITORY, MARCH 1, 1895–AUGUST 31, 1896

By the beginning of 1895 intense pressure had built up inside and outside Congress to liquidate the federal jurisdiction exercised in Indian Territory by courts situated in Arkansas, Texas, and Kansas. The immediate object of the reformers was to reshape the three divisions of the U.S. court at Muskogee into three judicial districts with the power to determine all federal cases, criminal and civil, originating within the Five Nations country. The real, and overt, purpose of the reforms was to advance the policy of bringing Territorial government to the area.

The Courts Act of March 1, 1895, was a compromise with the bill's opponents only to the extent that the outside courts were to retain superior jurisdiction in criminal cases for a further eighteen months. During that interval the new district courts, once their officials had been appointed, shared the duties previously discharged by the original Muskogee court.

Between March 1, 1895, and September 1, 1896, therefore, no fewer than six

federal district courts exercised jurisdiction in the Five Tribes area. The higher criminal jurisdiction was shared by the Western District of Arkansas, the Fort Scott
division of the District of Kansas, and the Paris division of the Eastern District of
Texas. The new Northern, Central, and Southern Districts of Indian Territory were
courts of civil and lower criminal jurisdiction.

Section 17 of the Act of March 1, 1889, had defined the line separating the Eastern
Texas and Western Arkansas districts accurately enough for ordinary map-sketching
purposes, but the legislators evidently were unfamiliar with the equivocal propensities
of creeks and roads in the Indian Territory:

> Beginning on Red River at the southeast corner of the Choctaw Nation; thence north
> with the boundary-line between the said Choctaw Nation and the State of Arkansas to
> the point where Big Creek, a tributary of the Black Fork of the Kimishi [sic] River,
> crosses the said boundary line; thence westerly with Big Creek and the said Black Fork
> to the junction of the said Black Fork with Buffalo Creek; thence northwesterly with
> said Buffalo Creek to a point where the same is crossed by the old military road from
> Fort Smith, Arkansas, to Boggy Depot, in the Choctaw Nation; thence southwesterly
> with the said road to where the same crosses Perryville Creek; thence northwesterly up
> said creek to where the same is crossed by the Missouri, Kansas and Texas Railway
> track; thence northerly up the center of the main track of the said road to the South
> Canadian River; thence up the center of the main channel of the said river to the west-
> ern boundary-line of the Chickasaw Nation, the same being the northwest corner of the
> said nation. . . .

This gave the two courts plenty to argue about, when they were not arguing first
with the officials of the original Muskogee court and then, from March 1895, those of
the three new Indian Territory district courts.

In the spring of 1896 an attempt to perpetuate the superior criminal jurisdiction
of the outside courts was only barely defeated in Congress. The three new Indian
Territory courts now looked forward eagerly to the day when they would take over
full jurisdiction. That day came on Tuesday, September 1, 1896, at two o'clock in the
afternoon. At Paris seventy-five deputies attended "a swell banquet" thrown by U.S
Marshal J. Shelby Williams; at Fort Smith, Judge Parker lay mortally sick. After that
the Fort Smith, Paris, and Fort Smith courts held a dwindling residual jurisdiction in
Indian Territory until they had cleared their existing caseloads.

The boundaries of the three judicial districts of Indian Territory from March 1,
1895, were added to the Land Office map of 1891 by an Office of Indian Affairs
official.

and, as ex-officio justices of the peace (as defined in the Arkansas statutes), to dispose finally of prosecutions for misdemeanors. Their duties in
cases of felony remained those of an examining magistrate.

Two of the provisions related to specific categories of crime. As an
exception to the general rule that, where the laws of the United States and
those of Arkansas prescribed differing penalties for a particular offense,
the United States statute should be followed, it was laid down that larceny
should be punished according to the Arkansas code. Federal law stipu-

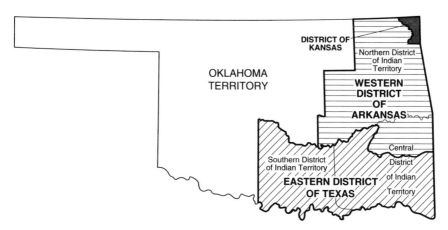

Map 5. Federal Judicial Districts of Indian Territory, March 1, 1895–
August 31, 1896

Under the structure laid down by the Courts Act of 1895 the Cherokee, Creek, and Seminole nations and the Quapaw Agency composed the Northern District of the Indian Territory, with Vinita, Miami, Tahlequah, and Muskogee as court towns; the Choctaw Nation, the Central District (South McAlester, Atoka, Antlers, and Cameron); and the Chickasaw Nation, the Southern District (Ardmore, Purcell, Ryan, and Chickasha).

The inaugural holders of the principal offices of the three districts:

Northern: judge, William Springer; marshal, Samuel Morton Rutherford; attorney, Clifford Jackson. (Springer became chief justice after Central District Judge Stuart's resignation and held his position until 1899.)

Central: judge, Charles Stuart; marshal, James McAlester; attorney, James V. Walker. (Stuart was appointed chief justice of the U.S. supreme court for the Indian Territory, but in September 1895 quit office to become a railroad attorney. Yancey Lewis, who replaced him as district judge, was succeeded after his removal in 1897 by William Clayton of Fort Smith, Arkansas. Walker resigned in June 1895 with effect from July 5, 1895, when William Horton succeeded him.)

Southern: judge, Constantine Buckley (Buck) Kilgore; marshal, Lucius Stowe; attorney, Andrew Cruce. (Stowe fell ill and died four months after taking his appointment. His brother Charles succeeded him. Kilgore died in September 1897, and was replaced by Hosea Townsend.)

The intentions and implications of the Courts Act of 1895 were well understood. One newspaper in northeast Texas, the Sherman *Courier,* put it tersely: "It is thought that the new judicial arrangement in the Indian Territory is the longest step yet taken toward territorial government and statehood."

Under a section of the Indian Appropriation Act approved on May 27, 1902, the Seminole and Creek nations and a small segment of the Cherokee Nation were detached from the Northern District to form a new Western District with courts at Muskogee, Wagoner, Sapulpa, Wewoka, Eufaula, and Okmulgee. Sallisaw, Claremore, Nowata, and Pryor Creek were added to the list of court towns in the Northern District; Tishomingo and Ada were established as court towns in the Southern District; and Durant became a court town in the Central District.

Charles Raymond was judge of the new Western District; the district attorney was William Mellette, and the marshal, Leo Bennett.

lated a maximum sentence of fifteen years' imprisonment, but set no minimum; the Arkansas law specified a maximum of five years in prison, but demanded a minimum sentence of one year. For petty theft (the theft of items worth no more than $10), which was not recognized by United States law as a distinct grade of crime, Arkansas law set the maximum penalty at one year's imprisonment. The theft of a horse or mule was also accorded a place of its own in the Arkansas statutes: conviction would mean at least five years in prison, and perhaps as much as fifteen years.

Secondly, the oversight in the Intoxicants Act of July 23, 1892, which had prohibited the introduction of ale, beer, and wine but not their manufacture, was now remedied. Lager and "Choctaw beer" had been manufactured in large quantities throughout Indian Territory, after the law of 1892 as before it. The Attorney-General could go no further than direct that the manufacture of these liquids could be prevented only when the product was found to be intoxicating. A situation rich in comic possibilities was ended by Section 8 of the Teller courts act, which forbade the manufacture, introduction, or disposal of "any vinous, malt, or fermented liquors, or any other intoxicating drinks of any kind whatever, whether medicated or not."[42]

William Springer, whose twenty uninterrupted years in the House had come to an end with his defeat in the election of 1894, was appointed judge for the Northern District. This was a reward from Cleveland for his long and intimate interest in the Oklahoma question, and for the much more recent conversion to the gold standard that may have cost Springer reelection. Constantine Buckley Kilgore of Texas, another former congressman, was made judge of the Southern District. They, along with Judge Stuart, the designated chief justice, were to sit as the Court of Appeals for the Indian Territory; but Stuart resigned in September 1895 and Springer became chief justice, with Yancey Lewis of Texas replacing Stuart at South McAlester.[43]

Judge Parker was happy to respond to an invitation from the House Committee on the Judiciary to present his views on the impending reforms:

> As you are well aware, as far as I am personally concerned, to take away this jurisdiction would remove a great burden from my shoulders, because for twenty years I have had to wrestle with one of the greatest problems of the age . . . but at the same time, while the Indian country is in its present condition, I can not see that it would inure to the benefit of that country or its peaceable and law-abiding people, but on the contrary, in my judgment, it would increase crime there.

> . . . And it is my judgment . . . that the strong judicial arm of the
> Government, as it has been wielded by what are sometimes called these
> outside courts, should remain extended over the Indian country . . . until
> that country is able to place its star on our flag—until its autonomy is
> changed from what it is now to statehood.[44]

Judge Bryant addressed himself in similar terms to a member of the
Chickasaw delegation then in Washington:

> If Congress puts the Indian Territory into a Territorial form of
> government, or takes the jurisdiction from Paris and Fort Smith and
> gives it exclusively to the courts of the Indian country, crime will rule
> the day. . . .
> The Indians and the law-abiding white men of your country have con-
> fidence in the juries at Paris and Fort Smith, because they are not involved
> in the local feuds and local interests, not related to nor acquainted with
> the defendants, and consequently can have no motive or do other than
> right.
> . . . I will add, personally, it would be to my interest to lose the ju-
> risdiction at Paris; it would relieve me of great labor and annoyance, but
> interest does not control me.[45]

These views were endorsed by express and railway companies whose
operations in the Indian Territory had been disrupted by bandits.[46] A bill
to retain the outside courts, supported by the Chickasaw government and
bearing the strong recommendation of the House Judiciary Committee,
was introduced by Little in January 1896. Despite all that Little and
Culberson could do, it was rejected, though only narrowly.[47] Even if the
Little bill had been passed by the House, the Senate would have given it
short shrift. Resistance there to any move to prolong the supremacy of the
outside courts had been mobilized by Senators Teller, Morgan, Vest, and
Platt, the joint addressees of a petition from fifty members of the Ardmore Bar Association.[48]

There was also a growing body of support in the Senate for the
program of the Dawes Commission, whose second annual report, even
more hostile than the first to the tribal courts and governments, had been
published recently.[49] In March 1896, one of the commissioners—now five
in number, with the appointment of three new men after the enforced
resignation of Meredith Kidd—testified at length before the House Committee on Indian Affairs. Among the exhibits was a letter from Edgar
Smith, second assistant district attorney at Fort Smith.

> Court opened for August term on 5th of August, and the regular panel
> of jury held until about the 20th of October, every day from 8.30 to
> 6 o'clock, being occupied with the trial of criminal cases. Court was open
> regularly from this time to November 2, but there was no time for civil
> business, this time being necessary for motions for new trial, sentences, etc.

Then on November 4 the November term commenced, with a new jury, and continues at this time. The work has occupied every day except November 28 [Thanksgiving Day] and December 25, and I suppose the present jury can be charged about the 15th day of this month [January, 1896]. The February term will commence February 2, and so on, ad infinitum.[50]

Another aspect of the strain thrown upon the Fort Smith and Paris courts in the middle 1890s is seen in a request made by Sinclair Taliaferro, district attorney for the Eastern District of Texas, to Attorney-General Olney. Taliaferro called on Olney in Washington to ask him to persuade a sympathetic congressman to introduce a bill providing for a verdict in a murder case of "guilty, without capital punishment." As the district attorney explained to a congressman in December 1895,

> I have on the docket of this court for trial at the next term, commencing in April, 73 murder cases, where parties are either in jail or under bond. In many of these the facts will not permit the court to submit the question of manslaughter to the jury, and the only question to be determined will be that of murder, which is now punishable only by death, and the severity of the penalty in many cases where the parties are undoubtedly guilty and should be punished, prevents the juries from either reaching a verdict or leads them to acquit the defendant.[51]

There were also, according to the recent report of the Dawes Commission, 128 alleged murderers ("nearly all of whom are eluding arrest") who had been indicted by the Paris court but were unavailable for trial. At Fort Smith, during the same year, the number of murderers convicted was a comparatively modest 20, but it was higher than any previous total.[52] Altogether 2,641 criminal and 22 civil cases were settled in Judge Parker's court during the three years from July 1, 1893, to June 30, 1896. Judge Bryant's record for the same period was 1,248 criminal and 6 civil cases. The Indian Territory courts tried 4,695 criminal and 3,586 civil cases, even though there were far fewer prosecutions during the months that followed the reorganization of March 1, 1895.[53]

The slackening yield of the Indian Territory courts in cases tried was marked with approval by some as proof that the deputy marshals, once placed on the salaried list, would cease hounding those guilty only of trivial infringements. For others, the decreasing haul of the courts in Indian Territory was conclusive evidence that, with a salary to cushion him, and freed of that urgency of incentive which springs from a scale of remuneration dependent solely upon results achieved, the deputy would slide into a life of languor. The chief reason may have been that the newly organized courts began to run smoothly only after they had acquired full jurisdiction in September 1896.

There were further jurisdictional clashes during this period. Ill feeling between the federal and Choctaw authorities was revived by the Eli Baldwin affair of 1894. Baldwin was murdered by a mob of fellow Choctaws led by the sheriff and judge of Cedar County. Once again, tribal politics were at the root of the difficulty. Baldwin and others of his party had committed acts of violence against their political enemies, who retaliated by killing Baldwin. Because Baldwin had regularly worked as posse for a deputy marshal of the Paris court, the authorities at Paris decided that there were grounds for prosecuting the murderers under the Indian Officers Protection Act of 1888 despite the *ex parte Mayfield* ruling.

In December 1894, the federal grand jury at Paris indicted the Choctaw sheriff and twenty-six others for murder. A good deal of indignation was aroused among the Choctaws by the intervention of the federal authorities, and the tribal senate appropriated $1,000 to pay for the defense; but public approval and official endorsement of mob law, in which a sheriff and judge were participants, were more damaging to the case for tribal autonomy than the interference by the United States court.[54] To borrow the comment a Cherokee newspaper passed at about this time, in the context of factional disturbances in Illinois district, "The nation has weight enough to carry without being weakened by internal divisions."[55]

Late in 1895, the imperfections of the existing federal court structure and some of its servants were exhibited in the Blue River case. This, too, arose in the Choctaw Nation, though none of those involved in it were Choctaws by blood. On Christmas day a man named Young was arrested by a deputy of the Central District for drawing a pistol during a brawl. A deputy of the Paris court then appeared at the head of an armed party and tried to take custody of Young on a warrant alleging larceny. A skirmish ensued in which Young and the Paris deputy were killed.

The upshot of the fray was "a most peculiar and interesting trial" at Paris, with six defendants charged with the murder of Young and two with the murder of the Paris deputy. Testimony was given that Young and the Central District deputy who had first arrested him were members of one of two opposing sets of feudists and that the Paris deputy had been a leader of the other faction.[56] While it may be wondered whether the marshals at Paris and South McAlester ought to have employed such men as these two in any circumstances, the real fault rested with those politicians who had prolonged a situation where there were overlapping, semi-concurrent jurisdictions within the confines of the federal court system.

When the Indian appropriation bill for 1896–97 came before Congress early in 1896, it was converted, as was becoming customary, into a vehicle for legislation of much more general nature. Senators lodged the customary protests that this was a practice in breach of their own rules; then added the customary saving clause that, having all due regard to the unusual importance of the measure before them at that particular time, a departure from the rules was justified. Only a bare handful of senators—Southern Democrats and New England Republicans—basing their objections on grounds of both procedure and principle, opposed the enactment of provisions that, while deriving their justification from abuses of power by the tribal governments, were intended to accelerate the total closure of those governments.

The most important of this latest batch of appropriation bill riders clad the Dawes Commission with quasi-judicial powers, constituting it a "Citizenship Court," and was the response of Congress to some of the most pungent passages of criticism in the commission's second annual report. These were the commissioners' observations on the current condition of the tribal roll of the Cherokee Nation:

> A tribunal was established many years ago for determining the right of admission to this roll, and it was made up at that time by judicial decision in each case. Since that time and since the administration of public affairs had fallen into present hands, this roll has become a political football, and names have been stricken from it and added to it, without notice or rehearing or power of review, to answer political or personal ends and with entire disregard of rights affected thereby. . . . The practice of striking names from the rolls has been used in criminal cases to oust courts of jurisdiction depending on that fact, and the same names have been afterwards restored to the roll when that fact would oust another court of jurisdiction of the same offense. Glaring instances of the miscarriage of prosecutions from this cause have come to the knowledge of the Commissioners and cases of the greatest hardship affecting private rights are of frequent occurrence. . . .
> The "intruders roll" is being manipulated in the same way.
> . . . The roll is now being prepared for that purpose by the Cherokee authorities, in a manner most surprising and shocking to every sense of justice, and in disregard of the plainest principles of law. The chief [Samuel Mayes] assumes to have authority to "designate" the names to be put upon the intruders' roll, and names are, by his order, without hearing or notice, transferred from the citizens' roll to that of intruders, so that, on January 1, 1896, the United States will be called upon to remove from the Territory, by force if need be, thousands of residents substantially selected for the purpose by the chief of the nation. . . . Persons whose names have been upon the citizens' roll by the judicial decree of the tribunal established by law for that purpose for many years, some of them for twenty or more . . . have been by the mere "designation" of the chief stricken from the citizens' roll and put upon that of the intruders.[57]

Corroboration was supplied by many Cherokees. For amplification, there was the voice of the Vinita *Indian Chieftain,* which carried all the way to Washington:

If the commission has misrepresented the Indians it has been largely the fault of the Indians themselves in not furnishing them with correct information. The truth is, if the commission had known some things that are true as regards the methods of some of our officials it would have made a report that would have "astonished the natives" for we all know that they didn't tell half that might have been told. . . .

The cattle men and the office holders have "had a picnic" out of this country about long enough and the congress of the United States has at last heard the cry of those who have been imposed upon so long, and the day of reckoning is near at hand. . . .

For years the capital of this nation has been a veritable sink hole of official venality. Citizenship of their nation has been bought openly from mercenary councilors, and occasionally a circuit judge takes a hand in selling out his country. Corruption at Tahlequah has assumed every form that will yield plunder, and good citizens have stood aghast at the saturnalia of corruption. . . . The boodlers have from time to time pooled their issues in the great spoils, and the courts, along with the council, have been perverted for money, and the channel of justice turned into cesspools of bribery and a menace to the liberties of the people and a travesty upon jurisprudence.[58]

The *Indian Chieftain* was only a recent and reluctant convert to the principle of reform from outside; in the past it had advocated a course of reform from within as offering the best hope of maintaining the political autonomy of the nation. It was the journal of the majority of intermarried or adopted white Cherokees, who were farmers or ranchers in a small or middling way or were in the professions. In contrast to them were the white citizens who, with the wealthier mixed-bloods, controlled the rising monopolies in the Cherokee, Choctaw, Creek, and Seminole nations, evoking this howl of derision from a Washington newspaper: *HEAP WHITE INDIANS.*[59]

Over in the Chickasaw Nation, a definitive economic breach between the intermarried citizens and the rest had been opened by a law withdrawing from the intermarried all the benefits of their citizenship. Information that the intermarried citizens had organized themselves for armed resistance to this confiscatory act gave cause for anxiety that another crisis was building in the Chickasaw country.[60]

It was against this background that Sebastian Little delivered a 12,000-word speech during the House debate on the Indian appropriation bill for 1896–97 proposing, on either side of an extended harangue against the Five Tribes governments, that Congress should set up "an impartial tribunal to compile a valid roll of the citizens of each tribe."[61]

After exhaustive debate in the Senate, an amendment offered by Orville Platt, which would confer upon the Dawes Commission the task of hearing and determining all questions of citizenship among the Five

Tribes, was ruled out of order by the Vice President only to be reinstated by the conference committee and accepted by both chambers after further argument in the Senate.[62]

Almost as controversial an innovation as this was a clause, inserted by the conference committee itself, declaring it "to be the duty of the United States to establish a government in the Indian Territory which will rectify the many inequalities and discriminations now existing in said Territory and afford needful protection to the lives and property of all citizens and residents thereof." In the opinion of Edward Walthall (D, Mississippi),

> With as much right and as much pretense of authority it [the conference committee] might just as well have declared what the policy of the United States should be with reference to the Cuban question, or with reference to the tariff, or any other subject not connected with the matter with which they were dealing.[63]

But, as Walthall's Mississippi colleague James George gloomily observed, few members of the Senate were "paying any attention at all to the subject . . . under consideration." When, on June 10, 1896, the bill was enacted into statute, the Dawes Commission ceased to be merely an executive board; it became a judicial tribunal as well.[64] Appeals from the decisions of the commission or the tribal citizenship tribunals could be taken to the federal courts. By this assertion of both executive and judicial supremacy, the United States had made itself the referee of tribal affairs.

The closing years of the Fort Smith court's jurisdiction in the Indian Territory were marked by public controversies whose principal instigator was the United States district judge. Parker was twice at issue with his superiors in those last two years, first with Justice Edward White (and in due course most of the other justices) of the Supreme Court, and then with the senior officers of the Department of Justice, including the Attorney-General. Both disputes stemmed from the acts of 1889 and 1891, which had divested Parker's court of its circuit powers and created an appeals system whereby the Supreme Court could overrule the district court in all cases; both were fueled by Parker's rising resentment of the Supreme Court's reversals of convictions and rulings determined at Fort Smith.

In the Lafayette Hudson case, where Parker had refused bail to a persistent criminal pending the outcome of an appeal against a conviction for assault, the defendant applied to the Supreme Court for a writ of *mandamus*. In the ordinary way, the application would have been decided by Justice David Brewer of the Eighth Circuit, who usually supported Parker; but Brewer being absent, the question was taken up by Justice

White. When White ordered Parker to approve Hudson's bail bond, the district judge refused on the ground that only the justice for his own circuit could issue such an order. In the middle of the impasse, while visiting Washington to appear before the Senate Judiciary Committee, Parker took occasion to criticize the Supreme Court in one of the interviews he gave to the press.

At last, on February 4, the Supreme Court as a body, with Brewer alone dissenting, found against Parker, compelling him to comply with Justice White's order. Hudson's conviction was upheld, but he escaped from custody soon afterward and remained at large.[65]

There were more bitter words from Parker against the Supreme Court when a murderer, one of the worst who had ever faced his court, killed a jail guard at Fort Smith while awaiting the result of an appeal. Parker was in St. Louis at the time of this murder and at once relayed his views to the *Globe-Democrat,* the leading Republican newspaper of that city.[66]

As the Supreme Court continued to send murder cases back to Fort Smith for retrial, Parker became satisfied that the fault lay as much with the senior officials of the Department of Justice for what seemed to him feeble presentation of the Government's case as with the strained meticulosity (in his eyes) of the Supreme Court. Early in February 1896, he favored the *Globe-Democrat* with what he called an "open letter" to Attorney-General Harmon, but failed to send a copy to Harmon himself. The letter contained "a few raps" at the Supreme Court, but Parker concentrated most of his fire upon Harmon's immediate junior, the Solicitor-General. A fortnight later, Assistant Attorney-General Edward Whitney replied with an open letter of his own, using the columns of the St. Louis *Republic,* a Democratic newspaper. Whitney's letter to Parker was an uncomplimentary to him as Parker's had been to the Solicitor-General. Parker's retort was a violent attack upon Whitney, released through some of the newspapers in western Arkansas.[67]

Thereafter the quarrel was prosecuted with greater civility but no less force through the calmer channels of official correspondence. When the exchanges between Solicitor-General Holmes Conrad and Whitney, at one end, and Parker and his district attorney at the other—over the Cul Rowe case—looked like becoming both protracted and disputatious, Harmon took up his pen:

> You understand of course that I cannot give personal attention to this class of cases, but it is only fair to say that the course of the Solicitor-General . . . was taken with my entire approval and, in fact, upon my suggestion. My attention was attracted, early in the term, to the frequent

reversals of cases from your court. . . . The consequence was that I immediately took an interest in the general subject and caused my several assistants to call my attention to cases as they arose. . . . I saw enough to readily agree with the opinions of my assistants. . . .

If the declamatory style of your instructions were abandoned, and the law given clearly and briefly, there certainly would be no trouble, for both the [Supreme] court and this Department are just as anxious as you are that justice should be properly administered and all criminals punished.[68]

Parker's twelve-page reply was devoid of contrition:

[Y]ou should not forget that your work in the profession has not been along the line of criminal law, that your experience in that direction is of the most limited character, that your judgment of what are errors in a charge of the court may be at fault. . . . These truths are entirely and fully applicable to your subordinates in the Department.

One or other of those subordinates—Conrad, Whitney, and Assistant Attorney-General J. M. Dickinson—Parker suggested, might be sent to Fort Smith to hear the dozen or fifteen capital cases set for the coming term of court and discuss with him any points arising from them.[69]

Harmon countered by engaging the judge on several technical issues. Later the Solicitor-General and the two assistants adopted the same line, but refined it into closer detail, as though to subdue the judge by attrition.[70]

It is easy to conclude from these exchanges that the judge had become too big for his court, but most people in Fort Smith, whatever their political sympathies, were on Parker's side. The press was divided, but not on partisan lines. For example, the Republican paper in St. Louis, which Parker chose as an outlet for his views, offered him only guarded sympathy, while its Democratic rival, which had acted as mouthpiece for Assistant Attorney-General Whitney, took the judge's part unreservedly.[71] In Washington, however, Parker's open quarrels with the Supreme Court and the Justice Department had done him far more harm than good and may have destroyed whatever chance there might have been of a congressional change of heart over the Teller courts act.

Among those in Indian Territory who stood to gain from the exclusion of the Fort Smith and Paris courts, the day of the transfer was avidly awaited. "After the first of next September," gloated one editor, "the Fort Smith saloons and chop houses along with their organ, the Elevator, will have mighty dry picking in this country."[72] The arrival of the epochal date was to be celebrated by a picnic and fair at Purcell, which was given several weeks' advance publicity: "September 1, 1896, marks the emancipation of 300,000 people from judicial bondage. Our relief from Arkansas and Texas serfdom is too heartily welcome to our people to permit the day of our great deliverance to pass unnoticed."[73]

As that day approached, the man who was probably the wealthiest intermarried citizen in the Five Nations circulated a lengthy and wide-ranging survey of the process by which the United States had taken a grip on affairs in the Indian Territory. After reviewing the visits of the various congressional committees and the passage of the Dawes Commission bill, he found "further evidence of the feelings of Congress on the matter, and its evident intention to at once right our wrongs and remedy the evils" in

> the rapid progress the United States has made in effecting changes in the Indian country by establishing a strong judiciary of its own within the bodies of our once happy people, and that, too, over our protest, thereby creating a stampede of confusion and consternation among our citizens. . . .
>
> If this, my fellow countrymen, is not enough to convince you that congress is determined to change the condition of affairs here and to break up our autonomy I would direct your attention to the survey of our lands being made by the United States government. . . .
>
> If you want still more, I would ask you to consider the evident frame of mind of Congressmen when they passed the bill returning the Dawes Commission against our wishes, with enlarged powers, and authority to settle the intruder question, to pass upon the question of citizenship.[74]

No one who did not know would have guessed that the speaker was the United States marshal of a district in Indian Territory. The Vinita *Indian Chieftain,* whose political direction by this time was the very reverse of his, offered a sarcastic testimonial to "a martyr . . . sacrificing himself willingly upon the altar of unselfish personal interest for his innate love of the Choctaws": "Those who know Jim McAlester say that he makes no pretension to being a humorist, and that he means every word he says."[75] As with so much political comment, the point was missed on purpose. What counted was what McAlester was saying, not his motives for saying it.

A week after the federal courts for the Indian Territory had assumed the jurisdiction formerly attached to Fort Smith and Paris, the same editor wrote:

> Judge Parker still has a court district composed of seventeen [*sic*] counties in Arkansas. One week in the year will be ample time for the trial of all federal cases arising there, as pine top whiskey selling by wild cat distilleries will be about all there will be to look after now. The $150,000 court house will be a rather lonesome place shortly.[76]

In fact, there was a heavy docket of cases awaiting trial, but Parker would not be attending to them. After seeming to have recovered from a heart ailment in June, he fell ill again the following month and on November 17, died.[77] The returns furnished annually by the district attorney

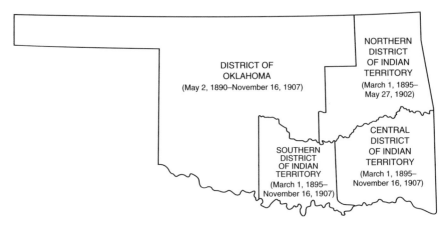

MAP 6. FEDERAL JUDICIAL DISTRICTS OF OKLAHOMA AND INDIAN TERRITORY, SEPTEMBER 1, 1896

at Fort Smith show that, between July 1, 1875, and June 30, 1896, a total of 12,031 criminal prosecutions were terminated in Parker's court, of which 8,791 had ended in the conviction of the defendant; a further 183 were standing on the docket waiting to be heard. Parker had also heard 674 civil cases in which the Government was a party.[78]

The statistics say little of his qualities, except his stamina. His worst fault appears to have been the stubbornness of pride not uncommon in those appointed to public office, particularly if they are unused to having their decisions questioned. On the whole, Parker was a much better servant than a bad system deserved; but when that system was improved, he rebelled against it.[79]

Judge Bryant, during his six years on the bench of the Paris court, had to contend with problems that in some respects were even worse than those encountered by Parker. More murder cases came to him than to Parker in the same period, but the paucity of convictions suggests that, where homicide was concerned, his juries were more wont to apply the rules of Texas custom than the principles of common law. All told, 2,408 criminal prosecutions of all classes were completed in the East Texas court during the seven years to June 30, 1896, but only 1,079 succeeded.[80] Perhaps one-fifth of these were Texas cases, almost all of them tried at Galveston, Tyler, or Jefferson. The remainder arose from writs issued at Paris for offenses in the Indian Territory.

The disappearance of the outside courts and consequent strengthening of the authority and influence of the three district courts of Indian

Territory opened the road for a further and more determined attack upon the tribal judiciaries. All three of the new district judges, joined by the recently retired judge of the Central District, criticized the tribal courts, though in varying degree. Judge Springer had this to say:

> [N]o greater reform or a more beneficial one could be enacted by Congress than that which would result from the entire abolition of the tribal courts and the conferring upon the United States court of entire and complete jurisdiction over all persons in the Indian Territory in all cases, both civil and criminal.
>
> The degree of civilization which has been attained by the citizens of the Five Civilized Tribes is far in advance of the crude and inefficient jurisdiction exercised by the tribal courts.

In the opinion of Judge Kilgore, "[T]he helpless and the illiterate Indian will fare better in the United States court than he does in the tribal courts." Judge Lewis commented rather mildly that the Indian courts had "ceased to exercise a restraining influence upon those subject to their jurisdiction in the commission of offenses" but cited cases whose circumstances would have justified a harsher tone.

Judge Stuart, now in private practice, was more forthright:

> I had not served twelve months upon the bench in this Territory before I became convinced that the dual government which the United States has attempted to maintain here was a great mistake. . . . I believe that the hour has struck, and the time is ripe for change. I am convinced that the Indian courts are a complete failure, and that they ought to be totally abolished.
>
> . . . Their judges are unlearned, their courts are loose, irregular, and dreadfully uncertain, and I never had an Indian judgment brought to me for enforcement or revision which gave any sign that it had been rendered by a court of justice. The whole thing is a farce from beginning to end . . . and I have heard more than one Indian judge testify in my court that all judicial officers in his tribe had their price.[81]

Judge Shackelford, who had stayed on in Muskogee after the expiry of his term, did not associate himself with the condemnation of the tribal courts. As chairman of the Muskogee bar, he helped to organize a memorial to Congress in which it was explained that the three Indian Territory judges had been overworked even before their courts acquired jurisdiction over the higher felonies. It would not do even to appoint just one additional judge because the extra business accruing after September 1, 1896, would leave four judges as overloaded as three had been before. Matters had been greatly worsened still further, the memorial continued, by the provisions of the act of June 10, 1896, which placed upon the federal courts the duty of considering appeals in citizenship cases: "The Dawes

Commission and the tribunals of the Five Civilized Tribes did not submit written opinions in these cases. The only order of the commissions was 'rejected' or 'allowed.' It will be incumbent, therefore, upon the United States court to give all of the cases a careful consideration."

Nearly 300 citizenship appeals affecting some 4,440 people had been taken by January 1, 1897, in the Northern District alone, with the result that 1,778 civil and criminal cases were awaiting a hearing. Rather more than one-third of these pending cases had been clogging up the docket since before the abolition of the original Muskogee court on March 1, 1895.[82]

There had been no bright tomorrow for the "day of emancipation." The apparent incompatibility of judicial complaint about the oppressive weight of the court dockets and judicial agitation for the abolition of the tribal courts is easily resolved: the judges wanted more jurisdiction, but less labor. The validity of the second of these demands was soon endorsed by Congress; the other was rather more dubious. Sometimes the tribal courts were as bad as the federal judges said they were, sometimes much better. Among enemies of the tribal system of government there had long been an inclination to decry the slackness of the Indian courts when they did not discharge the law and to condemn them for barbarity when they did. This critical ambivalence became acute during the last years of tribal self-government.

It is likely that by the spring of 1897 a majority could be mustered in both branches of Congress in support of any proposal to diminish or displace the governments of the Five Tribes. Yet when Congress delivered the triple blow that finally shattered the tribal governments, the weapon chosen by the reformers was another Indian appropriation bill.

Thus the appropriation bill for 1897–98 carried no fewer than three riders directed at the vitals of the governments of the Five Nations, all three given form and substance by the Senate Committee on Appropriations. First, a clause was inserted into an amendment to provide for the payment of the Dawes Commission's salaries: "That on and after January 1, 1898, the United States courts in said [Indian] Territory shall have original and exclusive jurisdiction and authority to try and determine all civil cases in law and equity thereafter instituted, and all criminal causes for the punishment of any offense committed after January 1, 1898, by any person in said Territory."[83]

Another amendment provided that, from the beginning of 1898, "all acts, ordinances, and resolutions" of the Five Tribes' governments, except adjournment resolutions and measures relating to negotiations with the Dawes Commission, should be "certified immediately upon their passage to the President of the United States, and shall not take effect if disapproved by him, or until thirty days after their passage."[84]

The third amendment answered the solicitations of the three serving federal judges in Indian Territory by providing for the appointment of an additional judge to the appellate court of the Territory, where as things first stood, a quorum could not be formed without the inclusion of the judge who had presided at the hearing of the case under review. The new appointee would be a "floater," holding court wherever assigned.[85]

William Bate (D, Tennessee), whose filibuster against the bill was not supported from the floor, pointed out that the President's ordinary duties would leave him without time to scrutinize the Five Tribes' legislative proceedings: "He would necessarily have to transfer it to the Secretary of the Interior, and he perhaps to the Indian Bureau, and the Indian Bureau to some chief clerk, and that chief clerk would really be the judge or the adjudicator of this action by the Indians in their councils."[86] As much could be said of most of the work of the Executive branch of the Government.

It was the Cherokee delegates George Benge and William Hastings who most tersely laid bare the logic of the first of these amendments. They were speaking only for the Cherokee Nation, but their words on this subject were as applicable to the Choctaws, Chickasaws, Creeks, and Seminoles: "In case this bill is passed you will observe that their judiciary is destroyed. Without courts, why enact laws? There will be no need then of any legislation. Hence their local self-government is absolutely destroyed."[87]

Four conferences were needed before the bill could be forced through, and it did not reach President William McKinley for approval until June 7, 1897. Before the ink had dried on his signature the "wall of fire" that had once engirdled the whole Indian Territory lay in ashes.[88] Nothing remained now but for Congress to pronounce the final demise of tribal self-government and to draw up plans for the disposal of the communal inheritance.

Neither the Creek nor the Seminole leaders waited for that to happen. Isparhecher, whom the Creeks had elected principal chief in 1895 to obstruct the Dawes Commission (which he had done) and to secure the repeal of the contract pasture law (which he had not done), was the first to throw in the towel. Negotiations with the Dawes Commission were authorized and an agreement was reached, subject to ratification, on September 27, 1897. A similar agreement was concluded on December 16 between the Dawes Commission and the Seminole Nation. As a concession, the courts of these two nations were to retain jurisdiction in all civil controversies except those "growing out of the title, ownership, occupation, or use of real estate" and the right to try all criminal cases except those for "homicide, embezzlement, bribery, and embracery hereafter committed."[89]

Discussions between the Dawes Commission and representatives of the Choctaw and Chickasaw nations had opened in the spring of 1897, and a tentative agreement was reached at Atoka. These terms had not been ratified by February 24, 1898, when Charles Curtis (R, Kansas) introduced H.R. 8581, in twenty-eight sections, "for the protection of the people of the Indian Territory, and for other purposes."[90]

On June 7 the Senate Committee on Indian Affairs proposed three additions to the bill. The first ordered the cessation of the tribal courts and abolition of all officers of the courts on July 1, 1898; the second ratified the Atoka Agreement and stated that if the Choctaws and Chickasaws had not ratified it by the end of a six-month period from the date of the passage of the act, the general provisions of the statute would apply to both nations; the third incorporated the text of the agreement with the Creek Nation.[91]

The Curtis bill provided for the maintenance of the forms of tribal government until March 4, 1906, the date by which the Dawes Commission was expected to complete its task of allotting the tribal lands and distributing the tribal funds. There was no debate in the House, and next to none in the Senate beyond a few words of protest from the veteran of another lost cause, William Bate, once a general in the Confederate army. Bate's speech before a sparsely attended and wholly uninterested chamber, on the proposal to abolish the tribal courts, was less an address than a recessional:

> That sweeps all the laws of the Indians away, all their courts of justice, all their juries, all their local officers, and all the rights they have under the treaties, which they have been given and guaranteed by the Government of the United States. Treaties which were entered into solemnly, which have been approved by the country, and which have lasted now ever since 1830 and 1835. . . . I do not want to make a speech here. I know it will be useless. . . .
>
> Now, then, we go along and encroach upon them inch by inch, Congress after Congress, until at last you have got to the main redoubt, and here it is destroyed. It is swept away in the twenty-seventh section and it is all gone.[92]

James Sherman (R, New York), Curtis, and Little were appointed conferees for the House; Richard Pettigrew (R, South Dakota), Jones of Arkansas, and Platt for the Senate.[93] Section 27 of the draft, amended to incorporate a partial concession—a three-month extension to the constitutional and jurisdictional status quo in the Choctaw, Chickasaw, and Creek nations—became Section 28:

That on the first day of July, eighteen hundred and ninety-eight, all tribal courts in Indian Territory shall be abolished and no officer of said courts shall thereafter have any authority whatever to do or perform any act therefore authorized by any law in connection with said courts, or to receive any pay for same; and all civil and criminal cases then pending in any such court shall be transferred to the United States court in said Territory by filing with the clerk of the court the original papers in the suit; Provided. That this section shall not be in force as to the Chickasaw, Choctaw, and Creek tribes or nations until the first day of October, eighteen hundred and ninety-eight.[94]

The object of the moratorium was to give the Chickasaws, Choctaws, and Creeks time to ratify their agreements with the Dawes Commission. Ratification of these instruments would enable the tribes to retain their courts, but for the Choctaws and Chickasaws would entail an even greater surrender of jurisdiction than that yielded by the Seminoles; for example, weapon carrying and disturbing the peace were brought within the orbit of the federal judiciary along with all disputes over coal or asphalt deposits. The Creeks would be on the same terms as the Seminoles.

President McKinley approved the act on June 28, 1898. A separate bill was needed for the ratification of the Seminole Agreement, and this became law on July 1 at the same time as the Indian Appropriation Act, though not as part of it. A section of the latter measure gave leave for appeals to be made from the federal courts in the Indian Territory to the United States Supreme Court in all citizenship cases.[95]

Although the progressive parties controlled the legislatures of the Choctaw and Chickasaw nations, a referendum on the Atoka Agreement produced a narrow majority against it. A second referendum, held under the provisions of the Curtis Act, approved the agreement by a large margin. This outcome allowed the two tribes to retain their own judicial systems in the attenuated form already outlined.[96]

For the Cherokees, whose government had consistently declined to treat with the Dawes Commission, there were no concessions. On July 1, 1898, the courts and offices attached to them were annulled. Trials and hearings then in progress were abandoned overnight. Outstanding warrants and processes remained unserved.[97]

The Creeks, in the end, chose these terms rather than the better ones their negotiators had earlier accepted. At Isparhecher's urging, the Creek council rejected the agreement that had been reached with the Dawes Commission. When the agreement was put to a referendum on November 1, 1898, a small majority of the electorate voted against it.[98]

The verdict of the referendum merely withheld ex post facto recognition from provisions which already had been operative for one month under Section 28 of the Curtis Act. Advance confirmation of this and the consequent irrelevance of the referendum had been supplied a few days before its submission by the justices of the Indian Territory court of appeals. On that occasion the court held that the United States had acted illegally in preventing the Creek authorities from executing three condemned criminals, ruled that the trio should be released into the custody of the Creek authorities, then ordered the men to be set at liberty because there were no longer any Creek authorities to take charge of them.[99] For its result to have any force, the referendum should have been held at least a month earlier.

Similar means were employed by United States officials to forestall the execution of a Choctaw named Walla Tonkawa, better known as William Goings, for a murder committed before the passage of the Curtis Act. The Choctaws, more determined and better advised than the Creeks, still had their judges and sheriffs. They heeded a writ of habeas corpus from a federal judge and yielded to a demand that Goings should be given a new trial; but, after he had been convicted for a second time, the officers of Nashoba County ignored a further writ and, at 2:33 P.M. on Thursday, July 13, 1899, the execution was carried out. A number of Choctaw officials were arrested afterward, but it was soon established that they had acted legally. Little sympathy is due the figure at the center of this battle of wills. Although he had been indicted for only two murders, he was reckoned to have committed nine or more. His execution by the Choctaws, in defiance of the United States authorities, was the last assertion by any of the Five Nations of the independence of tribal institutions.[100]

CHAPTER ELEVEN

Courthouse Government and the Move Toward Single Statehood

Indian Territory has no organized local government. What laws it possesses are given it by the Congress of the United States: while the Federal Judge within her borders and the Interior Department there and at Washington fill the interstice.—David W. Yancey, "Need of Better Government in the Indian Territory," The Forum, *February 1900*

[I]n fact, the only executive government in the Territory is a government by United States marshals.—John Austin Moon, Democratic congressman from Tennessee in House debate on a bill to establish the Territory of Jefferson (H.R. 956), March 14, 1902

[T]he standard of justice depends on the equality of power to compel and . . . in fact the strong do what they have the power to do and the weak accept what they have to accept. . . . Our opinions of the gods and our knowledge of men lead us to conclude that it is a general and necessary law of nature to rule wherever one can. This is not a law that we made ourselves, nor were we the first to act upon it when it was made. We found it already in existence, and we shall leave it to exist for ever among those who come after us.— Thucydides. The Peloponnesian War. *book V, chapter 7, "Dialogue Between the Melians and the Athenians."*

Abolition or reduction of the courts of the Five Nations broke the back of tribal government for, without an independent judiciary, the tribes were powerless to delay or seriously influence the course of whatever was ordained by the Congress and Executive of the United States. Partial, faltering, idle, or corrupt as many of them had sometimes been, these courts and the laws upon which they stood represented the clearest tangible expression of a national identity. Once the courts had been eliminated, or their scope severely restricted, by the Curtis Act and its appendages, none of the Five Tribes held a title stronger than an eight-year lease on a local suboffice of the federal Government.

Duality grounded upon an unhappy coalition of "outside" and "interior" federal courts on one flank and a miscellany of tribal courts on the other had not served the purposes of justice in an environment that was undergoing rapid social and economic change. It had been a bad system, partly redeemed but in no way retrieved by the ability and character of some individuals within it. Juristic unity built upon a handful of "interior" federal courts, where none of the demands of justice could be provided for by State or Territorial tribunals of justice, was sure to be worse, even in a stable populace. But under the stimulus of immigration the population of Indian Territory more than doubled from 180,000 in 1890 to almost 400,000 at the end of the century,[1] and continued its rapid growth through the early 1900s while the judicial system remained almost static after the dissolution or dilution of the tribal courts.

The problems of the federal courts were aggravated more than ever by the checkered and almost extemporized pattern of law they had to work with. Their text for the dispensation of most criminal and almost all civil law was Mansfield's *Digest of the Laws of Arkansas,* published in 1884, whose inadequacies as a reference work had been recognized so quickly in Arkansas that within a few years the State government had ordered a further compilation prepared.[2] In the Indian Territory, however, those sections of Mansfield that had been selected for use there remained in force until Statehood. Whenever the civil jurisdiction of the Indian Territory courts needed to be extended—as in the exercise of Section 14 of the Curtis Act,[3] under which any place with 200 or more inhabitants could apply for incorporation as a municipality—the legal terms were always adopted from Mansfield. It was in the broad field of incorporative and administrative law that Mansfield, as a primer for good government in Indian Territory, was at its most defective.

Another difficulty was caused by the failure of Congress to appropriate funds for the construction of serviceable jails in Indian Territory after the federal courts there had assumed full criminal jurisdiction in 1896. Acting in response to a Senate resolution, the Department of Justice had sent an examiner into the Territory, and the man had returned with detailed recommendations for jails to be built in the court towns, but the report had been set aside or overlooked.[4]

The worst fault in the new judicial arrangements was less that the inhabitants were without any say in the selection of judicial office-holders—the same was true of residents of Oklahoma or any other organized Territory of the United States—than their lack of a voice in the composition of the laws or the choice of the men who were to enforce them. A makeshift scheme for the regulation of society that might have been tolerable for three or four years was, at its outset, prescribed by statute for eight years at least and subordinated to the expected schedule of the Dawes Commission.

It was natural, therefore, that critical scrutiny should fasten upon the operations of the commission and upon the growing payroll which was its girth. One resident, a United States court commissioner, had nothing good to say of it:

> The commission secures from each succeeding Congress a new lease of official existence, together with a new, and always increased, appropriation. As the appropriations have increased so the clerical force of the commission has grown, until it has become, in fact as well as in reputation, the Rock-of-Ages for shipwrecked politicians from all parts of the United States. It has become a financial drain upon the general government and a thorn in the sides of the Indians and the white people of the Territory alike. It would be consonant with the ideas of good government for the Indian Territory to abolish this commission and allow the Secretary of the Interior to govern.[5]

But he was overcensorious, and the idea that the commission could simply be wound up and its duties reassigned to the Department of the Interior was a fantasy. Even a historian and critic hostile to the federal Government in its general policy toward the Five Tribes and, in particular, its use of the Dawes Commission, has concluded much more recently that the commissioners "conducted their tremendous task with a high degree of honesty and efficiency."[6] That can be taken as a just verdict on their attitude to the duties they were charged with and the way those duties were carried out. Their attitude to the public purse was less virtuous. In some supply contracts the interests of members of the Commission were paramount, and with many lesser appointments being awarded through the workings of patronage, the staff became larger and its appetite for funds correspondingly more voracious. In these respects, the Dawes Commission was a typical government agency, although it may have been better run than most. Tams Bixby, who joined the commission in 1897 and was its de facto head for several years before becoming its official chairman in 1901, was accused of many improprieties; but he was extremely good at getting things done, as well as fixing them, and he stayed in office until 1906.[7]

The provision in the Indian Appropriation Act of June 10, 1896, whereby either party in a citizenship case could appeal to the federal court for a reversal of a ruling by the Dawes Commission did not so much widen the remit of the commission as supplement the authority of the court. In the end, the Dawes Commission was ancillary to the federal judicial system, reinforcing the belief that Indian Territory was under courthouse rule. Appeals were lodged as a matter of course by Indian governments when the commissioners admitted applicants excluded from the tribal rolls, and a fair number of individuals appealed after the commissioners had turned them down. Between them they added appreciably to the labor and worry of the hard-pressed judges. In the Choctaw and Chickasaw nations nearly all the appellants admitted by the federal courts were subsequently rejected by a special Citizenship Court set up in 1902 under the terms of a Supplementary (or Supplemental) Agreement, an appendix to the original Atoka Agreement.[8]

Numerous legislative and administrative measures were adopted to make the courts more effective and economical. The marshals and their deputies in the Indian Territory had hardly been placed on salaries when there were cries for the reinstatement of the old system of payment by fee.

At first, these were disregarded by the congressional majority. An act of May 28, 1896, the product of years of agitation by citizens, politicians, and Attorneys-General for reform of the United States marshal's office, specifically excepted Indian Territory (and Alaska) from a set of new rules that applied throughout the country. Deputy marshals outside these two areas were now divided into the categories of office deputy and field deputy. The office deputy was a full-time salaried member of the staff, not necessarily engaged in clerical work; the field deputy was paid by fee and was usually a part-time officer. An additional office deputy could be employed only with the permission of the Attorney-General, who would also have the last word on how much salary was to be paid.[9] This contrasted pointedly with the arrangement then in force in the Indian Territory, where only the concurrence of the district judge was needed in a marshal's appointment of extra office deputies.[10] No one could have been very surprised when, in November 1896, the Attorney-General asked for the provisions of the new act to be extended to Indian Territory, and this was done in February of the following year.[11]

By an act of January 15, 1897, a United States trial jury in a case of murder or rape was at last allowed the option of bringing in a verdict of "guilty without capital punishment." Upon such a verdict being returned, the judge was required to sentence the prisoner to imprisonment at hard labor for life.[12]

In 1898 the outgoing Attorney-General, Joseph McKenna, asked Congress to provide $100,000 for the construction of jails in Indian Territory. Congress appropriated $60,000. McKenna's successor, John Griggs, designated Muskogee, South McAlester, and Ardmore as the locations for the new lockups. A year later he had to explain to Congress that nothing had been done because of difficulties encountered in finding suitable sites and obtaining the funds to pay for construction.[13]

A fourth judicial district was created on May 27, 1902, by bisecting the Northern District. One slice, comprising the Creek and Seminole nations and a little of the Cherokee Nation, now became the Western District. The "floating" judge was given charge of the new district, and Vinita became the headquarters of the Northern District.[14]

Several weeks after this, Congress remedied a flaw in the Teller Courts Act of March 1, 1895. One of its provisions stipulated that the punishment for larceny should follow the Arkansas statute rather than that of the United States, which Congress considered to be too mild. The purpose this provision was intended to serve was frustrated by a ruling from the Comptroller of the Treasury that, where officers of the Indian Territory courts had served papers on persons accused of larceny, the laws of Arkansas should also govern the size of the fees payable to the officers. Arkansas allowed an arresting officer 50 cents for serving the warrant and another 50 cents for conveying him to jail—not an unduly paltry sum, since the officer would be a precinct constable, and little time or travel would be required of him. In the Indian Territory, on the other hand, the arrest could be made only by deputy marshals, who were much more widely scattered and therefore generally unable to bring in the thief without being badly out of time and pocket at the end of the trip. And even then, 25 cents of the deputy's $1 fee would be deducted by the chief marshal as a commission. A further deterrent to the prosecution of theft cases was that the Arkansas statute allowed a fee of only 50 cents to the witness.[15]

The natural and obvious consequences were that the deputy marshal would not put himself out to make arrests for larceny, the witness would not put himself out to offer testimony in such cases, and "marauding outlaws" flocked to the Indian Territory until cattle and horses were being stolen "almost in droves." In this instance Congress reacted quickly. The act of June 21, 1902, restored the schedule of fees and expenses set out in the United States statutes, so that the deputy who traveled twenty miles to serve a warrant for larceny, returned with his prisoner, and committed him into safekeeping, would receive the net sum of $5.78 plus his actual expenses to a maximum of $2.00 instead of a flat fee of 75 cents and no expenses.[16]

Neither the officers of the Indian Territory courts nor the Department of Justice liked the rigidity of the Arkansas anti-horse-thief law, with its severe minimum sentence of five years' imprisonment, and dozens of prison terms were reduced by the President upon the recommendations of the Attorney-General, trial judge, and district attorney.[17] In February 1903, the mandatory minimum sentence was abolished in Indian Territory, except for second offenders.[18]

Thus the continuity of the policy of piecemeal reform was preserved amid growing evidence of the intrinsic unsoundness of the whole apparatus of justice. The one measure that might have alleviated the problem,—the addition of a fourth judicial district—made little difference: within two years, the courts were more overworked than they had been before the creation of the new judicial district.

During the year ended June 30, 1897, the three district courts completed 1,094 criminal prosecutions; but 1,013 went forward to the next year, when 1,558 cases were disposed of, with 1,492 still outstanding. The figures for the next four years were as follows:[19]

Year	Terminated	Pending at July 1
1899	1,923	1,671
1900	1,983	1,752
1901	1,815	2,546
1902	2,269	2,210

For the year ended June 30, 1903, the first in which the court for the recently formed Western District was fully operational, 2,769 criminal prosecutions were settled, but 3,276 remained on the docket for the following year. More than 2,500 private lawsuits were also cleared during that year, but nearly 3,000 others were still awaiting attention at the beginning of the next.[20]

By January 1904, the courts were almost choked by the congestion. In the Southern District as many as 2,523 criminal and civil cases were standing on the docket. Even in the Central District, generally the quietest of the four, 1,855 cases were pending.[21]

Charles Raymond, the judge in charge of the Western District, reported in a letter to the House Committee on the Judiciary that there were 300 criminal cases awaiting trial before him and that he expected the 400 cases then being considered by the grand jury to produce a further 350 indictments. Besides this, there were about 1,100 civil cases, many of them complicated, and the six United States commissioners of his district had, between them, 2,200 minor cases. Nor did this exhaust the judge's responsibilities. Over and above the demands of his own district, Raymond, as a justice of the court of appeals for Indian Territory, was "compelled . . . to decide and write opinions in between thirty and forty cases per year":

> I have worked since I came here every day, every night, every holiday, and every Sunday like a slave, because I promised that the dockets in this district should be kept up [with], but it [*sic*] is now increasing so rapidly on account of increase in population and increase in controversies which arise from the leasing of lands by the allottees until it is beyond one man's power to do the work. . . .
>
> Within the last two years, in order to keep up with the dockets, it has been necessary to move rapidly, and I have made it a rule to finish a murder case in a day, even if it took until past midnight to do so, and in living up to that resolution I have tried in that time 103 murder cases and 75 cases of assault with intent to kill, and in not a single instance has the trial in any of these important cases exceeded a day.[22]

Compared with this, the period when the conditions obtaining at Fort Smith and the other outside courts were regularly denounced as a "denial of justice" was an era of judicial tranquillity and ease. Rarely had there been more than 200 cases pending when the district attorney at Fort Smith compiled his annual report and Parker, although he always liked to move the proceedings along briskly, never attempted to rush a murder trial through in a single day.

As Congressman Little remarked, the Indian Territory needed either more courts or more considerate trial judges "because any man knows an ordinary murder case can not be judiciously and decently tried in one day."[23] Actually it needed both more courts and better judges; but the problems of the existing courts were not only intolerable: they were insurmountable. The rolling tide of litigation and crime had outpaced the capacity of the United States judicial system to provide a framework to contain it.

Seen in the light of the assumption that Indian Territory would be ready for Statehood in 1906, the simplest and cheapest means of diffusing the caseload was to appoint an extra judge for each of the four judicial districts for two years only, each district having five to seven court towns and enough work to absorb the energies of two full-time judges. Such was the solution written into an act approved by President Roosevelt on April 28, 1904. It was the last judicial reform applied to the Indian Territory.[24]

The establishment of Oklahoma Territory in 1890, like all other significant congressional enactments in relation to the Indian country, whether they were set in motion by the Senate or the House Committee on the Territories or by either Judiciary Committee, evolved from the understanding that the whole area set apart for the Indians in 1825 would in time enter the Union as a single State. When, in the summer of 1901, the Wichita-Caddo and Comanche-Kiowa-Apache reservations were opened for settlement and fully merged into Oklahoma, only the Osage Nation, two small reservations bordering it, and the country of the Five Tribes remained to be allotted.

By that time, few traces of the bolder overtones of the "Wild West" were to be seen in Oklahoma. Not much of the new Territory was cattle country—most of the Panhandle (the former Neutral Strip), the westernmost county of the onetime Cherokee Outlet, parts of what had been the Cheyenne and Arapaho and Comanche-Wichita country, and a few scattered pockets elsewhere. Outlawry, of which there had been a very great deal throughout the 1890s (although its personae and their individual misdeeds had been overdrawn by the newspapers for the delectation of a readership that wanted to be both thrilled and repelled), was now confined to isolated episodes of armed brigandage. These and similar phenomena composing the ordinary Easterner's vision of life on the Great Plains, were not interrelated; but an allusion to one was apt to evoke an image of the rest, and seen as a whole, they may have constituted an impediment to the transition from Territorial to State government.

It was small relief to the courts that many of the more desperate criminals were dealt with in the field, so never faced the bar of formal justice. The machinery of the less peremptory side of the judicial system was already creaking beneath the weight of routine criminal and civil business.

Edward Green, the first chief justice of Oklahoma Territory, often commented that the law of the Territory, like Oklahoma itself, was sui generis.[25] It was unique in that federal court (besides, as was usual, Territorial court) had to be held in each county. This, and much else, goaded one of the district judges, John Burford, into angry protest:

> The poor judge in Oklahoma must reside in his district; he must hold a court in each county; each United States offender must be prosecuted in the county where the offense is committed. . . .
> I hold court in seven counties, and attend one session of supreme court every six months. I travel overland from 60 to 150 miles to the county seats; am compelled to tent out and pay for team, feed, etc., for a number of days at a time. . . . My small salary of $3,000 per year has, after paying necessary expenses away from home, dwindled to about $2,000, and out of this we must support a family, live, and keep up the dignity of a supreme court.

... I am ordered to go out of my district next week for a whole week to hold court in another district. I must quit my district, leave my home at my own expense.

... If the War Department had not been courteous enough to supply transportation I would have been bankrupt.[26]

Burford asked for, and with the Attorney-General's help received, a sum similar to that paid to the judges in Indian Territory to cover traveling expenses and subsistence. But Congress was deaf to the pleas of Attorneys-General Harmon and McKenna for the abolition of the law dictating that there should be sittings of the federal court in each county.

Oklahoma acquired its twenty-third county in 1896 when, in accordance with a decision of the United States Supreme Court, Greer County was ceded by Texas. In 1902 the number of judicial districts in Oklahoma Territory was increased from five to seven.

Away from "old Oklahoma"—the district settled in 1889—there was often more statutory than material dignity to the institutions of justice and local government. Here is the city of Cloud Chief as it looked in 1898 to a young man who had just arrived there to make a career in the law:

> Indulge now in no illusions of grandeur. Twelve or fifteen small frame buildings, most of them of the box type, each with its inevitable false front, made up the business section. The saloons were the best equipped and best kept establishments there. Facing the others, stood the town's hotel, fitly named "Iron Hotel," one story, armored on the outside with sheets of corrugated galvanized iron.
>
> The court house—Ah, that courthouse! It was set in the middle of the naked square. There was not a tree nor a shrub, and no walks save a dirt path. . . . No other building was near, except that small place of convenience, now politely referred to as a "Chic Sales." This Temple of Justice, a scant one story, some sixteen by twenty feet in dimensions, was of sadly warped cottonwood lumber. Those who know the vagaries of a green cottonwood plank know well that no other material can equal the twists and turns, both sidewise and edgewise, it makes in drying. There were no partitions inside this building, yet it housed the County Clerk, Treasurer, Sheriff, and the Superintendent of Schools. In addition it had two small, iron cells for prisoners. It doesn't seem possible.
>
> Residence houses were some twenty in number—of one, two, and three rooms. There were, also, some twenty-five or such matter of dugouts and half dugouts. . . . The town's population did not exceed three hundred.[27]

As the writer noted, the district judges in Oklahoma "would go from the comfortable chambers in the counties out of their residences, out to the primitive and ill furnished county seat towns such as Cloud Chief, Arapaho, Taloga, Cheyenne, Grand, and others to hold a term of district court at least once a year."[28] None of these towns would grow to be much; several, such as Grand, would wither into the prairie. These places were born of hope. All the longer-term prospects were with Oklahoma City, Guthrie, Stillwater, Kingfisher, El Reno, Hennessey, and two or three of the towns in the former Cherokee Outlet.

Much of the future of the Territory, and its claim to Statehood, would depend upon how fully these towns succeeded in establishing themselves as trading centers. There was fecund soil, and, although the depressed state of the market kept crop prices low, most of the settlers stayed on. Among many of the smaller settlements in the western additions to the new Territory there was an air of fragility, arising perhaps from uncertainty whether the land would really support arable or other small-scale farming for any length of time.

Even more important for the economic well-being of the envisaged State was the natural wealth of the Indian Territory: the production of the coal mines in the Choctaw Nation was quadrupled between 1885 and 1900, and in the latter year a start was made on the exploitation of the oil reserves in the Osage Nation.[29]

Apart from the increase in the population, the most conspicuous evidence of economic growth was provided by the railroad industry. Railway mileage in the Indian Territory increased from 352 in 1885 to 432 in 1886 and 1,155 in 1889. By 1895 the combined mileage for Oklahoma and Indian Territory stood at 1,585, and during the year 1900 it passed the 2,000 mark.[30]

The Guthrie *Oklahoma State Capital,* perhaps the most politically aggressive paper in Oklahoma during the years of Territorial government, had coined the slick, if solecistic, term "the twin Territories" as early as the autumn of 1890.[31] But no amount of furious campaigning by the *State Capital* or the many like-minded papers in Oklahoma and Indian Territory could bring Statehood until the allotment of tribal land, and per capita distribution of tribal moneys, had been completed by the Dawes Commission.

This could not happen before 1906, and a number of political aspirants in Oklahoma, with a small band of allies in Congress, were unwilling to wait that long. They demanded Statehood for Oklahoma as it was then defined. Politicians in the Five Nations, including some of the tribal leaders, were at about the same time asking for the separate admission of Indian Territory, either at once or after an interim period of Territorial government.

Thus, although every significant statute relating to the trans-Mississippi tract allocated to the Five Tribes—before, including, and after creation of Oklahoma Territory—visualized and was intended to hasten the incorporation of the whole area as a single entity into the Union, there was no cessation of efforts to secure a distinct political identity for the section remaining to the Five Tribes after the treaties of 1866. Assertions that the admission of Oklahoma as a single State, instead of entry into the Union of two States on the basis of the division drawn in 1866, was the fortuitous outcome of a conglomeration of legislation or was accomplished by the operation of factors that became critical barely ahead of the event of Statehood, are the product of faulty analysis or none.[32] The contest was joined, broken off, and renewed on the same ground over a period of forty years; but the momentum, always, carried the issue towards the Enabling Act of 1906.

Only the chronological span of the closing stages was determined by political considerations that did not emerge before 1901. Many Eastern politicians of both main parties did not want as many as four additional Western States. To their mind, Oklahoma and Indian Territory should be joined into one State, and Arizona and New Mexico should also be combined if possible.

Another factor was that, while Oklahoma was preponderantly Northern in its attitudes and sympathies, Indian Territory was even more predominantly Southern, except in some of the coal-mining towns. It was a safe assumption that the Five Tribes area would be dominated by the Democratic party in State politics and would support the Democratic candidate in a Presidential election. Oklahoma, it could be supposed, would probably favor the Republican party, but by a smaller margin. Uncertainties in Congress about the overall political balance of the "twin Territories" introduced partisan calculations into the reckoning.

No progress was made in 1898 with a proposal by John Morgan to organize the Indian country into the Territory of Indianola, with Statehood to follow in due course.[33] In March 1902, the House Committee on the Territories recommended the passage of John Moon's bill to create the Territory of Jefferson out of the Indian Territory.[34] Soon afterward William Knox (R, Massachusetts) piloted through the House a bill "to enable the people of Oklahoma, Arizona, and New Mexico to form constitutions and State governments." The Knox bill allowed for, but did not require, attachments of portions of Indian Territory to the new State as the work of allotment was proceeding.[35] Neither bill advanced beyond the House of Representatives.

In November 1902, before the demise of the Moon bill, representatives of the governments of the Five Tribes met at Eufaula to formulate a line of resistance to any proposal that would place Indian Territory under organized government before March 4, 1906. Their protest to the Secretary of the Interior ran, in part:

Whereas, citizens of the United States, and not Indians, now resident in and upon the lands of the Five Tribes are making by petition and lobby efforts to induce the Congress of the United States to ignore the spirit and letter of these agreements [with the Dawes Commission] by placing the Indian Territory under the laws of Oklahoma Territory; failing in that, to organize a United States territory out of the present judicial organization known as the Indian Territory, either of which propositions would delay the work of the government now organized and satisfactorily proceeding under the direction of the Secretary of the Interior for the fulfillment of the agreements referred to . . . we insist upon our tribal governments continuing intact and our tribal conditions remaining unchanged until March 4, 1906, at which time, should Congress deem it wise to change the present form of government in the Indian Territory, we ask that a State be formed out of the territory composing Indian Territory without the preliminary steps of a Territorial term of government.[36]

Dennis Flynn, delegate to Congress from Oklahoma Territory, pushed for separate Statehood almost throughout his period of office but changed his tune just before he retired.[37] In 1903 the new delegate, Bird McGuire—a Republican, like Flynn, but from the opposing "progressive" wing of the party—failed to make headway with another bill to bring Statehood to Oklahoma Territory.[38] Shortly afterward James Robinson (D, Indiana) introduced a House bill for "double Statehood"—Statehood individually for each of the twin Territories. The Robinson bill was soon dropped, but it provided a concentration point for the various sides of the argument, and there was no doubt that the political classes and the politically vocal members of the people at large were at one in their marked preference for single Statehood for Oklahoma and Indian Territory conjoined; or if Congress could not deliver this before the Dawes Commission had finished its task, for Oklahoma alone on the understanding that Indian Territory would be annexed as soon as the commission's program had been concluded.[39]

After the House Committee on the Territories had heard the testimony of the opposing spokesmen for single and separate Statehood, with much the better of the argument going to the former, its chairman, Edward Hamilton (R, Michigan) introduced a bill which, in providing for the admission of Oklahoma and Indian Territory as one State and Arizona and New Mexico as another, hedged itself about with an unscalable barrier, for the two aims were politically irreconcilable.[40] Nearly a year later, after having been mutilated almost beyond recognition in the Senate, the bill became jammed in a conference committee. At this stage, during the congressional adjournment in that spring of 1905, the resistance of tribal politicians to amalgamation with Oklahoma took definite shape as an organized separate Statehood campaign for Indian Territory.[41]

The "Sequoyah movement" would never have acquired direction or impetus without the sponsorship of the leading white politicians in Indian Territory, and even then the majority of residents remained indifferent:

> Everyone talks about corn, cotton, wheat, alfalfa, cattle, hogs and hay, and it behooves the newcomer to fall into line and talk likewise if he desires to be listened to long. . . . It is now confidently asserted that we shall be fitted for statehood in 1906—the government, it is said, will make us fit by law—but even then, it is not likely that cotton and corn will be supplanted as the main topics of conversation.[42]

In November 1905, the constitution proposed for a State of Sequoyah was ratified by a vote of 57,000 to 9,000, but this demonstrated only that the Sequoyah movement enjoyed the support of 87 percent of one-third of the adult male population.[43]

Senior officeholders of the United States Government in Indian Territory had not taken much account of the general passivity. Judges Charles Raymond of the Western District and Hosea Townsend of the Southern District were accused by William ("Alfalfa Bill") Murray, a future State governor of Oklahoma, of "arbitrary oppression" in interfering with the work of the committee that was organizing the plebiscite for the Sequoyah constitution:

> When I recall the days of Federal Court Rule in the Indian Territory, I realize how sound was Jefferson's statement that if the people must choose between giving up their representatives in [the] law-making branch or the courts, they had best give up the former; for it would have been intolerable to have lived, at times, in some Districts in the [Indian] Territory without the right of Jury trials, unless one became an abject sycophant to the Court and his cohorts and I never knew a Murray that was good at that.[44]

Charles Haskell, principal organizer of the Sequoyah movement, and his colleagues, may have believed in the merit of the cause they had adopted and may have done all they could to advance it, but they never expected it to succeed. They knew that Congress would not accept a proposal for double Statehood; so, calculating that amalgamation of the "twin Territories" would produce a State whose governor would be a Democrat and whose legislature would contain a Democratic majority, they used the Sequoyah campaign to secure their power base in Indian Territory. Their longer-term objective was to squeeze out the established leaders of the Democratic party in Oklahoma Territory.[45]

This strategy attained its ends. President Theodore Roosevelt, to the chagrin of Republicans in Indian Territory hoping for double Statehood, cold-shouldered the Sequoyah proposals, but it is hard to see how he could have influenced Congress very much even if he had wished to do so. On January 22, 1906, Congressman Hamilton introduced a bill to enable the people of Oklahoma and Indian Territory to form a State constitution and government[46] and on June 16, 1906, Roosevelt added his signature to it. Charles Haskell was master of the Democratic party in the twin Territories and well on the way to becoming inaugural governor of the State of Oklahoma.[47]

The work of the Dawes Commission was far from complete by March 4, 1906. When, in accordance with the terms under which it had been given life, the commission expired on March 3, 1905, it was replaced by a single commissioner in the person of its former chairman, Tams Bixby.[48]

Despite the statutory insistence that they should be closed on March 4, 1907,[49] the tribal rolls were completed only in 1914, some five thousand names having been added in the meantime.[50] United States citizenship had been conferred upon all members of the Five Tribes on March 3, 1901.[51]

Tribal government subsided gently into desuetude even before the time appointed for its formal dissolution.

There were two disturbances of this placid surface, both quickly suppressed without loss of life.

First, during the winter of 1900–1901, Chitto Harjo (Crazy Snake), with several dozen supporters, made a foredoomed attempt to restore government upon traditional lines among the full-bloods of the Muskogee Nation. The federal authorities, fully backed by the Creek government, put down the movement with a mixture of speed, firmness, and tact.[52]

A second series of disruptions occurred in the autumn of 1902 in the wake of the general election in the Choctaw Nation when Green McCurtain and Thomas Hunter were rival candidates for the post of principal chief. As usual, each party claimed victory and accused the other of cheating. Gilbert Dukes, the incumbent chief, refused to make way for McCurtain and summoned the national light-horse to the capitol, which had been occupied by McCurtain partisans. Blair Shoenfelt, the Union agent, took a party of Indian police to Tuskahoma, and United States marshal Benjamin Hackett attended with a force of deputies. Shoenfelt thought the light-horse ought to be disarmed, but asked Hackett to do the work instead of doing it himself; and Hacket declined. The stalemate was unblocked by the arrival of two companies of soldiers from Fort Reno. Hunter had been inducted into office but had to step down when the supreme court of the Choctaw Nation upheld his opponent.[53]

Rumors about the scandalous conduct of all four federal district courts and their officers led to an investigation by examiners from the Department of Justice in the autumn of 1903. At the end of it, Marshal Hackett of the Central District, an assistant district attorney of the Western District, and a number of lesser officers were dismissed or required to resign. Marshal Benjamin Colbert of the Western District and District Attorney Pliny Soper of the Northern District narrowly escaped removal but were severely censured by Attorney-General Philander Knox. Several others, including Leo Bennett, marshal of the Northern District, were exculpated.[54]

Government from the federal courthouses was, by that time, tolerable only because of the imminence of its demise. Even with eight judges where there had been four, the courts fell further and further in arrear of an ever-thickening docket. At the close of the fiscal year on June 30, 1904, 3,661 criminal cases had been terminated, but 4,178 were pending. Twelve months later, the district attorneys reported that 3,989 criminal cases had been decided, leaving another 4,852 on the books. On June 30, 1906, a fortnight after the passage of the Enabling Act, it was recorded that 3,612 criminal cases had been resolved, with 5,512 unsettled at the beginning of what would be the last full year before Oklahoma took its place among the States. And that was only half the picture. The courts were as heavily beset on the civil side of their jurisdiction, with some 3,600 cases begun, 3,000 finished, and another 3,600 still untouched at the end of 1903–4 alone.[55] If judicial reform in its several phases had carried Indian Territory to the verge of Statehood, in the end it was the compelling necessity for judicial reform that made Statehood imperative.

About a week after the three federal district courts of Indian Territory had assumed the jurisdiction formerly borne by their rivals at Fort Smith, Paris, and Fort Scott, an editor in the Cherokee Nation mused, in apocalyptic vein: "All things must eventually come to an end. . . . The time will come, of course, when the great United States will be no more, when the boasted civilization of the greatest nation on earth will count for naught."[56]

Visionary phrase making neither demands the percipience nor implies the prescience to construct a time scale for the future, and the editor ventured no guess about how long it might be before tribal government had run its course. A decade later, in 1906, when the machinery for transition to Statehood was laid in place, none could have known what would emerge within the next year or so from the toiling and haggling of constitutional draftsmen.

Despite the sally into prophecy, the Vinita editor was speaking with the voice of his time. Expansion, consolidation, and further expansion were the goals toward which the gathering dynamic of American government and society was driving.

One of the staunchest advocates of Five Tribes governmental autonomy, the Atoka *Indian Citizen,* now counseled nationalism of a moderated, empirical, realistic, and accommodating sort. Its editor urged that the tribal governments yield to the United States while Washington was still of a mind to offer concessions, rather than suffer instant and utter annihilation because of their own obduracy. In an editorial of September 9, 1897, he pronounced the Atoka Agreement "THE BEST THING UNDER PRESENT CONDITIONS."

Enhancement of institutionalized federal authority and the global aggrandizement of the United States politically and economically were assuming a pattern with no place for five semiseparate enclaves. The intransigence of the Creeks and Cherokees was, in the editor's view, not merely regrettable but futile.

> [T]he old maxim that "times change and men change with them," is unfortunately as true with the American Indians as it was with the old Romans. The times have changed and are changing, and Indians can't make the maxim any less true any more than any other race of people in the world's history have been able to do. . . . History shows that the United States not only controls within her own dominions, but that she is exercising a dominating influence in the western hemisphere and is reaching out even into the islands of the seas and changing the political status in many cases.

Less than a year later the passage of the Curtis Act heralded the demise of tribal government, but the *Indian Citizen* had nothing to say about it. Seemingly in common with most small-town (and big-town) papers in the United States at that time, it was too carried away by the excitement of the American adventure in Cuba to pay much attention to local affairs. It is reasonable to suppose that when the Curtis Act was put before him for approval late in June 1898, President McKinley's mind was too preoccupied with the American advance upon Santiago to spare much thought for the death warrant of the five "independent domestic dependencies" that lay under his hand.[57]

By 1906 the United States had acquired quasi sovereignty over the isthmus of Panama, stepped into the role of intermediary between Russia and Japan, and established an economic suzerainty and debt collectorship over Central and South America. During the same span of eight years the balance of the population of the United States shifted from the country to the town, and the massive annual intake of immigrants, with eastern and southern Europe now supplying the greatest numbers, produced more labor than the market could or would accommodate.

Some connection could easily be predicated between any of these themes—expansionist aggression, continuing industrialization in the East and Middle West, and an excess of cheap labor—and the politico-legal strategy whose culmination was the suppression of five autonomous governments, the sale of the lands and other assets of their people, and the formation of a new State some 90 percent of whose inhabitants were born in the United States of parents who had been born in the United States. Only the first of the three elements was present, and then with only the slenderest of global implications, when that strategy was envisaged before the Civil War and formulated soon after it; but it may have been accelerated toward the fruition of its objectives by the emergence of new factors during the 1880s and then by the unrest and dislocations arising directly from the Depression of 1893.

Even if the rationale behind the dissolution of the governments of the Five Tribes absorbed something from all these intangible influences, they add up to much less than an explanation of the policy. In essence, the struggle was between the institutions of the United States and those of the Five Tribes. It might have been prolonged for a further few years if the Indians had been united in their opposition to intervention and domination from Washington, but it would have been over much sooner if the House of Representatives and the Senate had been united, in themselves and together (and the Executive with them), in a disposition to exploit the federal courts clauses of the treaties of 1866. The liquidation of the governments of the Five Nations of Indian Territory—accomplished through the restriction, reduction, and removal of their courts of law, until there was nothing left of tribal sovereignty but its torso—was but an episode in a phase in the aggrandizement of the federal Government. Eighty or ninety years beyond, without ensuring their permanency or its own, the same onward force has effected many changes in the character of the relationships between general and local government, the governing and the governed, and the governed among themselves. It has been part of a process that can never be complete.

Notes

ABBREVIATIONS

AG	Attorney-General of the United States
AR	*Annual Report*
BIC	Board of Indian Commissioners
CG	*Congressional Globe*
Chron.	*Chronicles of Oklahoma*
CIA	Commissioner of Indian Affairs
CR	*Congressional Record*
DJ	Department of Justice
HD	*House Document*
HED	*House Executive Document*
HJ	*House Journal*
HMD	*House Miscellaneous Document*
HR	*House Report*
LR	Letters Received
LS	Letters Sent
OHS	Oklahoma Historical Society; IAD: Indian Archives Division
SD	*Senate Document*
SED	*Senate Executive Document*
SEJ	*Senate Executive Journal*
SI	Secretary of the Interior
SMD	*Senate Miscellaneous Document*
SR	*Senate Report*
Stats.L.	*Statutes at Large of the United States of America* (*RS: Revised Statutes,* 1873–74)

CHAPTER ONE. FROM REMOVAL TO RECONSTRUCTION

1. F. N. Thorpe, comp. ed., *Federal and State Constitutions,* vol. 1, 261.

2. *Stats.L.* III, 493.

3. John W. Morris and Edwin C. McReynolds, *Historical Atlas of Oklahoma* (1965; rev. ed., with Charles R. Goins, 1976) is an invaluable work of reference and, as the only collection of its kind, accompanied the preparation of the text of the present study throughout. The revisions carried into the edition of 1976 alter nothing of the original content matter relating to the period 1866–1906.

4. *CR,* vol. 8, app., 111. No such passage occurs in Jefferson's writings as so far published, but thoughts expressed in a letter to John Dickinson dated August 9,

1803, are so similar in substance and wording as to amount almost to a paraphrase. See Paul Leicester Ford, comp., ed., *Writings of Thomas Jefferson,* vol. 8, 261–63.

5. The standard histories of the Five Tribes are Angie Debo, *Rise and Fall of the Choctaw Republic;* Debo, *Road to Disappearance* (Muskogee, or Creek, Nation); Arrell M. Gibson, *Chickasaws;* Edwin C. McReynolds, *Seminoles;* and Morris L. Wardell, *Political History of the Cherokee Nation* (the 1977 reprint has a fine Bibliographical Foreword by Rennard Strickland).

These books have been utilized in conjunction with other sources in the summary given in this introductory chapter of the history of the Five Tribes from the time of the removal to the year 1860. The other, occasional sources have been cited whenever applicable.

Among works of a more general character, Francis Paul Prucha, *The Great Father,* and Christine Bolt, *American Indian Policy and American Reform,* contain several important chapters and passages on the Five Tribes and Indian Territory.

6. *Stats.L.* 9, 871. For the background to these difficulties, see T. L. Ballenger, "Death and Burial of Major Ridge," *Chron.,* Spring 1973, 100–105; Gerald A. Reed, "Financial Controversy in the Cherokee Nation," ibid., Spring 1974, 82–98; Gay E. Moulton, "Chief John Ross and Cherokee Removal Finances," ibid., Fall 1974, 342–59.

7. Michael D. Green, *Politics of Indian Removal,* 69–186; A. P. Du Chateau, "Creek Nation on the Eve of the Civil War," *Chron.,* Fall 1974, 290–315.

8. Rex Syndergaard, "Final Move of the Choctaws, 1825–1830," *Chron.,* Summer 1974, 207–219; W. David Baird, *Peter Pitchlynn,* 13–69, 95–125.

9. *Stats.L.* 7, 573; 11, 611.

10. Baird, 71–75.

11. For a good concise general account of the removals, see Prucha, *Great Father,* vol. 1, 183–243.

12. *Laws of the Choctaw Nation, Session VII.*

13. Debo, *Rise and Fall of the Choctaw Republic,* 125, 179–80. But see art. 38 of treaty of 1866, quoted below.

14. *Constitution of the Chickasaw Nation, 1866,* General Provisions, sec. 7.

15. *Constitution of the Muskogee Nation, 1867,* art. 3, 49th Cong., 1st sess., *SR* 1278, pt. 2, 164. For the exceptions, see *Laws of the Muskogee Nation, 1867,* chap. 7, art. 2, which lists them by name.

16. R. Halliburton, Jr., "Black Slavery Among the Cherokees," *Chron.,* Winter 1974–75, 483–96.

17. Rennard Strickland, *Fire and the Spirits,* 56–57.

18. Ibid., 58–59.

19. Ibid.; Bobby L. Blackburn, "Oklahoma Law Enforcement since 1803," Ph.D. diss., University of Oklahoma, 29–38; Carolyn Thomas Foreman, "Lighthorse in the Indian Territory," *Chron.,* Spring 1956, 17–43; *Stats.L.* 9, 871, art. 2.

20. *Stats.L.* 7, 210; *Constitution of the Choctaw Nation, 1860,* art. 5; *Act of the Choctaw Nation,* October 24, 1860; Blackburn, 39–41; Foreman; Lewis Anthony Kensell, "Reconstruction in the Choctaw Nation," *Chron.,* Summer 1969.

21. *Constitution of the Chickasaw Nation, 1867,* art. 6, sec. 17; C. T. Foreman, "Notes on the Chickasaw Light-horsemen," *Chron,* Winter 1956–57, 484.

22. Foreman, "Notes on the Organization of the Seminole Lighthorse," *Chron.,* Autumn 1956, 340–43.

23. 45th Cong., 3d sess., *SR* 744; 49th Cong., 1st sess., *SR* 1278, pt. 2; Strickland.

24. *Stats.L.* 4, 564 (*RS* 2139), 731–38 (*RS* 2145, etc.). The first Indian Trade and Intercourse law was enacted on July 24, 1790. These early acts, with extracts from documents relating to them, are reproduced in Francis Paul Prucha, *Documents of United States Indian Policy,* 14–35.

25. B. P. Curtis, *Reports of Decisions of the Supreme Court of the United States,* vol. 16; Howard 4, 571–72.

26. *CR* 13, 2526.

27. *Stats.L.* 9, 594–95.

28. *Stats.L.* 10, 269–70.

29. Act of Congress, April 30, 1790 (*Stats.L.* 1, 113, embodied in *RS* 5339).

30. For an early example, see the act of March 3, 1855, "Forgery in the Indian country," *Stats.L.* 10, 700–701.

31. *Stats.L.* 18, 146–47.

32. The provisions applicable in the various nations, derived from the different treaties and little changed since the removals, are summarized in *AR,* SI 1890, 99. The matrix was sec. 2, act of June 30, 1834, *Stats.L.* 4, 279 (*RS* 2129).

33. Art. 15 of Creek and Seminole treaty, 1856; art. 7 of Choctaw and Chickasaw treaty, 1855.

34. 45th Cong., 3d sess., *SR* 744, 428.

35. *Stats.L.* 11, 80 (*RS* 2149).

36. *AR,* SI 1877, 503–4; 49th Cong., 1st sess., *SR* 1278, pt. 2, 135–36.

37. R. C. Childers to Samuel Checote, September 4, 1880, Creek Nation, Foreign Relations, doc. 30455 (IAD, OHS).

38. Leo G. Bennett to Robert P. Porter, May 29, 1891, in *Report on Indians Taxed and Indians Not Taxed . . . at the Eleventh Census, 1890,* 284–85. Most of the earlier statutes still in force in 1873 are contained in *RS* 2039–2157.

39. *RS* 2152, from *Stats.L.* 4, 732.

40. A. M. Gibson, "Indian Territory United Nations 1845," *Chron.,* Winter 1961–62, 389–413; Curtis L. Nolen, "Okmulgee Constitution," ibid., Fall 1980, 264–81.

41. *Official Records of the War of the Rebellion,* ser. 4, vol. 1, 426–43, 445–65, 513–27, 669–87.

42. *CG,* 39th Cong., 2d sess., 915, 1021–22.

43. *AR,* SI 1865, 496–537; Nolen.

44. Seminole treaty, *Stats.L.* 14, 755–58; Choctaw and Chickasaw treaty, ibid., 769–84; Creek treaty, ibid., 785–92; Cherokee treaty, ibid., 799–809.

45. Creek Docs. 30626–28, 30640, Creek, Foreign Relations: Seminole (IAD, OHS).

46. The U.S. Supreme Court so ruled in 1900.

47. B. B. Chapman, "Final Report of the Cherokee Commission," *Chron.,* December 1941, 356–65.

48. For the disposition of the "freedman" issue, see Debo, *Road to Disappearance,* 172–76; *Rise and Fall of the Choctaw Republic,* 87–89, 99–107; Wardell, 203–4; Gibson, 258–63; McReynolds, 318–19; Parthena Louise James, "Reconstruction in the Chickasaw Nation: The Freedman Problem," *Chron.,* Spring 1967, 44–57; Hanna R. Warren, "Reconstruction in the Cherokee Nation," ibid., Sum-

mer 1967, 180–89; Kensell; Gail Balmain, "Creek Treaty of 1866," *Chron.,* Summer 1970, 184–96; Harry Henslick, "Seminole Treaty of 1866," ibid., Autumn 1970, 280–94.

49.   For the origin of this suggestion, see *AR,* SI 1865, 541.

50.   The seventh article is partly ambiguous, but this is what it seems to mean when placed beside a map of the Cherokee Nation. Wardell, 203, interprets the article a little differently.

51.   Legus M. Perryman to Dennis W. Bushyhead, May 2, 1887, Cherokee, (Tahlequah) Indian Police; Bushyhead to Perryman, May 6, 1887, Creek, Foreign Relations: Cherokee, Doc. 30524.

52.   See Chapter 3.

53.   See Chapter 6.

54.   1866–1870; 1872–1874.

55.   John B. Meserve, "Governor Cyrus Harris," *Chron.,* December 1937, 373–86.

56.   Meserve, "Chief Allen Wright," *Chron.,* December 1941, 314–21.

57.   Incorporated in Choctaw and Chickasaw treaty of 1866, art. 8, sec. 10.

58.   Then the prescribed mode of capital punishment in the Choctaw Nation; see Chapter 4.

59.   Wright to William Ward, Tinnenubbee, Filia, etc, May 3, 1867, Choctaw Nation, Letters of the Chiefs. See also docket book, supreme court of the Choctaw Nation, second district, 16–17 (IAD, OHS).

60.   *AR* SI 1865, 436–96; ibid., 1869, 486–520, *Report of the Bureau of Indian Commissioners,* 847–63.

61.   Milton W. Reynolds, "Indian Territory," *Western Monthly,* November 1870, 262–63.

62.   Edward King, "Great South, the New Route to the Gulf," *Scribner's Monthly,* July 1873, 278.

63.   *AR,* SI 1866, 283. The figure given for the Choctaws and Chickasaws is 29,000, but it is obvious from material relating to other years that this total is much too high; and if it were not incorrect, it would increase the grand total by 7,000. A misread numeral or misprint must account for the discrepancy; cf. *AR,* SI 1872, 421–24.

64.   Ibid., 1868, 736–37.

65.   Ibid., 1869, 846–48.

CHAPTER TWO. **AN *IMPERIUM IN IMPERIO?***

1.   Allen Wright to the U.S. Senate and House of Representatives, March 7, 1867, Choctaw Nation, Letters of the Chiefs.

2.   *Stats.L.* 15, 125–68.

3.   Robert K. Heimann, "Cherokee Tobacco Case," *Chron.,* Autumn 1963, 299–322.

4.   *CG,* 41st Cong., 1st sess., 334; 41st Cong., 3d sess. 600–605, 699–701.

5.   Checote to Wright, April 14, 1870, Choctaw Nation, Foreign Relations.

6.   *AR,* BIC 1870, 113–28 (app. 35); "Okmulgee Constitution," *Chron.,* September 1925, 216–28.

7.   *CG,* 41st Cong., 3d sess., 601.

8.   Ibid., 699.

9. Jurors and salaried officers had to be residents of the appropriate counties of the State; deputy marshals did not have to be but generally were. There were, however, a few deputy marshals who were Indian citizens and lived in the Indian Territory.

10. *CG,* 41st Cong., 3d sess., 700; *AR,* BIC 1870, 117.

11. 42d Cong., 2d sess., *HED* 153.

12. 42d Cong., 2d sess., *SMD* 85.

13. John H. Beadle, *Undeveloped West,* 362–63.

14. Ibid., 364. See also Reynolds.

15. *CG,* 41st Cong., 3d sess., 1195–96, 1460–61.

16. *AR,* SI 1869, 847.

17. Ibid., 1870, 754.

18. Ibid.

19. Ibid., 1871, 984; 1872, 492, 618–19.

20. Ibid., 1871, 986; 1872, 622.

21. *Stats.L.* 13, 29.

22. *AR,* SI 1868, 736–37.

23. *Stats.L.* 19, 244.

24. 42d Cong., 2d sess., *SED* 70, pt. 2, 3–8.

25. 43d Cong., 1st sess., *HR* 626, 189–91; *AR,* BIC 1870, 117; *AR,* SI 1872, 618–19.

26. *Constitution of the Cherokee Nation,* 1880, art. 2, sec. 29.

27. 42d Cong., 2d sess., *SED* 70, 18–20.

28. For the Going Snake courthouse affray, see Fort Smith, Arkansas, *New Era,* April 17, 19, 1872; letters, documents, and newspaper reports in 42d Cong., 2d sess., *SED* 70, 1–20; *AR,* SI 1872, 619; Beadle, 408–9; Daniel F. Littlefield and Lonnie F. Underhill, "Trial of Ezekiel Proctor and the problem of Judicial Jurisdiction," *Chron.,* Autumn 1970, 307–22. The last-mentioned item does not offer a balanced evaluation of the evidence.

29. 42d Cong., 2d sess., *SMD* 166.

30. *CG,* 42d Cong., 3d sess., 611–17.

31. Ibid., 617.

32. Ibid., 657.

33. Ibid., app., 13–14.

34. *AR,* SI 1869, 485–86; 43d Cong., 2d sess., SMD 66; *New York Times,* January 17, February 13, 1875.

35. 43d Cong., 2d sess., *SMD* 34.

36. Ibid., *SMD* 72.

37. Ibid., *SMD* 112.

38. 44th Cong., 1st sess., *SMD* 23.

39. Ibid., *SMD* 42.

40. Enfaula, Creek Nation, *Indian Journal,* May 10, 1877.

41. Ibid., November 17, 1877; the closing sentence exaggerates the legal impediment, but not the practical difficulties.

42. 45th Cong., 1st sess., *SR* 744, vols. 1–4; the testimony is recorded on pp. 1–800 of the same document; cited hereinafter as *Patterson Report.*

43. H. Craig Miner, *Corporation and the Indian,* 73, 94–95.

44. Marston to Charles Thompson, October 21, 1878; Thompson to Marston, November 11, 1878; Cherokee Nation, Foreign Relations.

45.   The respective capitals of the Cherokee, Muskogee, Choctaw, and Chicka-saw nations. Wewoka, the Seminole capital, was barely a hamlet. Tuskahoma suc-ceeded Chahta Tamaha as capital of the Choctaw Nation in 1884.

46.   David J. Rothman, *Politics and Power*, 212.

47.   *Patterson Report*, app., 260–319.

48.   *CR* 6, 608; 8, 1057, 2388, 2404; app. 108–14.

49.   46th Cong., 2d sess., *SED* 124, *SR* 332.

50.   Ibid., *HR* 755, 1–9.

51.   *CR* 13, 503.

52.   *Stats.L.* 22, 181–85; see Chapter 6.

CHAPTER THREE. **FEDERAL LAW IN THE INDIAN TERRITORY, 1866–1883**

1.   *Stats.L.* 1, 113 (*RS* 5339).

2.   Ibid., 4, 115 (*RS* 5345).

3.   Ibid., 1, 113 (*RS* 5343).

4.   Ibid., 18, 473.

5.   Ibid., 29, 487.

6.   James T. Mitchell and Henry Flanders, comps., *Statutes at Large of Pennsylvania*, vol. 15, 174–81.

7.   L. P. Sandels and Joseph M. Hill, *a Digest of the Statutes of Arkansas*, 534–40.

8.   C. F. W. Dassler, *Compiled Laws of Kansas, 1881*, 328–30.

9.   C. L. Sonnichsen, *I'll Die Before I'll Run*, 8–9.

10.   Sandels and Hill, 536 (from an act of December 17, 1838).

11.   *Compiled Laws of New Mexico*, secs. 1063–69.

12.   *AR*, AG 1883, 24.

13.   *Stats.L.* 25, 33.

14.   Ibid., 17, 289–320.

15.   Ibid., 12, 301.

16.   Ibid., 24, 635–42.

17.   Ibid., 9, 594–95.

18.   Ibid., 15, 44.

19.   Ibid., 25, 655–56.

20.   The various provisions, derived from an act of September 24, 1789, are summarized in *RS* 551–62, 767–99.

21.   *CG*, 41st Cong., 2d sess., 2094, 4171–72; 41st Cong., 3d sess., 1135, 1195–96, 1417, 1460–61, 1471, 1668, 1680–81, 1751, 1761, 1765, 1769, 1801, 1910.

22.   *Stats.L.* 16, 471–72.

23.   *SEJ* 17, 683–84

24.   Ibid., 18, 46, 47, 50.

25.   43d Cong., 1st sess., *HR* 626, 72; cited hereinafter as *Sener Report*.

26.   *AR*, SI 1866, 16; 1867, 19; 1868, 18; 1869, 13.

27.   *Sener Report*, 268.

28.   *Stats.L.* 16, 164.

29.   *AR*, AG 1870, 2.

30.   Ibid., 1871, 4.

31.   43d Cong., 2d sess., *HED* 178, 5; *Sener Report*, 266–68.

32. Akerman to James H. Huckleberry, August 22, 1871, LS, DJ, *Instructions to United States Attorneys and Marshals,* Letter Book B2, 332.

33. *Sener Report,* 310–15.

34. Beadle, 367–71; Reynolds, 270; Edward King, 260 ff; James L Allhands, "History of the Construction of the Frisco Railway Lines in Oklahoma," *Chron.,* September 1925, 229–39; James D. Morrison, "Union Pacific, Southern Branch," ibid., June 1936, 173–88; Walter A. Johnson, "Brief History of the Missouri-Kansas-Texas Railroad Lines," ibid., Autumn 1946, 340–58; Craig Miner, "Struggle for an East-West Railway into the Indian Territory, 1870–1882," ibid., Spring 1969, 560–81; Nancy Hope Self, "Building of the Railroads in the Cherokee Nation," ibid., Summer 1971, 180–205.

35. *Sener Report,* 225–27, 239–40.

36. George H. Williams to Roots, March 4, 1872, LS, DJ, *Instructions to United States Attorneys and Marshals,* Letter Book C, 206–07; April 10, 1872, ibid., 259.

37. Williams to William A. Britton, August 30, 1872, ibid., 443–44.

38. *AR,* SI 1872, 481, 621–23; Edward King, 260–61, 269, 271–73.

39. Story was questioned about this case by the Sener committee, but gave evasive answers.

40. *Sener Report,* 239, 241; Samuel W. Harman, *Hell on the Border,* 167–81.

41. *Sener Report,* 264; 43d Cong., 2d sess., *HED* 175, 6.

42. *Sener Report,* 76–81.

43. *AR,* AG 1872, 7.

44. *Sener Report,* 264.

45. *Sener Report,* i; *SEJ* 18, 314; Williams to Story, June 26, 1874, LS, DJ, *General and Miscellaneous,* Letter Book I, 352. Incorrect dates are given in 43d Cong., 2d sess., *HED* 175, 3.

46. 43d Cong., 2d sess., *HR* 2.

47. *HEJ* 18, 390.

48. *Sener Report,* 31, 35.

49. Ibid., 36–37.

50. Ibid., 278–98.

51. Ibid., 308.

52. Fort Smith *New Era,* August 20, 1873.

53. "Gar," in *New York Times,* November 1, 1873.

54. *Sener Report,* 65–89, 287–92, 298–307.

55. *Stats.L.* 10, 166 (*RS* 841).

56. *Sener Report,* 31–33.

57. Ibid., 5, 39, 44.

58. *SEJ* 19, 73, 80.

59. *Sener Report,* 44, 61, 130–31, 133–36.

60. HJ, 43d Cong., 1st sess., 869, 1145, 1194; Williams to Story, June 17, 1874, LS, DJ, *Instructions to Judges and Clerks,* Letter Book 1, 31.

61. *Sener Report,* ix–x.

62. 43d Cong., 2d sess., *HED* 175, 1

63. Ibid., 2; Harman, 42–44.

64. 43d Cong., 2d sess., *HED* 175, 23, 25; *SEJ* 19, 428, 511; Williams to DuVal, August 31, 1874, LS, DJ, *General and Misc.,* Letter Book K, 447.

65. Williams to DuVal, June 24, August 8, September 2, October 2, October 9, November 9, 1874, March 19, 1875; LS, DJ, *General and Misc.,* ibid., 361, 419, 452, 490–91, 499, 538, 668; 43d Cong., 2d sess., *HED* 175, 2–14, 18–78.

66. 43d Cong., 2d sess., *HED* 175, 20.

67. Washington letter, in *New York Times,* January 12, 1874.

68. *SEJ* 20, 19, 31, 32, 40, 45; Williams to Parker, March 24, 1875, LS, DJ, *General and Misc.,* Letter Book K, 673.

69. *AR, AG* 1872–75, Exhibit B; *Sener Report,* 268.

70. 43d Cong., 2d sess., *HED* 175, 6–7.

71. For a convenient but not absolutely accurate summary of this side of the court's work, see Harman, 167–81. The list of executions in the Fort Smith *Elevator,* March 20, 1896, is correct to that date.

72. *AR, AG* 1876–83.

73. Pierrepoint to Parker, May 20, 1875, LS, DJ, *Instructions to United States Judges,* Letter Book I, 147.

74. *New York Times,* July 26, 1875.

75. Pierrepoint to Parker, September 12, 1875, LS, DJ, *Instructions,* Letter Book I, 171.

76. *Report of the Board of Inquiry . . . to Investigate Certain Charges against S. A. Galpin.*

77. S. A. Galpin, *Report upon the Condition and Management of Certain Indian Agencies in the Indian Territory,* 33.

78. Ibid., 34–35.

79. *AR,* SI 1873, 379.

80. Galpin, 35n.

81. *AR,* SI 1876, 477.

82. *Stats.L.* 11, 363 (*RS* 2153).

83. Williams to Story, November 3, 1873, LS, DJ, *General and Misc.,* Letter Book K, 177.

84. *Stats.L.* 10, 164–65; also *RS* 829–41.

85. *AR, AG* 1883, 22–23; 1884, 44–45; 1891, XXVI–XXVII; 1892, XXIII; 1893, XXIII–XXIV; 1895, 5–6; *CR* 28, 2302, 2360–61, 2390–2402; 2410–2531; app., 288–90, 3166–5897 (H.R. 6654, H.R. 6248).

86. Galpin; 45th Cong., 3d sess., *SR* 744, iv–v and passim; LS, DJ, Pierrepoint to Parker; Charles Devens to Parker, October 5, 1878, LS, DJ, *Instructions,* Letter Book I, 384–85; June 24, July 18, 1879, 442, 449; *New York Times,* July 26, 1875.

87. *Stats.L.* 19, 230.

88. Ibid., 240.

89. *AR,* SI 1868, 737.

90. See Chapter 7.

91. Eufaula *Indian Journal,* April 19, 1877; 49th Cong., 1st sess., *SR* 1278, pt. 2, 387; Fort Smith *Elevator,* March 1, 1887.

92. Eufaula *Indian Journal,* October 13, 1877.

93. 51st Cong., 1st sess., *SED* 164, 2–6; see also 49th Cong., 1st sess., *SR* 1278, pt. 2, 409–10.

94. W. P. Adair to Charles Thompson, May 17, 1879; Cherokee Nation, Federal Relations (IAD, OHS); testimony before probate judge, Blue County, Choctaw

Nation, October 3, 1877; Coleman Cole to general council of the Choctaw Nation, October 1878, Letters of the Chiefs; 45th Cong., 3d sess., *SR* 744, 91–92.

95. Adair to Thompson; for another noteworthy jurisdictional dispute of the 1870s, see *Ex Parte Kenyon* (1878), judgment of I. C. Parker, copy in Cherokee, Foreign Relations.

96. Act of Cherokee Nation, December 6, 1882, Cherokee Nation, Federal Relations, as cited.

97. Ibid., December 13, 1884.

98. 49th Cong., 1st sess., *SR* 1278, pt. 2, 378; cited hereinafter as *Dawes Report,* pt. 2.

99. Ibid., 390.

100. Fort Smith *New Era,* April 10, 1878.

101. *AR,* AG 1885, 30; see also 49th Cong., 1st sess., *Dawes Report,* pt. 2, 7. The basement jail was replaced in 1887 by a newly built three-story brick structure. The courthouse itself was moved in 1889 to the third floor of the new Government Building; but the original courthouse still stands, and is now a museum.

102. 45th Cong., 3d sess., *SR* 744, 80, 82–83, for this and similar assertions.

103. *AR,* AG 1875–1878, Exhibit B.

104. *AR,* SI 1879, 186.

105. *CR* 10, 1298; 13, 102, 1449, 1607, 1634, 2725, 4511–12.

106. *Stats.L.* 22, 400.

CHAPTER FOUR. CONSTITUTIONS AND LAWS OF THE FIVE NATIONS

1. *Dawes Report,* pt. 2, xix.

2. Anna Laurens Dawes, "Unknown Nation," *Harper's New Monthly Magazine,* March 1888, 604.

3. Beadle, 388.

4. *Constitution of the Cherokee Nation, 1839, 1880,* art. 3; *Constitution of the Choctaw Nation, 1860,* art. 3, sec. 15; *Constitution of the Chickasaw Nation, 1867,* art. 4; *Constitution of the Muskogee Nation, 1867,* art. 1, Secs. 2, 3.

5. *Cherokee Constitution,* art. 5, sec. 1.

6. Act of December 4, 1877.

7. *Compiled Laws of the Cherokee Nation, 1880,* chap. 3, art. 3 (secs. 31, 32).

8. *Cherokee Constitution,* art. 5, sec. 2 (amended).

9. *Cherokee Compiled Laws,* chap. 3, art. 2 (sec. 29).

10. Ibid., art. 4 (sec. 43); chap. 1, art. 4; *Constitution,* art. 5.

11. Act of November 24, 1873.

12. Act of December 3, 1874.

13. Act of December 2, 1880.

14. Act of December 12, 1883

15. *Cherokee Compiled Laws,* chap. 4, arts. 2, 3.

16. Ibid., art. 5.

17. Ibid., art. 6.

18. Ibid., art. 30.

19. Under the earlier code, a first conviction for theft carried a penalty of

thirty-nine lashes; a second conviction, one hundred lashes; and a third conviction, death by hanging.

20. *Constitution and Laws of the Cherokee Nation, 1875;* the changes embodied in the later revision of 1880 were few, but significant.

21. *Constitution of the Choctaw Nation, 1859 (promulgated 1860),* art. 4, secs. 1–20; art. 5, secs. 1–16; act of October 24, 1860.

22. Debo, *Rise and Fall of the Choctaw Republic,* 175–76.

23. Act of October 31, 1877.

24. Acts of October 23, 1858 (murder), October 26, 1858 (manslaughter).

25. Act of October 16, 1846.

26. Act of October 13, 1865.

27. Act of October 26, 1858.

28. Act of October 26, 1858.

29. Act of October, 1840.

30. Act of October, 1841.

31. Act of November 3, 1857.

32. *Constitution of the Chickasaw Nation, 1867,* art. 6, secs. 1–13, 16–17; acts of October 7, 1876. Most of the acts approved in October 1876 and hereinafter cited were restatements of the existing law.

33. Act of October 12, 1876.

34. Act of October 9, 1876.

35. Chickasaw, Auditor, Doc. 12706, "List of National and County Officers," September 22, 1891 (IAD, OHS).

36. Acts of October 12, 1876, October 17, 1876.

37. Act of October 17, 1876.

38. Act of October 7, 1876.

39. Act of October 7, 1876.

40. Act of October 7, 1876.

41. Act of October 17, 1876.

42. *Constitution of the Muskogee Nation, 1867,* art. 3, sec. 1.

43. Ibid., sec. 2.

44. Ibid., art. 2, sec. 3.

45. *Laws of the Muskogee Nation, 1867,* chap. 3, art. 3, sec. 1.

46. Debo, *Road to Disappearance,* 181.

47. *Muskogee Laws,* chap. 2, art. 3, secs. 2, 3, 4, 6, 7.

48. *Muskogee Constitution,* art. 4, secs. 2, 3, 4, 5; *Muskogee Laws,* chap. 3, art. 3, sec. 6.

49. *Muskogee Laws,* chap. 4, art. 1.

50. Act of October 12, 1867.

51. *Muskogee Laws,* chap. 4, art. 3.

52. Act of October 12, 1867; *Muskogee Laws,* chap. 4, arts. 5–7.

53. *Muskogee Laws,* chap. 4, art. 4.

54. Dawes (A.), 603.

55. *Dawes Report,* pt. 2, 161–64. Rape, like theft, was punishable by death on the fourth conviction.

56. *Report on Indians Taxed and Indians Not Taxed,* 271, 317.

57. Fort Smith *Elevator,* January 19, 1894.

58. John N. Thornton, "In the Seminole Nation," Tahlequah, Cherokee

Nation, *Indian Arrow,* August 20, 1896; the article was reprinted from the Eufaula *Indian Journal,* of which Thornton was editor. See also William M. Springer, U.S. judge, Northern District, Indian Territory, to R. F. Pettigrew, U.S. Senate, February 12, 1897, 54th Cong., 2d sess., *SD* 164, 12.

59. *Revised Statutes of the Seminole Nation, 1903* (manuscript and typescript in IAD, OHS).

60. Ibid., chaps. 9, 12.

61. Thornton; *AR,* SI, 1889, 202.

62. *Seminole Revised Laws,* chap. 6.

63. Thornton.

64. *Muskogee Laws,* chap. 4, art. 1, secs. 1–3.

65. Act of the Choctaw Nation, November 20, 1867.

66. Cherokee Laws, chap. 5; act of the Chickasaw Nation, October 12, 1876, sec. 6.

67. *Dawes Report,* pt. 2, 232.

68. *Muskogee Constitution,* art. 2, sec. 3.

69. *Cherokee Constitution,* art. 1, sec. 16.

70. Fort Smith *Elevator,* August 10, 1901; *Seminole Revised Laws,* chap. 49; William H. Wood, "Seminole Nation," in Porter, 317; Thornton.

71. *AR,* SI 1893, 82–90.

72. *Dawes Report,* pt. 2, 369.

73. *Patterson Report,* 771.

74. Ibid., 783.

75. 49th Cong., 1st sess., *HR* 1076, 222–23.

76. *Dawes Report,* pt. 2, 208.

77. Ibid., 219.

CHAPTER FIVE. **THE ADMINISTRATION OF JUSTICE BY THE FIVE NATIONS**

1. *AR,* BIC 1870, 138 (app., 37).

2. *AR,* SI 1867, 320–21; 1868, 743–44.

3. *AR,* SI 1869, 855.

4. Ibid., 840.

5. Ibid. 1870, 762; 1871, 8.

6. Ohland Morton, "Government and the Creek Indians," *Chron.,* March 1930, 42–64, June 1930, 190–226; Morton, "Reconstruction in the Creek Nation," ibid., June 1931, 171–79; John B. Meserve, "Chief Pleasant Porter," ibid., September 1931, 318–34; Meserve, "Chief Isparhecher," ibid., March 1932, 52–76; Clarence W. Turner, "Events among the Muskogees during Sixty Years," ibid., March 1932, 21–32; Meserve, "Chief Samuel Checote, with sketches of Chiefs Lochar Harjo and Ward Coachman," ibid., December 1938, 400–409; Gail Balman, "Creek Treaty of 1866," ibid., Summer 1970, 184–96; Joel D. Boyd, "Creek Indian Agents, 1934–1874," ibid., Spring 1973, 37–58.

7. *AR,* SI 1883, 39–41, 146; *Report of Board of Indian Commissioners,* ibid., 670–95; Meserve, "Chief Samuel Checote"; Turner; Debo, *Road to Disappearance,* 268–81.

8. *Patterson Report,* 100–101, 104–5, 134–38, 792–95.

9. Dispatches from Tahlequah and Vinita, in *New York Times,* November 25, December 4, 1874.

10. Ibid., January 2, 3, 1875; E. R. Roberts, chief clerk, Union Agency, to E. P. Smith, CIA, January 3, January 5, 1875, ibid.

11. Wardell, 40–54; Meserve, "Chief Dennis Wolfe Bushyhead," *Chron.,* September 1936, 349–58; Meserve, "The Mayes," ibid., March 1937, 56–64; Harold Keith, "Memories of George W. Mayes," ibid., Spring 1946, 40–54.

12. Wardell, 207–8.

13. 42d Cong., 2d sess., *SED* 70, pt. 2, 8–9.

14. *AR,* SI 1873, 574; *Patterson Report,* 396–402; William P. Ross, principal chief, to E. R. Roberts, acting agent, Union agency, January 14, 1875, Cherokee, Federal Relations.

15. *Patterson Report,* 793.

16. Quoted in Fort Smith *Elevator,* September 24, 1897.

17. In 1880 (*Dawes Report,* pt. 2, 45). By 1890, the total had risen to 2,686 (*Indians Taxed,* 255).

18. Vinita, Cherokee Nation, *Indian Chieftain,* November 7, 1895.

19. Mostly ex-slaves.

20. Act of November 1, 1875.

21. *Annual Report of the High Sheriff,* 1877.

22. Ibid., 1887.

23. Vinita *Indian Chieftain,* August 12, 1897.

24. G. A. Jenks, assistant attorney general, to M. H. Sandels, U.S. district attorney, Fort Smith, June 19, August 1, 1888, LS, DJ, *Instructions to U.S. Attorneys and Marshals,* Letter Book 1, 49, 263; *Dawes Report,* pt. 1, 168–80.

25. S. A. Cross to C. J. Harris, principal chief, January 27, 1894, Cherokee, Outlaws (IAD, OHS).

26. *Annual Reports of the High Sheriff,* 1877, 1879, 1886, 1887, 1892, 1893, 1895, 1897 (those for other years are missing); Vinita *Indian Chieftain,* July 30, 1896, in which the prison register as it stood shortly before that date is reproduced; *AR,* SI 1886, 369; Anna Dawes, 600.

27. Creek, Pardons, Docs. 34570–715 (IAD, OHS).

28. Thornton.

29. *Dawes Report,* pt. 2, 232.

30. Fort Smith *Elevator,* May 28, 1886; May 27, 1887.

31. Atoka, Choctaw Nation, *Indian Champion,* September 12, November 7, 1885; Docket Book, supreme court of the Choctaw Nation, third judicial district, 94–97.

32. Docket Books, supreme court of the Choctaw Nation, first, second, and third districts, 1866–1905 (IAD, OHS).

33. Choctaw Nation, Miscellaneous Court Records, vol. 12, 294; *Kiamitia* was a variant spelling of Kiamichi.

34. Ibid., vol. 14, 1.

35. Ibid., 9.

36. Atoka *Indian Champion,* January 31, 1885.

37. St. Louis *Globe-Democrat,* July 4, August 7, 1893.

38. Ibid., October 30, 31, 1891; February 29, 1892; March 12, 15, 1893; March 12, 1894.

39. *Dawes Report,* pt. 2, 233.

40. St. Louis *Globe-Democrat,* June 27, July 25, 1893, February 3, 1894; Fort Smith *Elevator,* July 21, 1893.

41. St. Louis *Globe-Democrat,* August 26, 1893. Locke, like the assassins (only one of whom was executed), belonged to the National (conservative) party.

42. As quoted in Chapter 1.

43. John H. Mashburn, "Reminiscences," *Chron.,* December 1927, 400–404.

44. *Report of Attorney-General of Chickasaw Nation,* Pontotoc County, April 23, 1877 (Chickasaw vol. 36, 12, IAD, OHS). The 'dead, dead, dead' formula was also pronounced in a Choctaw court when David Dyer was sentenced in December 1894; the Atoka *Indian Citizen,* January 10, 1895, quoted the judge's remarks in full.

45. Fort Smith *Elevator,* September 4, 1885.

46. St. Louis *Globe-Democrat,* December 11, 1890, December 24, 1891; Guthrie *Oklahoma State Capital* (weekly), December 12, 1890; Fort Smith *Elevator,* April 19, 1895; Oklahoma City *Daily Oklahoman,* April 10, 1895; *CR* 24, 2030.

47. St. Louis *Globe-Democrat,* January 4, 1891. There was criticism from responsible Chickasaws as well as outsiders; see Charley Brown, sheriff, and J. W. Greenwood, constable, Tishomingo County, to R. M. Harris, governor, June 19, 1897, Harris to J. W. Byrd, national jailor, June 22, 1897, Docs. 7271, 7272, Chickasaw, Jailor. Byrd was summoned before the governor to answer official charges that he had let prisoners escape.

48. Minute Book of District Court of Chickasaw Nation, 1885–1889, 14–15, 51, 167–314 (IAD, OHS).

49. *Report of Attorney-General of Chickasaw Nation,* October 31, 1868; *Records of Attorney-General, 1869–1878.*

50. Act of September 30, 1884.

51. *Dawes Report,* pt. 2, 208.

52. Creek, Light-horse, Docs. 31561, January 8, 1875; 31582, 31585, October 21, 1876, March 31, 1877; 31590, June 16, 1877; 31593, June 23, 1877; 31849, May 31, 1882; 31875, September 15, 1882, 31883, October 7, 1882; 31877, September 19, 1882.

53. St. Louis *Globe-Democrat,* April 21, 1891.

54. See Chapter 10.

55. Creek, Pardons, Docs. 34596, 34597, July 13, 1881.

56. *Indians Taxed,* 257.

57. Creek, Pardons, Doc. 34661, April 17, 1890; 34667, 34668, August 30, 1890; 34650, August 24, 1887.

58. Ibid., 34611, September 27, 1882; 34612, October 10, 1882; 34613, October 17, 1882.

59. St. Louis *Globe-Democrat,* April 21, 1891.

60. Ibid., April 19,21; Fort Smith *Elevator,* April 24, 1891.

61. Marston to Harjo, October 5, 1876, Creek, Liquor and Gambling, Doc. 32288, September 19, 1876; Creek, Foreign Relations, Doc. 30433; Charles Thompson to Coachman, May 27, 1879, ibid., Doc. 30445.

62. *Stats.L.* 19, 11.

63. Creek Docs. 30449, 30454–60, 30475–502, 30512, 30539–96, Creek, Foreign Relations: Cherokee.

64. Severs to Checote, May 23, 1880, Creek, Liquor and Gambling, Doc. 32294.

65. Act of October 19, 1880, ibid., 32296.

66. Act of October 8, 1880, ibid., 32995.

67. *AR,* SI 1867, 329.

68. Statement by John F. Brown and others, September 30, 1886, Indian Office Doc. 26544(4), copy in LR, DJ Year File 4450/86.

69. *Dawes Report,* pt. 2, 68.

70. *AR,* SI 1870, 764–65; ibid. 1871, 999.

71. Fort Smith *Elevator,* November 26, 1886.

72. *New York Times,* June 7, 1887.

73. Guthrie *News,* in Vinita *Indian Chieftain,* October 15, 1896. No particulars have been traced of the other five. The Seminole Nation was not so isolated that even one criminal could be sentenced to death, much less executed, without word of it being carried to the telegrapher or correspondent.

74. St. Louis *Globe-Democrat,* September 18, 1896; The woman was erroneously described as a Seminole in the Fort Smith *Elevator,* September 24, 1896.

75. Jumper to Checote, August 1882, Doc. 30677, Creek, Foreign Relations: Seminole.

76. *Stats.L.* 11, 689.

77. Docs. 30598–30727, Creek, Foreign Relations: Seminole.

78. Doc. 30626, July 14, 1879, ibid.

79. Doc. 30627, August 5, 1879, ibid.

80. Doc. 30628, Chupco to Coachman, October 24, 1879, ibid.

81. Docs. 30599–603, ibid.

82. Doc. 30640, ibid.

83. John F. Brown to Thomas Yahola, judge, Wewoka district, Creek Nation, July 6, 1894, February 8, 1895; Wisdom to Brown, February 20, 1895, enclosing copy of Wisdom to Shul-ku-le-sa, U.S. Indian Police, Docs. 30713–15, ibid.

84. Summary of missing Doc. 30725, December 16, 1896, ibid.

85. *Stats.L.* 11, 611.

86. See, for instance, Douglas H. Johnston, governor, Chickasaw Nation, to all sheriffs and constables, June 10, 1899, for the arrest and delivery to the Choctaw authorities of a fugitive from the Choctaw Nation, upon a writ of extradition from the Choctaw principal chief, Doc. 7231, Chickasaw, Foreign Relations.

87. An example occurs in R. M. Harris, governor, Chickasaw Nation, to Green McCurtain, principal chief, Choctaw Nation, October 6, 1896, Doc. 7225, ibid.

88. Docs. 30431, May 25, 1876; 30434, November 6, 1876; 30451, May 10, 1880; 30474, March 17, 1882; Creek Foreign Relations: Cherokee.

89. Docs. 30454–57, 30539–96, ibid.

90. See especially Docs. 30502–12, ibid.

91. Letter dated September 24, 1881, Doc. 30467, ibid.

92. Doc. 30469, ibid.

93. Allen Wright to Lewis Downing, January 22; Vann to Wright, March 7, 1868, Cherokee, Foreign Relations.

94. *Laws of the Muskogee Nation, 1880,* 85.

95. Chupco to Checote, March 30, 1880, Doc. 30638, Creek, Foreign Relations: Seminole.

96. Doc. 30489, October 8, 1884, Creek, Foreign Relations: Cherokee.

97. *AR,* SI 1886, 377–378; Doc. 30844, Creek, Foreign Relations: Miscella-

neous; "Act approving the 'Compact' &c and making an appropriation," December 4, 1886, Cherokee, Foreign Relations.

98.   J. F. McCurtain to Checote, March 15, 1883, Doc. 30737, Creek, Foreign Relations: Choctaw.

99.   Edmund McCurtain to J. M. Perryman, December 3, 1884, n.d. 1885, Docs. 30741, 30742, ibid.

100.   J. M. Perryman to William Guy, June 10, 1887, Doc. 30759, Creek, Foreign Relations: Chickasaw.

101.   Robert L. Owen to Bushyhead, June 9, 1886; William Vann to Bushyhead, September 19, 1886, Cherokee, Outlaws.

102.   Dew M. Wisdom to C. J. Harris, October 27, November 17, 1894, ibid.

103.   Docs. 32092, 32096, 32097, 32130, Creek, Light-horse.

104.   The press coverage was vast; see, for example, St. Louis *Globe-Democrat,* Vinita *Indian Chieftain,* and Fort Smith *Elevator.* At least three New York dailies— the *Times, Tribune,* and *Herald*—printed lengthy dispatches on the "Cook gang" in the autumn of 1894. See also Chapter 10.

105.   St. Louis *Globe-Democrat,* November, 18, 20, 1888; *United States vs. Alexander Lewis: Murder,* testimony of J. T. Hollomon in preliminary examination, December 31, 1890, and in trial, *Records of the United States District Court for the Western District of Arkansas,* 82–157.

106.   Eufaula *Indian Journal,* June 28, 1877; Docs. 30801–3, Creek, Foreign Relations: Miscellaneous.

107.   Gibson to National Council of the Muskogee Nation, October 11, 1893, Resolution of National Council, November 2, 1893, Doc. 32087, Creek, Light-horse.

CHAPTER SIX. **INDUSTRY, IMMIGRATION, AND TRIBAL SOVEREIGNTY, 1866–1886**

1.   Allhands, in *Chron.*

2.   *Statistical Abstract of the United States,* 1878–1900, annual figures for railroad mileage constructed and in operation; Miner; Allhands.

3.   See Chapter 1.

4.   *CR* 13, 2566–67, quoting journal of the Choctaw house of representatives, November 9, 10, 1881; 47th Cong., 1st sess., *SED* 44, 1–12; 45th Cong., 3d sess., *SMD* 73, 1–3; Meserve, "Governor Benjamin Franklin Overton and Governor Benjamin Crooks Burney," *Chron.,* June 1938, 221–29.

5.   *Stats.L.* 22, 181–85.

6.   *AR,* SI 1884, 22–23.

7.   *Stats.L.* 23, 69–72, 73–76.

8.   46th Cong., 2d sess., *SED* 124.

9.   Eufaula *Indian Journal,* August 18, 1877; *Patterson Report,* 12–13, 78–84, 240–78; Paul Nesbit, "J. J. McAlester," *Chron.,* June 1933, 757–64; Meserve, "Chief Coleman Cole," ibid., March 1936, 10–21.

10.   Eufaula *Indian Journal,* September 8, 1877.

11.   *Dawes Report,* pt. 2, 266–73. A correspondent whose interview with James McAlester appeared in the *New York Times,* May 15, 1887, reported that five gallons of rum had been seized a few days earlier.

12. See Chapter 9.

13. 45th Cong., 3d sess., *SMD* 52.

14. *CR* 17, app., 188–89; Edward Everett Dale, "Ranching on the Cheyenne-Arapaho Reservation, 1880–1885," *Chron.*, March 1928, 35–59; "The Cheyenne-Arapaho Country," ibid., December 1942, 360–71; *AR,* SI 1884, 124; 1885, 311, 316, 326; 1886, 337.

15. Eufaula *Indian Journal,* April 5, 1877.

16. Ibid.

17. Roy Gittinger, *Formation of the State of Oklahoma,* 96.

18. *CR* 15, 19.

19. *AR,* SI 1886, 12–13.

20. *CR* 17, app. 195–97.

21. *CR* 17, 4067–68.

22. Ibid., app. 178–79.

23. *AR,* SI 1885, 316.

24. Berlin B. Chapman, "How the Cherokees Acquired and Disposed of the Outlet," *Chron.*, March 1937, 30–50; June 1937, 205–25; September 1937, 291–321; March 1938, 36–51; June 1938, 135–62; William W. Savage, Jr., *Cherokee Strip Live Stock Association: Federal Regulation and the Cattleman's Last Frontier.*

25. *CR* 19, 6750.

26. *CR* 27, 993, 996–99; Norman A. Graebner, "History of Cattle Ranching in Eastern Oklahoma," *Chron.*, September 1943, 300–311; Graebner, "Public Land Policy of the Five Civilized Tribes," ibid., Summer 1945, 107–18; Creek, Cattle, Docs. 34902, 34906, 34952, 35030 (IAD, OHS).

27. Graebner, "History of Cattle Ranching," 303; see also *AR,* BIC 1870, 138, which adds that the value of *all* stock stolen by both armies during the war was estimated as $15 million.

28. 49th Cong., 1st sess., *HR* 1076, 240–42, cited hereinafter as *Holman Report.*

29. *Patterson Report,* 758–60.

30. *AR,* SI 1886, 82–86.

31. Law of October 17, 1876; Eufaula *Indian Journal,* March 23, 1877; Meserve, "Governor Benjamin Franklin Overton."

32. Meserve, "Chief Coleman Cole."

33. Eufaula *Indian Journal* December 7, 1876.

34. Ibid., April 5, 1877.

35. *Patterson Report,* 425–27; *AR,* SI 1876, 467.

36. Eufaula *Indian Journal,* April 19, 1877.

37. Ibid., September 15, 1877.

38. Ibid., September 29, 1877.

39. *Patterson Report,* 428.

40. Parthena Louise James, "White Threat in the Chickasaw Nation," *Chron.*, Spring 1968, 73–85. In 1880 the annual permit tax was reduced from $25 to $5.

41. *Patterson Report,* app., 268–71, including reproduction of Cherokee Nation "Penal Law" of December 12, 1878.

42. *CR* 16, 894.

43. James D. Morrison, "Problems in the Industrial Progress and Development of the Choctaw Nation," *Chron.*, Spring 1954, 70–91.

44. *Patterson Report,* vol. 3, 111–14.

45. An exception was the Cherokee census of 1880, a summary of which appears in *Dawes Report,* pt. 2, 45–50; this showed a population of 5,352 noncitizens in a total of 25,438.

46. 46th Cong., 2d sess., *HR* 755, 2; *AR,* SI 1880, 217–18; 1883, 145; 1885, 329.

47. *AR,* SI 1880, 217.

48. Ibid., 1885, 334.

CHAPTER SEVEN. **CONGRESSIONAL INTERVENTION AND
JUDICIAL CONFLICT, 1878–1886**

1. *Stats.L.* 20, 65; *CR* 7, 3313, 3521, 3659, 3692.

2. Jenness, 445

3. *AR,* SI 1878, 471, 551; 1879, 165, 173.

4. Ibid., 1880, 10, 88, 191, 197.

5. *Stats.L.* 20, 296.

6. *AR,* SI 1881, 14–15.

7. Ibid., 1882, 148.

8. Tufts to Hiram Price, CIA, January 9, 1882; Cherokee delegates to Price, January 13, 19, February 4, March 16, April 7, 1882 (Cherokee, Indian Police, Federal Relations); Bushyhead to Checote, March 17, 1882, Rabbit Bunch to Checote, August 7, 1882 (Creek, Foreign Relations: Cherokee; IAD, OHS).

9. See Chapter 5; Debo, *Road to Disappearance,* 231.

10. *AR,* SI 1883, 7–10; correspondence in 48th Cong., 1st sess., *SED* 108, 1–15.

11. *Stats.L.* 26, 96.

12. *AR,* SI 1884, 12–13.

13. Ibid., 1885, 23–24.

14. *CR* 16, 934–35.

15. Ibid., 936.

16. Ibid., 1749, 2385–88, 2518–19, 2533, 2568–69; *Stats.L.* 23, 385.

17. *Stats.L.* 23, 284.

18. *AR,* SI 1886, 376–78.

19. *Dawes Report,* pt. 1, i.

20. *Holman Report,* i.

21. *Dawes Report,* pt. 2, 5–425.

22. Ibid., pt. 1, ii.

23. Ibid., xx–xxi.

24. Ibid., xxiii–xxiv.

25. *Holman Report,* i–ix, 211–44.

26. Ibid., xxxix–xl.

27. Ibid., lviii–lxii.

28. *CR* 17, 375, 384, 2752, 3514, 4063–71, 5214–20, app., 174–201; 18, 269, 334–47.

29. 49th Cong., 1st sess., *HR* 1684, 11–26.

30. *Dawes Report,* pt. 2, app., 1–6.

31. *CR* 19, 1558. For a concise and generally very good review of tribal opposition to the Territorialization movement during the period 1879–1889, see Mary Jane Ward, "Fight for Survival: The Indian Response to the Boomer Movement," *Chron.,* Spring 1989, 30–51.

32. *AR,* SI 1886, 378; *Stats.L.* 16, 437 (*RS* 5522); *Laws of the Muskogee Nation, 1867,* arts. 2, 11.

33. *AR,* SI 1887, 52–54, 200; J. M. Perryman to D. W. Bushyhead, January 31, 1887 (requisition and enclosures); I. C. Parker to Bushyhead, May 3, 1887; W. H. H. Clayton, of Clayton and Brizzolara, Attorneys at Law, to Bushyhead, May 18, 1887; Perryman to Bushyhead, May 18, 1887; J. C. Cunningham, Eureka Springs, Arkansas, to Bushyhead, May 19, 1887—all in Cherokee, Foreign Relations, Creek, Foreign Relations: Cherokee, Docs. 30513–38; Fort Smith *Elevator,* January 7, September 23, 1887; Atoka, Choctaw Nation, *Independent,* January 8, 1887; Cherokee, Federal Relations, Owen to Bushyhead, June 18, 1887; *United States vs. Richard Vann: Murder,* Capias, December 25, 1887. Vann, one of the murderers, was a resident of Canadian district, and jurisdiction in his case was eventually claimed by the federal court at Fort Smith, under the special provisions for Canadian district in the treaty of 1866 (see Chapter 1). Alfred Cunningham, the other murderer, was a native of Tahlequah district, one-thirty-second part Cherokee, who, after a hearing at Fort Smith, was turned over to the Indian authorities, with the results stated.

34. *CR* 18, 216, 375–78, 1270, 1398–99, 2470, 2754–55; *Stats.L.* 24, 449.

35. Documents and correspondence in LR, DJ year file 4450/86; Garland to Parker, July 20, 1886, LS, DJ, *Instructions to Judges and Clerks,* Letter Book 3, 153–54; Fort Smith *Elevator,* June 4, 1886; Atoka *Independent,* June 5, 1886; *AR,* AG 1888, 241.

36. The views expressed were not those of the Union agent, Robert Owen.

37. *CR* 18, 376–77; the quotation is from "Locksley Hall, Sixty Years After" (published 1886), ll. 103, 127.

CHAPTER EIGHT. **A DOUBLE THRUST AT TRIBAL SOVEREIGNTY**

1. *Stats.L.* 24, 388.

2. Ibid, 25, 783–87.

3. Ibid., 757–59, 1004–6.

4. Ibid., 26, 81–100.

5. *CR* 19, 206, 693, 2989.

6. Ibid., 206, 364, 424, 445, 566, 648, 834, 966, 1343.

7. *Stats.L.* 25, 33.

8. Galveston, Texas, *News,* in Austin, Texas, *Daily Statesman,* December 27, 1887; St. Louis *Globe-Democrat,* December 26, 27, 1887.

9. *CR* 19, 2347, 2352, 2989, 4314, 4466–67, 4500, 4514, 4911; *Stats.L.* 25, 167.

10. *CR* 19, 483, 1980, 2346, 2989, 4314, 4467, 4468, 4816; *Stats.L.* 25, 178.

11. *CR* 19, 232.

12. Ibid., 2353, 2989.

13. Report of Cherokee Delegation to National Council, November 18, 1888, 1–2, Cherokee, Federal Relations (IAD, OHS).

14. Ibid., 5.

15. 50th Cong., 1st sess., *HR* 263, 1–15 (both reports).

16. *CR* 20, 1402, 1501–6.

17. Cherokee Nation senate bill 37, February 9, 1888, Cherokee, Federal Relations.

18. *CR* 20, 1711.

19. Ibid., 1644–45.

20. Ibid., 1709.

21. Ibid., 1711.

22. Ibid., 1711–12. Paris had not yet become a "place of revolving jurisdiction" (in the senator's phrase). Graham still was one.

23. Ibid., 1714–15.

24. Illustrative map in Henry King, "The Indian Country," *Century Illustrated Monthly Magazine,* August 1885, 604. See also George H. Shirk, "Seymour," *Chron.,* Spring 1977, 93–99.

25. *a Compilation of the Messages and Proclamations of the Presidents,* vol. 8, 807–10; *CR* 20, 2046; *AR,* SI 1889, 209; *Stats.L.* 25, 757–59.

26. *AR,* SI 1889, 209.

27. *CR* 20, 2046.

28. Letter as dated, Cherokee, Federal Relations.

29. Clements and Peabody to Joel B. Mayes, October 20, 1891, Cherokee, Federal Relations.

30. *CR* 20, 2317–18, 2385–87, 2398–99, 2458–59, 2671.

31. On May 3, 1892, the Quapaw Agency was placed in the newly created third division of the judicial District of Kansas, with Fort Scott as court town; *CR* 23, 1871, 3211, 3283, 3371, 3467, 4191; *Stats.L.* 27, 24–25.

32. *Stats.L.* 25, 783–85; *Indians Taxed,* 259.

33. Atoka *Indian Citizen,* April 19, 1890.

34. *Stats.L.* 25, 757–59.

35. *CR* 20, 2367–68, 2399–2400, 2592, 2608–09; *Stats.L.* 25, 1004–6.

36. *Messages and Proclamations of the President* 9, 15–18; *AR,* SI 1889, 79.

37. Guthrie *Oklahoma Capital,* April 27, May 4, 11, 1889; St. Louis *Globe-Democrat,* April 22–27, 1889; Arthur W. Dunham (or Durham), "A Pioneer Railroad Agent," *Chron.,* March 1924, 48–62, repr. "Oklahoma City Before the Run of 1889," ibid., Spring 1958, 72–78; Dan W. Peery, "First Two Years," ibid., September 1929, 278–322, December 1929, 419–457, March 1930, 94–120; Frank J. Best, "Recollections of April 22, 1889," ibid., March 1943, 28–32; Rube Carl White, "Experiences in the Opening of Oklahoma," ibid., Spring 1949, 56–59; Berlin B. Chapman, "Legal Sooners of 1889 in Oklahoma," ibid., Winter 1957–58, 382–415; "Oklahoma City, from Public Land to Private Property," ibid., Summer 1959, 219–29, Autumn 1959, 330–52, Winter 1959–60, 442–78; Brad Agnew, "Voices from the Land Run of 1889," ibid., Spring 1989, 4–29; Donald E. Green, "Oklahoma Land Run of 1889: A Centennial Re-interpretation," ibid., Summer 1989, 116–49; Hamilton S. Wicks, "Opening of Oklahoma," *Cosmopolitan,* September 1889, 460–470 (repr. but without photographs, *Chron.,* June 1926). Green errs in stating that the lands were opened under "the Springer Amendment to the Indian Appropriation Act (H.R. 1874)." The Indian Appropriation Act of March 2, 1889, was H.R. 12578, and the amendment was Peel's, not Springer's. H.R. 1874 was designated "a bill to change the eastern and northern judicial districts of Texas, and for other purposes" but was more commonly called the Muskogee (court) bill.

For an essential element in the homesteading process often neglected by historians, see Gordon Moore, "Registers, Receivers, and Entrymen: U.S. Land Office Administration in Oklahoma Territory, 1889–1907," *Chron.,* Spring 1989, 52–75.

38. Wicks.

39. Peery, September 1929, 295.

40. Berlin B. Chapman, "Guthrie: From Public Land to Private Property," *Chron.,* Spring 1955, 63–86.

41. Guthrie *Oklahoma Capital,* July 27, August 3, 1889.

42. According to the Guthrie *Oklahoma Capital* of June 1, 1889, there were 15,000 at Guthrie directly after the opening and 20,000 by the date of the article; probably both figures were overstated.

43. W. C. Jones to My Dear Etta, April 29, 1889, *Chron.,* Summer 1957, 233–34. For a contemporaneous view of Oklahoma City and Kingfisher, also from the pen of a Government official writing privately, see "Captain Charles W. Whipple's Notebook: The Week of the Run into Oklahoma in 1889," presented by Muriel H. Wright, *Chron.,* Summer 1970, 146–53.

44. Guthrie *Oklahoma Capital,* November 2, 1889.

45. Richard Harding Davis, "The West from a Car Window," 109–10; Peery, September 1929, 296–299, 309–17; Wicks; Guthrie *Oklahoma Capital,* May 11, November 30, 1889.

46. Guthrie *Oklahoma Capital,* July 6, September 21, 1889.

47. An immense quantity of newspaper space was lavished on Mattox. For the beginnings of his criminal career, see the Oklahoma City *Oklahoma Chief,* in Guthrie *Oklahoma Capital,* June 15, 1889; for its apparent close, see *AR,* AG 1898, 196. The quotation is from the Guthrie *News,* in Gainesville, Texas, *Hesperian,* January 21, 1894.

48. For an excellent, but not definitive, account of this phase, see Glenn Shirley, *West of Hell's Fringe.*

49. *CR* 20, 1644.

50. *SEJ* 20, 32, 42.

51. *AR,* AG 1889, 4–5, 14–15; Muskogee *Our Brother in Red,* in Atoka *Indian Citizen,* June 8, July 6, 1889.

52. Muskogee *Phoenix,* ibid., September 21, 1889; the jail is so described ibid., June 15, 1889, from *Our Brother in Red.*

53. *AR,* AG 1889, 2–15; 1890, 1–16.

54. St. Louis *Globe-Democrat,* September 2, 1890.

55. Guthrie *Oklahoma State Capital,* September 21, 28, October 12, 1889.

56. *Stats. L.* 25, 1004.

57. Chapman, "How the Cherokees Acquired and Disposed of the Outlet," *Chron.,* September 1937, 298–314.

58. *CR* 21, 123, 688, 1066–67.

59. Ibid., 1066.

60. Ibid., 1083.

61. Ibid., 1272.

62. St. Louis *Globe-Democrat,* July 27–30, 1888.

63. Garland to Charles B. Pearre, October 15, 1888, LS, DJ, *Instructions to Attorneys and Marshals,* Letter Book 1, 569.

64. St. Louis *Globe-Democrat,* December 12, 1890; March 3, 6, 1891. Both the press coverage and the official record of the case attained vast proportions; the incoming correspondence in LR, DJ 1820/87, alone, extends to some 1,175 pages.

65. Elmer E. Brown, "No Man's Land," *Chron.,* June 1926, 89.

66. *CR* 21, 1273.

67. Ibid., 1274.

68. Ibid., 1276.

69. *Messages and Proclamations* 9, 97.

70. Secs. 33, 31, respectively, of the act as passed and approved, Stats.L. 26, 94–96.

71. *CR* 21, 1452.

72. Ibid., 1464.

73. Ibid., 1464–65.

74. John B. Meserve, "Governor William Leander Byrd," *Chron.,* December 1934, 432–43; "Governor William Malcolm Guy," ibid., March 1941, 10–13.

75. *CR* 21, 1502–5.

76. Ibid., 1503.

77. Ibid., 1505.

78. Ibid., 1508.

79. Ibid., 1517–18.

80. Ibid., 1510, 1519.

81. Ibid., 2220.

82. Ibid., 2336.

83. Ibid., 2409.

84. The missing letter of March 25, 1890, is quoted in Clements and Peabody to Joel B. Mayes, October 20, 1891, Cherokee, Federal Relations.

85. Mayes to Peabody and Clements, March 28, 1890, ibid.

86. Clements and Peabody to Mayes, October 20, 1891, ibid.

87. *CR* 21, 3553–58.

88. Ibid., 3716; the allusion is to a speech by the central character in Shakespeare's *Othello, The Moor of Venice,* 1.3.129–59.

89. Ibid., 3861.

90. Isaac Struble, ibid., 3627.

91. Ibid., 3719.

92. *Messages and Proclamations* 9, 156–60.

93. Ibid., 275–78.

94. Cherokee, Federal Relations; Chapman, "How the Cherokees Acquired"; Dale, "Cherokee Strip Live Stock Association"; Savage.

95. *Messages and Proclamations* 9, 406–24.

96. Joe B. Milam, "Opening up of the Cherokee Outlet," *Chron.,* September 1931, 268–77, December 1931, 454–71, March 1932, 114–36.

97. *Stats.L.* 28, 20–21.

98. A. G. C. Bierer, "Early Day Courts and Lawyers," *Chron.,* March 1930, 3.

CHAPTER NINE. **PROBLEMS OF GOVERNMENT AND JURISDICTION, 1886–1893**

1. *AR,* SI 1886, 374.

2. Ibid., 1887, 197.

3. *AR,* AG 1883, 46–47, 110–15; 1884, 48–49, 108–11; 1885, 50–53, 76–81; 1886, 24–27, 46–50.

4. Fort Smith *Elevator,* March 1, 1887.

5. *AR,* AG 1887, 4–7.

6. Ibid., 1888, 5–7, 34–35; 1889, 32–33; 1890, 28–29.

7. Ibid., 1883–1888. The nature of forfeiture proceedings in the Fort Smith federal court is well enough conveyed by the titles of the suits. Here are three from 1887–1888: *United States vs. One wagon, two ponies, eleven dozen brooms, etc.; United States vs. Six horses, one wagon, one set of harness, three guns, two pistols, and four saddles; United States vs. Two black mules, one wagon, two sets of harness, and three gallons of brandy.* The goods at issue were seizures from peddlers of one sort or another.

8. Ibid., 1889, 4–5; 1890, 4–5.

9. Ibid., 1889, 2–5, 8–15; 1890, 1–5, 8–15.

10. Ibid., 1890, 1–5, 8–15; 1891, 18–21.

11. See Chapter 5.

12. For contemporary comment on Seminole affairs, see *CR* 28, 2070, 54th Cong., 1st sess., *SD* 182, 41–42. An attempt to verify a report that certain records of the general or national council of the Seminole Nation had come to light was fruitless. As matters stand, the Seminole material held by IAD, OHS comprises the *Revised Laws* of 1903, an allotment ledger, some unsupported disbursement warrants, and letters from Seminole officials in files maintained by other tribes. There is also correspondence and other documents preserved by the U.S. Government, such as the files of the Indian agencies.

13. 50th Cong., 1st sess., *SMD* 53.

14. *AR,* SI 1888, lxi–lxiii; Fort Smith *Elevator,* September 14, 1888; St. Louis *Globe-Democrat,* September 1888.

15. Creek, Pastures and Cattle, Docs. 34902, 34906, 34952, 35030.

16. *AR,* SI 1895, 158–59, where the date of the act of the national council is given erroneously as May 2, 1892.

17. *Stats.L.* 11, 699.

18. *CR* 27, 998.

19. Petition to national council of Cherokee Nation, *CR* 27, 1991.

20. The Fritz Sittel case is in 52d Cong., 2d sess., *HR* 2384, 1–11.

21. *Indians Taxed,* 245–57.

22. *AR,* SI 1892, 247.

23. Ibid., 1893, 150

24. *Indians Taxed,* 259.

25. Ibid., 273–74;

26. *AR,* SI 1887, 56–57.

27. 55th Cong., 2d sess., *SD* 84, 1–15: James, "Reconstruction in the Chickasaw Nation."

28. *Indians Taxed,* 256.

29. *AR,* SI 1887, 195–96; Bixby, comp., *Laws, Decisions, and Regulations Affecting the Work of the Commissioner to the Five Civilized Tribes, 1893 to 1906,* 140.

30. *AR,* SI 1887, 196; 1892, 253; Fort Smith *Elevator,* January 27, 1899.

31. Meserve, "Governor William Leander Byrd," 439–40; "Governor William Malcolm Guy," 11.

32. *AR,* SI 1890, 103.

33. Ibid., 90.

34. Except for the ex-slaves and a few whites taken fully into the Muskogee and Seminole tribes by specific legislative enactment.

35. Fort Smith *Elevator,* November 7, 1890.

36. 52d Cong., 2d sess., *HR* 2384, 1–9; *CR* 24, 2029–30.

37. *AR,* SI 1892, 262.

38. *AR,* SI 1892, 260–63; 1893, 82–90; Atoka *Indian Citizen,* August 11, 18, September 8, 15, 22, 29, October 13, December 22, 1892; July, 6, 13, 20, 27, 1893; November 8, 1894; Vinita *Indian Chieftain,* September 15, 1892; St. Louis *Globe-Democrat,* September 13–30, 1892; November 6, 1894; Fayetteville, Arkansas, *Democrat,* September 7, 1893; Gainesville, Texas, *Hesperian,* November 7, 13, 1894; J. F. Holden, "B.I.T.: The Story of an Adventure in Railroad Building," *Chron.* March 1933, 652–53; John B. Meserve, "Chief Wilson Nathaniel Jones," ibid., December 1936, 426–28.

39. Garland to Sandels, June 29, 1887, LS, DJ, *Instructions to Marshals and Attorneys,* Letter Book X, 149.

40. *AR,* SI 1894, 143.

41. Atoka *Indian Citizen,* July 6, 1889.

42. Ibid., July 13, 1889.

43. Fort Smith *Elevator,* July 25, 1890.

44. St. Louis *Globe-Democrat,* December 24, 1889, January 4, 1890; Atoka *Indian Citizen,* June 14, 21, 1890; *AR,* SI 1890, 98–99.

45. Atoka *Indian Citizen,* July 18, August 1, 15, 22, 29, September 5, October 17, 1891; St. Louis *Globe-Democrat,* July 25, 1891; Fort Smith *Elevator,* August 7, 28, 1891; *AR,* SI 1891, 248–49.

46. See also Atoka *Indian Citizen,* September 12, 19, 1891; St. Louis *Globe-Democrat,* August 25, 28, 1891; Fort Smith *Elevator,* September 18, 1891; *AR,* SI 1892, 259.

47. *AG,* SI 1892, 260; Fort Smith *Elevator,* October 2, 1891.

48. St. Louis *Globe-Democrat,* December 20, 1891; January 25, 1892; Atoka *Indian Citizen,* January 28, 1892.

49. St. Louis *Globe-Democrat,* March 11, 1892; Fort Smith *Elevator,* June 17, 1892; Atoka *Indian Citizen,* May 12, 19, June 2, 1892.

50. *AR,* SI 1892, 259–60; *Stats.L.* 27, 260–61; Atoka *Indian Citizen,* July 28, August 4, 11, 1892.

51. *CR* 24, 269.

52. St. Louis *Globe-Democrat,* March 10, 1893.

53. Ibid., January 28, February 2, 6, April 7, 1892, July 1, 1893; Fort Smith *Elevator,* February 12, 1892, July 7, 1893.

54. *AR,* SI 1892, 248–49.

55. S. F. Phillips, Solicitor-General and Acting Attorney-General, to A. Parsons, Choctaw agent, August 27, 1873; George H. Williams to William Story, October 8, December 19, 1873, LS, DJ, *General and Misc.,* Letter Book K, 80–81, 143–44, 227; *Sener Report,* 144, 235–36.

56. Charles Devens to Parker, April 23, June 24, July 18, 1879, LS, DJ, *Instructions to Judges and Clerks,* Letter Book 1, 426, 442, 449.

57. 50th Cong., 1st sess., *SMD* 153, 14–15.

58. *AR*, SI 1886, 375; 1888, 136.

59. Wilson to Miller, June 9, 1890; Parker to Miller, June 13, 1890; Clayton to Miller, June 14, 1890; 51st Cong., 1st sess., *SED* 164, 2–5.

60. Ibid., 1–2.

61. *AR*, AG 1890, xix–xx.

62. Jackson to Olney, September 29, December 15, 1893, 53d Cong., 2d sess. *HED* 67, 2–4.

63. *AR*, AG 1893, xix–xxiii.

64. *CR* 24, 27–28

65. Ibid., 83.

66. Vinita *Indian Chieftain,* August 1, 1895.

67. *CR* 24, 100.

68. Ibid., 101–2.

69. Perkins had failed to secure reelection to the House for 1889, but at the beginning of 1892 was appointed to the Senate to fill the vacancy created by the death of Preston Plumb. His utterances in the Senate on the question of the Indian Territory were rather milder in tone than his speeches from the popularly elected body.

70. *CR* 24, 268–70.

71. Ibid., 2316, 2381–87; *Stats.L.* 27, 640–46.

72. *SEJ* 29, 232–34; Loren N. Brown, "Dawes Commission," *Chron.,* March 1931, 76.

73. *AR,* AG 1890, 1–7, 14–15, 32–33; 1891, 16–19, 28–29, 40–51; 1892, 20–25, 32–33, 46–51; 1893, 16–20, 28–29, 45–49.

74. Ibid., 1894, 52–55; 1895, 90–91.

75. Ibid.; on October 31, 1891, the federal grand jury at Paris returned 170 or 171 true bills of indictment, not more than 3 or 4 of which could have originated in the four Texas counties included in the Paris division of the Eastern District of Texas.

76. *Stats.L.* 24, 635–41.

77. St. Louis *Globe-Democrat,* February, 1, 3, 1889.

78. Ibid., May 18, October 6, 1890.

79. Ibid., January 25, 1889.

80. Ibid., February 3, April 30, 1889; January 17, 1890.

81. *AR,* AG 1889, 259; 1894, 159.

82. Fort Smith *Elevator,* May 5, 1893, Fayetteville *Democrat,* July 11, 1895.

83. See, for example, *Ed Alberty, alias Charles Burns, vs. United States,* Supreme Court of the United States, No. 853, October term, 1895; testimony, charge, and other trial papers in *U.S. vs. Frank Carver, U.S. vs. Alexander Allen, U.S. vs. Robert H. Hall, U.S. vs. Robert Marshall Hall, U.S. vs. Eli Lucas,* Records of the Western Judicial District of Arkansas, U.S. National Archives, Fort Worth Division; see also, Harman, 466–95, 521–82.

84. Reports of Clerk of Pardons/Pardon Attorney, *AR,* AG 1885–1906.

85. Fred Harvey Harrington, in *Hanging Judge,* and others.

86. See note 83.

87. *CR* 19, 5611, 7551, 7636–37, 8263, 9098.

88. *CR* 20, 566–67, 993–94; *Stats.L,* 25, 655–56. Later, on March 3, 1891, Congress created a Court of Appeal for each of the federal circuits. One effect of this reform was that an appeal in *any* Fort Smith case could be decided by the

Supreme Court; certain grades of appeal (e.g., on a writ of error in capital cases, as first set out in the February 1889 act) went there automatically. *Stats.L.* 26, 826–30; *AR,* AG 1891, v–vi.

89. 54th Cong., 1st sess., *HR* 108, 5–8.

90. Fort Smith *Elevator* April 16, 1886, November 20, 1891.

91. Atoka *Indian Citizen,* June 20, 1890.

92. 141 U.S. 106, 107.

93. Writ of Habeas Corpus, I. C. Parker to Jesse Mays [*sic*], High Sheriff, Cherokee Nation, August 14, 1888, Cherokee, Prison and High Sheriff, IAD, OHS; Fort Smith *Elevator,* June 15, August 17, 1888; January 11, 1889.

For another such case, see Atoka *Indian Citizen,* June 21, 1890.

94. Vinita *Indian Chieftain,* November 11, 1892; April 6, 1893; June 25, August 6, 1896; St. Louis *Globe-Democrat,* November 20, 1892; January 1, March 18, 1893; Fort Smith *Elevator,* March 24, 1893; 54th Cong., 2d sess., *SD* 164, 6–7.

95. Vinita *Indian Chieftain,* March 9, 30, November 2, 9, 1893; January 2, 1896; St. Louis *Globe-Democrat,* October 20, 1893; Fort Smith *Elevator,* September 29, November 10, 1893; December 20, 1895; 54th Cong., 2d sess., *SD* 164, 7; Annual Report of the High Sheriff, 1894, Cherokee, Prison and High Sheriff). In the event, both men died in prison of natural causes before the dates set for their execution.

CHAPTER TEN. **JUDICIAL REFORM AND THE END OF TRIBAL SELF-GOVERNMENT, 1894–1899**

1. Kidd to Turpie, February 24, March 3, 1894, 53d Cong., 2d sess., *SMD* 114; for other remarks by Kidd, see Fort Smith *News Record,* June 5, 1894, Vinita *Indian Chieftain,* September 20, 1894.

2. 53d Cong., 2d sess., *SR* 377 (*Teller Report*), 6–7.

3. 53d Cong., 2d sess., *SMD* 166, 2.

4. *CR* 26, 7997.

5. St. Louis *Globe-Democrat,* August 7, 1894.

6. Report of Cherokee delegation to Principal Chief Samuel H. Mayes, December 1895, Cherokee, Federal Relations, IAD, OHS.

7. W. A. Duncan, printed address, 1894, ibid.

8. Gainesville *Hesperian,* October 26, 1894.

9. Ibid., November 18, 1894.

10. See Chapter 5, note 104.

11. Wisdom to C. J. Harris, November 17, 1894, Cherokee, Outlaws, IAD, OHS; the Roman of the allusion was Marcus Porcius Cato the elder (234–149 B.C.), but the Latin as given by Wisdom is an elementary misquotation or mistranslation.

12. Ardmore, Chickasaw Nation, *Daily Ardmoreite,* in Gainesville *Hesperian,* November 21, 1894.

13. 54th Cong., 3d sess., *SMD* 24, 1–43.

14. Ibid., 9–10.

15. For instance, *Post-Dispatch* (independent, nominally Republican) in Fayetteville *Democrat,* November 7, 14, 1895; *Republic* (Democratic), ibid., January 30, 1896; *Globe-Democrat* (Republican), April 12, 1889, and frequently thereafter.

16. For the origin of this statement, see *CR* 27, 999; for Parker's rejoinder, see Parker to W. A. Duncan, December 21, 1894, *CR* 28, 4307.

17. John B. Meserve, "Perrymans," *Chron.*, July 1937, 167–81.

18. *CR* 27, 197–98; these individuals are named, and their holdings detailed, in many other places.

19. Thornton, "Among the Seminoles."

20. 53d Cong., 3d sess., *SMD* 24, 11. For a scandal in the Choctaw and Chickasaw Nations, derived from the Choctaw and Chickasaw Railroad project, and involving the two legislatures, Mike Conlan, Newton Childs, Eliphalet Wright, and others, see 54th Cong., 1st sess., *SD* 182, 32–39.

21. St. Louis *Globe-Democrat,* January 4, 1895.

22. Ibid.; 54th Cong. 1st sess., *SD* 182, 8, 27–28.

23. St. Louis *Globe-Democrat,* January 12, 1895.

24. *CR* 27, 951–52; the writer of the letter was Rezin W. McAdam, an Ardmore lawyer.

25. Ibid., 961.

26. Ibid., 996–1004.

27. Ibid., 2554.

28. Harris and Cherokee delegation to Grover Cleveland, February 2, 1895, Cherokee, Federal Relations.

29. Harris and J. F. Thompson to Vilas, February 5, 1895, ibid.

30. Tribal delegates and representatives to Wilkinson Call, Francis M. Cockerill (*sic*), and Henry M. Teller, February 15, 1895, ibid.

31. Gainesville *Hesperian,* February 8, 1895.

32. *CR* 23, 241, 1429, 4480.

33. *CR* 27, 1931.

34. Gainesville *Hesperian,* February 8, 1895.

35. Report of Cherokee delegation, December 1895; see note 6.

36. Gainesville *Hesperian,* February 13, 1895.

37. *CR* 27, 2088.

38. Ibid., 2556–62.

39. Report of the Cherokee delegation, December 1895.

40. Ibid.

41. Gainesville *Hesperian,* February 27, 1895; *CR* 27, 2842–43, 2871–72, 2961.

42. *Stats.L.* 28, 693–98; Sandels and Hill, 543–44.

43. *SEJ* 30, 4, 5, 7, 36, 48: Fayetteville *Democrat,* September 19, 1895; Gainesville *Hesperian,* October 5, 29, 1895.

44. Parker to Department of Justice, January 21, 1896, 54th Cong., 1st sess., *HR* 1063, 4–8.

45. Bryant to Holmes Colbert, March 9, 1896, *CR* 28, 4307.

46. 54th Cong., 1st sess., *HR* 1063, 2–3.

47. *CR* 28, 754, 3463, 5964–68; St. Louis *Globe-Democrat,* March 14, 1896; Atoka *Indian Citizen,* June 4, 1896.

48. 54th Cong., 1st sess., *SD* 173, 1–7.

49. Ibid., *SD* 12.

50. Ibid., *SD* 182, 25. Matters had only lately reached this pass; in the past, Parker had taken many leaves of absence.

51. Taliaferro to N. M. Curtis, December 23, 1895, 54th Cong., 1st sess., HR 108, 1.

52. 54th Cong., 1 sess., *SD* 12, 17.

53.   *AR,* AG 1894, 26–29, 38–40; 1895, 58–60, 70–71; 1896, 28–33, 40–41; *CR* 28, 2461–62, 5964. The 3586 civil cases dealt with by the Indian Territory courts included 3,473 in which the United States was not a party. Private suits have been excluded from the summaries for the Western Arkansas and East Texas courts. It is not known exactly how many U.S. prosecutions in these two courts related to the Arkansas or Texas side of their function, but about one-tenth of Parker's cases and about one-fifth of Bryant's may reasonably be apportioned to prosecutions originating inside their States.

54.   St. Louis *Globe-Democrat,* August 28, September 1, December 9, 1894; Gainesville *Hesperian,* October 26, 1894.

55.   Tahlequah *Telephone,* August 9, 1894.

56.   St. Louis *Globe-Democrat,* December 28, 1895; January 2, 3, 11, 1896; Fort Smith *Elevator,* January 10, 31, 1896.

57.   54th Cong., 1st sess., *SD* 12, 16.

58.   Vinita *Indian Chieftain,* February 13, 1896; this editorial was read to the House of Representatives on February 20, *CR* 28, 1990.

59.   Washington *Post,* February 24, 1896 (headline).

60.   Act of Chickasaw Nation, October 1, 1895; 54th Cong., 1st sess., *SD* 12, 14–15.

61.   *CR* 28, 1988–93.

62.   Ibid., 4263–71, 4298–4312, 5828–35, 5886–96, 5929–33, 6085–86, 6183, 6227–39, 6242–43, 6247–48, 6299, 6327, 6357, 6362, 6365.

63.   Ibid., 5831.

64.   *Stats.L.* 29, 339–40.

65.   Fort Smith *Elevator,* February 16, August 24, 31, 1894; February 8, 1895; Vinita *Indian Chieftain,* October 18, December 13, 1896; Tahlequah *Telephone,* August 14, 1894; St. Louis *Globe-Democrat,* January 12, 1895; Gainesville *Hesperian,* February 6, 1895; Fayetteville *Democrat* July 25, 1895.

66.   St. Louis *Globe-Democrat,* July 27, 30, 1895.

67.   Ibid., February 5, 1896; St. Louis *Republic,* February 18, 1896; Fayetteville *Democrat,* March 5, 1896. The two earlier articles were reprinted in the Vinita *Indian Chieftain,* February 6, 20, 1896.

68.   Harmon to Parker, March 25, 1896, LS, DJ, *Instructions to Judges and Clerks,* Letter Book 9, 343–47.

69.   Parker to Harmon, April 2, 1896, LR, DJ, Year File 600/96.

70.   Harmon to Parker, May 1, 1896, LS, DJ, *Instructions,* Letter Book 9, 531–37; Conrad to Parker, July 16, 1896, Dickinson to Parker, August 27, September 3, 1896, ibid., Letter Book 10, 136, 255–59, 280–82.

71.   St. Louis *Globe-Democrat,* February 29, 1896; St. Louis *Republic,* in Vinita *Indian Chieftain,* February 27, 1896.

72.   Vinita *Indian Chieftain,* May 21, 1896.

73.   Ibid., July 23, 1896, and other issues.

74.   Address of J. J. McAlester, July 27, 1896, copy in Creek, Foreign Relations, IAD, OHS.

75.   Vinita *Indian Chieftain,* August 6, 1896.

76.   Ibid., September 10, 1896. An act of June 19, 1886, had reduced the Arkansas side of the jurisdiction from nineteen counties to sixteen (not seventeen).

77.   Ibid., June 4, 18, July 23, November 19, 1896; St. Louis *Globe-Democrat,* November 19, 20, 1896; Fayetteville *Democrat,* November 19, 1896.

78. *AR,* AG 1875–1896.

79. There has been no recent biography of Isaac Charles Parker. His successor, former Congressman John H. Rogers, was appointed by President Cleveland on November 27, 1896, confirmed in office on December 16, and held the post until his death in 1911.

80. *AR,* AG 1890–1896.

An item in the Purcell *Register,* in Atoka *Indian Citizen,* September 10, 1896, said that "during the jurisdiction of the [Paris] court in this [Indian] country two thousand cases have been handled and about 1500 sent to the penitentiary." This latter figure can only be right if the official returns supplied at the end of each year for the *Annual Reports* were wildly wrong. The paper was correct in stating that nine executions had taken place at Paris.

81. 54th Cong., 2d sess., *SD* 164, 5–20; the letters quoted were all written during February 1897 and addressed to Richard Pettigrew, chairman of the Senate Committee on Indian Affairs.

82. Ibid., 1–4.

83. *CR* 30, 711.

84. Ibid., 734.

85. Ibid., 1001.

86. Ibid., 735.

87. 55th Cong., 1st sess., *SD* 24, 1–5.

88. This term was used by Samuel Maxey in the House debate on the Saint Louis and San Francisco Railway bill, April 3, 1882, *CR* 13, 2525.

89. 55th Cong., 2d sess., *SD* 78, 1–10.

90. Ibid., *HR* 593, 1–4; *CR* 31, 2154.

91. *CR* 31, 5582–88.

92. Ibid., 5593.

93. Ibid., 5593.

94. Ibid., 6173, 6174; *Stats.L.* 30, 495–519.

95. *CR* 31, 1611–16, 1626; *Stats.L.* 30, 567–69, 591–97.

96. Brown, "Dawes Commission," 100; *AR,* SI 1898, 75–79, 435; Atoka *Indian Citizen,* July 14, 21, August 18, 25, September 1, 8, 1898.

97. Evidence of confusion and anomaly abounds. See, for example, Fort Gibson *Post,* in Vinita *Indian Chieftain,* July 14, 1898; Claremore *Progress,* ibid.; William P. Thompson, "Courts of the Cherokee Nation," *Chron.,* March 1924, 73 (from an address delivered in 1910); T. L. Ballenger, "Life and Times of Jeff Thompson Parks," ibid., Summer 1952, 192.

98. Brown, 101–2.

99. Fort Smith *Elevator,* November 26, 1897; October 28, 1898.

100. Ibid., November 12, 1897; March 24, 1899; Fayetteville *Democrat,* July 20, 1899; file of contemporary materials on the Goings case compiled by Mary Lee Boyle, IAD, OHS.

CHAPTER ELEVEN. **COURTHOUSE GOVERNMENT AND THE MOVE TOWARD SINGLE STATEHOOD**

1. *AR,* SI 1901, 219

2. Sandels and Hill.

3. *Stats.L.* 30, 499–500.

4. 54th Cong., 1st sess., *SD* 202, 1–4.

5. David W. Yancey. "Need for Better Government in the Indian Territory," *Forum,* February 1900, 738.

6. Angie Debo, *And Still the Waters Run,* 31; recent support for this judgment may be found in Kent Carter, "Deciding Who Can Be Cherokee: Enrollment Records of the Dawes Commission," *Chron.,* Summer 1991, 174–205.

7. Miner, *Corporation and the Indian,* 192–97; Robert L. Williams, "Tams Bixby," *Chron.,* September 1941, 205–12; Muriel H. Wright, "Notes on the Closing of the Roll of the Five Civilized Tribes," *Chron.,* Autumn 1964, 344–47.

8. For the Supplementary Agreement and citizenship court, see Loren N. Brown, "The Choctaw-Chickasaw Court Citizens," *Chron.,* December 1938, 425–43; Debo, *Rise and Fall of the Choctaw Republic,* 263–64, 270–72.

9. *Stats.L.* 29, 181–83.

10. Ibid., 28, 695 (sec. 2, act of March 1, 1895).

11. *AR,* AG 1896, vi–vii; *Stats.L.* 29, 577–78.

12. *Stats.L.* 29, 487.

13. *AR,* AG 1897, XXV; 1898, XXVI.

14. *Stats.L.* 32, 275–76 (part of Indian Appropriation Act, 1902–3).

15. 57th Cong., 1st sess., *HR* 2281, 1–6.

16. *Stats.L.* 32, 595.

17. Exhibit Q, *AR,* AG 1898; Exhibit P, ibid., 1899–1902; Exhibit 7, ibid., 1903.

18. *Stats.L.* 32, 792–93.

19. *AR,* AG 1899, 72–75; 1900, 68–71; 1901, 66–69; 1902, 20–23.

20. Ibid., 1903, 144–49, 158–60.

21. Ibid., 1904, 172–83, 190–92.; *CR* 38, 5004–6.

22. *CR* 38, 5005–6.

23. Ibid., 5005.

24. Ibid., 5845; *Stats.L.* 33, 573.

25. Bierer, 2. He said it so often that "Old Sui Generis" became his professional nickname.

26. 53d Cong., 3d sess., *HED* 267, 1–3.

27. Thomas Allison Edwards, "Early Days in the C & A," *Chron.,* Summer 1949, 151–52.

28. Ibid., 157.

29. Miner, *Corporation and the Indian,* passim.

30. *Statistical Abstract of the United States,* 1885–1900.

31. Guthrie *Oklahoma State Capital,* November 22, 29, 1890. This newspaper began life in Winfield, Kansas, as the Guthrie *Oklahoma Capital* in March 1890, arrived in Guthrie on April 22, 1889, at the same time as the first batch of "Sooners," and inflated itself into the Guthrie *Oklahoma State Capital* shortly afterward, some seventeen years before Guthrie became, for a brief period, the capital of a State.

32. Dan W. Peery, "Oklahoma: A Foreordained Commonwealth," *Chron.,* March 1936, 22–48; Charles Wayne Ellinger, "Drive for Statehood for Oklahoma," ibid., Spring 1963, 15–37.

33. *CR* 31, 1615–16.

34. Ibid., 36, 341; 57th Cong., 1st sess., *HR* 956, 1–4.

35. *CR* 35, 5136–46; 57th Cong., 2d sess., *SD* 36, 188–225.

36. 57th Cong., 2d sess., *SD* 8, 1–3.

37. George O. Carney, "Oklahoma's Territorial Delegates and Progressivism, 1901–1907," *Chron.,* Spring 1974, 38–51.

38. *CR* 37, 349.

39. Ibid., 38, 785; Thomas H. Doyle, "Single versus Double Statehood," *Chron.,* March 1927, 18–41; June 1937, 117–48; September 1927, 266–86; Charles Wayne Ellinger, "Congressional Viewpoint Towards the Admission of Oklahoma as a State, 1902–1906," ibid., Fall 1980, 282–95.

40. *CR* 38, 4281.

41. Ibid., 39, 2785–90.

42. Josiah Flynt, "Town Life in the Indian Territory," *Cosmopolitan,* June 1905, 138.

43. Amos Maxwell, "Sequoyah Convention," *Chron.,* Summer 1950, 299–340.

44. William H. Murray, "Constitutional Convention," *Chron.,* June 1931, 132.

45. Danney G. Goble, "New Kind of State: Settlement and Statemaking in Oklahoma to 1907," Ph.D. diss., University of Missouri, Columbia, 297–301.

46. *CR* 40, 1407.

47. *Stats.L.* 34, 267–86.

48. Ibid., 33, 1067; Williams, "Tams Bixby"; Wright, "Notes on the Closing Rolls of the Five Civilized Tribes," 347.

49. *Stats.L.* 34, 137.

50. Debo, *And Still the Waters Run,* 47.

51. *Stats.L.* 31, 1447.

52. *AR,* SI 1901, 235–37; Eufaula *Indian Journal,* January 25, February 1, March 8, 1901; February 28, March 21, 1902; John B. Meserve, "Chief Pleasant Porter," *Chron.,* September 1931, 318–34; Mace Davis, "Chitto Harjo," *Chron.,* June 1935, 139–45; Debo, *And Still the Waters Run,* 54–57.

53. *AR,* SI 1903, 243–45; Meserve, "McCurtains," *Chron.,* September 1935, 297–310; "Chief Gilbert Wesley Dukes," ibid., March 1940, 53–56.

54. 58th Cong., 2d sess., *HD* 528, 1–28.

55. *AR,* AG 1904, 172–92; 1905, 114–19; 1906, 92–97.

56. Vinita *Indian Chieftain,* September 10, 1896.

57. In commenting upon this definition of the status of the Five Nations, expounded fifty years earlier by Chief Justice John Marshall, Senator George Vest declared: "I do not understand it. I have never understood it, and in the providence of God I never expect to understand it." *CR* 13, 2570, 2576, April 4, 1882.

Bibliography

MANUSCRIPT SOURCES

General Records of the Department of Justice, National Archives, Washington, D.C.

Letters Received: Year Files 4450/86, 600/96.
Letters Sent:
  General and Miscellaneous, 1870–1913, Letter Books I, K, Q, and 17.
  Instructions to United States attorneys and marshals, 1870–1904, Letter Books B2, C, X, 1, 2, 3.
  Judges and Clerks, 1874–1904, Letter Books 1, 3, 7, 9, 10.

Records of the United States District Court for the Western Judicial District of Arkansas, National Archives, Fort Worth, Texas

Miscellaneous ledgers and journals:
  Bar Dockets, 1876–1878.
  Clerk's Docket, 1889–1897.
  Docket Index, 1889–1897.
  Index to Cases, 1865–1872.
  Index to Judgment Dockets, 1866–1905.
  Minutes, 1873–1898.
  Writ Dockets, 1873–1897.
Individual cases, trial papers:
  U.S. vs. Alexander Allen (testimony and charges to jury, first and second trials).
  U.S. vs. Frank Carver (testimony, first trial; charge to jury [incomplete], first trial; instructions to jury, third trial).
  U.S. vs. Robert H. Hall (testimony).
  U.S. vs. Robert Marshal(l) Hall (testimony).
  U.S. vs. Mary A. Kettenring et al. (testimony, first and second trial; charge to jury, first trial).
  U.S. vs. Mary A. Kittenring (sic) *et al.* (testimony before U.S. commissioner).
  U.S. vs. Alexander Lewis (testimony before U.S. commissioner; testimony, first trial).
  U.S. vs. Eli Lucas (ruling on jurisdiction; testimony; charge to jury).
  U.S. vs. Buz Lucky [Luckey] (testimony, charge to jury).
Copies of Reports of Supreme Court of the United States:

285

Ed. Alberty, alias Charles Burns vs. U.S. (No. 853, October Term, 1895).
Frank Carver vs. U.S. (No. 721, October Term, 1895).

Records of the Five Civilized Tribes, Indian Archives Division, Oklahoma Historical Society, Oklahoma City

Records of the Cherokee Nation:
  Federal Relations, 1866–1898.
  Foreign Relations, 1866–1909.
  Indian Police, 1882–1899.
  Outlaws, 1886–1894.
  Pardons, 1877–1901.
  Prison and High Sheriff, 1874–1909.
  Railroads, 1867–1868, 1871–1880.
Records of the Chickasaw Nation:
  Auditor, 1881–1908 (Documents 12705–12939).
  Decisions of the Supreme Court, 1868–1878.
  Federal Relations, 1866–1909.
  Foreign Relations, 1892–1905.
  Jailor, 1890–1907 (Documents 7259–7335).
  Minute Book of the District Court, 1885–1889.
  Sheriffs, 1888–1902 (Documents 11901–12088).
  Miscellaneous records and memoranda.
Records of the Choctaw Nation:
  Foreign Relations, 1870–1902 (Documents 17712–17724).
  Miscellaneous Court Records (Documents 15820–15856).
  Records of the Principal Chiefs (Letters of the Chiefs, etc.), 1866–1880.
  Records of the Supreme Court, 1865–1905.
Records of the Creek (Muskogee) Nation:
  Foreign Relations, 1876–1906 (Documents 30431–30891).
  Intruders, 1876–1908 (Documents 30903–31157).
  Light-horse, 1871–1900 (Documents 31515–32287).
  Liquor and Gambling, 1876–1901 (Documents 32288–32314).
  Pardons, 1870–1898 (Documents 34570–34750).
  Pastures and Cattle, 1871–1904 (Documents 34751–35143).
  Records of the Supreme Court, 1871–1898.
Records of the Seminole Nation:
  Revised Laws, 1903.
  Miscellaneous surviving documents.

OFFICIAL PUBLICATIONS

United States Government

Congressional Globe, 38th Cong., 2d sess.; 41st Cong., 1st, 2d, and 3d sess.; 42d
  Cong., 2d sess.
Congressional Record, vols. 6, 8–10, 13–24, 26–27, 30, 31, 35, 37–40.

House and Senate Documents, Executive Documents, Miscellaneous Documents, and Reports, 41st Cong., 2d sess., *SMD* 76, March 8, 1870; *HMD* 76, May 23, 1870; *SMD* 143, May 28, 1870;

42d Cong., 2d sess., *HED* 153, February 21, 1872, *SMD* 85, February 21, 1872; *HR* 61, May 2, 1872; *SED* 70, May 7, 1872 (2 pts.); *HR* 89, May 27, 1872; *SMD* 166, June 3, 1872.

42d Cong., 3d sess., *HMD* 110, March 3, 1873.

43d Cong., 1st sess., *HR* 626, June 1, 1874 *(Sener Report)*.

43d Cong., 2d sess., *SMD* 34, January 15, 1875; *SMD* 65, February 2, 1875; *SMD* 66, February 2, 1875; *SMD* 71, February 6, 1875; *SMD* 72, February 9, 1875; *HED* 175, February 23, 1875; *SMD* 112, February 24, 1875.

44th Cong., special sess., *SMD* 3, March 8, 1875.

44th Cong., 1st sess., *SMD* 23, January 6, 1876; *SMD* 42, January 27, 1876; *HR* 43, February 1, 1876; *SMD* 53, February 14, 1876; *HR* 299, March 21, 1876.

45th Cong., 1st sess., *HMD* 18, November 27, 1877.

45th Cong., 2d sess., *HR* 95, January 22, 1878; *SED* 74, May 10, 1878.

45th Cong., 3d sess., *SED* 46, January 27, 1879; *SMD* 52, January 29, 1879; *SR* 744, February 11, 1879 *(Patterson Report); SMD* 70, February 13, 1879; *SMD* 73, February 19, 1879; *HR* 188, March 3, 1879.

46th Cong., 1st sess., *HMD* 13, May 8, 1879.

46th Cong., 2d sess., *SR* 332, March 3, 1880; *SMD* 46, March 3, 1880; *SED* 124, March 19, 1880; *HR* 755, April 6, 1880; *HR* 755, pt. 2, April 10, 1880.

46th Cong., 3d sess., *SED* 14, January 5, 1881.

47th Cong., 1st sess., *HED* 131, March 21, 1882.

48th Cong., 1st sess., *HED* 92, February 14, 1884; *SED* 108, February 15, 1884; *HED* 112, March 8, 1884; *SR* 575, May 26, 1884; *HR* 1307, April 15, 1884; *HMD* 38, pt. 1, July 3, 1884.

49th Cong., 1st sess., *HR* 1076, March 16, 1886 *(Holman Report); HR* 1684, April 15, 1886; *SR* 1278, pts. 1 and 2, June 4, 1886 *(Dawes Report)*.

50th Cong., 1st session, *SMD* 16, December 20, 1887, *HED* 90, January 18, 1888; *HR* 263, February 7, 1888; *HED* 208, March 8, 1888; *HR* 1007, March 10, 1888; *SMD* 153, July 9, 1888.

50th Cong., 2d sess., *HR* 34, December 21, 1888; *HED* 47, January 2, 1889.

51st Cong., 1st sess., *SED* 78, March 12, 1890; *HR* 814, March 13, 1890, *HR* 901, March 21, 1890; *SED* 117, May 13, 1890; *SED* 164, June 23, 1890.

51st Cong., 2d sess., *HMD* 104, February 6, 1891; *HR* 3819, February 16, 1891; *HR* 3823, February 17, 1891.

52d Cong., 1st sess., *SR* 281, February 25, 1892; *HED* 144, February 26, 1892; *HR* 1413, May 17, 1892; *SMD* 161, May 24, 1891; *SR* 1079, July 26, 1892, *SMD* 221, August 2, 1892.

52d Cong., 2d sess., *HR* 2384, January 20, 1893.

53d Cong., 2d sess., *HR* 242, December 20, 1893; *HR* 348, February 3, 1894; *HED* 67, January 10, 1894; *HED* 107, February 9, 1894; *HED* 125, February 24, 1894; *SMD* 114, March 7, 1894; *SMD* 166, April 27, 1894; *SR* 377, May 7, 1894 *(Teller Report); SED* 120, June 27, 1894.

53d Cong., 3d sess., *SMD* 24, December 10, 1894; *HED* 168, January 4, 1895; *HED* 23, January 15, 1895; *HED* 247, January 24, 1895; *SMD* 137, February 27, 1895.

54th Cong., 1st sess., *SD* 12, December 5, 1895; *HR* 108, January 22, 1896; *HD* 167, January 23, 1896; *SR* 290, February 18, 1896; *HR* 571, February 29, 1896; *SD* 173, March 16, 1896; *SR* 532, March 20, 1896; *SD* 182, March 24, 1896; *SD* 190, March 26, 1896; *HR* 1063, April 1, 1896, *SD* 202, April 9, 1896; *SR* 909, May 11, 1896.

54th Cong., 2d sess., *HR* 2489, January 12, 1897; *SD* 164, February 27, 1897.

55th Cong., 1st sess., *SD* 24, April 6, 1897; *HD* 83, July 12, 1897.

55th Cong., 2d sess., *SD* 78, January 21, 1898; *SD* 84, January 24, 1898; *SD* 98, January 27, 1898; *SD* 99, pt. 1, January 28, 1898; *SD* 99, pt. 2, February 2, 1898; *SD* 99, pt. 3, February 7, 1898; *HD* 318, February 22, 1898; *HR* 593, March 1, 1898; *HD* 341, March 14, 1898; *HD* 360, March 18, 1898.

57th Cong., 1st sess., *HR* 956, March 14, 1902; *HR* 2281, May 28, 1902.

57th Cong., 2d sess., *SD* 36, December 10, 1902; *SD* 38, December 15, 1902.

58th Cong., 2d sess., *HD* 428, February 11, 1904.

[Department of the Interior]. *Annual Reports of the Secretary of the Interior* (including annual reports of the commissioner of Indian affairs, superintendents, and agents), 1865–1906.

———. *Annual Reports of the Board of Indian Commissioners,* 1870, 1881, 1882, 1885. (All others, except the first, for 1868, were included in the *Annual Reports of the Secretary of the Interior* .)

[Department of Justice]. *Annual Reports of the Attorney-General,* 1870–1906.

[Post Office Department]. *Annual Reports of the Postmaster-General,* 1875, 1886–1899.

[Department of the Treasury]. *Statistical Abstract of the United States,* 1878–1900.

Galpin, Samuel A. *Report upon the Condition and Management of Certain Indian Agencies in the Indian Territory now under the Supervision of the Orthodox Friends.* 1877.

Journal of the Executive Proceedings of the Senate of the United States of America, vols. 16–25, 27–36.

Journal of the House of Representatives, 43d Cong., 1st sess.; 51st Cong., 2d sess.

Kappler, Charles J., comp., ed. *Indian Affairs: Laws and Treaties.* 4 vols. 1904–1929.

Laws, Decisions, and Regulations Affecting the Work of the Commissioner to the Five Civilized Tribes. 1906.

Official Records of the War of the Rebellion. Ser. 4, vol. 1. 1900.

Report of Board of Inquiry convened by authority of the Secretary of the Interior, June 7, 1877 to Investigate certain charges against S.A. Galpin, chief clerk of the Indian Bureau, Washington. 1878.

Report on Indians Taxed and Indians Not Taxed in the United States (except Alaska) at the Eleventh Census: 1890. 1894. *Report of the Population of the United States at the Eleventh Census: 1890* Compendium, pt. 1. 1895.

Richardson, James D. *A Compilation of the Messages and Proclamations of the Presidents.* 10 vols., supplement. 1896–1903.

Statutes at Large of the United States of America. Vols. 1, 4, 5, 9–14, 17–20, 22–34. (Revised Statutes of 1873–74 are in vol. 18, pt. 1.)

Thorpe, Francis Newton, comp., ed. *The Federal and State Constitutions and other Organic Laws of the States, Territories and Colonies now or heretofore forming the United States of America.* 9 vols. 1909.

Governments of the Indian Nations

Constitution and Laws of the Cherokee Nation, 1874. 1875.
Compiled Laws of the Cherokee Nation, 1880. 1881.
Constitution and Laws of the Chickasaw Nation, 1857. 1857.
Constitution, Laws, and Treaties of the Chickasaws, 1877. 1878.
General and Special Laws of the Chickasaw Nation, 1878–1884. 1884.
Constitution and Laws of the Choctaw Nation, together with the Treaties of 1855, 1865 and 1866. 1869.
Constitution and Laws of the Muskogee Nation, 1872. 1872.

State and Territorial Governments

Compiled Laws of New Mexico 1897.
Dassler, C. F. W. *Compiled Laws of Kansas 1881.*
———. *General Statutes of Kansas, 1901, Authenticated.*
McCartney, W. A., John H. Beatty, and J. Malcolm Johnston. *The Statutes of Oklahoma 1893.*
Mitchell, James T., and Henry Flanders. *Statutes at Large of Pennsylvania.* Vol. 15, 1794–97. 1911.
Sandels, Leonidas Polk, and Joseph M. Hill. *A Digest of the Statutes of Arkansas, 1893.* 1894.
Wilson, W. F. *Wilson's Revised and Annotated Statutes of Oklahoma.* 1903.

NEWSPAPERS

(Inclusive dates enclosed within brackets indicate a broken run containing at least half the issues published during the period stated.)
Atoka, Choctaw Nation, *Choctaw Champion,* July 15–August 18, 1898.
Atoka *Indian Champion,* [January 10–May 16, 1885; September 12–November 7, 1885].
Atoka *Independent,* June 5, October 9, 1886; January 8, July 20, 1887; February 11, May 5, 12, 19, 1888.
Atoka *Indian Citizen,* March 2, 1889–March 30, 1899 (almost complete).
Claremore, Cherokee Nation, *Progress,* [June 17, 1893–May 26, 1894].
Coffeyville, Kansas, *Daily Journal,* [June 23, 1893–February 3, 1894].
El Reno, Oklahoma, *News,* December 4, 11, 18, 25, 1896.
Eufaula, Muskogee Nation, *Indian Journal,* December 7, 1876; [March 22–July 5], August 11, 18, September 8, 15, October 13, November 17, December 15, 29, 1877; October 26, 1900–June 27, 1902.
Fayetteville, Arkansas, *Democrat,* February 4–June 23, 1892; July 20, 1893–July 12, 1894; July 11, 1895–July 20, 1899.
Fort Gibson, Cherokee Nation, *Indian Arrow,* April 12, 1888; February 7, 1889; August 23, 1890.
Fort Smith, Arkansas, *Daily News Record,* May 31, [June 11–July 3, 1894]; [August 5, 1894–September 29, 1896].
Fort Smith *Elevator* July 1, 1881; [August 14, 1885–April 21, 1899]; June 23, 1899; May 11, 25, 1900; January 4, 1901–December 19, 1902.
Fort Smith *New Era,* April 17, 19, 1872; August 20, 1873; April 10, 1878; June 1, 1881.

Gainesville, Texas, *Daily Hesperian,* [January 4, 1894–December 14, 1895]

Guthrie, Indian Territory–Oklahoma, *Oklahoma Capital* or *Oklahoma State Capital* (first published at Winfield, Kansas), (weekly edition) [March 30, 1889–March 7, 1891].

Little Rock, Arkansas, *Arkansas Gazette,* February 18–April 19, 1896.

New York Times [1866–1898].

Oklahoma City *Daily Oklahoman* and *Weekly Oklahoman,* [January–December 1895].

Saint Louis, Missouri, *Globe-Democrat,* December 26, 27, 1887; January 1, 1888–March 23, 1898 (all issues).

Sedan, Kansas, *Weekly Times-Journal,* August 26, 1892–January 12, 1894 (all issues).

Tahlequah, Cherokee Nation, *Courier,* September 19, October 17, December 3, 1893.

Tahlequah *Indian Sentinel,* October 21, December 16, 1891; May 9, 1895.

Tahlequah *Telephone, Arrow-Telephone,* or *Arrow,* August 2, 9, 16, 1894 *(Telephone);* September 19, November 23, 1894 *(Arrow-Telephone)* ; July 7, 1894; May 24, May 31, August 2, 16, 1895; May 16, August, 15, 22, September 12, 1896 *(Arrow).*

Vinita, Cherokee Nation, *World,* July 18, 25, 1891.

Vinita *Indian Chieftain,* January 2, 1890–June 28, 1900 (all issues).

Washington, D.C., *Post,* December 1, 1895–February 29, 1896.

DISSERTATIONS AND THESES

Blackburn, Bobby L. "Oklahoma Law Enforcement Since 1803." Ph.D. diss., University of Oklahoma, 1979.

Buice, Sammy David. "The Civil War and the Five Civilized Tribes—A Study in Federal Indian Relations." Ph.D. diss., University of Oklahoma, 1970.

Goble, Danney G. "A New Kind of State: Settlement and Statemaking in Oklahoma to 1907." Ph.D. diss., University of Missouri, 1976.

Smith, Geraldine M. "Violence on the Oklahoma Territory—Seminole Nation Border: The Mont Ballard Case." Master's thesis, University of Oklahoma, 1957.

Snodgrass, William George. "A History of the Cherokee Outlet." D.Ed. diss., Oklahoma State University, 1972.

BOOKS

(*Note:* What follows is not a directory of all the relevant books read or consulted but a select list, confined chiefly to those that were useful. Several are derived from an author's original observations or personal experience; others nudged the present writer toward a line of thought or documents he might otherwise have missed. One, which readers may like to identify for themselves, is included solely on the strength of its author's admission that the Indian Territory lay outside the terms of its hypothesis. Added to these are one or two recommendable general studies of U.S. "Indian policy" and the best of the few worthwhile volumes on the livelier side of law enforcement in Indian Territory and Oklahoma Territory.)

American Digest System, 1906: Decennial Edition of the American Digest. 26 vols. (21–25). St. Paul: West, 1911.

Anson, Bert. *The Miami Indians.* Norman: University of Oklahoma Press, 1970.

Baird, W. David. *Peter Pitchlynn; Chief of the Choctaws.* Norman: University of Oklahoma Press, 1972.

Barsh, Russel Lawrence, and James Youngblood Henderson. *The Road: Indian Tribes and Political Liberty.* Berkeley: University of California Press, 1980, 1982.

Beadle, John Hanson. *The Undeveloped West or Five Years in the Territories.* Philadelphia: National, 1873.

Blandford, Linda A., and Patricia Russell Evans, ed. *The Supreme Court of the United States: An Index to Opinions Arranged by Justice.* 2 vols. New York: Kraus International, 1983.

Bolt, Christine. *American Indian Policy and American Reform.* London: Allen and Unwin, 1987.

Brightly, Frederick C. *A Digest of the Decisions of the Federal Courts from the Organization of the Government to the Present Time.* Philadelphia: Kay and Brother, 1868.

Century Edition of the American Digest: A Completed Digest of all Reported American Cases from the Earliest Times to 1896. 50 vols. St. Paul: West, 1897–1904.

Curtis, B. P. *Reports of Decisions of the Supreme Court of the United States.* 22 volumes. Boston: Little, Brown, 1854–1886.

Davis, Richard Harding. *The West from a Car-Window.* New York: Harper, 1892.

Debo, Angie. *The Rise and Fall of the Choctaw Republic.* Norman: University of Oklahoma Press, 1934, 1961.

———. *And Still the Waters Run.* Princeton, N.J.: Princeton University Press, 1940, 1972.

———. *The Road to Disappearance.* Norman: University of Oklahoma Press, 1941, 1982.

Ford, Paul Leicester, comp., ed. *The Writings of Thomas Jefferson.* 10 vols. New York: G. P. Putnam's Sons, 1892–1899.

Friedman, Leon, and Fred L. Israel, eds. *The Justices of the United States Supreme Court, 1789–1969.* 4 volumes. New York: Chelsea House, R. R. Bowker, 1969.

Gibson, Arrell Morgan. *The Chickasaws.* Norman: University of Oklahoma Press, 1971.

Gittinger, Roy. *The Formation of the State of Oklahoma, 1803–1906.* Berkeley: University of California Press, 1917.

Green, Michael D. *The Politics of Indian Removal.* Lincoln: University of Nebraska Press, 1982.

Hagan, William T. *Indian Police and Judges: Experiments in Assimilation and Control.* Lincoln: University of Nebraska Press, 1966, 1980.

Harman, Samuel W. *Hell on the Border: He Hanged Eighty-eight Men.* Fort Smith, Ark.: Phoenix, (1898) 1899. (A reprint of the abridged edition of 1920 was published by Frank L. Van Eaton, Stockton, Calif., 1953. The Indian Heritage Edition, ed. Jack Gregory and Rennard Strickland, 1971, is a short selection of excerpts from the original work.)

Harrington, Fred Harvey. *Hanging Judge.* Caldwell, Idaho: Caxton, 1952

Hoxie, Frederick E. *A Final Promise: The Campaign to Assimilate the Indians, 1880–1920.* Lincoln: University of Nebraska Press, 1984.

Johnson, Steven L. *Guide to American Indian Documents in the Congressional Serial Set, 1817–1899.* New York: Clearwater, 1977.

Kvasnicka, Robert M., and Herman J. Viola, eds. *The Commissioners of Indian Affairs, 1824–1977.* Lincoln: University of Nebraska Press, 1979.

McReynolds, Edwin Clarence. *The Seminoles.* Norman: University of Oklahoma Press, 1957.

Mathews, John Joseph. *The Osages: Children of the Middle Waters.* Norman: University of Oklahoma Press, 1961.

Miner, H. Craig. *The Corporation and the Indian: Tribal Sovereignty and Industrial Civilization in Indian Territory, 1865–1907.* Columbia: University of Missouri Press, 1976.

Morris, John Wesley, and Edwin Clarence McReynolds. *Historical Atlas of Oklahoma.* Norman: University of Oklahoma Press, 1965.

Morris, John Wesley, and Charles Robert Goins. *Historical Atlas of Oklahoma.* 2d ed. 1976.

Prucha, Francis Paul. *Documents of United States Indian Policy.* Lincoln: University of Nebraska Press, 1975.

———. *A Bibliographical Guide to the History of Indian-White Relations in the United States.* Chicago: University of Chicago Press, 1977.

———. *Indian Policy in the United States.* Lincoln: University of Nebraska Press, 1981.

———. *Indian-White Relations in the United States: A Bibliography of Works Published, 1975–1980.* Lincoln: University of Nebraska Press, 1982.

———. *The Great Father: The United States Government and the American Indians.* 2 vols. Lincoln: University of Nebraska Press, 1984.

Rothman, David J. *Politics and Power.* Cambridge, Mass.: Harvard University Press, 1966.

Savage, William W., Jr. *The Cherokee Strip Live Stock Association: Federal Regulation and the Cattleman's Last Frontier.* Norman: University of Oklahoma Press, 1973.

Shirk, George H. *Oklahoma Place Names.* Norman: University of Oklahoma Press, 1965.

Shirley, Glenn, *Law West of Fort Smith.* New York: Henry Holt, 1957.

———. *Heck Thomas: Frontier Marshal.* Philadelphia and New York: Chilton, 1962.

———. *West of Hell's Fringe.* Norman: University of Oklahoma Press, 1978.

Strickland, Rennard, *Fire and the Spirits: Cherokee Law from Clan to Court.* Norman: University of Oklahoma Press, 1975.

Thoburn, Joseph B. *A Standard History of Oklahoma.* 2 vols. Chicago: American History Society, 1916.

Wardell, Morris L. *A Political History of the Cherokee Nation, 1838–1907.* Norman: University of Oklahoma Press, 1938, 1977.

White, Eugene Elliott. *Experiences of a Special Indian Agent.* Norman: University of Oklahoma Press, 1965 (first published 1893 as *Service on the Indian Reservations*).

Wright, Muriel Hazel. *A Guide to the Indian Tribes of Oklahoma.* Norman: University of Oklahoma Press, 1951.

ARTICLES

Miscellaneous Contemporary Publications

Candee, Helen Churchill. "Social Conditions in Our Newest Territory." *The Forum* 25, no. 4 (June 1898): 426–37.

Dawes, Anna Laurens. "An Unknown Nation." *Harper's New Monthly Magazine* 76 (March 1888): 598–605.

Downing, A. "The Cherokee Indians and Their Neighbors." *American Antiquarian* 57, no. 6 (November 1895): 307–16.

Duncan, D. W. C. "The Cherokee Outlet." *Andover Review* 16 (October 1891): 342–51.

Flynt, Josiah. "Town Life in the Indian Territory." *The Cosmopolitan* 39, no. 2 (June 1905): 137–44.

Hamilton, Gail [Mary Abigail Dodge]. "Prisoner Among the Indians." *North American Review* 146 (January 1888): 55–66.

———. "Sunday in Cherokee Land." *North American Review* 146 (February 1888): 194–202.

———. "The Lion's Side of the Lion Question." *North American Review* 146 (March 1888): 294–309.

Harsha, William Justin. "Law for the Indians." *North American Review* 134 (March 1882): 272–92.

Jenness, Theodora R. "The Indian Territory." *Atlantic Monthly* 43 (April 1879): 444–52.

Johnson, W. H. "The Saloon in Indian Territory" (Notes and Comments, IV). *North American Review* 146 (March 1888): 341–42.

King, Edward. "The Great South, the New Route to the Gulf." *Scribner's Monthly* 6, no. 3 (July 1873): 257–88.

King, Henry. "The Indian Country." *Century Illustrated Monthly Magazine* 30, no. 4 (August 1885).

Platt, Orville H. "Problems in the Indian Territory." *North American Review* 160 (February 1895): 195–202.

Reynolds, Milton W. "The Indian Territory." *Western Monthly* 4 (November 1870): 260–66.

Toler, Sallie F. "A Glimpse of the New Country." *Era Magazine* 12, no. 4 (October 1903): 313–17.

Wicks, Hamilton S. "The Opening of Oklahoma." *The Cosmopolitan* 7, no. 5 (September 1889): 460–70.

Yancey, David W. "Need of Better Government in the Indian Territory." *The Forum* 28, no. 6 (February 1900): 737–40.

Chronicles of Oklahoma

Adams, Harry. "The Brush Court in Indian Territory," 46, no. 2 (Summer 1968): 201–5.

Agnew, Brad. "Voices from the Land Run of 1889," 67 (Spring 1989): 4–29.

Allhands, James L. "History of the Construction of the Frisco Railway Lines in Oklahoma," 3, no. 3 (September 1925): 229–39.

Anderson, Mona Washbourne. "General Stand Watie," 10, no. 4 (December 1932): 540–48.

Anon. "Henry E. Asp" (Obituary), 1, no. 3 (June 1923): 256–57.

———. "John H. Burford" (Obituary), 1, no. 3 (June 1923): 254.

———. "Luda P. Davenport" (Memorial), 4, no. 3 (September 1926): 292–93.

———. "Napoleon Bonaparte Maxey" (Necrology), 10, no. 4 (December 1932): 611.

———. "James Stirman Standley" (Necrology), 10, no. 4 (December 1932): 614–17.

———. "George W. Steele" (Obituary), 1, no. 3 (June 1923): 253.

———. "Charles Bingley Stuart. Resolution of Respect for and in Appreciation of . . . ," 15, no. 2 (June 1937).

Baird, W. David. "Are There Real Indians in Oklahoma?" 68, no. 1 (Spring 1990): 4–23.

Ballenger, T. L. "The Life and Times of Jeff Thompson Parks," 30 no. 2 (Summer 1952): 173–99.

———. "The Death and Burial of Major Ridge," 51, no. 1 (Spring 1973): 100–105.

Balman, Gail. "The Creek Treaty of 1866," 48, no. 2 (Summer 1970): 184–96.

Beck, T. E. "When the Territory Was Young," 14, no. 3 (September 1936): 360–64.

Benedict, John D. "Reminiscences," 33, no. 4 (Winter 1955–56): 475–88.

Best, Frank J. "Recollections of April 22, 1889," 21, no. 1 (March 1943): 28–32.

Bierer, A. G. C. "Early Day Courts and Lawyers," 8, no. 1 (March 1930): 2–12.

Board of Indian Commissioners. "Appendix 37" (to second annual report, 1870), 5, no. 1 (March 1927): 79–104.

Bobo, L. D. "Reminiscences of Pioneer Days," 23, no. 3 (Autumn 1945): 276–90.

Boyd, Joel D. "Creek Indian Agents, 1834–1874," 51, no. 1 (Spring 1973): 37–58.

Brewer, Phil D. "Edward Overholser" (Necrology), 9, no. 2 (June 1931): 212–13.

Broemeling, Carol B. "Cherokee Indian Agents, 1830–1874," 50, no. 4 (Winter 1972–73): 437–57.

Brown, Elmer E. "No Man's Land," 4, no. 2 (June 1926): 89–99.

Brown, Kenny L. "'He has Builded his own Monument': Will T. Little and the Legacy of '89," 67, no. 3 (Fall 1989): 248–63.

Brown, Loren N. "The Dawes Commission," 9, no. 1 (March 1931): 71–105.

———. "The Choctaw-Chickasaw Court Citizens," 16, no. 4 (December 1938): 425–43.

———. "The Establishment of the Dawes Commission for Indian Territory," 18, no. 2 (June 1940): 171–80.

———. "An Appraisal of the Lands of the Choctaws and Chickasaws by the Dawes Commission," 22, no. 3 (Autumn 1944): 177–91.

Brown, Thomas Elton. "Seminole Indian Agents, 1842–1874," 51, no. 1 (Spring 1973): 59–83.

Bullard, Clara Williamson Warren. "Pioneer Days in the Cherokee Strip," 36, no. 3 (Autumn 1958): 258–69.

Bark, Jerry L. "Oklahoma Seminole Indians," 51, no. 3 (Fall 1973): 211–23.

Carney, George O. "Oklahoma's Territorial Delegates and Progressivism, 1901–1907," 52, no. 1 (Spring 1974): 38–51.

Carr, Sarah Jane. "Bloomfield Academy and Its Founder (John Harpole Carr)," 2, no. 4 (December 1924): 366–77.

Carroll, Lew F. "The Diary of an Eighty-niner," 15, no. 1 (March 1937): 66–68.

————. "An Eighty-niner Who Pioneered the Cherokee Strip," 24, no. 1 (Spring 1946): 87–101.

Carter, Kent. "Deciding Who Can Be Cherokee: Enrollment Records of the Dawes Commission," 69, no. 2 (Summer 1991): 174–205.

Caywood, Elzie Ronald. "The Administration of William C. Rogers, Cherokee Nation," 30, no. 1 (Spring 1952): 29–37.

Chapman, Berlin B. "How the Cherokees Acquired and Disposed of the Outlet," 15, no. 1, 30–50; no. 2, 205–25: no. 3, 291–321; 16, no. 1, 36–51; no. 2, 135–62.

————. "Unratified Treaty with the Creeks, 1868," 16, no. 3 (September 1938): 337–39.

————. "The Final Report of the Cherokee Commission," 19, no. 4 (December 1941): 356–65.

————. "The Pottawatomie and Absentee Shawnee Reservation," 24, no. 3 (Autumn 1946): 293–305.

————. "Guthrie, from Public Land to Private Property," 33, no. 1 (Spring 1955): 63–86.

————. "The Legal Sooners of 1889 in Oklahoma," 35, no. 4 (Winter 1957–58) 382–415.

————. "Oklahoma City, from Public Land to Private Property," 37, no. 2 (Summer 1959): 219–228; no. 3 (Autumn 1959): 330–52; no. 4 (Winter 1959–60): 442–78.

————. "Opening the Cherokee Outlet: An Archival Study," 40, no. 2 (Summer 1962): 158–81; no. 3 (Autumn 1962): 253–85.

Cherokee Strip Live Stock Association. (Map of Cherokee Outlet, with details of leases and brands of lessees), 9, no. 3 (September 1931): 268.

Christian, Emma Ervin. "Memories of My Childhood Days in the Choctaw Nation," 9, no. 2 (June 1931): 155–65.

Clark, J. S. "The Career of John R. Thomas," 52, no. 2 (Summer 1974): 172–79.

Clifton, Adelia. "A Pioneer Family in Old Greer County," 39, no. 2 (Summer 1961): 150–57.

Colcord, Charles Francis. "Reminiscences," 12, no. 1 (March 1934): 5–18.

Collin, Ellsworth. "The Hook Nine Ranch in the Indian Territory," 33, no. 4 (Winter 1955–56): 456–66.

Collins, Hubert Edwin. "Ben Williams, Frontier Peace Officer," 10, no. 4 (December 1932): 520–39.

Conlon, Czarina C. "Peter Perkins Pitchlynn" (Necrology), 6, no. 3 (September 1928): 215–24.

Cooper, Charles M. "The Big Pasture," 35, no. 2 (Summer 1957): 138–46.

Cornish, Melven. "Douglas H. Johnston" (Necrology), 18, no. 1 (March 1940): 99.

Crockett, Bernice Norman. "The Story of Rock Cut," 38, no. 3 (Autumn 1960): 253–64.

Crockett, Norman L. "The Opening of Oklahoma: A Businessman's Frontier," 56, no. 1 (Spring 1978): 85–95.

Daily, Harry P. "Judge Isaac C. Parker," 11, no. 1 (March 1933): 673–89.

Dale, Edward Everett. "The Cherokee Strip Live Stock Association," 5, no. 1 (March 1927): 58–78.

————. "Ranching on the Cheyenne-Arapaho Reservation, 1880–1885," 6, no. 1 (March 1928): 35–59.

———. "The Cheyenne-Arapaho Country," 20, no. 4 (December 1942): 360–71.

Davis, Caroline. "Education of the Chickasaws, 1856–1907," 15, no. 4 (December 1937): 415–48.

Davis, Mace. "Chitto Harjo," 13, no. 2 (June 1935): 139–45.

Davis, Moita Dorsey. "Boss Neff," 26, no. 2 (Summer 1948): 159–73.

Decker, Frank G. "Letter from Los Angeles," 7, no. 4 (December 1929): 458.

Denton, J. L. "Notes on James Lafayette Denton—The Cowman," 36, no. 4 (Winter 1958–59): 476–78.

Doran, Michael F. "Population Statistics of Nineteenth Century Indian Territory," 53, no. 4 (Winter 1975–76): 492–515.

Doyle, Thomas H. "Single versus Double Statehood" (statement before House Committee on the Territories, January 26, February 1, 1904), 5, no. 1 (March 1927): 18–41; no. 2 (June 1927): 117–48: no. 3 (September 1927): 266–86.

———. "The Supreme Court of the Territory of Oklahoma," 13, no. 2 (June 1935): 214–18.

Du Chateau, A. P. "The Creek Nation on the Eve of the Civil War," 52, no. 3 (Fall 1974): 290–315.

Duncan, James W. "Interesting Ante-Bellum Laws of the Cherokees," 6, no. 2 (June 1928): 178–80.

Dunham, Arthur W. "A Pioneer Railroad Agent," 2, no. 1 (March 1924): 48–62.

Durham, Arthur W. "Oklahoma City Before the Run of 1889," 36, no. 1 (Spring 1958): 72–78 (almost identical with the preceding item; contemporary materials indicate that the author was registered under both names in Oklahoma City in 1889).

Edwards, Thomas Allison. "Early Days in the C & A," 27, no. 2 (Summer 1949): 148–61.

Ellinger, Charles Wayne. "The Drive for Statehood for Oklahoma," 41, no. 1 (Spring 1963): 15–37.

———. "Congressional Viewpoint Towards the Admission of Oklahoma as a State, 1902–1906," 58, no. 3 (Fall 1980): 282–95.

Ellis, Clyde. "'Our Ill-Fated Relative': John Rollin Ridge and the Cherokee People," 68, no. 4 (Winter 1990–91): 376–95.

Estill, A. Emma. "The Great Lottery," 9, no. 4 (December 1931): 365–81.

Fessler, W. Julian. "The Work of the Early Choctaw Legislature from 1869 to 1873," 6, no. 1 (March 1928): 60–68.

Finney, Frank F. Sr. "Progress in the Civilization of the Osage and Their Government," 40, no. 1 (Spring 1962): 2–21.

Fischer, LeRoy H. "Indian Agents of the Five Civilized Tribes—Introduction: Choctaw and Chickasaw and Cherokee Agents," 50, no. 4 (Winter 1972–73): 410–14.

———. "Indian Agents of the Five Civilized Tribes—Introduction: Creek and Seminole Agents," 51, no. I (Spring 1973): 34–36.

Fischer, LeRoy H., et al. "The Governors of Oklahoma Territory," 53, no. 1 (Spring 1975): entire issue.

Flynn, Dennis T. "William Grimes" (Necrology), 9, no. 2 (June 1931): 221–23.

Ford, Jeanette W. "Federal Law Comes to Indian Territory," 48, no. 4 (Winter 1980–81): 432–39.

Foreman, Carolyn Thomas. "Gen. James M. Shackelford," 12, no. 1 (March 1934): 103–11.

———. "Mrs. Anna C. Trainor Matheson" (Necrology), 18, no. 1 (March 1940): 101.

———. "Jeremiah Curtin in Indian Territory," 26, no. 3 (Autumn 1948): 346–56.

———. "John Jumper," 29, no. 2 (Summer 1951): 137–52.

———. "Texanna," 31, no. 2 (Summer 1953): 178–88.

———. "Marshalltown, Creek Nation," 32, no. 1 (Spring 1954): 52–57.

———. "The Light-horse in the Indian Territory" (Cherokee, Choctaw, and Creek), 34, no. 1 (Spring 1956): 17–43.

———. "Notes on the Organization of the Seminole Light-horse," 34, no. 3 (Autumn 1956): 340–43.

———. "Notes on the Chickasaw Light-horsemen," 34, no. 4 (Winter 1956–57): 484.

Foreman, Grant. "Clarence W. Turner," 10, no. 1 (March 1932): 18–20.

———. "Oklahoma's First Court," 13, no. 4 (December 1935): 460–66.

———. "Horace Speed," 25, no. 1 (Spring 1947): 5.

Franks, Kenny A. "Confederate Treaties with the Five Civilized Tribes," 50, no. 4 (Winter 1972–73): 458–74.

———. "The Implementation of the Confederate Treaties with the Five Civilized Tribes," 51, no. 1 (Spring 1973): 21–33.

Frederick, J. V. "The Vigilantes in Early Beaver," 16, no. 2 (June 1938): 190–96.

Gibson, Arrell M. "Indian Territory United Nations 1845," 39, no. 4 (Winter 1961–62): 398–413.

Gill, Joseph A. Jr. "Joseph Albert Gill" (Necrology), 12, no. 3 (September 1934): 375–76.

Graebner, Norman Arthur. "History of Cattle Ranching in Eastern Oklahoma," 21, no. 3 (September 1943): 300–311.

———. "The Public Land Policy of the Five Civilized Tribes," 23, no. 2 (Summer 1945): 107–18.

Grant, Valerie J. "The Editor and the Magic City: Frank H. Greer and the Beginnings of Guthrie, Oklahoma Territory," (Spring 1980): 34–52.

Graves, William H. "Indian Soldiers for the Gray Army: Confederate Recruitment in Indian Territory," 69, no. 2 (Summer 1991): 134–45.

Gravley, Ernestine. "Fifty Years Ago in Shawnee and Pottawatomie County," 31, no. 4 (Winter 1953–54): 381–91.

Green, Donald E. "The Oklahoma Land Run of 1889: A Centennial Re-interpretation," 67, no. 2 (Summer 1989): 116–49.

Guthrey, E. Bee. "Early Days in Payne County," 3, no. 1 (April 1925): 74–80.

Halliburton, R. Jr. "Black Slavery among the Cherokees," 52, no. 4 (Winter 1974–75): 483–96.

Hammond, Sue. "Socioeconomic Reconstruction in the Cherokee Nation, 1865–1870," 56, no. 2 (Summer 1978): 158–70.

Hampton, Carol. "Indian Colonization in the Cherokee Outlet and Western Indian Territory," 54, no. 1 (Summer 1976): 130–48.

Harrel, Melvin. "Oklahoma's Million Acre Ranch," 29, no. 1 (Spring 1951): 70–78.

Harriman, Helga H. "Economic Conditions in the Creek Nation, 1865–1871," 51, no. 3 (Fall 1973): 325–34.

Hartshorne, G. E. "Skullyville and Its People in 1889," 28, no. 1 (Spring 1950): 85–88.

Hastings, James K. "The Opening of Oklahoma," 27, no. 1 (Spring 1949): 70–75.

———. "Log Cabin Days in Oklahoma," 28, no. 2 (Summer 1950): 143–53.

Hefley, Maurice. "A Pioneer of the Land Openings in Oklahoma," 40, no. 2 (Summer 1962): 150–56.

Heimann, Robert K. "The Cherokee Tobacco Case," 41, no. 3 (Autumn 1963): 299–322.

Henderson, James C. "Reminiscences of a Range Rider," 3, no. 4 (December 1925): 253–88.

Henslick, Harry. "The Seminole Treaty of 1866," 48, no. 3 (Autumn 1970): 280–94.

Hodges, Bert. "Notes on the History of the Creek Nation and Some of Its Leaders," 43, no. 1 (Spring 1965): 9–18.

Holden, James Franklin. "The B.I.T.—The Story of an Adventure in Railroad Building," 11, no. 1 (March 1933): 637–66.

Hosmer, Brian C. "Rescued from Oblivion? The Civilizing Program in Indian Territory," 68, no. 2 (Summer 1990): 138–53.

Hoxie, Frederick E. "The End of the Savage Indian Policy in the United States Senate, 1880–1900," 55, no. 2 (Summer 1977): 157–79.

[Hudson, Peter]. "The Recollections of Peter Hudson," 10, no. 4 (December 1932): 501–19.

Hysmith, Mrs. Logan G. "Biography of Capt. William Graham Baird," 4, no. 3 (September 1926): 286–88.

James, Parthena Louise. "Reconstruction in the Chickasaw Nation: The Freedman Problem," 45, no. 1 (Spring 1967): 44–57.

———. "The White Threat in the Chickasaw Nation," 46, no. 1 (Spring 1968): 73–85.

Johnson, Bobby H. "Reports of the Governors of Oklahoma Territory, 1891–1899," 44, no. 4 (Winter 1966–67): 365–79.

Johnson, Walter A. "Brief History of the Missouri–Kansas–Texas Railroad Lines," 24, no. 3 (Autumn 1946): 340–58.

[Jones, William Clark]. "A Letter from a United States Marshal in 1889," 35, no. 2 (Summer 1957): 233–34.

[Kansas City Star, Sunday, February 7, 1897]. "Report on the Five Civilized Tribes, 1897," 48, no. 4 (Winter 1970–71): 416–30.

[Kansas City Times, Monday, July 22, 1889]. "The Magic City: Guthrie," 36, no. 1 (Spring 1958): 65–71.

Keith, Harold. "Memories of George W. Mayes," 24, no. 1 (Spring 1946): 40–54.

Kelley, E. H. "When Oklahoma City Was Seymour and Verbeck," 27, no. 4 (Winter 1949–50): 347–53.

Kensell, Lewis Anthony. "Reconstruction in the Choctaw Nation," 47, no. 2 (Summer 1969): 133–53.

Kinchen, Oscar A. "The Squatters in No Man's Land," 26, no. 4 (Winter 1948–49): 385–98.

Knight, Oliver. "Fifty Years of Choctaw Law," 31, no. 1 (Spring 1953): 76–95.

———. "History of the Cherokees, 1830–1846," 34, no. 2 (Summer 1956): 159–82.

Lanchet, Joseph. "The Diary of Joseph Lanchet, May 1884," 5, no. 2 (June 1927): 238–50.

Laracy, John. "Sacred Heart Mission and Abbey," 5, no. 2 (June 1927): 234–38.

Lehman, Leola. "A Deputy U.S. Marshal in the Territories" [William Bartley Murrill], 43, no. 3 (Autumn 1965): 289–96.

Lemon, G. E. "Reminiscences of Pioneer Days in the Cherokee Strip," 22, no. 4 (Winter 1944–45): 435–57.

Lester, Patricia. "William J. McClure and the McClure Ranch," 58, no. 3 (Fall 1980): 296–307.

Lewis, Anna. "Trading Post at the Crossing of the Chickasaw Trails," 12, no. 4 (December 1934): 447–49.

Littlefield, Daniel F., and Lonnie F. Underhill. "The Trial of Ezekial Proctor and the Problem of Judicial Jurisdiction," 48, no. 3 (Autumn 1970): 307–22.

Lucas, Robert C. [as told to Lucille Gilstrap]. "Homesteading the Strip," 51, no. 3 (Fall 1973): 285–304.

McFadden, Marguerite. "Intruders or Injustice?" 48, no. 4 (Winter 1970–71): 431–49.

McNeil, Kenneth. "Confederate Treaties with the Tribes of the Indian Territory," 42, no. 4 (Winter 1964–65): 408–20.

McRill, Leslie A. "The Story of an Oklahoma Cowboy, William McGinty, and His Wife," 34, no. 4 (Winter 1956–57): 432–442.

———. "Old Ingalls: The Story of a Town That Will Not Die," 36, no. 4 (Winter 1958–59): 429–45.

Mashburn, John H. "Chickasaw Courts," 5, no. 4 (December 1927): 400–404.

Maxwell, Amos. "The Sequoyah Convention," 28, no. 2 (Summer 1950): 161–87; no. 3 (Autumn 1950): 299–340.

Mayes, Mayme B. "Notes on Joel Bryan Mayes," 44, no. 3 (Autumn 1966): 325–27.

Meserve, John Bartlett. "Chief Pleasant Porter," 9, no. 3 (September 1931): 318–34.

———. "Chief Isparhecher," 10, no. 1 (March 1932): 52–76.

———. "The McIntoshes," 10, no. 3 (September 1932): 310–25.

———. "Governor William Leander Byrd," 12, no. 4 (December 1934): 432–43.

———. "The McCurtains," 13, no. 3 (September 1935): 297–310.

———. "Chief John Ross," 13, no. 4 (December 1935): 421–37.

———. "Chief Coleman Cole," 14, no. 1 (March 1936): 9–21.

———. "Chief Dennis Wolfe Bushyhead," 14, no. 3 (September 1936): 349–58.

———. "Chief Wilson Nathaniel Jones," 14, no. 4 (December 1936): 419–33.

———. "Chief William Potter Ross," 15, no. 1 (March 1937): 21–29.

———. "The Mayes," 15, no. 1 (March 1937): 56–64.

———. "The Perrymans," 15, no. 2 (June 1937): 166–81.

———. "Governor Cyrus Harris," 15, no. 4 (December 1937): 373–86.

———. "From Parker to Poe," 16, no. 1 (March 1938): 89–96.

———. "Governor Benjamin Franklin Overton and Governor Benjamin Crooks Burney," 16, no. 2 (June 1938): 221–29.

———. "Chief Lewis Downing and Chief Charles Thompson (Oochalata)," 16, no. 3 (September 1938): 317–25.

———. "Chief Samuel Checote, with Sketches of Chiefs Locher [sic] Harjo and Ward Coachman," 16, no. 4 (December 1938): 400–409.

———. "Chief Colonel Johnson Harris," 17, no. 1 (March 1939): 17–21.

———. "Chief Thomas Mitchell Buffington and Chief William Charles Rogers," 17, no. 2 (June 1939): 135–46.

———. "Governor Robert Maxwell Harris," 17, no. 4 (December 1939): 361–63.

———. "Chief Gilbert Wesley Dukes," 18, no. 1 (March 1940): 53–56.

———. "Governor Jonas Wolf and Governor Palmer Simeon Mosely," 18, no. 3 (September 1940): 243–49.

———. "Governor Dougherty (Winchester) Colbert," 18, no. 4 (December 1940): 348–56.

———. "Governor William Malcolm Guy," 19, no. 1 (March 1941): 10–13.

———. "Chief Benjamin Franklin Smallwood and Chief Jefferson Gardner," 19, no. 3 (September 1941): 213–19.

———. "Chief Allen Wright," 19, no. 4 (December 1941): 314–21.

———. "Chief George Hudson and Chief Samuel Garland," 20, no. 1 (March 1942): 9–17.

———. "The Governors of Oklahoma Territory," 20, no. 3 (September 1942): 218–27.

Milam, Joe B. "Opening of the Cherokee Outlet," 9, no. 3 (September 1931): 268–77; no. 4 (December 1931): 454–71; 10, no. 1 (March 1932): 114–36.

Milligan, James C., and L. David Norris. "Connecticut Yankee in the Indian Territory," 68, no. 3 (Fall 1990): 266–75.

Miner, [H.] Craig. "The Struggle for an East-West Railway into the Indian Territory, 1870–1882," 47, no. 1 (Spring 1969): 560–81.

———. "'A Corps of Clerks': The Bureaucracy of Industrialization in Indian Territory, 1866–1907," 53, no. 3 (Fall 1975): 322–31.

Mitchell, Sara Brown. "Early Days of Anadarko," 28, no. 4 (Winter 1950–51): 390–98.

Monahan, Ernest D. Jr. "The Kiowa-Comanche Reservation in the 1890s," 45, no. 4 (Winter 1967–68): 451–63.

Moore, Gordon. "Registers, Receivers, and Entrymen: U.S. Land Office Administration in Oklahoma Territory, 1889–1907," 67, no. 1 (Spring 1989): 52–75.

———. "Letter to the President, 1890," 68, no. 2 (Summer 1990): 190–98.

Morgan, Omar L. "The Saline Court House Massacre," 33, no. 1 (Spring 1955): 87–95.

Morris, Cheryl Haun. "Choctaw and Chickasaw Indian Agents, 1831–1874," 50, no. 4 (Winter 1972–73): 415–36.

Morrison, James D. "Problems in the Industrial Progress and Development of the Choctaw Nation," 32, no. 1 (Spring 1954): 70–91.

———. "The Union Pacific, Southern Branch," 14, no. 2 (June 1936): 173–88.

Morton, Ohland. "The Government and the Creek Indians," 8, no. 1 (March 1930): 42–64; no. 2 (June 1930): 190–226.

———. "Reconstruction in the Creek Nation," 9, no. 2 (June 1931): 171–79.

Moulton, Gay E. "Chief John Ross and Cherokee Removal Finances," 52, no. 3 (Fall 1974): 342–59.

Murchison, A. H. "Intermarried Whites in the Cherokee Nation Between 1865 and 1887," 6, no. 3 (September 1928): 299–327.

Murdock, Victor. "Dennis T. Flynn," 18, no. 2 (June 1940): 107–13.

Murphy, James. "Reminiscences of the Washita Campaign and of the Darlington Indian Agency," 1, no. 3 (June 1923): 259–78.

Murray, William H. "The Constitutional Convention," 9, no. 2 (June 1931): 126–38.

Nesbitt, Paul. "Governor Haskell Tells of Two Conventions," 14, no. 2 (June 1936): 189–217.

————. J. J. McAlester," 11, no. 2 (June 1933): 758–64.

————. "Daniel William Peery," 20, no. 1 (March 1943): 3–8.

Nolen, Curtis L. "The Okmulgee Constitution," 58, no. 3 (Fall 1980): 264–81.

Osborne, Alan. "The Exile of the Nez Perce in Indian Territory, 1878–1885," 56, no. 4 (Winter 1978–79).

Owen, James McKee. "Reminiscences of an '89er of Oklahoma City," 34, no. 2 (Summer 1956): 217–21.

Parker, Linda. "Indian Colonization to Northeastern and Central Indian Territory," 54, no. 1 (Spring 1976): 104–29.

Peery, Dan W. "The First Two Years," 7, no. 3 (September 1929): 278–332; no. 4 (December 1929): 419–57; 8, no. 1 (March 1930): 94–128.

————. "Oklahoma: A Foreordained Commonwealth," 14, no. 1 (March 1936): 22–48.

Perry, Mrs. A. E. "Colonel Forbes LeFlore, Pioneer and Statesman," 6, no. 1 (March 1928): 75–88.

[Posey, Alexander Lawrence]. "The Journal of Alexander Posey, January 1 to September 4, 1897," 45, no. 4 (Winter 1967–68): 393–432.

Prucha, Francis Paul. "The Board of Indian Commissioners and the Delegates of the Five Civilized Tribes," 56, no. 3 (Fall 1978): 247–64.

Quillin, Henry A. "John Owen Quillin: Cowboy," 40, no. 1 (Spring 1962): 36–40.

Ragland, Hobart D. "Missions of the Society of Friends Among the Indian Tribes of the Sac and Fox Agency," 33, no. 2 (Summer 1955): 169–82.

Rand, Jerry [W. Judson]. "Samuel Morton Rutherford," 30, no. 2 (Summer 1952): 149–59.

Records, Ralph H. "Range Riding in Oklahoma," 20, no. 2 (June 1942): 159–71.

————. "The Round-up of 1883: A Recollection," 23, no. 2 (Summer 1945): 119–38.

————. "Recollections of April 19, 1892," 21, no. 1 (March 1943): 16–27.

Reed, Gerald A. "Financial Controversy in the Cherokee Nation, 1839–1846," 52, no. 1 (Spring 1974): 82–98.

Richards, O. H. "Early Days in Day County," 26, no. 3 (Autumn 1948): 313–24.

————. "Memories of an '89er," 26, no. 1 (Spring 1948): 2–12.

Robinson, Ella M. "The Daugherty Ranch, Creek Nation," 38, no. 1 (Spring 1960): 75–77.

Roff, Joe T. "Reminiscences of Early Days in the Chickasaw Nation," 13, no. 2 (June 1935): 169–89.

Rose, F. P. "Early History of Catesby and Vicinity," 29, no. 2 (Summer 1951): 177–98.

Rulon, Philip H. "Angelo Cyrus Scott," 47, no. 1 (Spring 1969): 494–514.

Russell, Orpha B. "William G. Bruner, Member of the House of Kings, Creek Nation," 30, no. 4 (Winter 1952–53): 397–407.

Savage, William W. Jr. "Leasing the Cherokee Outlet, An Analysis of Indian Reaction, 1884–5," 46, no. 3 (Autumn 1968): 285–92.

Self, Nancy Hope. "The Building of the Railroads in the Cherokee Nation," 49, no. 2 (Summer 1971): 180–205.

Shadburn, Don L. "Cherokee Statesmen: The John Rogers Family," 50, no. 1 (Spring 1972): 12–40.

Shirk, George H. "Seymour," 55, no. 1 (Spring 1977): 93–99.

Smith, Robert E. "A Life for a Pair of Boots: The Murder of Shepalino," 69, no. 1 (Spring 1991): 26–47.

Sparger, Julia K. "Young Ardmore," 43, no. 4 (Winter 1965–66): 394–415.

Squire, C. A. "Old Grand, Ghost Town," 28, no. 4 (Winter 1950–51): 399–417.

Stiles, George W. "Early Days in the Sac and Fox Country, Oklahoma Territory," 33, no. 3 (Autumn 1955): 316–38.

Swartz, Lillian Carlile. "Life in the Cherokee Strip," 42, no. 2 (Summer 1964): 62–74.

Syndergaard, Rex. "The Final Move of the Choctaws," 52, no. 2 (Summer 1974): 207–19.

Taylor, Nat A. "The Old Bar X Ranch," 49, no. 1 (Spring 1971): 83–91.

Thompson, Tommy R. "Milk and Honey and a Few Bad Apples: The Image of Oklahoma in Popular Magazines," 68, no. 3 (Fall 1990): 276–95.

Thoburn, Joseph B. "John Joseph Gerlach," 10, no. 1 (March 1932): 36–43.

———. "Frank H. Greer," 14, no. 3 (September 1936): 265–94.

———. "Albert Linwood Kates," (Necrology), 16, no. 1 (March 1938): 131.

———. "Mary Emily Hensley," (Necrology), 17, no. 1 (March 1939): 124–25.

Thompson, William P. "Courts of the Cherokee Nation," 2, no. 2 (March 1924): 63–74.

Travis, V. A. "Life in the Cherokee Nation a Decade After the Civil War," 4, no. 1 (March 1926): 16–30.

Turner, Clarence W. "Events Among the Muskogees During Sixty Years," 10, no. 1 (March 1932): 21–32.

Viles, Mildred Milam. "Some Experiences of C. H. Rienhardt in Early Oklahoma," 15, no. 4 (December 1937): 466–76.

Wade, J. S. "Uncle Sam's Horse-race for Land: The Opening of the 'Cherokee Strip,'" 35, no. 2 (Summer 1957): 147–53.

Warde, Mary Jane. "Fight for Survival: The Indian Response to the Boomer Movement," 67, no. 1 (Spring 1989): 30–51.

Wardell, Morris L. "The History of No-Man's Land, or Old Beaver County," 1, no. 1 (January 1921): 60–89.

Warren, Hanna R. "Reconstruction in the Cherokee Nation," 45, no. 2 (Summer 1967): 180–89.

Welsch, Glenn A. "Otis Hoover Richards," 39, no. 2 (Summer 1961): 112–16.

White, Robe Carl. "Experiences in the Opening of Oklahoma," 27, no. 1 (Spring 1949): 56–69.

Williams, Nudie E. "United States vs. Bass Reeves," 68, no. 2 (Summer 1990): 154–67.

Williams, Robert L. "John E. Love," (Necrology), 10, no. 4 (December 1932): 604–6.

———. "Judge Jesse James Dunn," 18, no. 1 (March 1940): 3–7.

———. "George Buchanan Noble," 19, no. 3 (September 1941): 221.

———. "Tams Bixby," 19, no. 3 (September 1941): 205–12.

———. "George Adrian Smith," (Necrology), 24, no. 4 (Winter 1946–47): 500–501.

Williams, Ronnie. "Pictorial Essay on the Dawes Commission," 53, no. 2 (Summer 1975): 225–38.

Wilson, L. W. "Reminiscences of Jim Tomm," 44, no. 3 (Autumn 1966): 290–306.

———. "A History of Wagoner, Oklahoma, from S. S. Cobb," 50, no. 4 (Winter 1972–73): 486–96.

Wilson, T. Paul. "Delegates of the Five Civilized Tribes to the Confederate Congress," 53, no. 3 (Fall 1975): 353–66.

Wise, Donald A. "Bird's Eye Views of Oklahoma Towns," 68, no. 4 (Fall 1989): 228–47.

Wright, J. B. "Ranching in the Choctaw and Chickasaw Nations" (with a biographical note on Alinton Telle), 37, no. 3 (Autumn 1959): 294–300.

Wright, Muriel H. "Old Boggy Depot," 5, no. 1 (March 1927): 4–17.

———. "The Removal of the Choctaws to the Indian Territory, 1830–1833," 6, no. 2 (June 1928): 103–28.

———. "Organization of Counties in the Choctaw and Chickasaw Nations," 8, no. 3 (September 1930): 315–32.

———. "Review of *The Rise and Fall of the Choctaw Republic,* by Angie Debo," 13, no. 1 (March 1935): 108–20.

———. "John D. Benedict: First United States Superintendent of Schools in the Indian Territory," 33, no. 4 (Winter 1955–56): 472–88.

———. "A Report to the General Council of the Indian Territory Meeting at Okmulgee," 34, no. 1 (Spring 1956): 7–16.

———. "Notes on the Closing of the Rolls of the Five Civilized Tribes, Allotment of Lands in Severalty and the Closing of Each of Their Governments," 42, no. 3 (Autumn 1964): 344–47.

———. "Captain Charles W. Whipple's Notebook: The Week of the Run into Oklahoma in 1889," 48, no. 2 (Summer 1970): 146–53.

———. "The Indian International Fair at Muskogee," 49, no. 1 (Spring 1971): 14–47.

Wright, Muriel H., and Peter J. Hudson. "A Brief Outline of the Choctaw and Chickasaw Nations in the Indian Territory," 7, no. 4 (December 1929): 388–413.

Young, Claibourne Addison. "A Walking Tour of the Indian Territory," 36, no. 2 (Summer 1958): 167–80.

Bibliographical Note
to the Second Printing

This reprint permits a word or two to be said about several first-rate works that did not come my way in time to be recognized earlier.

Regard for the dictates of verbal economy dissuaded me from comment on the *Indian-Pioneer History* in the archives of the Oklahoma Historical Society. A second edition of Theda Perdue's *Nations Remembered* (1993; first published in 1980) compels second thoughts. *Indian-Pioneer History* is of immense value just as raw material, but its potential can be fully released only when it is read alongside other, more formal sources; and its value then is beyond price. *Nations Remembered: An Oral History of the Cherokees, Chickasaws, Choctaws, Creeks, and Seminoles,* an annotated selection of extracts, is invaluable as an introduction to the *History.* Perdue's commentary is always sound.

Mixed-Bloods and Tribal Dissolution, by William E. Unrau (1989), is a model study of the life and politics of Charles Curtis, one-eighth Kaw (Kansa), whose impact upon "Indian Affairs" was manifest even twenty years after his name had been stamped ineffaceably on the Indian Territory Government Act of June 1898.

In 1992 the text of Samuel W. Harman's *Hell on the Border,* unabridged and with all the original illustrations, became available for the first time since the turn of the century. This reprint is further enhanced by Larry Ball's Introduction.

Since then, Larry Ball has also contributed a good Foreword to a long-overdue—and, therefore, doubly welcome—reprint of *Hanging Judge,* by Fred Harvey Harrington (1996).

Index